FATHER JOHN SAMMON

A MANUAL OF CHURCH HISTORY

VOL. II.

A MANUAL

OF

CHURCH HISTORY

BY

DR. F. X. FUNK

PROFESSOR OF THEOLOGY AT THE UNIVERSITY OF TÜBINGEN

AUTHORISED TRANSLATION

FROM THE 5TH GERMAN EDITION

BY

LUIGI CAPPADELTA

VOL. II.

KEGAN PAUL, TRENCH, TRÜBNER & CO. LTD.
DRYDEN HOUSE, GERRARD STREET, LONDON, W.
B. HERDER
17 SOUTH BROADWAY, ST. LOUIS, MO.
1910

Nihil obstat.

J. P. ARENDZEN
Censor Deputatus

Imprimatur.

EDMUNDUS CANONICUS SURMONT
Vicarius generalis

Westmonasterii, die 16 *Maii,* 1910

CONTENTS

III.—THE MIDDLE AGES (*Continued*)

Contents

Contents

A MANUAL

OF

CHURCH HISTORY

III. THE MIDDLE AGES

THIRD PERIOD

From Boniface VIII to the End of the Middle Ages,
1294–1517

CHAPTER I

THE PAPACY[1]

§ 137

Boniface VIII and his Quarrel with Philip IV of France—Fifteenth General Council[2]

When Celestine V resigned the papal crown, a successor was found in the person of cardinal Benedetto Gaetani, henceforth to be known as **Boniface VIII** (1294–1303). Though an adept in Canon Law, his hastiness and forceful measures led to his being repeatedly humiliated at the hand of secular princes. From his pontificate dates the decline of the political power of the papacy.

He found himself faced by a stupendous task. On all

[1] Literature, §§ 85, 109: Hefele-Hergenröther, CG. VI–VIII; Christophe, Hist. de la papauté au XIVe siècle, 3 vol. 1853; Hist. de la papauté pendant le XVe siècle, 2 vol. 1863; M. Tangl, Päpstl. Kanzleiordnungen v. 1290–1500, 1894.

[2] Mg. on Boniface by Dupuy, 1655; Baillet, 1718; Tosti, 2 vol. 1846; Drumann, 2 vol. 1852; H. Finke, Aus den Tagen Bonifaz' VIII, 1902; MIŒ. 1905, pp. 201–24 (on Philip the Fine); D.Z.f.G. N.F. ii, 16–38; (Bull Ausculta fili); E. Renan, Études sur la politique relig. du règne de Philippe le Bel, 1899; Döllinger, Anagni (Engl. Trans. in Addresses, 1894); R. Holtzmann, Wilhelm von Nogaret, 1898; R. Scholz, Publizistik zur Zeit Philipps d. Sch. u. Bonifatius' VIII, 1903; MIŒ. 1905, pp. 488–98; 1906, pp. 85–96 (on the supposed heresy of Boniface VIII).

sides quarrel and conflict prevailed, and he was doing no more than his duty when he strove to make peace, especially as nothing could be done to deliver the Holy Land until the animosities of the Western rulers had been laid to rest. First and foremost he desired to mediate between France and England. As his remonstrances were unavailing, and as the clergy were being subjected to systematic extortion in the interest of the different war parties, he took the course of issuing (1296) the Bull, known as *Clericis laicos (infestos esse oppido tradit antiquitas)*, from the words with which it begins. He therein forbade the clergy, on pain of the ban, to contribute anything whatsoever to the laity without previously securing his permission, forbidding also princes or secular officials to impose any kind of tax on clerics, or to claim or receive aught from them. The way for this prohibition had indeed been, in some sense, made ready by the previous enactments of Alexander III, Innocent III, and Alexander IV.[1] The new decree, however, went much further, the times were anything but favourable to its execution, and in England, and still more in France, it encountered opposition. **Philip the Fine** even retaliated by forbidding the export of silver and treasure from his country, and prohibiting strangers to sojourn in his dominions. His action was crowned with success, and though the Bull was not immediately withdrawn, it was soon made ineffectual by new decrees. Boniface not only explained that his prohibition was not intended to interfere with the duties imposed by fealty, but he expressly granted permission to the clergy to make free gifts to the king, and even to do so at the king's demand, provided the request was made in a friendly way. In cases of need—the judgment of what precisely constituted a need being left to the king— he consented to such demands being made without first seeking the approbation of the Apostolic See.

As this conflict was nearing its end, Boniface came into collision with a portion of the powerful Colonna family. Cardinal Giacomo Colonna and his party bore a grudge against the Pope on account of an adverse judgment in some matter concerning the family property. As the Colonnas were

---

[1] *Lateran. III*, c. 19 ; *Lat. IV*, c. 46 ; In the *Corp. i. c. c.* 4, 7. X *de immun. eccl.* 3, 49 ; c. 1 in VI *de immun.* 3, 23.

also much attached to the house of Aragon, and maintained treasonable intercourse with James II and Frederick III of Sicily, the Pope determined, for the sake of his own safety, to occupy some of the strongholds held by the Colonna family. This was the signal for an outburst of fury. The Colonnas even questioned the validity of the Pope's election—arguing that the resignation of his predecessor was against law—and clamoured for the convocation of a General Council. Boniface retorted by depriving them of all their dignities and possessions, directed a crusade to be preached against them, and finally succeeded in capturing and levelling with the ground their main stronghold Palestrina (1298).

Though this quarrel had turned to the Pope's advantage, he was soon to experience a second and more disastrous defeat at the hands of the king of France. Philip having instituted proceedings on various charges against Saisset, bishop of Pamiers, who had been sent by Boniface to remind the king of a projected crusade (1301), the Pope not only demanded that his envoy should be set free, but actually took measures against the king himself. Alleging the many acts of oppression which the king had practised on the Church and on his people generally, the Pope summoned the French bishops to a synod to be held at Rome in the autumn, 1302, and there to decide on the measures to be adopted to preserve the freedom of the Church, and to reform both king and kingdom. Philip himself, by the Bull *Ausculta fili*, was invited to attend and answer the charges. To tell the truth, the king's misgovernment was quite sufficient to justify a mediæval pope in thus summoning him before his court, but France had always been jealous of her privilege of independence, whilst the chances of any success attending the Holy See in its claim to suzerainty were all the more remote, now that the French throne was occupied by a prince noted equally for his strength of will and want of scruple in his selection of means. Philip, far from making overtures to the Pope, rejected his proceeding as an affront to the independence of the kingdom. By means of a trick, the nation as a whole was soon won over to the sovereign, the Bull *Ausculta fili* being replaced by a forgery entitled *Deum time*, of which the principal clause runs : *Scire te volumus, quod in spiritualibus et temporalibus nobis subes ;* this document, together with an insolent answer beginning : *Sciat maxima tua fatuitas,* was circulated throughout the country. Such was the outcry, that Rome sought to smooth matters. The cardinals explained that superiority was only claimed *ratione peccati,* and not *temporaliter,* or, as it came to be afterwards expressed, that the Church claimed the right of interfering indirectly, though not directly, in secular concerns. The Pope forebore to excommunicate the king by name, but, as in the Bull *Unam sanctam,* he expressly alluded to the subjection of the secular to the spiritual power— insisting that no other arrangement met the order willed by God, and that any other scheme could only be an outcome of Manichæan dualism—instead of mending matters, he only made them worse. In the summer, 1303, at a parliament which met at Paris, the Pope was charged with a series of atrocious crimes, with heresy, blasphemy, intercourse with demons, immorality, cruelty, the murder of his predecessor, simony, hatred of France and her king, &c., and a General Council was demanded to investigate the charges. Boniface forthwith protested against the imputations, several of which were manifestly absurd, and it was decided to solemnly excom- municate the king on the feast of our Lady's Nativity. On the previous day the Pope was, however, surprised and taken prisoner at Anagni by the French chancellor William of Nogaret and the vengeful Sciarra Colonna, and though he secured his liberty three days later, and was received with acclamation on his return to Rome, the shock proved too much for him, and it was left to his successors to end the quarrel.

Benedict XI (1303–4),[1] though he had been friendly to his predecessor, considered it advisable to adopt a different course with respect to the main matter at issue. Mindful of being the vicar on earth of Him, *cuius est proprium misereri et parcere,* he withdrew by the Brief *Dudum* (*Extrav. comm.* 5, 4) a portion of the sentence pronounced on the Colonnas (excom- munication, exile, and inability to hold office). He likewise issued a number of decrees of which the object was to pacify the French. **Clement V** went even further in the same direction. He completely reinstated the Colonnas, and to please France quashed the Bull *Clerieis laicos* and issued

[1] Mg. by FUNKE, 1891 ; KINDLER, 1891.

the Brief *Meruit* (c. 2, *Extrav. comm.* 5, 7), declaring that the Bull *Unam sanctam* should never be interpreted to the prejudice of the kingdom (1306). As Philip still insisted (1307) on Boniface being formally arraigned, the depositions of the witnesses were taken (1310). Finally, after the Pope had succeeded in obtaining that the painful case should be tried before his own court, the matter was settled in the spring, 1311, by the unconditional annulment of all the sentences pronounced against France since the opening of the struggle (All Saints, 1300), Philip being declared guiltless of the outrages committed against Boniface, and even Nogaret being absolved on protesting his innocence ; in return for these concessions the case of Boniface was to be allowed to drop. Even then, the king's ire does not seem to have been soothed, and it is probable that the matter again came up for discussion at the General Council which Clement assembled at **Vienne** (1311-12) to deal with the Templars and with other affairs. The charge of heresy was dismissed as unfounded.

The Bull **Unam sanctam** (c. 1, *Extrav. comm.* 1, 8, and in the *Specimina palaeographica regestorum Rom. Pont,* ed. DENIFLE, 1886, tab. 46) has given rise to many discussions and has been diversely interpreted. The concluding clause : *Porro subesse Romano pontifici omni humanae creaturae declaramus, dicimus, definimus et pronuntiamus omnino esse de necessitate salutis*, which constitutes the main difficulty, speaks quite generally of the subjection of all human creatures to the Apostolic See, and may therefore be understood as implying a subjection only in things spiritual. But taking the clause in connection with the justificatory antecedent context, then it must be allowed that the subjection which it demands extends also to things temporal. FUNK, *A. u. U.* I, 483–89.

§ 138

The Babylonian Exile—Conflict of the Papacy with Lewis of Bavaria [1]

By the time that the quarrel excited by Boniface had been settled, the seat of the Roman Curia was no longer at Rome or even in Italy, but in France, a fact which, perhaps, to some

[1] *Vitae paparum Avenion.* ed. BALUZIUS, 2 vol. 1693 ; *Lettres des papes d'Avignon,* 1899 ff. (*Bibliothèque des écoles franç. d'Athènes et de Rome,* III) ; ANDRÉ, *Études sur le XIVe siècle,* 2nd ed. 1888 ; C. MÜLLER, *Der Kampf*

extent accounts for the issue of the business. The change of abode made the papacy to a certain extent dependent on the French court, and this dependence was soon to be made otherwise manifest.

The Babylonian exile, as this period is usually called, began with the election of Bertrand de Got, archbishop of Bordeaux, as **Clement V** (1305–14).[1] The conclave lasted eleven months, and the votes were ultimately bestowed on him, because the Italian and French cardinals were so divided among themselves that it was impossible to secure the requisite majority for any one of their number, whereas the archbishop seemed to both parties to be rightly minded regarding the great questions then pendent. On the one hand, he was a supporter of Boniface VIII, on the other, he was a Frenchman, and at the same time a dependent of England, to which Gascony then belonged. It does not seem to have been his intention to transfer permanently the seat of the Curia to France, for he allowed the papal treasure to remain in Italy (at Assisi), and several times expressed a determination to take up his quarters at Rome. As a matter of fact, however, he never crossed the Alps, the dissensions and uncertainty which prevailed in Italy being anything but inviting. He was consecrated at Lyons, and his usual residence after 1309 was **Avignon.**

His pontificate was followed by a vacancy even longer than that which had preceded his election. It was only after two and a quarter years that cardinal Jacques de Ossa of Cahors was chosen Pope, and assumed the name of **John XXII** (1316–34). At the time of his election a dispute had already arisen in Germany which was to lead to yet another conflict between Papacy and Empire. When it became necessary to select a successor for Henry VII (1308–13), two men were elected, **Lewis of Bavaria** and Frederick the Fine, of Austria, a grandson

---

Ludwigs d. B. mit der röm. Kurie, 2 vol. 1879–80 ; J. SCHWALM, *Die Appellation K. Ludwigs d. B. v.* 1324 *in ursprüngl. Gestalt*, 1906; VERLAQUE, *Jean XXII*, 1885 ; *Hist. J.* 1897, pp. 37–57 (on the treasure of John XXII) ; RIEZLER, *Vatik. Akten zur deutschen Gesch. in der Zeit K. Ludwigs d. B.* 1891 ; WERUNSKY, *Karl IV*, I–III, 1880–92 ; WURM, *Kard. Albornoz*, 1892 ; *Studi stor.* XIV (1905), 29–68 (*Albornoz*, 1358–67) ; *Z. f. KG.* XXI (on Ludwig's abettors, adversaries, and means in his struggle with the Curia) ; W. FELTEN, *Forsch. zur Gesch. Ludwigs d. B.* 1900 ; W. OTTE, *Der hist. Wert d. alten Biographien Klemens V*, in the *Kirchengesch. Abh.*, ed. by SDRALEK, 1902.

[1] H. FINKE, *Aus den Tagen Bonifaz' VIII*, pp. 269–90 (election) ; EHRLE, *Archiv f. Lit. u. KG. d. MA.* V (1889), 1–166.

of Rudolf of Habsburg (1314), both of whom decided to uphold their candidatures. The battle of Mühldorf in 1322 was a
victory for the Bavarian, but, even so, he was not able to obtain
the crown immediately. Frederick was indeed his prisoner,
but the conflict proceeded between the houses of Habsburg
and Wittelsbach. Nor was the Pope disposed to acknowledge
the victor without further ado. Before doing so, he expected
the king to admit the papal right of administering the kingdom
of Italy so long as the imperial throne remained unoccupied.
The vicar or viceroy, whom Lewis had sent across the Alps, was
peremptorily summoned by the Pope to desist from all acts of
government (October 8, 1323). This order, which practically
called into question the connection of Italy with the Empire,
could not but be considered an affront by a German king,
especially as the Pope had simultaneously nominated to the
Italian vicariate king Robert of Naples, who was under the ban
of the Empire. Lewis was not satisfied with protesting against
the infringement of his rights, and on being excommunicated
(March 23, 1324), he launched an appeal from Sachsenhausen
and proceeded to adopt aggressive tactics. As John had
reproached him for his relations to the Viscontis of Milan, in-
sinuating that he had afforded protection to heretics, he in his
turn accused the Pope of having fallen into heresy through his
Constitution on the poverty of Christ (§ 148), and challenged
his right to the tiara. These proceedings altered the character
of the conflict, negotiations made way for a state of war, and all
likelihood of any papal acknowledgment of Lewis's election,
especially bearing in mind the influence on John exercised by
France and Naples, became exceedingly remote. Not only did
the Pope refuse to withdraw his sentence, he also declared that
Lewis had forfeited the German throne, and laid an excommunication and interdict on all his supporters. On the king
proceeding to Rome to claim the imperial crown (1327), new
censures were launched against him, depriving him of all his
titles and properties, and on his receiving the crown from
Sciarra Colonna, the governor of the city of Rome, a crusade
was proclaimed against him (1328). The success of these
measures was small. The Bulls were indeed nailed to the
church doors at Avignon, but the larger portion of Germany
remained loyal to Lewis. On the other hand, the latter's

proceedings were not one whit more effective. Many of his supporters disapproved of his action in putting up an anti-Pope soon after his coronation. Pietro da Corvara, or Nicholas V, the anti-Pope, found so little sympathy, that two years later he submitted to John (1330). On the death of Frederick of Austria, Lewis himself took the lead in offering to treat with the Pope. But, to begin with, he was loath to resign the crown, which was made a condition of the negotiations, and when, later on, he was more disposed to assent (1333), other obstacles came in the way. His own plan, which was to offer the crown to duke Henry of Lower Bavaria, his cousin and the son-in-law of John of Bohemia, was opposed by the king of Naples and by the Italian cities which were mostly disposed to be unfriendly to the Empire. Nor was the king's offer to resign meant at all seriously, for it was soon withdrawn. His change of attitude was a result of the difficulties into which John had recently been plunged through his teaching concerning the *Visio beatifica*. In a sermon (All Saints, 1331) he had advocated the view that the souls of the just attain to the vision of God, not forthwith after death, but only subsequently to the Last Judgment, an opinion which he afterwards withdrew.

Benedict XII (1334–42), his successor and the builder of the papal palace at Avignon, was more inclined to come to a settlement, though he did not succeed in his endeavour. The difficulties of the situation were increased by the opposition of the enemies of the Bavarian, especially by that of the king of France. Nor did the increasing pressure of the German Estates on the Curia much improve matters, though it seems to have had some influence. At Lahnstein the Estates bound themselves, by an everlasting oath, to defend the honour, rights, and dignities of the Empire (1338). A day later, by declaring at Rense that the king-elect received the imperial rights by the mere fact of his election, they practically denied the Pope any right of confirming the election of the German king.[1] Even when Lewis allied himself with Philip VI (1341), and entrusted the king of France with the negotiations on his behalf, it was still found impossible to come to an understanding. Owing to

---

[1] K. Höhlbaum, *Der Kurverein von Rense*, 1338, in *Abh. Göttingen*, N. F. VII, 1903–4; *N.A.* 1905, pp. 85–112.

the mutual distrust existing between Paris and Avignon, the French king's intercession was of no avail. Lewis, moreover, by marrying his son Lewis of Brandenburg to Margaret Maultasch, wife of prince John Henry of Bohemia and heiress to the Tyrol, committed, in the following year, a deed which infringed one of the laws of Christian marriage, and rendered nugatory any further attempts at a reconciliation.

Nevertheless, on the election of a new pontiff, efforts were again made to secure peace, though with no better success. The demands made of Lewis by the splendour-loving **Clement VI** (1342–52) were so great that they were rejected even by the German Estates. But as the latest doings of the emperor had caused deep dissatisfaction among the people, and as there seemed no other means of obtaining peace, the majority of the prince-electors forsook Lewis and chose in his place **Charles IV** (1346–78), king of Bohemia and grandson of Henry VII. As Lewis met a sudden death in the ensuing year, whilst his successor, Günther of Schwarzburg, died prematurely in 1349, after having, before his end, made peace with his opponent, Charles was soon in undisputed possession of the throne. At Easter, 1355, he received the imperial crown at Rome from the hand of a cardinal acting under papal instructions, and in the next year, to regulate the royal election which had caused thirty-five years of wrangling, he issued the Golden Bull, which excluded all foreign interference, and made the election to depend solely on the votes of the majority of the prince-electors.

At about this time the absence of the popes from Italy led to changes in the extent of the Papal States. Clement VI bought Avignon on behalf of the Apostolic See from queen Joanna of Naples (1348). The comté Venaissin, to the east of the town which had formerly belonged to count Raymond of Toulouse, had already been ceded to the Pope by the treaty of Paris in 1229. Whilst in France the papal territory was being enlarged, in Italy it was in dire distress. In several localities risings took place, the people shaking off their allegiance to the Pope. In Rome itself, after the overthrow of the nobility, the government was seized by Cola di Rienzi (1347), who assumed the title of Tribune, and though he fell seven months later, the

city continued to be disturbed.   At the beginning of the pontificate of **Innocent VI** (1352–62), a new Tribune arose in
Francesco Baroncelli.   At his downfall, Cola again assumed
the government, though his second term of office was even
shorter than his first.   The revolt stirred up by his tyranny was
the cause of his death, whereupon cardinal Albornoz, by dint of
energy and tact, little by little succeeded in again establishing
the papal sovereignty ;   to the wisdom of this same cardinal the
Papal States owed a new code of law, commonly known from
his Christian name as the *Constitutiones Ægidianae*, which
continued in use until the commencement of the nineteenth
century.

During the next pontificate the question of the Pope's
residence entered a new stage.   The exile had already lasted too
long.   Save in France, the absence of the Pope from Rome was
regarded as something contrary to nature.   Many were the
appeals for a return to the Eternal City, the emperor Charles IV,
the poet Petrarch, and St. Bridget, who since her husband's
death had been living the life of an ascetic in Rome, all joined
in beseeching the Pope to revert to Rome.   **Urban V** (1362–70)
gave way before this widespread feeling and quitted Avignon
(1367), only to return thither again towards the close of his life.
The evil therefore continued, and soon new dangers threatened
the temporal sovereignty of the popes in Italy.   The rule of the
legates had aroused much discontent in the Papal States, and
the republic of Florence took advantage of this feeling to stir
up the Romans to rebellion, the revolt soon spreading throughout the country.   **Gregory XI** (1370–78), a nephew of Clement
VI, was obliged to exert his might to the utmost in order to cope
with it.   He excommunicated Florence, laid it under an interdict (1376), and sent bands of Breton mercenaries into Italy.
But it was now seen that the best, and, in fact, the only way of
appeasing the trouble—as St. Catherine of Siena, who acted as
intermediary between the contending parties, urged—was for
the Pope to return to Rome.   This he did in the autumn, 1376.
The state of Italy continued, however, to afford ground for
anxiety, though the Florentines, after a short time, consented to
come to terms.   It is even said that on this account Gregory
meditated a return to Avignon, and shortly before his death
predicted the coming schism.

The supposed Bull *Quia in futurorum,* or *Ne praetereat,* of John XXII, which decrees the separation of Italy from the German Empire, is a document drafted at the chancery of king Robert of Naples. Cp. W. FELTEN, *Die Bulle Ne praetereat,* 1885–87 ; Th. LINDNER, *Deutsche Gesch. unter den Habsburgern u. Luxemburgern,* I (1890), 322 ; *Th. Qu.* 1886, p. 659.

From the time of the return from Avignon, the residence of the popes has no longer been the Lateran, but the Vatican.

§ 139

The Great Schism—The Councils of Pisa and Constance [1]

The schism, whether predicted or not, actually came to pass. The very next papal election resulted in extraordinary disorders. The Romans demanded with threats the selection of one of their own countrymen, or at least of an Italian. A large mob spent the night in sight of the conclave, and gave clamorous expression to the Romans' wishes. The cardinals were thus induced to bring their task to a close by the election on the first day (April 8) of Bartolommeo Prignano, archbishop of Bari, who took the name of **Urban VI** (1378–89) ; it was to be the last instance of the choice of one not belonging to the college of cardinals. Before the choice was yet known, the Romans in their impatience broke into the conclave, and as, in the confusion which ensued, the cardinal of St. Peter's, a Roman, was pointed out as the elect, he was overwhelmed with the customary congratulations, the cardinals in the meantime having betaken themselves to flight. The mistake was, however, soon corrected, and the Romans expressed themselves satisfied. The new Pope was enthroned on the following day, and crowned at Easter (April 18). The cardinals, who assisted at the ceremonies, did so, doubtless, under pressure of circumstances, but, on the other hand, there can be no doubt that they acknowledged Urban as

---

[1] THEODERICUS DE NYEM, *De schismate,* ed. G. ERLER, 1890 ; GAYET, *Le grand schisme d'Occident,* I–II, 1889 ; L. SALEMBIER, *item.* 3rd ed. 1902 (Engl. Trans. *The Great Schism of the West,* 1908) ; VALOIS, *La France et le grand schisme d'Occident,* 4 vol. 1896–1902 ; SOUCHON, *Die Papstwahlen in der Zeit des grossen Schismas,* 2 vol. 1898–99 ; F. BLIEMETZRIEDER, *Das Generalkonzil im grossen abendländ. Schisma,* 1904 ; Th. LINDNER, *Gesch. d. d. Reiches vom Ende des 14 Jahrh. bis zur Reformation,* I–II, 1875–80 ; MICE. 1900, pp. 599–639 (on the schism of 1378, and the conduct of Charles IV).

Pope, as may be seen especially from their requesting favours of him, taking part in his consistories, &c. Hence, whatever may have been wanting at the moment of election was certainly made good by the subsequent action of the electors, and Urban must accordingly be reckoned a duly elected pontiff.

The new Pope soon deceived the hopes which had been built on him. He did not tarry to make proof of an overbearing zeal, and such a quality, at a time when the utmost moderation and circumspection was required, was even more than usually dangerous. For their part the cardinals were not the men to abide the Pope's high-handedness, whilst the French members of the Sacred College were impatient for a change which might favour their own national and political aims. Hence the events which had attended the Pope's election were seized as a pretext for annulling it, the Sacred College meeting at Fondi and electing, September 21, cardinal Robert of Geneva as **Clement VII** (1378–94).

The consequences of this step were far-reaching. As both Clement and Urban stood by their respective elections, a double papacy was the result, having one its headquarters in the Eternal City and the other at Avignon, whither the anti-Pope migrated (1379) as soon as he found it impossible to maintain himself at Rome. The Church likewise separated itself into two obediences, France, Savoy, Spain, Scotland, and certain German States acknowledging Clement, and the rest of Europe, Urban. As, moreover, each of the popes excommunicated his opponent, together with all his adherents, it came about that the whole of the West was under an excommunication. This position of affairs was as unbearable as it was unnatural, and the wish to put an end to it was increased by the grievous burden of expenditure which the political enterprises of the popes and the upkeep of a twofold court laid on the shoulders of the people, to say nothing of the many quarrels regarding bishoprics and other ecclesiastical emoluments to which the strange situation gave rise. At Paris Henry of Langenstein (*Epistula pacis*, 1379) and Conrad of Gelnhausen (*Epistula concordiae*, 1380) were demanding the assembling of a General Council, and in 1381 the university, too, decided to support their appeal. But the evil had to grow far worse to compel both parties to agree to make an end of it. The kingdom of Naples, to begin with, was the occasion of disastrous complications. As Queen Joanna espoused the cause of the anti-Pope, Urban excommunicated and deposed her, and bestowed her crown on Charles of Durazzo, giving also several cities in the kingdom to an unworthy nephew of his own. For her support Joanna thereupon, with the consent of Clement VII and the French king, adopted Lewis of Anjou as her son. It is true that Lewis himself and most of his army perished during the course of the expedition to Lower Italy, but the disorders nevertheless persisted throughout the pontificate, Lewis II taking his father's place. Not long after a quarrel broke out between Urban and Charles (1385), and on Charles's death the war was carried on by his son Ladislaus. Yet another complication now came to add to the trouble. Owing to the conduct of Urban, and possibly having been won over by Charles of Durazzo, six cardinals evolved a plan to bring the Pope's action under some kind of control. Their plot was, however, discovered and they were tortured, imprisoned, and finally put to death. Under these circumstances, the Pope's death was greeted with a certain relief. Its effect on the situation was, however, not great, and the hope that the Roman cardinals would refrain from proceeding to a new election, and would acknowledge Clement VII, turned out to be idle. After a few weeks, **Boniface IX** (1389–1404) was elected at Rome ; and as the newly-elect, conscious of his better right, would hear of no mediation, the matters stood in much the same position as before. In Naples, however, the war came to an end, Ladislaus making peace with Boniface, and then overcoming his opponent.

At Avignon, in the meantime, difficulties were likewise being experienced. After the death of Clement (1394), in spite of the very strong feeling against any new election, cardinal Peter de Luna was chosen as **Benedict XIII** after an interval of twelve days.[1] Before entering the conclave, like the other cardinals, he had taken an oath to do his best to restore unity to the Church, and for the sake of it to resign his office at any time should the majority of the cardinals demand of him this

---

[1] EHRLE, *Archiv. f. Lit. u. KG. d. MA.* V–VII, 1889–1900 ; M. DE ALPARTILS, *Chronica actitatorum temporibus D. Benedicti XIII*, ed. F. EHRLE, I, 1906.

sacrifice.   This promise led to the opening of negotiations, but
the Pope proved so refractory that France, Castile, and Navarra
withdrew from his obedience (autumn, 1398) ; most of the
cardinals abandoned him, and he was kept a prisoner in his
palace.   This 'Subtraction,' as the measure was called, was
one which could not endure, and it soon found adversaries,
especially as it injured so many interests, and it was ultimately
revoked in the spring of 1403.   Benedict, who, shortly before,
had escaped from prison, and had quitted Avignon never to
return, now opened negotiations on his own account, and dispatched an embassy to Rome (1404).   His proposal was that his
opponent should meet him at some safe spot, or that the matter
should be referred to arbitration.   These terms were rejected
by Rome, the discourteous behaviour of Benedict's legates contributing to discredit his advances.   On Boniface's death, which
occurred a few days after, he was succeeded by **Innocent VII**
(1404–6),[1] during whose reign the troubles at Rome drove all
other events into the background.   The situation seemed
all the more hopeless when king Wenzel was deposed and
replaced by Rupert of the Rhine Palatinate (1400–10), thus
causing a political division in an empire already torn by
ecclesiastical schism.

A better outlook opened out on the election of cardinal
Angelo Corrario as **Gregory XII** to the see of Rome (1406).
Previous to his election, he had bound himself even more
stringently than his predecessors to restore the Church's unity,
and no sooner was he Pope than he put himself into connection
with Benedict, and by the treaty of Marseilles (1407) it was
settled that both popes should hand in their resignation at
Savona.   In many places people now began to breathe more
freely, and the pernicious schism seemed to be nearing its end.
The treaty was, however, never carried into effect.   Under the
influence of the counsels of his greedy relatives and of king
Ladislaus of Naples, who foresaw that the union would endanger
his crown, Gregory never got beyond Lucca.   Benedict, indeed,
came as far as Porto Venere to meet him, but further he refused
to go.   Matters seemed as far off as ever from being smoothed,
when something happened which altered the whole aspect of the
question.   At about this time Gregory decided to create new

---

[1] E. GÖLLER, *K. Sigismunds Kirchenpolitik*, 1404–13, 1902.

cardinals, thereby alienating from his cause his old friends in the Sacred College. This quarrel turned out to be the first step towards reunion. The Roman cardinals came to Livorno (1408), where they met the cardinals of the opposite faction, and decided to summon a General Council for the mending of the schism to meet at **Pisa** in 1409.[1] An attempt was made to secure the support of the two popes, though they were not to be induced to attend, even when invited by the Council itself. On the contrary, each assembled a council of his own, Gregory at Cividale near Aquileia, and Benedict at Perpignan.[2] Hence both, for having disregarded in their actions the article of Faith regarding *Una sancta Ecclesia*, were deposed as ' notorious schismatics and heretics,' and Peter Philargo, cardinal archbishop of Milan, was elected as **Alexander V** (1409–10).

The new Pope was indeed not acknowledged everywhere, and the schism was therefore by no means at an end. In fact, so far from unity being attained, the Council had only succeeded in making three factions where previously there had been two, and this state of affairs continued to prevail when, in 1410, Alexander was succeeded by Balthasar Cossa as **John XXIII**.[3] In spite of all this the action of the cardinals did not lose its significance. The step they had taken was a practical protest against the schism, and after having been repeated with greater emphasis, it was to be productive of the desired result. This happened at the Sixteenth General Council, which held its sessions from the autumn of 1414 until the spring of 1418 at **Constance**,[4] was one of the most memorable ecclesiastical assemblies known to history, and in some sense a parliament of the whole of the West, this being largely due to the fact that,

[1] F. STUHR, *Organisation u. Geschäftsordnung des Pisaner u. Konstanzer Konzils*, 1891 ; *R. Qu.* 1895, pp. 351–75.

[2] On the Council of Cividale, see *Hist. J.* XIV, p. 320 ff. ; *R. Qu.* 1894, pp. 217–58 ; on that of Perpignan, *Archiv f. Lit. u. KG. des MA.* V, 1889.

[3] *Z. f. KG.* XXI (on his election and personal character).

[4] H. v. d. HARDT, *Magnum oecum. Constant. Concilium, &c. sex tomis comprehensum*, 1697–1700 ; Chronicle of the Council by ULRICH v. RICHENTAL : ed. M. R. BUCK, 1882 (*Bibl. des lit. Vereins*, vol. 158), illustrated ed. by WOLF, 1869, H. SEVIN, 1881 ; phototype reproduction, Leipzig, 1895 ; H. FINKE, *Forsch. u. Quellen z. G. d. Konst. Konzils*, 1889 ; *Acta conc. Constanciensis*, I, 1896 ; *Bilder vom Konst. Konzil*, 1903 ; HEFELE, *CG.* vol. VII ; ASCHBACH, *Gesch K. Sigismunds*, 4 vol. 1838–45 ; B. FROMME, *Die span. Nation u. das Konst. Konzil*, 1896 ; TRUTTMANN, *Das Konklave auf dem Konzil zu Konstanz*, 1899 ; WYLIE, *Council of C. to Death of J. Hus*, 1900.

in the meanwhile, an end had been made of the division within
the Empire, and that the premier prince of Christendom was
in a position to perform with greater strength his duty as
supreme protector of the Church.

John XXIII himself attended at Constance, under the
impression that the Council would confirm him in his position.
In this he was, however, deceived. As Gregory and Benedict
refused to bow to the sentence of the Council of Pisa, further
attempts had to be made to induce them to resign, and they
would hear of nothing of the sort unless the third Pope did the
same as they. John soon found that his resignation was also
expected. After a little while formal charges of misconduct
began to be made against him, and it became clear that his
chance of re-election was exceedingly remote. Under these
circumstances he found it convenient to quit Constance one
day when his ally duke Frederick of Austria had diverted the
attention of the town by a tournament. His intention in so
doing was, without a doubt, to cause the dissolution of the
Council which had offended him by re-arranging the manner
of voting ; to prevent the undue predominance of the over-
numerous Italian bishops, it had enacted that the votes should
be taken by nations, and that in each nation not only the
prelates, but also the procurators of the chapters and universities, and also the envoys of civil princes should be allowed
the suffrage. John had, however, miscalculated, and though
his flight caused great consternation, the Council was prevailed
on to continue its sessions, owing principally to the efforts of
the emperor **Sigismund**—present in person at its deliberations
—and of several prominent ecclesiastics. To guard against
any action on the Pope's part, the step was taken of proclaiming
that the Council had been duly summoned and declared open,
that John's departure, or that of any other prelate, could
not avail to dissolve it, that until the Church had been reformed
in both head and members, the Council was to remain in
session, that it was not to be transferred to another place
save for weighty reasons and by its own decision (Sess. III),
that it held its power directly from Christ, and that every
Christian, and even the Pope himself, was obliged on pain of
punishment to obey it in those things for which it had met
(Sess. IV–V). These decrees, though they were in disagreement

with the law regarding the relations of Pope and Council
as it had been settled by mediæval practice, were in some sense
an historical necessity. Judging by previous experience, a
Council seemed the only means of restoring the unity of the
Church, and as the right of the Council had been challenged
by the Pope, it could only fulfil the task for which it had been
summoned by claiming a right superior to his. In point of
fact this superiority had already been tacitly assumed by the
Council of Pisa, but the conduct of the Pope now furnished an
occasion for distinctly formulating it. The object of these
decrees was to prevent the breaking up of the Council, and to
render possible its task. As soon as this was done, formal
proceedings were started against John, who was deposed
on the charge of having furthered the schism by his cowardly
flight, and of having been guilty of simony and of evil life
(twelfth Session, May 29, 1415). Gregory XII abandoned
his cause of his own accord (fourteenth Session, July 4, 1415).
It was hoped that Benedict XIII would likewise be induced to
resign, and, with this in view, Sigismund even journeyed to
Perpignan, where the anti-Pope had been in residence since
1408. As Benedict, however, remained obdurate, it was
found necessary to proceed against him also. In this case the
duty of the Council was considerably facilitated by the action
of the Spanish princes, who, before the end of 1415, had been
persuaded to sever their connection with Benedict by the
treaty of Narbonne. He was ultimately deposed in the
summer, 1417. In the course of the next autumn a new
pope was elected, though not until after long and vehement
discussion. Sigismund, and the Germans generally, claimed
that the reform of the Church should first be proceeded with ;
another point in dispute concerned the electors, namely to
what extent their numbers should be increased by the addition
of deputies of the Nations. The former demand was withdrawn
on the Council consenting to issue a decree before the conclusion
of the Council, obliging the future Pope to complete the
reform of the Curia. With regard to the latter point it was
ultimately agreed that thirty other members of the Council
should join the cardinals in performing the election. The
unanimous choice of the conclave fell on cardinal Odo Colonna,
who assumed the title of **Martin V.**

By these measures the Council had succeeded in one of its principal tasks, the *causa unionis*. Its success was not however entire, for Benedict continued to hold his own in the stronghold of Peñiscola (between Tarragona and Valencia)—whither he had withdrawn after the treaty of Narbonne,—and at his death, in 1424, mainly owing to the doing of the king of Aragon, who had fallen out with Martin V, he was succeeded by Muñoz, a canon of Barcelona, who called himself Clement VIII. A dissentient cardinal even put up yet another anti-Pope known as Benedict XIV. By this time the number of schismatics had been reduced to about 2000. Clement VIII submitted as early as 1429, and so far as the other anti-Pope is concerned, his following was so small that none of his contemporaries found it worth their while to narrate his later adventures, with the result that he henceforth disappears from history.

The words used by Martin V at the last session of the Council of Constance—when requested by the Poles to condemn the libellous pamphlet which had been directed against their race by the Prussian Dominican Falkenberg—to the effect that he approved all that the Council had decided *in materiis fidei concilialiter*, but not *aliter nec alio modo*, cannot be interpreted as though the Pope had thereby wished to declare his position with regard to the dealings of the Council as a whole. The truth is that Martin V never expressed any public opinion concerning them. Cp. FUNK, *A. u. U.* I, 489–98.

§ 140

The Councils of Basel and Ferrara-Florence—The Schism of Felix V [1]

In the decree *Frequens* (Sess. XXXIX) the Council of Constance enacted that, in future, General Councils should be held frequently, the next two in five years and seven years respectively, and afterwards at intervals of not more than ten years. In accordance with this regulation, a Council was opened at Pavia in 1423, and owing to an epidemic was transferred to Siena. The assembly was, however, a small one,

---

[1] *Monumenta Concil. gener. saec. XV* (I–III, 1857–96) ; *Concilium Basiliense, Studien u. Quellen z. G. des Konzils v. B.*, ed. J. HALLER, &c. I–V, 1896–1904 ; ARNOLD, *Pontifikat Eugens IV*, 1897 (*Repertorium Germanicum*, I) ; *Byz. Z.* V (1896), 572–86 (for the attempt at union in 1439) ; VANNUTELLI, *Il concilio di Firenze*, 1899 ; HEFELE, *CG.*, vol. VII ; *A. f. öst. G.* 1890, pp. 1–236 (on the German kings and the neutrality of the prince-electors) ; *SB. Wien*, vol. 135, 1896.

and as soon as the question of reform had bred a conflict, this was seized on as a pretext for dissolving it in the spring, 1424, before anything worth speaking of had been accomplished. The next Council was to meet at **Basel.** It is true that Martin V was not disposed to look at it with a favourable eye, for the last Councils, by assuming an influence paramount to his own, had occasioned him not a little misgiving. At the same time, as everywhere, save at Rome, people were inclined to attach great importance to Councils, he did not consider it politic to oppose it, and at the expiry of the allotted term he accordingly appointed cardinal Giuliano Cesarini to preside at Basel. As for the rest, the Pope died soon after and was succeeded by cardinal Gabriel Condulmer as **Eugene IV** (1431–47).

The new Council began under auspices even more unfavourable than the previous. Eugene indeed confirmed the president, though at the same time he made allusion to a change which had occurred in the circumstances of the Council—doubtless thereby referring to the treaty which his predecessor had concluded with the Greeks, according to which a Council was to be held in the interests of reunion in some city on the coast of Lower Italy. At Basel itself the only prelate to make his appearance at the appointed time was the abbot of Vezelay in Burgundy. The state of affairs in the town and neighbourhood was also depicted in very dark colours by Beaupère, a canon of Besançon, who had been dispatched to Rome, and all this gave occasion to the Pope, even before the end of 1431 (December 18), to dissolve the Council, and to call another to meet the Greeks at Bologna in the summer, 1433. As it happened, however, the Council already four days before this, on the return into its midst of Cesarini from a crusade against the Husites, had held its first public session, and was now no longer disposed to separate without having previuosly performed its duty. The decree of dissolution aroused the assembled Fathers to protest that it was apparently Rome's intention to render the Council nugatory, in spite of its being the only means of carrying through the necessary reforms. Even cardinal Cesarini strongly advised the Pope to withdraw his decree. The Council subsequently held its ground. To obviate an attack, it re-enacted the decrees of Constance proclaiming the superiority of Councils over the Pope, and in this it was supported by the princes, especially by Sigismund, who was then preparing to assume the imperial crown. Eugene was, in consequence of this, induced to yield gradually ; after failing to impose his choice of Bologna, he agreed first that the Council should be held in a German city, and finally allowed it to take place at Basel, after having previously expressly excluded this city. An interesting change is also apparent in the formulæ with which the Pope safeguards his own supremacy ; to begin with he ' willed and commanded ' (*Volumus et mandamus*), or ' willed and was pleased to allow ' (*Volumus et contentamur*), the celebration of the Council, whereas towards the end of 1433, when the situation at Rome had become one of great peril, he was content to ' decree and declare ' (*Decernimus et declaramus*), thus giving his unconditional assent to the meeting. Hereby the conflict between the two powers was at an end, and the assembled Fathers were enabled to pass a number of useful reforming decrees. Their ordinances, however, lacked sanction, and were not generally observed, for the peace between Pope and Council was not to last ; some of the reforms, by endangering his revenues, were obnoxious to the Pope, this being especially the case with the conciliar statutes abolishing annates. At the same time the Fathers themselves fell to quarrelling over the question of the Reunion Council, the majority favouring the choice of Avignon and the minority an Italian town, and this dissension gave the Pope an advantage. On May 29, 1437, Eugene confirmed the decision of the minority, and on the Council inviting him to attend and answer for his action, he took the simple course of dissolving the assembly (September 18). Cesarini, who had previously given timely warning to the Pope, now endeavoured to persuade the Council to be conciliatory. His intervention being to no purpose, he left the Council with all his friends, among whom was Nicholas of Cusa, and proceeded to the Reunion Council in Italy. His departure did not alter the attitude of the opposition, the Council remaining in session, and instituting an inquiry concerning Eugene.

The Reunion Council was opened at **Ferrara** in 1438. The Greeks were well represented. Besides the patriarch Joseph II of Constantinople, the emperor John Palæologus also attended in person. Negotiations were, however, only carried on with extreme difficulty, and the Council seemed frequently on the point of breaking up ; the Greeks were held back only by the fear of the Turks, and the hope of ridding themselves of the danger with the help of the West. Following their emperor's advice they avoided, to begin with, any reference to doctrinal differences, and when finally the matter of the *Filioque* came up for discussion, they confined themselves to questioning the right of adding it to the Creed. At **Florence**, whither the Council migrated in 1439, they consented at last to discuss the dogmatic aspect of the question, and after much ado, united— with the one exception of Marcus Eugenicus of Ephesus—in acknowledging the Western doctrine as correct. After this the other points of controversy were dealt with, purgatory, the commencement of the *Visio beatifica*, the use of unleavened bread in the Eucharist, and the primacy of the Roman Church ; on an understanding being reached, Eugene publicly notified the re-establishment of the union by the decree *Laetentur coeli*. The Council had thus attained the object for which it had been summoned, but, doubtless to act as a counterpoise against that of Basel, it continued in session, and after the departure of the Greeks, received the submission of other oriental Churches, of the Armenians (autumn, 1439), the Jacobites (1442), the Meso-potamians from between the Tigris and Euphrates (1444), the Chaldæans (Nestorians) and Maronites of the Island of Cyprus (1445). It is in connection with the latter event that we last hear of the Council, which already two years previously (1443) had been transferred from Florence to the Lateran at Rome, at the time when Eugene returned to the city after nine years' absence due to a revolt.

To return to the Council of Basel, which was now sitting under the presidency of cardinal Lewis of Arles,[1] at the com-mencement of 1438 it pronounced the suspension of Eugene. This measure was not, however, well received outside of the assembly, the memory of the last schism with its misfortunes being as yet too fresh to dispose people to look forward to another. Some of the princes directly challenged the action of the Council, and the principal Western Powers tried their best to make peace, the French at the Council of Bourges (1438), and

---

[1] G. Pérouse, *Le card. Louis Aleman, président du concile de Bâle*, 1902.

the Germans at the Diets of Frankfort (1438) and Mainz (1439). The conflict, however, proceeded apace. The Fathers of Basel deposed Eugene IV, in 1439, as a heretic and schismatic for having opposed the decrees of Constance, now considered as articles of Faith. On the Pope's retorting by excommunicating them as heretics for having erected their opinions into dogmas, they elevated duke Amadeus of Savoy, a widower, to the position of anti-Pope under the title of **Felix V** (1439–49).[1] In spite of this, Christendom was gradually returning to the cause of Eugene. France and other states immediately assured him of their obedience and they were soon followed by Aragon and Scotland (1443), the obedience of the former being secured after king Alfonso had succeeded in defeating duke René of Anjou, his rival to the throne of Naples (1442), and had received from the Pope on the battlefield the satisfaction of all his demands. The Germans continued to offer their mediation, and on the proposal to call a General Council, which had been reiterated by the Diet of Mainz in 1441, being rejected both by Basel and by Eugene, they determined to remain neutral, though ultimately they, too, went over to the Pope. This alteration of policy was largely due to Frederick III (1440–93) ; in 1445 he made overtures to the Pope, and his attitude was gradually imitated by the princes of his empire. As late as the spring, 1446, the college of prince-electors at the Diet of Frankfort was inclined to deal defiantly with Eugene for having deposed two of its members, the archbishops of Cologne and Treves, for the part they had taken in the Council of Basel. Yet at the next Diet in the autumn of the same year, two prince-electors (those of Mainz and Brandenburg) and two bishops declared for the Pope. Other princes soon followed their example, the result being the so-called Concordat of Princes agreed to at Frankfort in February, 1447. The completion of the work, owing to the death of Eugene a few days later, was left to his successor, **Nicholas V** (1447–55), formerly Tomaso Parentucelli of Sarzana. Having already been employed in the negotiations with Germany, no better choice of a peacemaker could have been made. In 1448 the Concordat of Vienna was signed, thereby laying the foundation for the reconciliation of the German nation with the papacy, as the treaty was gradually

[1] H. Manger, *Die Wahl Amadeos v. S. zum Papst*, 1903.

assented to by all the princes. This treaty also had an effect on the Council of Basel. Banished from that city, it migrated to Lausanne (1448), and after having long been a mere shadow (it had held no solemn session since 1443), it finally ended its existence by acknowledging Nicholas V (1449).

The danger into which the conflict between Pope and Council had brought the unity of Western Christendom was thus dispelled without any further evil consequences. Felix V found supporters only in Savoy and Switzerland, and he was to be the last of the anti-Popes, for the Reformation was soon to put an end to schisms within the bosom of the Church. Whilst, however, for a while, peace reigned in the West, the union with the Eastern Church was soon again dissolved. This union, like that which had been formerly negotiated at Lyons, rested on too shaky a foundation to be lasting. The Greeks had been impelled to the decision they took at Florence only through dread of the Turk. At home, both clergy and people were full of fanatical hatred of the Westerns, and to them reunion could not fail to be abhorrent. The union received its death-blow when it became apparent that the West was not disposed to perform the office which the East expected from it. The patriarchs of Alexandria, Antioch, and Jerusalem, who through their delegates had signified their support of the Council of Florence, now withdrew their assent (1443), and the same was done, shortly before his death, by the emperor John Palæologus (1448). His brother Constantine XII, who succeeded him, indeed re-established the union, but it did not survive the fall of Constantinople into the hands of Mohammed II (May 29, 1453), the patriarchal see being forthwith bestowed on Gennadius, a great foe of Western influence.

The fall of the Eastern Empire, by removing a protecting bulwark, threatened danger to the West. To guard against this it was of the utmost importance that the Western States should unite their forces, and this Nicholas strove by might and main to effect, labouring more especially to cement the various Italian powers ; he also decreed a crusade against the hereditary foe of Christendom ; further proceedings were, however, hindered by his early death. This Pope was the first humanist to occupy the Apostolic See, was a friend of art and learning, and was much concerned in beautifying the city of Rome, which also owes to him the foundation of the Vatican Library. He it was who crowned Frederick III (1452), this being the last imperial coronation to take place at Rome.[1] At one time his position at Rome was endangered by the conspiracy of Porcaro, but the danger was averted by timely discovery (January, 1453).

Opinions regarding the Council of Basel are apt to differ according to the point of view under which it is considered, in its mode of convocation, its membership, or its decisions. Some hold it not to have been œcumenical at all, others believe that it was really œcumenical in its earlier stages, *i.e.* until the dissolution pronounced in 1437, and the latter, which is the more prevalent opinion, is preferable, if we are to consider, as is usually done, the Council of Ferrara-Florence as œcumenical. As the Council of Basel was transferred by Eugene IV to Ferrara, the Council of Ferrara-Florence must be considered as the continuation of that of Basel, the two together constituting the Seventeenth General Council. Cp. HEFELE, I, 62-66.

§ 141

End of the Middle Ages—The so-called Political Popes— Fifth Lateran Council [2]

The Turkish danger, which had given occupation to the closing days of Nicholas V, was to be the main concern of the next popes also. **Calixtus III** (1455-58), a scion of the Spanish house of Borgia, again proclaimed a crusade, sent missionaries into every country to preach it, and fitted out a fleet to fight the Turks. One of the preachers, the Franciscan John Capistran, was pre-eminently successful in winning over people to the cause. At the same time, it was only in Hungary, then so sorely pressed, that any sort of enthusiasm could be aroused. With the help of John Capistran and of cardinal Carvajal, the papal legate, John Hunyadi successfully engaged the Turks at Belgrad (1456). Unfortunately, it was impossible

---

[1] J. MARTENS, *Die letzte Kaiserkrönung in Rom* (1452), 1900.
[2] PASTOR, *Gesch. der Päpste*, &c. 1886-1906, 1899-1904 (Engl. Trans. *Hist. of the Popes from the Close of the Middle Ages*, 1906 ff.). SÄGMÜLLER, *Die Papstwahlen von 1447 bis 1555*, 1890.

to follow up the victory. Hunyadi and Capistran both died that same year, and the rest of Christendom was deaf to the Pope's warnings. The German bishops were wroth with the Pope on account of the Concordat of Vienna, the Sorbonne appealed to a General Council against the tax demanded for a crusade, whilst Venice, the mightiest sea-power of the age, had actually concluded a treaty with the Turks a year after the fall of Constantinople. The salvation of Christendom was not Calixtus's only concern ; he also put himself to much trouble to find suitable situations for his relatives. Two of his nephews he promoted to be cardinals, and a third he presented with a princedom. As his example was followed by the next popes, his pontificate may be said to have inaugurated a new era of nepotism.

Æneas Sylvius Piccolomini, known as **Pius II** (1458–64),[1] continued the agitation for a crusade, and, soon after entering into office, summoned a conference of all Christian princes to meet at Mantua to debate the Turkish question (1459), nor was there any time to lose, seeing that Servia, Bosnia, and Epirus were already in the hand of Mohammed II. The result was that a three-year war was decided on. Matthias Corvinus, king of Hungary (1459–90), proved himself a worthy successor of his father ; in Albania many deeds of valour were performed by George Castriota, known among the Turks on account of his bravery as Scanderbeg (*i.e.* prince Alexander). The majority of the sovereigns, however, carefully avoided the risks of active service, and the Pope's design of arousing them by putting himself at the head of the crusade was thwarted by his own death. He died when on the point of embarking at Ancona. As he had previously been on the side of the Council of Basel and of Felix V, and had even defended in written works opinions very different from those which he advocated as Pope, some were not slow to point to the significance of the alterations which had occurred in his views. To cut short such reproaches, he issued, in 1463, a Bull of retractation *In minoribus agentes*, in which with the words, *Æneam reicite, Pium recipite*, he recanted the opinions of his youth, and entreated all to put their trust in him as supreme

[1] G. Voigt, *Enea Silvio de P. als P. Pius II*, 3 vol. 1856–63 ; A. Weiss, *Æneas S. P. als P. Pius II*, 1897.

pontiff. He also published the Bull *Execrabilis* (1460), condemning the prevalent practice of appealing from the Holy Sęe to a General Council.

Paul II (1464–71), formerly cardinal Barbo of Venice, had also, at the conclave, to give an undertaking to push forward the war with the Turks. In this matter he was, however, even less successful than his predecessors, and the Turks continued their progress. The Pope, seeing how impossible was the promise he had made, refused to be any longer bound by it, and to the great dudgeon of the cardinals, compelled them to annul it. The officials known as Abbreviators were likewise highly indignant with Paul for having dissolved their college for certain malpractices (1466), and loaded him with reproaches. Platina took his revenge by drawing a most unfavourable picture of this pontificate in his *Vitae pontificum*. This was, however, the worst that happened.

The next conclave resulted in the bestowal of the tiara on a Franciscan, Francesco della Rovere, who took the name of **Sixtus IV** (1471–84).[1] He was a patron of the arts and of learning, enriched the Vatican Library, threw it open to the public, beautified the city of Rome, and built in the Vatican a chapel which received his name, and is renowned for its frescoes. The East also occupied his thoughts, and though no more attention was paid to his appeal than to those of his predecessors, other circumstances occasioned a change for the better. The victorious sultan Mohammed II, the terror of the Christians, died in 1481, and his death weakened the Turks, owing to the family quarrels to which it gave rise. The town of Otranto, which shortly before had been captured by the Moslems (1480), had again to be evacuated. Prince Jem, after an abortive attempt to secure the crown, actually fled to Rhodes to summon the help of the Christian sovereigns against his brother the sultan Bajazet. From Rhodes he was sent to France, whence he passed into the custody of Rome (1489). Sixtus, like the other popes of the period, was not averse to honouring and enriching his own family. Several

---

[1] A. v. REUMONT, *Lorenzo de Medici il Magnifico*, 2 vol. 2nd ed. 1883 (Engl. Trans. 1876); J. SCHLECHT, *Andrea Zamometic und der Basler Konzilsversuch vom Jahre*, 1482, I, 1903.

of his nephews he appointed cardinals, and on another, Girolamo Riario, was bestowed the vicariate of Imola. It was the latter's ambition that drew Sixtus into several political adventures of very questionable character. In supporting the Pazzi in their anti-Medicean conspiracy at Florence (1478), he may have deprecated the shedding of blood, but the plot nevertheless cost Giuliano de' Medici his life. His part in this business and his subsequent severity against Lorenzo de' Medici and the Florentine republic for punishing the offenders involved him in a war with Florence, and soon after in others with Naples (1482) and Venice (1483–84). The wars were made worse by the feuds existing at Rome between the Colonna and Orsini families. There was even some talk of assembling a council against the Pope. The Dominican Andrew Zamometic (Zuccalmaglio), archbishop of Granea (Krania), who for some time had been imperial ambassador at Rome, to avenge himself for the treatment he had experienced in return for certain strictures on the Curia, sought to convoke a General Council at Basel (1482). Throughout the pontificate dissension and confusion never ceased, and on the Pope's death Rome was thrown into a state of anarchy.

His successor **Innocent VIII** (1484–92), cardinal Cybo, endeavoured to restore order, though with small success. The worse elements rapidly gained the upper hand. War again broke out with Naples, and at Rome itself everything seemed obtainable for money. There even came into existence a society of papal functionaries dealing in forged Bulls. Their crime was indeed severely punished, but the Pope himself was too much devoted to his relatives (besides a son whom he married to a daughter of Lorenzo de' Medici, he also had a daughter) to have either the strength, or the will, to uproot the evils.

The state of things became even worse when Rodrigo Borgia ascended the throne of Peter as **Alexander VI** (1492–1503). Conspicuous as was his worldly wisdom, his morality was shocking, even when judged by the very lax standards of the time. He had several children, and after having by bribery obtained his election, his one concern was to provide for the four borne him by Vannozza Catanei. His son Cæsar,

who occupies a place of special importance in the history
of this pontificate, was preconised archbishop of Valencia, and
created cardinal.   After the violent death of his brother Juan
(1497), and after the Pope had sufficiently recovered from the
shock caused by the crime, Cæsar was relieved of the burden
of his ecclesiastical dignities, and by Lewis XII of France was
appointed duke of Valence, and married to a princess of the
French house, receiving also from the Pope the duchy of the
Romagna.   The plan of both father and son was to establish
a kingdom of central Italy.   Cæsar set about the work by
murder and warfare, seemingly with a fair chance of success,
but before it could be achieved, Alexander had passed away.
Transactions such as these could hardly fail to affect injuriously
the prestige of the Holy See, but even yet the Pope's authority
ranked very high, as we see from the action of Spain and
Portugal in referring to his arbitration the division of the
New World which had just been discovered (1493–94).

As for the remaining children of Alexander and Catanei, Godfrey
(Juffré) received the hand of Sancia of Aragon, a natural daughter
of King Alfonso II of Naples, together with the princedom of
Squillace.   Lucrezia (Mg. by GREGOROVIUS, 3rd ed. 1875 (Engl.
Trans. *Lucretia Borgia*, 1903)) was finally bestowed on Alfonso
de Este, hereditary prince of Ferrara (1501), her third husband.
Her second marriage with the duke of Bisceglia ended tragically
by his murder at the hand of Cæsar Borgia (1500) ; as for her
first marriage with Giovanni Sforza of Pesaro, it was considerately
annulled by the Pope, the same being done for two previous
espousals.   For the sake of Juan, whom Ferdinand the Catholic
had appointed duke of Gandia, a number of towns were united
to form a new dukedom of Benevento (1497) ; Juan was, however,
murdered five weeks later.   If the deed was not the outcome
of some love adventure, then suspicion must rest on the Orsini.
Some months after the murder, and especially after the assassination of his brother-in-law in 1500, the crime came to be attributed
to Cæsar.   The material at our disposal, however, furnishes no
proof against him, though at the same time it does not exclude
the possibility of his having been implicated in the business.
PASTOR, III, 375–88 (Engl. Trans. V. pp. 493 ff.) ; *Hist. J.* 1900,
pp. 1–21.

Pius III, formerly cardinal Piccolomini,[1] reigned only
twenty-six days, and was succeeded by Giuliano della Rovere

---

[1] *Archivio Stor. Ital.* 1903, III. pp. 102–38.

as **Julius II** (1503–13). Like Alexander, he was wholly given up to politics, though the object of his ambitions was not the enriching of his family, so much as the promotion of the arts and the strengthening of the papacy by the restoration and aggrandisement of the Papal States, which during the last few decades had been sadly reduced. Perugia and Bologna he easily recovered, and by entering the League of Cambrai he also succeeded in obtaining back the Romagna which had been in the occupation of Venice (1509). Having achieved his end, the Pope assumed the immediate government of the Papal States, now in a stronger position than ever. In spite of these successes, the sword was never sheathed. The wish to expel the French from northern Italy drew Julius into new undertakings in which he encountered resistance even from the French bishops. The French National Council of Tours in 1510 discussed the measures to be adopted against him in certain eventualities, and a Council summoned by a few refractory cardinals to meet at Pisa, in the autumn, 1511— later on removed to Milan, and then after the departure of the French from Italy transferred to Lyons (1512)—even pronounced the Pope's suspension as a 'new Goliath.' Julius was, however, not to be foiled, and to deprive his opponents of the pretext that had been afforded them by the non-fulfilment of the promise made at his election, viz. to summon within two years a General Council for the reform of the Church, he opened in the spring, 1512, a Council in the **Lateran.**[1] He thereby deprived his enemies of their main grievance, though the question of reform was scarcely mooted at the assembly.

Leo X (1513–21),[2] a son of Lorenzo de' Medici, lived to see the end of the schism. Lewis XII, by coming to an understanding with the Pope in 1513, cut the ground from under the feet of the opposition Council of which the existence depended on the good-will of the king of France. His successor, Francis I, was even persuaded to renounce (1516) the Pragmatic Sanction agreed to at Bourges in 1438, by which certain restrictions had been placed on the exercise of the papal

---

[1] GUGLIA, *Studien zur Gesch. d. V Laterankonzils*, 1899–1906 (*SB. Wien*) ; *MIŒ.* 1900, pp. 679–91 (for the debate on the Turkish question at the Fifth Lateran Council).

[2] Mg. by ROSCOE, 1805 ; AUDIN, 1845 ; NITTI, 1892 ; *Z. f. d. G.* 1893–94 ; A. SCHULTE, *K. Maximilian als Kandidat für den päpstl. Stuhl* (1511), 1906.

power in France.　As for the pressing reforms of the Church, they received scant regard.　The Lateran Council, though it sat for five years, did practically nothing.　Leo himself was more interested in art and learning, in the government of the Papal States, and in the promotion of his family, on which he bestowed the duchy of Urbino as a papal fief (1516), than in religion.　'Let us enjoy the papacy, since it has pleased God to bestow it on us,' he is reported to have remarked to his brother Giuliano on his election, and these words, even if they be not truly authentic, certainly describe his general habits and inclinations.　Similar feelings were shared by most of the cardinals, and a lurid light is thrown on the then state of the Church by the conspiracy of Petrucci and other cardinals against the Pope's life (1517).　At any rate, Leo, however worldly-minded, was not immoral.

The Lateran Council (1512–17), as may be seen from a comparison of its results with those of the Council of Trent, made no serious attempt at reforming the Church.　The Council was also very meagrely attended, there being usually present only about one hundred prelates, mostly Italians.　In spite of this it is commonly reckoned an œcumenical Council, being assigned the fifth place among the Councils of the Lateran.

CHAPTER II

HERETICAL MOVEMENTS—RELATIONS WITH THE JEWS

§ 142
John Wiclif [1]

THE need of ecclesiastical reform which—as we have seen from
the previous chapter, and shall have occasion to see again
(§ 158)—was so sorely felt, and yet so little heeded by those
in power, incited certain private individuals to undertake
reforms on their own account, their unenlightened zeal sometimes causing them to outstep due bounds. Of these the
first and most noteworthy was the Englishman John Wiclif
(1320/30–84). Seeing how the Church had been spoiled by
the possession of wealth, he put forth doctrines concerning
property and the royal supremacy which threatened the
independence of the Church in the administration of her
temporalities. His view was that the Church should be poor
as in the time of the Apostles, that the possession of property
was her ruin, and that it would be better for the State to undertake the support of the clergy. He was especially adverse to
property being held by monks, and as his keenest opponents
were found in the ranks of the Regulars, it was not long before
he began to attack monasticism as an institution. On the
outbreak of the Great Schism (1378) he assailed not only the
anti-Pope, but also Urban VI, and the papacy itself. It was
probably at this time, if not before, that he put forth his
thesis that papal or episcopal excommunication can do no
harm to him whom God Himself does not excommunicate,

---

[1] Mg. by LECHLER, 2 vol. 1873 (Engl. Trans. 1878); R. BUDDENSIEG, 1885;
H. FÜRSTENAU (on Wiclif's doctrine regarding the division of the Church and
the position of the secular power), 1900; *Z. f. KG.* XVII, 282 ff.; *SB. Wien*,
1897, vol. 136.

and that such measures are no hindrance to preaching and hearing the Word of God. By preference he spoke of the Church as the company of the predestined, a definition which, driven to its consequences, made the validity of the sacraments and the legitimacy of any ecclesiastical office depend on predestination, or, in other words, on a state of grace. He himself, however, never drew this inference from his premises ; on the contrary, he repeatedly acknowledged the saving-power of the sacraments whenever they are rightly adminis-tered. He held Scripture to be the unconditional and highest authority, and, to put it within the ken of all, he procured its translation into English, doing a part of the work himself. As opposed to Transubstantiation he taught the remainder-theory, according to which the Bread and Wine remain essenti-ally present even after consecration. Auricular confession he held to be a late invention, and celibacy he denounced as immoral and pernicious. He also opposed the honouring of the saints, of relics and pictures, the practice of making pilgrimages and offering masses for the dead, and, lastly, the doctrine of purgatory.

His proceedings were early the object of inquiries (1377–78), but with no result, as Wiclif was under high protection. This reason probably also accounts for his never having been submitted to any persecution for his views. Several (24) of his theses were condemned by the 'Earthquake Council' of London in 1382, though his name was not mentioned in connection with them. He himself spent the closing days of his life at his vicarage of Lutterworth, devoting himself to literary work, especially to the composition of his *Trialogus*. Subsequently to the Council of London, his friends at the University of Oxford were compelled to renounce his doctrine, though this measure was not effective in stamping it out. The preachers whom he had sent forth, the so-called Lollards (from *Lolium*, tares, *i.e.* sowers of tares), continued · their labours after the master's demise, and though his teaching was soon to be forcibly driven out of England, it was favourably received in certain parts of the continent.

The number of Wiclif's writings is considerable (Cp. LECHLER, II, 553–73). Their publication has been undertaken only of recent years, chiefly with the help of the Wiclif Society. To the works mentioned by J. LOSERTH, *Gesch. des späteren MA.*(1197–1492), 1903, pp. 390 ff., others must be added, amongst them being *De veritate S. Scripturae* (ed. BUDDENSIEG, 3 vol. 1904).

§ 143

Hus and the Husites [1]

In the latter half of the fourteenth century, the crimes being committed in the Church were denounced by several of the Bohemian clergy, among them by Conrad of Waldhausen (†1369), Milicz of Kremsier (†1374), and Matthias of Janov (†1394). Later on these men were followed by John Hus, a University professor and preacher at the Bethlehem chapel in Prague (1402). Whereas, however, his predecessors, with all their zeal for reform, had never strayed from the path of orthodoxy, he preferred to adopt, almost in their entirety, the tenets of Wiclif, whose works—owing to the intercourse between the Universities of Oxford and Prague, which had been increased by the marriage of Richard II with Anna of Luxemburg, a sister of king Wenzel—had early found their way into Bohemia. The only point of difference was that Hus held fast to the doctrine of Transubstantiation.

Naturally enough, opposition was not wanting to Wiclifism in its new home. The University of Prague censured a series of Wiclifite theses (1403), among them being those already condemned by the Earthquake Council. But the admirers of the new doctrine were not to be discouraged, and, belonging as they mostly did to the Bohemian nation, they profited by the action of king Wenzel, who reversed, to the disadvantage of the Germans, the old proportion of three to one in the votes at convocation, thus driving away the Germans from the University (1409). Nor was a stop put to the movement by the

---

[1] *J. Hus Opp.* edd. FLAŠJHANS & KOMINKOVA, 1903 ff. ; C. KROFTA, *Acta Urbani VI et Bonifatii IX*, I, 1903 (*Monum. Vatic. res Bohemicas illus-trantia*, t. V) ; PALACKÝ, *Gesch. v. Böhmen*, vol. III. 1845; HÖFLER, *Geschicht-schreiber der hus. Bewegung*, 3 vol. 1856–66 (*Fontes rer. Austr.* II, VI–VII) ; *Mag. Joh. Hus*, 1864; H. R. WORKMAN, *The Dawn of the Reformation*, II : *The Age of Hus*, 1902 ; HEFELE, *CG.* vol. VII ; LOSERTH, *Hus u. Wiclif*, 1884 (Engl. Trans. *Wiclif and Hus*, 1884); *A. f. öst. Gesch.* 82 (1895), 327–417 (on the spread of Wiclifism in Bohemia and Moravia, 1410–19); TOMEK, *J. Ziska*, 1882; *MICE.* 1900, pp. 445–57 (on the trial at Vienna of Jerome of Prague, 1410–12).

burning of a number of Wiclifite works and by all preaching being forbidden save in the parish churches (1410), nor even when excommunication was launched against Hus (1411) and interdict threatened on every locality which should afford him shelter (1412). On the contrary, the indulgences granted by John XXIII, on the occasion of the promulgation of a crusade against king Ladislaus of Naples, gave Hus and his friends new grounds for complaint. They denounced the indulgences, and the papal Bull was burnt by a mob led by the knight Waldstein. These doings induced a few, such as Stanislaus of Znaim and Stephen of Palecz, to withdraw from Hus's circle. Hus himself, who in the meantime had appealed against the Pope to a General Council, and to Christ the highest judge, was obliged to quit Prague, as the clergy, on account of the interdict, refused to hold Divine service. He was, however, harboured by friendly noblemen, on whose estates he wrote his *De ecclesia*, a work similar to Wiclif's like-named book. His party gained the upper hand when Wenzel, resenting the manner in which his overtures had been rejected, took the course of banishing Stanislaus, Palecz, and Hus's other opponents, and gave the Czechs equal votes with the Germans in the government of the city of Prague.

On the assembling of the Council of Constance, attempts were again made to bring the trouble to an end ; the emperor Sigismund, being heir to the crown of Bohemia, was especially desirous of securing peace. Hus was accordingly invited to attend personally at Constance to clear himself and his nation of the ill-repute which he had earned for it. Hus accepted the call, but any hope he may have cherished of being exculpated was certainly not fulfilled. Several theses extracted from his works were submitted to him as erroneous, and finally thirty of them were solemnly anathematised. As he refused to recant when called upon to do so, he was condemned as a heretic and burnt (July 6, 1415). Eleven months later (May 30, 1416) a like fate overtook his friend Jerome of Prague.

The originator of the trouble had now been removed, but the trouble itself was by no means at an end. The news of Hus's execution caused a great outcry in Bohemia, and for a time the Church was in grave danger. Most of the clergy who were unfavourably disposed to Hus were driven away,

and even the archbishop of Prague had to fly for his life.
The queen openly espoused the cause of Hus, who had been
her confessor, and nearly the whole of the Bohemian and
Moravian nobility was represented in the letter dispatched to
Constance, in which Hus was praised as a virtuous and orthodox
man, and in which the talk of a Bohemian heresy was roundly
denounced as a monstrous lie and invention of Hell. Simultaneously a league was formed for the defence of the freedom
of the pulpit, to oppose unjust excommunication, &c., and
the presenting of the chalice to the laity—a practice which
until then had been indulged in only by Jacob of Mies (known
as Jacobellus) and a few other priests—was now adopted
generally as a symbol of the Husite union. In the meantime,
Wenzel, though he did not favour the movement, did practically nothing to hinder it, whilst the Catholic league, formed
to withstand the pretensions of the Husites, was too small
and insignificant to be of any service. For several years
the Husites remained in almost undisputed possession. When,
at last, more energetic measures were resolved on, and
the expelled priests were restored to their positions (1419), the
Husites still continued to hold their ground. Led by the
knights Nicholas of Pistna and John Ziska, they claimed
fuller rights, and on their demand for the release of certain
prisoners being refused, they stormed the council-house of
Prague-Neustadt, seven councillors finding their death in
the tumult. When, soon after, Sigismund inherited the
crown of his brother Wenzel, the Husites refused to acknowledge him. Crusading armies dispatched against them (1420–21)
returned home defeated, and the Bohemians themselves,
assuming the offensive (1427), began a series of raids into
the neighbouring countries, in the hope of inducing the Church
to come to terms.

After a new crusade in 1431 had ended in failure, it was
judged politic to enter into negotiations. In the beginning
of 1433 many Husite deputies arrived at Basel, among them
being their great theological luminary Rokyzana, parish
priest of the Teynkirche at Prague, and Procopius the Great,
chieftain of the Radical party, or Taborites, so called after
the stronghold of Tabor erected during the religious wars.
Their demands were that Communion should be administered

under both species, that grievous sin should be punishable at law, that no restriction should be placed on preaching, and that the clergy should be incapable of holding property. These demands led to prolonged debate ; when negotiations were resumed at Prague in the autumn, 1433, the articles agreed to were as follows : 1. Persons having attained the use of reason may, in Bohemia and Moravia, receive Communion under both species, provided they acknowledge Christ to be wholly present under each species; 2. Mortal sins, especially such as are notorious, must be hindered so far as possible, sinners being punished by their rightful superiors ; 3. The Word of God is free to all the clergy who are qualified to preach and who have been approved and sent forth by their superiors, provided their preaching be in accordance with the Church's rulings; 4. Church property is, according to the principles laid down by the Fathers, to be rightly administered, nor may it be usurped by others. At the Parliament of Iglau in 1436 the latter portion of the last article was interpreted to mean that Church property must not be unjustly detained by others, and with this modification the compact of Prague was at last ratified. The Husites had recently fallen out among themselves, and the Taborites and Orphans (*i.e.* Ziska's ; he died in 1424) had been utterly defeated at Lipan (1434) by the moderate party composed of the citizens of Prague and the nobles. This victory must, to some extent, account for the ultimate success of the negotiations.

After an understanding had been reached, the name of Husites gradually disappears from history, and in its stead we find other names. From the use of the chalice or the practice of communicating under both species, they were called Calixtines or Utraquists, whilst the other Catholics were dubbed Unists or Subunitae. The permission for the use of the chalice by the laity did not, however, satisfy all, and soon some, such as Chelczicky, began to denounce saint-worship, Masses for the dead, property, oaths, the death penalty, military service, and, generally, all public offices. A few also denied the presence of Christ in the Eucharist. In Kunwald, near Senftenberg, whither the irreconciliables betook themselves under the leadership of Gregory, a nephew of Rokyzana (1457), a simpler mode of worship was introduced, thus laying the foundation of a new religious society or confraternity, that of the **Bohemian**

Brethren.[1] This society was finally established as a sect when, with the help of the Waldensians, it set about ordaining priests on its own account (1467). Though in its beginnings it was insignificant, it soon grew in importance, especially when it consented to accommodate itself to the requirements of social life, *i.e.* subsequently to the Council of Reichenau (1494). On the other hand, the Catholics of Bohemia were not successful in retaining the use of the chalice for the laity. Communion under both species was abolished by the edict of restitution issued by Ferdinand II in 1629.

The **safe conduct** granted to Hus by Sigismund promised protection for the journey, for the return journey naturally only on the assumption that it took place. The emperor also, by word of mouth, promised Hus a free hearing, probably even in the case of Hus's refusing to submit to the ruling of the Council. This promise was, however, not valid according to Canon Law. The Council claimed a right to deal with Hus (it did so expressly, September 25, 1415, in spite of the formal escort provided by the sovereign ; on the other hand, it dismissed as untenable the view that promises made to heretics generally are not binding), and the emperor could not gainsay it without endangering the continuance of the assembly. Hence the impossibility in which the emperor found himself of fulfilling his verbal promise must absolve him from the imputation of unfaithfulness. Cp. W. BERGER, *J. Hus u. K. Sigismund*, 1871 ; *Hist. Vierteljahrschrift*, III (1898), 41–86.

§ 144

Later Reformers [2]

Wiclif and Hus by their opposition to the Church are to be considered in some sense as forerunners of the Reformers of the sixteenth century. The same may be said of others of later date and whose historical importance is not to be compared with that of the two men just spoken of.

I. The Netherlander, Jan (Pupper) of Goch,[3] who founded, and acted as confessor to, a convent of women at Mechlin († 1475), refused to acknowledge as true any doctrine not vouched for by Scripture. He rejected the idea that there was any merit in vows or in the Religious Life (*De libertate*

---

[1] Mg. by GINDELY, 2 vol. 1857–58 ; GOLL (*Quellen u. Unters. z. G. der B. Br.*), 2 vol. 1878–82 ; CHARVÉRIAT, *Les affaires religieuses en Bohême*, 1886 ; *Monatsschrift der Comenius-Gesells.* 1894, pp. 172–209.

[2] K. ULLMANN, *Reformatoren vor der Reformation, vornehmlich in Deutschland u. den Niederlanden*, 2 vol. 1841–42.

[3] O. CLEMEN, *Johann Pupper von Goch*, 1896 (*Leipziger Studien a. d. Gebiet d. Gesch.* II, 3).

*christiana ; Dialogus de quattuor erroribus circa legem evangeli-
cam exortis*).

II. Johann (Ruchrat) of Wesel († 1481)[1] advocated yet
more strongly the Bible as the sole rule of faith. A Jubilee
(1475) furnished him with a pretext for declaiming against
indulgences, for which he could find no argument either in
Scripture or elsewhere, and which he described—as Petrus
Cantor († 1197) had done before—as a pious fraud (*Dis-
putatio adversus indulgentias*). He also denied, in his sermons,
the binding character of the commandments of the Church,
especially of the law of fasting and of the celibacy of the
clergy ; besides this, he attacked the sacramental character
of Extreme Unction, and railed against the sacramentals and
the Church's festivals. On being brought before the Inquisition at Mainz he consented to recant (1479), and was accordingly
merely condemned to be kept in prison at the Augustinian
monastery in that city.

III. Wessel Gansfort of Gröningen († 1489),[2] who formerly,
by an error, was known as Johann Wessel, questioned the
infallibility of General Councils, taught that every righteous
man shared to some extent in the power of the keys, that
indulgences are merely a remission of the canonical penalties,
that no punishment is administered in purgatory for sins
which have been remitted in this world, that purgatory is
intended only to cleanse souls from their remaining sins
and evil inclinations, that prayer for the dead can have for
its object only to ask of God that He should enable them
to attain more speedily to inner perfection, &c. His admirers
styled him *Lux mundi*, whilst to his opponents he was the
Magister contradictionum. Luther opined that this writer
was animated by his own spirit ; however this may be, Wessel,
so far as Justification and other important doctrines are concerned, never ceased to think as a Catholic.

Nicholas Russ (Rutze) of Rostock, in his *Büchlein vom Reife*
(ed. NERGER, 1886 ; *Z. f. hist. Th.* 1850, pp. 171–237), advocated
views resembling Wessel's. He attacked monasticism, the hierarchy,
indulgences, and the veneration of saints and relics.

---

[1] *Kath.* 1898, I, 44–57 ; *Z. f. k. Th.* 1900, pp. 644–56 ; *Hist. Vierteljahrschr.*
1900, pp. 521–23.
[2] J. FRIEDRICH, *Johann Wessel*, 1862 ; *Kath.* 1900, II, 11 ff.

§ 145

Relations with the Jews—The Spanish Inquisition [1]

During the Middle Ages the Jews had repeatedly to suffer at the hands of the populace. The crusaders, too, were frequently misled by their zeal to commit acts of cruelty against them, and the protests of St. Bernard and of the popes were unavailing to prevent the injustice. The Jews also drew down on themselves many persecutions owing to the oppressive usury which some of them practised. In time of calamity, more especially during the prevalence of the Black Death in the middle of the fourteenth century, among the many crimes with which they were charged was the sacrificing of Christian children, desecrating the Host, and starting epidemics.

Hand in hand with persecution went the attempt to convert them, this being the case more especially in Spain, where the Jews had always been numerous. During the persecution in 1391 in many localities they were merely offered the alternative of choosing between death and baptism, and a considerable number, under compulsion, actually passed over to Christianity. Others were won by gentler means, principally through the preaching of St. Vincent Ferrer, who began his missionary labours among them in 1412. Owing to the pressure so frequently brought to bear on them, their conversion was, however, seldom whole-hearted, and as soon as outward compulsion was removed, many would, openly or secretly, return to their former mode of life. It thus came about that in Spain there were many Jewish half-Christians, known locally as Maranos or as new Christians.

The people were not much more kindly disposed to these new converts than to the real Jews, especially as they showed consummate ability in securing the highest and most

[1] GRÄTZ, *Gesch. d. Juden*, 2nd ed. vol. V–IX, 1871–77; LLORENTE, *Hist. crit. de l'Inquis. de España*, 10 vol. 1822 (Engl. Trans. *Hist. of the Inquisition of Spain*, 1826); RODRIGO, *Hist. verdadera de la Inquisicion*, 3 vol. 1876–77; H. Ch. LEA, *The Moriscos of Spain, their Conversion and Expulsion*, 1901; *A History of the Inquisition of Spain*, I, 1906; E. SCHÄFER, *Beiträge zur Gesch. des Protestantismus und der Inquis. in Spanien*, 3 vol. 1902; *Hist. J.* 1903, pp. 583–97; DÖLLINGER, *Studies in European Hist.* (Engl. Trans. p. 210 ff.)

influential positions in the State. In order, therefore, to secure their complete conversion, shortly after the revolt which broke out in Cordova in 1473 against the nobles and Maranos, and soon spread over the whole of Andalusia and even into Castile, Isabella and Ferdinand the Catholic determined to re-establish in their states the Inquisition, which was now no longer in existence in Castile, and was scarcely known in Aragon. Permission to re-erect it having been obtained from Sixtus IV (1478), it was formally re-introduced in 1480. The first Inquisitor-General, who was at the same time the organiser of the new Spanish institution, was the Dominican, Thomas de Torquemada. Success did not, however, attend his efforts. Embittered by the proceedings, the Maranos of Saragossa hatched a conspiracy against the life of the Inquisitor Peter Arbues (1485), with the result that in 1492, by an edict, all Jews, save those who were willing to embrace Christianity, were banished from Spain. Most preferred exile to apostacy. In 1609 the same measure was adopted against the Moriscos, as those of the Moors were called who, under compulsion, had outwardly conformed to Christianity. With these, too, the Inquisition had busied itself shortly after its introduction. The proceedings of the Spanish Inquisition were repeatedly blamed for their severity, even by the Holy See. Very little attention was, however, paid to these remonstrances, the inquisitors being more disposed to hearken to the Spanish rulers than to the Pope. The activity of the institution has, moreover, been much misrepresented by its enemies, the number of its victims in particular being grossly exaggerated.

The character of the Spanish Inquisition was first and foremost ecclesiastical. At the most, owing to the extent to which the secular power was concerned in it, it may be spoken of as a mixed institution. The statement that it was primarily a department of the State (Hefele, Gams, Knöpfler) is quite unjustifiable. Cp. PASTOR, *Gesch. der Päpste*, II, 624–30 (Engl. Trans. iv, p. 403 ff.).

CHAPTER III

CHURCH ORGANISATION

§ 146

The Roman Primacy [1]

THOUGH the Roman See retained its supremacy, the storms of the period did not pass without some of its prerogatives being called into question. In narrating the history of the popes, we have already pointed out that the pretension to a political supremacy had been rejected by France, and that Germany had likewise denied to the Pope any right of ratification in the election of the emperor. The disputes, which resulted in these decisions being taken, had also other consequences. Occam, in his *Dialogus*, not only questioned the temporal power of the Church, he also proposed as a matter for debate whether Christ had ever ordained a primacy. Marsilius of Padua and John of Jandun, in the *Defensor pacis*, utterly denied the Divine institution of the primacy. They also questioned the fact of the Pope being the successor of St. Peter, seeing that the latter's stay at Rome cannot be proved from Scripture. By subordinating the spiritual to the temporal power they also threatened the Church's freedom and independence. Their views, however, met with but little sympathy. The current was still in the opposite direction. In the *Summa de potestate ecclesiastica*, dedicated to John XXII by Augustinus Triumphus, and in the work *De planctu ecclesiae*, composed at the same Pope's instigation by Alvarus Pelagius, the plenitude of all power is ascribed to the Holy See, the Pope being described

---

[1] SCHWAB, *Gerson*, p. 23 ff.; SCHWANE, *Dogmengesch. d. mittl. Z.* p. 557 ff.; Mg. on d'Ailly by TSCHACKERT, 1877; SALEMBIER, 1886; SCHEUFFGEN, *Beiträge zur Gesch. d. grossen Schismas*, 1889; KNEER, *Entstehung der konziliaren Theorie*, 1893; *Hist. Z.* 76 (1895), 6–61.

as the true and highest monarch of the West, and the emperor as his vassal.

Far worse than these paltry quarrels between the two powers was the agitation which was aroused in the bosom of the Church at the outbreak of the Great Schism. The needs of the time produced a theory which found wide acceptance, to wit that the papal power is not absolute even over the Church, the Pope being inferior to a General Council. The elements of this theory are found in Occam's dialogue, but it is first encountered complete in the *Epistula concordiæ* of Conrad of Gelnhausen (1380) and in the *Consilium pacis* of Henry of Langenstein (1381). The theory received a new lease of life at the Council of Pisa, and at the Council of Constance—at which it was advocated by the Paris chancellor Gerson and by cardinal d'Ailly (Petrus ab Aliaco), bishop of Cambrai—it was formally approved. At the same time it was not to the tastes of all, as we may see from the fact that, at the Council of Constance, certain of the cardinals absented themselves from the session in which it was sanctioned. That it was not more vehemently opposed at the time may be explained by the then state of the Church. Upon the theory depended, in some sense at least, the existence of the Council of Constance, and, consequently, also the union of the Church. It was ultimately set aside by Leo X at the Fifth Lateran Council : *Romanum pontificem, tanquam super omnia concilia auctoritatem habentem, conciliorum indicendorum, transferendorum ac dissolvendorum plenum ius et potestatem habere* (Sess. XI, anno 1516).

Some few individuals were not satisfied with subjecting Pope to Council. The author of the tract *De modis uniendi ac reformandi ecclesiam in concilio universali*, written in 1410 (ed. by v. d. HARDT, *Conc. Const.* I, V, 68–142, and variously ascribed to Dietrich of Nyem, the historian of the schism, to Andrew Escobar, and to an unknown third person ; cp. J. HALLER, *Papsttum u. Kirchenreform*, I, 505–24), distinguishes between the universal Catholic Church and the Roman Catholic Church, conceding to the former, *i.e.* to the whole of Christendom, inerrancy and the possession of the sure means of salvation, whereas he believes that the latter can err, fall into schism and heresy, and even cease to exist (c. 1–2). The substance of this thesis is found even in Conrad of Gelnhausen.

§ 147

Benefices and the Roman See [1]

Benefices loom large in the history of this period. The Roman See even previously (§ 122) had taken on itself the right of appointing to vacancies in foreign dioceses, by means of Expectancies, Provisions (*Mandata de providendo*), and Reservations. This practice was now vastly enlarged. Boniface VIII enacted that the reservation made by Clement IV should hold good whenever a beneficiary died within two days' journey of the place of residence of the Curia.[2] Clement V decreed further that all bishoprics, abbacies, and Church preferments generally should fall under this reservation.[3] The conferring of an expectancy for a definite benefice was indeed forbidden by Boniface VIII on account of the abuses it entailed, yet the practice was sanctioned, provided the promise was merely to confer the first benefice falling vacant after a certain date.[4] Simultaneously the *Cumulus beneficiorum*, or the holding of benefices ' in Commendam,' assumed greater proportions than heretofore, giving rise to complaint even at the Council of Vienne. It is true that John XXII forbade the holding of more than one benefice to which a cure of souls was attached, but the prohibition was not comprehensive enough to restrain effectually the evil. Cardinals and sons of princes were exempted from the law ; the former, because their service on behalf of the Church as a whole was to the best interests of all particular Churches ; the latter, because they deserved to be privileged on account of their high birth. The number of Reservations was to be enlarged yet more. John [5] claimed the right of bestowal of all the church

---

[1] C. LUX, *Constitutionum apost. de generali beneficiorum reservatione ab an.* 1265 *usque ad an.* 1378 *emissarum, collectio et interpretatio*, 1904 ; THOMASSIN, *Vet. et nova discipl.* II, i, c. 43 sqq. ; II, iii, c. 10 sqq. ; HINSCHIUS, *KR.* III ; L. KÖNIG, *Die päpstliche Kammer unter Klemens V u. Johann XXII*, 1894 ; J. P. KIRSCH, *Die päpstlichen Kollektorien in Deutschland während des* 14 *Jahrh.* 1894 ; *Die päpstlichen Annaten in Deutschland w. d.* 14. *Jahrh.* 1903 ; J. HALLER, *Papsttum u. Kirchenreform*, I, 1903 ; SAMARAN and MOLLAT, *La fiscalité pontificale en France au XIVe siècle*, 1905.

[2] C. 34 *de praeb.* in VI, 3, 4.

[3] C. 3 *de praeb.* in *Extrav. comm.* 3, 2 ; cp. c. 4, *ibid.* 1, 3.

[4] C. 2, 3 *de praeb.* in VI, 3, 7.

[5] C. 4 *de praeb. in Extrav. comm.* 3, 2 ; c. 4, *ibid.* 1, 3.

offices in which a vacancy was caused by his decree. He enlarged the scope of Clement's reservation by explaining that under *Beneficia apud sedem apostolicam vacantia* should be comprised all preferments which became vacant through the action of the Holy See, for instance through the deposition, transference, or promotion of its occupant, through the papal rejection of an election, &c.; also such offices as fell vacant owing to the death of a cardinal or official of the Curia. These enactments were ratified by Benedict XII in his Constitution *Ad regimen*.[1] Subsequent popes issued no new decrees concerning the matter, but the existing legislation was aggravated by the regulations made by the papal Chancery.[2] These alterations may be largely explained by the Babylonian exile. During the foreign residence of the popes, there was a great falling off in the revenues derived from the Papal States, whilst the expenses of the papal court were much increased, and when once a breach had been made in the prohibition of holding pluralities, it was only natural to cover the deficit in the papal treasury by providing the curial officials with productive sinecures. The evil became even worse during the Great Schism when the expenses of two Curias had to be met.

The various Churches were also called upon to support the Roman See in other ways. As had been the case previously, from time to time special tithes were exacted from them. Clement V was the first to reserve to the Holy See the revenues of vacant benefices, *fructus medii temporis*, and this reservation soon came to apply everywhere, and to all church offices. Besides this, all benefices which were in the appointment of the Roman See had to pay annates, bishoprics and exempted abbeys having to hand over the total revenues of the first year (*fructus primi anni*), or an equivalent pre-arranged tax, whilst other benefices paid the *medii fructus* or revenue of the first half-year, a tax which Boniface IX in 1392 exacted from all his nominees, and which, probably in consequence of this, was known as *Annatae Bonifatianae*. The Curia further claimed the property left by defunct prelates (*ius spolii*), and, likewise, the procurations payable to bishops when visiting the

---

[1] C. 13 *de praeb. in Extrav. comm.* 3, 2.
[2] *Regulae Cancellariae apostolicae* (from John XXII to Nicholas V), ed. E. von OTTENTHAL, 1888; TANGL, *Die päpstl. Kanzleiverordnungen v.* 1200–1500, 1894.

churches of their dioceses; the latter claim, however, was possibly only urged in France. These taxes were none of them entirely new; some of them had formerly been due to the bishops, others, like the annates, had their origin in the gifts which, even in Antiquity, it was customary for clerics to bestow at their ordination; at Rome it had long been the practice to expect certain dues from those ordained there. All these pre-existing taxes were now centralised and enforced more generally.

These taxes were not submitted to with good grace, yet— save only in England, where the statute of provisors (1351) had set a limit to the Pope's powers of appointing to benefices— they continued to exist in spite of the opposition. The reforming Councils of the fifteenth century did their best to diminish them, but with only meagre success. The Council of Constance forbade only the papal reservation of the episcopal procurations and any interference, either papal or episcopal, in the *Spolia* of other dioceses (1417). Martin V for his part withdrew any claim to the *fructus medii temporis*. It is true that the Council of Basel abolished the annates and a portion of the reservations, acknowledging only those which were according to common law (*i.e.* according to the *Corpus iuris*, excluding the *Extravagantes*), or which were due from Churches situated in the Papal States. The decrees in question were not, however, ratified by the Pope, and further negotiations were accordingly necessary. The end of these, so far as Germany was concerned, was reached in the treaty of Aschaffenburg, or, as it is more correctly called, the **Concordat of Vienna** (1448).[1] This, like the Concordat of Constance, conceded to the Roman See the right of appointing to the following:

(1) To all church offices falling vacant through the death of their occupants either *in Curia*, or in any other way *apud sedem apostolicam*.

(2) To all bishoprics and exempt abbeys when the election has not been canonical, or has not taken place before the expiry of the legal term. The right to be, however, reserved to the Pope, acting on the advice of his cardinals, to set aside a valid election, when a more worthy candidate is in the field.

(3) To the lower capitular benefices falling vacant in the

---

[1] Koch, *Sanctio pragmat. Germ.* 1789.

first, third, fifth, &c. months of the year, the nomination of the higher officials of the Chapter, according to the original wording of the Concordat, being left to those who regularly confer the dignities in question, but, according to the Bull of ratification issued by Nicholas V, devolving on the Roman See. In the event, the latter appointments were always made by Rome.

(4) In lieu of the *fructus primi anni*, the Curia was to receive, from the Chapters and monasteries of men—though under no circumstance more than once in the course of a year —a fixed tax, whilst any other preferment in the gift of Rome, provided its value amounted to twenty-four florins a year, was likewise to discharge the *medii fructus* by means of a tax.

The concessions, which were thereby made to the Roman See, were in certain quarters regarded with disfavour, and as Rome in the course of time gradually increased its demands, discontent grew more intense and more general. We thus meet with repeated complaints against the encroachments of Rome on the German Church, and the grievance which resulted had not a little to do with the success of the Protestant Reformation in the sixteenth century.[1]

In France an understanding was arrived at much later than in the Empire. In the Pragmatic Sanction of Bourges (1438) the French adopted, with a few modifications, the decrees of Basel. The annates were abolished, and replaced by a tax amounting only to a fifth of what had formerly been paid, this practice being persisted in throughout the fifteenth century, in spite of the efforts of the popes to obtain more favourable treatment. True it is that, in 1461, the Sanction was nominally abrogated by Lewis XI, but, this notwithstanding, it continued in force. Only under Leo X did Rome succeed in ridding itself of the obnoxious treaty, and even then only at great costs. In the **Concordat** entered into by Leo with Francis I (1516), the king was empowered to appoint all the bishops, abbots, and priors throughout his dominions, whilst the Pope was to have the right of confirming the appointments, and of appointing his own candidate in case of two unworthy candidates being successively proposed for

---

[1] B. GEBHARDT, *Die Gravamina der d. Nation gegen den römischen Hof*, 2nd ed. 1895.

a preferment. The Pope's right was also acknowledged to fill the offices falling vacant *apud sedem apostolicam*, and his right of provision over certain French cathedral and collegiate prebends was likewise ratified.

A Pragmatic Sanction, protesting against the usurpations and exactions practised on France by the Holy See, and supposed to have been drawn up by St. Lewis in 1269, and first heard of in 1452, is a forgery dating from the years immediately following the negotiations at Bourges in 1438. Cp. *MIŒ*. 1887, pp. 353-96 ; J. HALLER, I, 202, note 1 ; P. SCHMITZ, *Zur Vorgeschichte des Konkordates von Bourges*, 1902.

A cleric holding for a time a benefice, besides that to which he had been regularly appointed, was said to hold the former *in commendam* (*i.e.* until otherwise bestowed), the latter being held *in titulum*. As is clear, the difference between the holding of a benefice *in commendam*, and a *cumulus beneficiorum* is more verbal than real.

§ 148

Monasticism [1]

A. SUBSEQUENT HISTORY OF THE MENDICANT AND BENE-
DICTINE ORDERS

In the period now under consideration monasticism had fallen from the position it had once occupied. Excepting the Carthusians, and to some extent the Cistercians, the older Orders had not proved equal to their task. With increasing wealth, luxury had entered the monasteries, and discipline was relaxed. Many of the Benedictine establishments were now little better than hostels for the maintenance of the gentry and higher middle class.

The **Franciscans** were still split into two camps. Boniface VIII quashed the decision of his predecessor by which the Spiritual or stricter party had been merged into the Order of the Celestine Hermits, and did his best to unite again all the Franciscans under one rule. His successors also worked for a like end. Clement V, after having in his Bull *Exivi de Paradiso* explained, as Nicholas III had done before, the points of the

[1] For literature, see § 127.

rule which were in dispute, pronounced excommunication on
all gainsayers. John XXII acted with even greater severity.
These measures were, however, not completely successful, for
the schism was not removed, and a portion of the followers
of the stricter observance, known as the Fraticelli, Bizochi, &c.,
actually fell into heresy (cp. § 136). John himself came into
violent conflict even with the milder party over the question
of Christ's poverty. Dealing with a question then being
considered by the Inquisition of Narbonne, a chapter of the
Order, assembled at Perugia (1322), solemnly declared that
Christ and His Apostles had possessed no property. This
declaration was pronounced heretical by the Pope,[1] and action
was immediately taken against its propounder, Peter John
Olivi, who was then already dead. The difference of opinion
gradually made a separation inevitable. The French Observantines were granted a certain independence by the Council
of Constance (1415)—a like privilege was soon after bestowed
on the Spaniards—and were empowered to elect their own
general-vicar. By his Constitution *Ite et vos in vineam meam*
(1517), Leo X authorised the division into two distinct Orders,
the Observantines and Conventuals.

Something similar happened to the **Carmelites.** The
Great Schism, to begin with, occasioned a split in this Order,
as it also did in others, and though this was healed by the
restoration of unity to the Church, it was soon to be renewed.
A relaxation of the rule which had been obtained from Eugene
IV (1431) proved obnoxious to many members of the Order,
with the result that the Carmelites followed the example of
the Francisans, and separated into Observantines and Conventuals.

Though, on the whole, the state of the older Orders was far
from satisfactory, there were exceptions to the rule. In the
fifteenth century the desire for Reform seized the Orders,
the greatest promotors of the movement being the Observantines, among them Bernardine of Siena († 1444) and John
Capistran († 1456).[2] Mention must also be made of the Benedictine congregation of Santa Giustina in Padua (1412), founded

---

[1] C. 4, *Extrav. Joh. XXII*, tit. 14 ; cp. CHRISTOPHE, *Hist. de la papauté au
XIVe siècle*, I, 313 ff.
[2] E. JACOB, *Joh. v. Capistran*, 1903–5.

by the Venetian Barbo, and of the congregation of Bursfeld,[1] erected in 1440, which were instrumental in introducing far-reaching reforms into the monastic life of Italy and northern Germany.

B. The Orders of Knighthood

Even after the loss of Palestine a task still remained for the knights to accomplish. For long after, the hopes of the West were fixed on the re-conquest of Palestine ; nevertheless, as the Saracens were pushing steadily westwards, they had to be met on other fields. At the same time it seemed advisable to re-establish the Orders of Knights on a different footing and to unite them in one society, especially as the belief was rife that the fall of Acre was an outcome of the bickerings between the Knights of St. John and the Templars. Nicholas IV was the first to adopt measures to this end, but his plan was never to be realised, as one of the two Orders was soon to perish.

I. Against the **Templars**[2] charges of a shocking character had been brought by Squin of Floiran. It was alleged that at their initiation candidates were compelled to deny Christ, to spit on a crucifix, and adore an idol, besides binding themselves to sodomite and other unmentionable practices. This gave Philip IV of France a pretext for interfering with the Order, of whose power he had long been jealous, and whose property he coveted. On an inquiry being sanctioned by Clement V, the king, ostensibly in concert with the Pope, though really quite independently, cast the knights into prison (autumn, 1307), confiscated their belongings, and called on the other sovereigns to follow suit. His prisoners he put to the question, *i.e.* compelled by torture to make compromising revelations. Clement protested against these proceedings as an outrage on the rights of the Pope and an insult to the Holy See, and demanded that the captives and their properties should be

---

[1] Berlière, *Des origines de la Congrég. de Bursfeld, Revue Bénéd.* 1899 ; Linneborn, *Die Reformation der westfäl. Benediktinerklöster im* 15 *Jahrh. durch die Bursfelder Kongregation,* 1901.

[2] K. Schottmüller, *Untergang des Templerordens,* 2 vol. 1887 ; J. Gmelin, *Schuld oder Unschuld des Templerordens,* 1893 ; Döllinger, *The Order of Knights Templars* (Engl. Trans. in *Addresses* 1894) ; *D. Z. f . G.* XI (1894), 242–75 ; *MICE.* 1905, pp. 213–15.

handed over to himself, seeing that their Order enjoyed exemption. The protest seems, however, to have been merely a matter of form, for only a few weeks later the Pope himself issued an edict condemning the Templars, wherever resident, to be imprisoned ; in the summer, 1308, alleging the results of the trials at Poitiers and Chinon, he ordered a general trial of all the Templars, and his subsequent attitude to the Order is sufficiently clear from the decrees afterwards issued. According to their tenor no one was to give assistance to a Templar by either counsel or deed, and those who persisted in denying the charges were to be tortured into a confession. The judgment was to be left to a General Council to meet at Vienne in the autumn, 1310, but which, owing to the length of the trial, was delayed until the autumn of the ensuing year. Even then the issues were not quite clear. By far the greater number of the assembled Fathers were of opinion that, considering the nature of the imputations hitherto gleaned, the Order should be heard on its own behalf, and that to condemn it unheard, as heretical, would involve a crime against God, and an act of injustice. Only a small minority, consisting mostly of Frenchmen, was in favour of summary judgment, but this minority, backed as it was by the personal presence of Philip the Fine, who insisted on the immediate removal of the Order, succeeded in gaining the day. The result was that the Order was, not indeed by a definitive judgment (*per modum definitivae sententiae*), but by a special Apostolical ordinance (*per modum provisionis seu ordinationis apostolicae*), abolished (spring, 1312), its properties being made over to the Knights of St. John, save only those situate in the Spanish peninsula which the Pope reserved to himself in view of an object of his own. In the Bull publishing this decree (*Vox in excelso*), among the reasons alleged for dissolving the Order were the following : that the Templars had fallen into disrepute on account of their alleged heresies, that they were an object of scandal to sovereigns and bishops, and that, owing to the conquest of the Holy Land, they could no longer fulfil the task for which they existed. In the discourse with which the Pope introduced his Bull before publishing it, Clement alleged a further, and much more telling reason, *viz.: Ne scandalizetur rex Franciae*. Without a doubt Philip IV was the moving power behind these measures, making his influence felt even after the dissolution. The decision as to what was to be done with the dignitaries of the Order, a decision which by right belonged to the Pope, was usurped by the king. The court to whom they were handed condemned them to be imprisoned for life ; two of them, one being the grand-master Jacques de Molay, ended their lives in the flames for having refused to repeat the confessions which had been previously wrung from them (1314). During the actual trial hundreds of the Knights had already been burnt as backsliders (as many as fifty four perishing together at Paris), or had died under torture or in the dungeon. There is now very little doubt as to the true motives of all this cruelty, yet, at the time, people were not wanting who really believed the charges to be well-founded.[1]

II. The goods of the Templars did not devolve in their entirety on the **Knights of St. John,**[2] much of their property being seized by the sovereigns. In the Spanish peninsula where the Order had been exonerated by the Council of Tarragona (1312), their possessions were bestowed on the local Orders of Knights, or used to found new Orders, such as the Order of Christ in Portugal. The papal decision, nevertheless, was greatly to the advantage of the Knights of St. John, and with the new means at their disposal, they soon earned new laurels in the struggle with the infidel. During this period (1310–1522), the headquarters of the Order were at Rhodes. On the capture of the island by sultan Soliman II, Malta, together with the islands of Gozo and Comino, was made over to them by Charles V (1530). Hence the name of Knights of Malta by which they were sometimes known. When Malta came into the possession of France (1798), and then into that of England (1814), the Knights had already lost all their power and, as a result of the political changes which followed the French Revolution, they soon dwindled away to nothing. The remaining Orders of Knighthood at about the same time were transformed into mere orders of merit.

---

[1] H. Prutz, *Geheimlehre u. Geheimstatuten des Tempelherrenordens,* 1879 ; *Entwicklung u. Untergang d. T.* 1888 ; Jungmann, *Diss.* 31 ; *Z. f. k. Th.* 1881.

[2] Reumont, *Die letzten Zeiten des JO.* 1844 ; Doublet, *Mém. hist. sur l'invasion et l'occupation de Malte par une armée française en* 1798, 1883.

C. New Orders and Congregations

The most noteworthy of the religious societies which sprang into being during this period were :

I. The congregation of the **Brethren of the Common Life,** or of the Knights-brothers.[1]   Their founder was Gerard Groot of Deventer (1340–84).   Having, after his conversion, resolved to devote himself to the preaching of penance, he gathered around him at his house a few scholars and young clerics whom he engaged in the transcribing of manuscripts. His disciple Florentius Radewin, with his consent, formed these young men into a community.   New houses soon sprung up, and the society began to win fame for the instruction it imparted to studious youth.   Groot, by assigning a part of his house as an asylum for virgins and widows, also laid the foundation of a society of Sisters of the Common Life.   The foundation, owing to its possessing a monastic form, though without the customary binding vows, was vehemently assailed by the Mendicants.   To give his establishments a rallying point, Groot conceived the idea of erecting a monastery, or rather a chapter, regulated by the rule of St. Augustine.   His plan was realised after his death by the house at Windesheim (1386), which became the nucleus of a very considerable society.   In Germany the institution owed its success mainly to Johann Busch.

II. The **Minims,** or *fratres minimi,* founded by Francis of Paula, and approved by Rome in 1474, were commonly known in France as *Bons hommes,* and in Spain as Fathers of the Victory ; they were, when at their best, in possession of some 450 houses.

III. The **Olivetans,** or congregation of our Lady of Mount Olivet, came into existence through the foundation of a monastery on Monte Oliveto in the neighbourhood of Siena by Giovanni Tolomei (Bg. by Maréchaux, 1888).   The congregation was chiefly confined to Italy and Sicily.

IV. The **Jesuats** were founded for nursing the sick and the care of the poor by Giovanni Colombino of Siena in the latter half of the fourteenth century, and approved by Urban V in 1364.   Bg.

---

[1] K. Grube, *G. Groot u. s. Stiftungen,* 1882 ; *J. Busch,* 1881 ; Bonet Maury, *G. de Groot d'après des documents inédits,* 1878.

of Colombino by RAMBUTEAU, 1892 ; *L'Université*, 1895, XX, 66–87.

V. The **Alexian Brothers,** also known as Cellites, or Lollards (men of prayer), a congregation of lay-brothers devoted to the care of the sick and the burial of the dead, came into existence in the Netherlands at about the same time, owing to the prevalence of the Black Death, and were granted the rule of St. Augustine by Sixtus IV. Cp. *KL.* I, 532.

VI. The **Jeronymites**, or hermits of St. Jerome, four congregations which originated in the fourteenth century in Spain and Italy, and soon spread to other countries. Of these the oldest and most important grew out of the union of some tertiaries of St. Francis formed by Peter Ferdinand Pecha, a chamberlain to Peter Cruel (1370–73).

VII. The **Bridgittines** originated at a monastery erected by St. Bridget of Sweden at Vadstena in 1363. They were widespread in the North, and were sometimes known as the Order of the Saviour, owing to the belief that their foundress had received the rule in a vision from our Lord Himself. In its constitution the Order resembled that of Fontevraud, having double monasteries, and the administration of the whole settlement being in the hands of the abbess. Mg. on St. Bridget by CLARUS, 1856 ; HAMMERICH-MICHELSEN, 1872 ; B. RINGSEIS, 1890 ; G. BINDER, 1891 ; FLAVIGNY, 1892 ; T. HÖJER, *Studier i Vadstena Klosters och Birgittenordens historia* 1905 (down to 1350).

§ 149

The Parish Clergy and the Mendicants [1]

The share in the parish work taken by the Religious Orders, particularly by the Mendicants, had aroused considerable discontent even in the previous period. Complaints were made of various encroachments, it being urged that the Friars took on themselves nearly the whole of the work of the parish, granted excessive indulgences, used their rights to the disadvantage of episcopal jurisdiction, &c. The power, which had been granted them by Clement IV and Martin IV, to preach and hear confessions, even without the permission of the parish priest, provided they had leave of the bishop, was of a nature to lead to conflict. Instead of acting as

---

[1] EUBEL, *Gesch. der oberrheinischen Minoritenprovinz,* 1886 ; *R. Qu.* 1895, pp. 393–405 ; C. PAULUS, *Welt und Ordensklerus beim Ausgange des 13 Jahrh. im Kampfe um die Pfarrrechte,* 1901.

assistants to the parish clergy, the Mendicants soon became their rivals, and their competition was all the more annoying in that it affected the income of the parishes.[1]   The complaints induced Boniface VIII to place certain restrictions on the activity of the Franciscans and Dominicans ; they were to preach in parish churches only by leave of the parish priest, nor were they to preach even elsewhere whilst service was in progress at the church ; in order to hear confessions they were first to obtain the bishop's permission, or rather that of the Pope ; interments were indeed to be allowed in their churches, but of the fees and legacies, a fourth was to be given to the clergy of the parish.[2]   These ordinances which, in the meantime, had been recalled by Benedict XI, were re-enacted by Clement V at the Council of Vienne.[3]   Neither the seculars nor the regulars were, however, satisfied with this settlement.   Either side sought to increase its own rights at the other's expense.   The discontent of the parish clergy increased, when, as soon was the case, the other Mendicants, *i.e.* the Augustinians and Carmelites, were granted the same rights as the Friars Minor and Friars Preachers. Some of the Franciscans, to entice the simple, even spread abroad superstitious notions as to the value of their habit to those at the point of death.[4]   Hence the quarrel proceeded apace, the Holy See being frequently compelled to intervene. Sixtus IV in 1478 undertook to define more clearly the rights and duties of either party, but having himself been a Franciscan he proved too favourable to the Mendicants, dispensing them from the *Quarta funeralium*, and even giving them the power to absolve from sins reserved by the bishop.   The only result of the measure was to increase the discontent of the seculars. Ultimately at the Fifth Lateran Council, Leo X again reduced the rights of the regulars (1516).

[1] HEFELE, VI, 130, 241, 256.
[2] C. 2, *Extrav. comm. de sepult.* 3, 6.
[3] *Ibid.* c. 1 *de privil.* 5, 7.
[4] Cp. HEFELE, VI, 982 ; VII, 582.

CHAPTER IV

ECCLESIASTICAL LITERATURE

§ 150

Scholasticism [1]

Two men, both of them Franciscans and natives of England, exercised a far-reaching influence on the learning of the period. Of these one was **John Duns Scotus,** who taught at Oxford and at Paris, and died in the same year in which he was summoned to Cologne (1308).[2] As his title of *Doctor subtilis* denotes, he was remarkable for his subtlety. He succeeded in establishing a new school distinct from that of the Thomists, nor was it long before his doctrines were embraced throughout his Order. There were now in existence two schools between which the main points of difference concerned the doctrine of Justification and the Immaculate Conception of the Blessed Virgin, a question which had been debated even in the previous period. With regard to the former matter, whereas the Thomists generally followed St. Augustine, the Scotists preferred to lay greater stress on the human factor; with regard to the latter, the Immaculate Conception was denied by Thomas Aquinas and asserted by Scotus.[3] The latter matter gave rise to frequent and violent disputes; Sixtus IV was compelled (1483) to forbid the use of the epithet of heretic by the contending parties; even at the beginning

---

[1] K. WERNER, *Die Scholastik des späteren MA.* 4 vol. 1881–87.

[2] Opp. ed. WADDING, 12 fol. 1639; ed. nova 26 tom. 1891 ff. R. SEEBERG, *Theologie des Duns Scotus,* 1900; *Th. Qu.* 1902, pp. 259–79 (for his Theology); *Z. f. k. Th.* 1906, pp. 454–69 (for his views respecting the Immaculate Conception).

[3] RADA, *Controversiae inter S. Thomam et Scotum,* 1599; W. TÖBBE, *Die Stellung des hl. Thomas zur unbefleckten Empfängnis der Gottesmutter,* 1892; *Th. Qu.* 1879, pp. 355–401.

of the sixteenth century the spite engendered by the question was responsible for the execution of four of the Friars at the Dominican monastery at Bern.[1]

The second great Franciscan was Scotus's disciple **William Occam,** called after his birthplace, the village of Ockham in Surrey, who undertook the defence of Lewis of Bavaria in his conflict with the papacy, and was variously known as *Doctor invincibilis*, and *Venerabilis inceptor* († c. 1347). It has been usual to define the latter title by adding the word *Nominalium*, for whereas previously Realism had been the prevalent theory, through Occam's efforts, Nominalism now came to the fore.   As a matter of fact, however, using the expressions brought into currency by the new logic which had been taught at Paris since the middle of the thirteenth century, and of which the classical handbook was the *Parva logicalia* of Peter the Spaniard (better known as John XXI), Occam described general ideas, not as *nomina*, but as *termini* which take the place (*supponere*) in our minds of the things which they denote, or as signs (*signa*) of an unknown reality.   Only in the fifteenth century, for the purposes of discrediting it as heretical, was the new system styled Nominalism.[2]   All the same, it had all along been opposed to Realism.

Scholasticism had, moreover, but little inventive power left. As the numerous universities which sprang up during the fourteenth and fifteenth century show, minds were not at a standstill, but in spite of this the amount of useful work forthcoming was very small.   After scholasticism had reached its prime with Thomas Aquinas and Duns Scotus, teachers came to confine their efforts to the propagation and defence of the doctrines of one or other of these masters.   What they added mostly consisted of subtle distinctions not seldom devoid of any meaning.   This is no matter for surprise.   Without a fuller and more exact knowledge of history further real progress was not possible ; only towards the end of the period was the way cleared, by the awakening of historical criticism in the fifteenth century.

---

[1] N. PAULUS, *Ein Justizmord an vier Dominikanern*, 1897 ; R. STECK, *Der Berner Jetzerprozess*, 1902 ; *Die Akten des Jetzerprozesses*, 1904.
[2] Cp. E. HERMELINK, *Die theol. Fakultät in Tübingen vor der Reformation* (1477-1534), 1906, pp. 96 ff., 139 ff.

Apart from the church reformers, who will be dealt with in § 158, other well-known exponents of learning were :

(1) **Durandus** of St. Pourçain (*Doctor resolutissimus*), a Dominican professor at Paris, and later on (1326–34) bishop of Meaux. His great work was a commentary on the *Sentences* of Peter Lombard.

(2) **Thomas Bradwardine** (*Doctor profundus*), professor at Oxford, and finally archbishop of Canterbury, though he died the very year of his appointment. He was a strict Augustinian.

(3) **Gabriel Biel,** professor at Tübingen, and the last sententiary of the Middle Ages († 1495). *Th. Qu.* 1865 ; *KL.* II, 804 ff.

Finally, mention must be made of two men, who, though they both struck a new path, remained on the whole within the sphere of scholasticism. One was the Spaniard **Raymond of Sabunde,** a Toulouse professor († c. 1450), who, in his *Liber creaturarum*, sought to demonstrate the doctrines of Christianity by an appeal to reason and to Nature, and thus became the founder of Natural Theology (M. Huttler, *Die Religionsphil. d. R. v. S.* 1851 ; *Z. f. hist. Th.* 1859). The other was **Nicholas of Cusa,** dean of the collegiate church of St. Florin at Coblence, a zealous member of the Council of Basel, later on a follower of Eugene IV, and ultimately cardinal and bishop of Brixen († 1464). Equally conspicuous by the extent and the depth of his learning, he set himself the task of constructing a system which should bring controversy to an end. He laid great stress on the limits of human knowledge, and upheld the view that the essence of things is beyond the power of our understanding ; hence the title of his principal work : *De docta ignorantia.* Mg. by Scharpff, 1843 ; Düx, 2 vol. 1847 ; Übinger, 1888 ; *KL.* IX, 306–15.

§ 151

The Mystics [1]

Whilst scholasticism had already entered on its period of decay, mysticism was bearing its choicest fruit, more especially in Germany, and among the Dominicans. The greatest mystics of the time were :

I. **Master Eckhart,**[2] who ultimately settled at Cologne († 1327). To some extent his speculation went astray into the maze of pantheism, though this would not seem to have been intentional. Subsequently to his death, twenty-eight of his

---

[1] Pfeiffer, *Deutsche Mystiker des 14 Jahrh.* 2 vol. 1845–57 ; Greith, *Die deutsche M. im Predigerorden*, 1861 ; Preger, *Gesch. der d. M. im MA.* 3 vol. 1874–92 ; R. Langenberg, *Quellen u. Forschungen zur Gesch. d. d. M.* 1902.

[2] A. Pummerer, *Der gegenwärtige Stand der Eckhart-Forschung*, 1903.

theses were condemned by John XXII (1329), seventeen as heretical and the remainder as erroneous and savouring of heresy.

II. **John Tauler** [1] of Strasburg (1290–1361), a preacher of great power.

III. Henry Seuse [2] (or **Suso**), surnamed Amandus (1295–1366), who seems to have been born at Constance (not at Überlingen), certainly lived as a Dominican at that town, and died at Ulm. Of all the German mystics he was the sweetest and most attractive.

IV. **Jan van Ruysbroek,** [3] prior of the canons regular at Groenendael near Brussels († 1381), who, owing to the profundity of his utterances, was known in his own circle as the ' spokesman of the Holy Ghost.'

V. The unknown author of a German Theology [4] was an inmate of the house of the German knights at Frankfort at the end of the fourteenth or beginning of the fifteenth century.

VI. **John Gerson,** [5] professor and chancellor of the University of Paris († 1429), who, while not depriving mysticism of a certain speculative element, nevertheless gave it a preponderantly practical or ethical character.

VII. **Thomas à Kempis,** [6] a canon at Agnetenberg near Zwolle († 1471), the writer of many mystical works, among which must be reckoned the *Imitation of Christ*, a book which stands in a category apart, and than which few have found more readers. The authorship of the work has been the subject of much controversy, some having assigned it, though without reason, to Gerson, whilst others still more unfoundedly had ascribed it to a certain Benedictine abbot John Gersen at Vercelli, a personage of whom history knows nothing, and who was probably only Gerson's shadow.

The spirit which animated these men soon spread to others. The evils of the time, the political unrest in Germany, and the

---

[1] Mg. by K. SCHMIDT, 1841.

[2] Ed. K. BIHLMEYER, 1907.

[3] Mg. by AUGER, 1892 ; OTTERLOO, 1896.

[4] Ed. in German F. PFEIFFER, 4th ed. 1900 ; A. HEGLER, *Sebastian Francks lat. Paraphrase der deutschen Theologie*, 1901.

[5] Mg. by SCHWAB, 1858 ; MASSON, 1894.

[6] Opp. ed. SOMMALIUS, 1600; M. J. POHL, 1902 ff.; HIRSCHE, *Prolegomena*, 3 vol. 1873–94 ; WOLFSGRUBER, *Giovanni Gersen*, 1880 ; FUNK, *A. u. U.* II, 373–444 ; *Hist. J.* 1906, pp. 322–33.

interdict under which the nation groaned, to say nothing of
the plagues and allied diseases which wrought havoc throughout
Christendom, all contributed to predispose people to mysticism.
Among clergy and laity, seculars and religious, men and women,
we find in the fourteenth century a great outburst of enthusiasm
for the doctrines of the mystics and a desire everywhere
expressed to postpone the things of this world and to give
oneself entirely to God. Those who favoured this movement
styled themselves the ' Friends of God.'[1] Among the most
active and zealous was the secular priest Henry of Nördlingen,
the merchant Rulman Merswin of Strasburg, who wrote the
book on the Nine Rocks, and founded the house of the knights
of St. John on the grüner Wört († 1382), and also certain nuns,
such as Christina Ebner and Adelheid Langmann of the convent
of Engelthal near Nuremberg, and Margaret Ebner of the
convent of Medingen near Dillingen. In the higher regions
watered by the Rhine, the soul of the movement was a man
who wrote many books, who seems to have been closely connected with Merswin, and who is commonly known as the
Friend of God from the (Bernese) Oberland. His life is,
however, wrapt in mystery. Of late years his whole history
and all his works have been explained as a fiction of Merswin's,[2]
or of Nicholas of Louvain, Merswin's secretary, who afterwards
became a priest, and head of the house established by his
former master.[3]

§ 152

Exegesis and Bible-criticism

I. In the exegetical field the Franciscan **Nicholas Lyra**
(*Doctor planus et utilis*, † 1340) was labouring at Paris with
conspicuous success at the very beginning of the period. By
laying it down as a principle that interpretation must start

---

[1] A. JUNDT, *Les amis de Dieu au XIVe siècle*, 1879.
[2] DENIFLE, *Taulers Bekehrung*, 1879 ; JUNDT, *R. Merswin et l'Ami de Dieu
de l'Oberland*, 1889. On the other side see PREGER, III, and cp. *Deutsche LZ.*
1893, pp. 717–21.
[3] K. RIEDER, *Der Gottesfreund vom Oberland*, 1905. On the opposite side :
A. SCHÖNBACH, in *Lit. Rundschau*, 1905, p. 167 ff.; Ph. STRAUCH, in *RE.f. pr.
Th.* XVII, 224–27.

from that literal meaning of the text with which the Middle Ages had been so little concerned, and by endeavouring to ascertain the true meaning of the words of Holy Writ, he opened a way for later workers. His commentary, entitled *Postilla*, deals with the whole of Scripture. On its completion he turned his attention to the mystical interpretation of the Bible. At a later date the *Moralitates*, as his last work was originally styled, was divided up into sections, one being appended to each chapter of the *Postilla*. The work was received with great applause. A century later Paul, bishop of Burgos, a convert Jew († 1435), issued a new edition of it, correcting many of its details with his *Additiones*, or glosses, which the Saxon Franciscan M. Döring in his *Replicae defensivae* submitted to strictures more bitter than just. The commentary continued long in vogue, and before the end of the fifteenth century it had been printed eight times, having first been issued from the press at Rome (5 fol. 1471–73). How much Luther was indebted to it is shown by the saying: *Si Lyra non lyrasset, Lutherus non saltasset.* Later commentators were Alfonsus Tostatus, professor at Salamanca and bishop of Avila († 1455),[1] and the Carthusian Dionysius Rickel († 1471), commonly known as Denis the Carthusian.[2]

According to the mediæval view adopted even by Lyra, the mystical sense of Scripture is subdivided into the moral, allegorical and anagogical sense. The following verse explains the meaning of these terms :

> Littera gesta docet ; quid credas, allegoria ;
> Moralis, quid agas ; quo tendas, anagogia.

II. We owe much to two scholars for their efforts to correct the text of Scripture. Under the direction of cardinal Ximenes, archbishop of Toledo,[3] a learned commission produced the Complutensian Polyglot (1514–17). The work was edited at Alcala, the former Complutum, whence its title. Erasmus of Rotterdam also published (1516) a Greek edition of the New Testament.

---

[1] Opp. 13 fol. Venet. 1507, and often since.
[2] Opp. 13 fol. Coloniae, 1613 ; Neuville-sous-Montreuil, 1896 ff. ; KROGH-TONNING, *Der letzte Scholastiker*, 1904.
[3] Mg. by HEFELE, 2nd ed. 1851 (Engl. Trans. 1860).

§ 153

Humanism [1]

At no time in the Middle Ages had the ancient classics been wholly forgotten. But whereas previously they had not exercised any far-reaching influence on education, they now began to be more earnestly and thoroughly studied, with the result that they soon became a power to be reckoned with. At the very inception of the period, Petrarch († 1374), the famous Latin poet of the Middle Ages, and Boccaccio († 1375), author of the sarcastic and obscene *Decamerone*, were warm advocates of the ancient stylists, and their enthusiasm proved infectious among the Florentines. To begin with, attention was given only to the Latin classics, but towards the end of the century Greek literature also became the subject of study. The Byzantine Emanuel Chrysoloras was summoned to Florence, and many Italians, such as Guarino of Verona and Francesco Filelfo, betook themselves to Constantinople to investigate Greek wisdom at its source. Nor were natives of Greek-speaking lands utterly unknown in other parts of Italy. The attempts to re-unite Christendom secured for a while the stay of the Platonist Gemistus Pletho, and Bessarion, the metropolitan of Nicæa, even settled permanently in Italy. Though Florence had originally been the centre of the movement, which had there obtained the support of the Mediceans Cosimo († 1464) and Lorenzo the Magnificent († 1496), yet at Rome, too, subsequently to Nicholas V, humanism was in high honour. Other humanists of note were the Camaldolese monk Traversari († 1439), Leonardo Bruni of Arezzo, Francesco Poggio Bracciolini, and Lorenzo Valla († 1465), the first to call seriously into question the Donation of Constantine.

Outside of Italy the movement made itself felt most in Germany. Here it had its beginning in the schools of the Brethren of the Common Life, where the classics were zealously

---

[1] J. BURCKHARDT, *Die Kultur der Renaissance in Italien*, 7th ed. by L. GEIGER, 2 vol. 1899; G. VOIGT, *Die Wiederbeleb. des klass. Altert.* 2 vol. 3rd ed. by LEHNERDT, 1893; L. GEIGER, *Renaissance u. Hum. in Italien u. Deutschland*, 1882; FROUDE, *Life and Letters of Erasmus*, 1894; EMERTON, *Desiderius Erasmus*, 1899; J. KNEPPER, *J. Wimpheling*, 1902; R. ROCHOLL, *Bessarion*, 1904; SEEBOHM, *Oxford Reformers*, 3rd ed. 1887.

studied, though to some extent it was introduced from Italy, whence so many university students returned home enamoured of the new learning. By the end of the fifteenth century the whole country was involved, the headquarters of the movement being the schools of Schlettstadt, Deventer, and Münster, and the University of Erfurt; and its principal exponents the Gotha canon Conrad Mutian († 1526), the acknowledged leader of the humanists in the neighbouring town of Erfurt; John Reuchlin († 1522), the promoter of Hebrew studies; Desiderius Erasmus († 1536), a master of Latin style and no less learned in Greek, as eminent for his scholarship as for his literary activity, and famed among his contemporaries as a prince in the realm of learning; finally, Ulrich von Hutten († 1523), the political chief of the humanists and declared adversary of Rome.

As the conduct of many of the humanists shows, the new learning was by no means incompatible with the Christian faith, though the latter was to some extent endangered. Enthusiasm for Antiquity led many, more especially in Italy, to exchange altogether, or in part, the Christian view of the world for the old pagan philosophy, or at least to profess a scepticism not far removed from unbelief. The Roman academy, founded by Pomponius Leto, and presided over by him as *Pontifex maximus*, not only imposed pagan names on its members, but in its whole attitude was disposed to favour paganism rather than Christianity. Modern Aristotelians, particularly Peter Pomponatius († 1524), refused to consider the immortality of the soul and other similar doctrines as being more than mere theological truths, improbable in philosophy, a point of view which was condemned by the Fifth Council of the Lateran (1513, Sess. VIII). Other humanists were merciless in scourging with criticism and satire the ecclesiastical abuses of the times. Among the latter Erasmus earned himself a name by his *Laus stultitiae* (1509) and other similar diatribes.

Under these circumstances pretexts were not wanting to attack the humanists. It could also be safely predicted that the collision between old and new would be all the more violent, owing to the fact that some of the scholastics clung tenaciously even to the least tenable of their theories. A sign of the times was the dispute which broke out between the Ingolstadt professors G. Zingel and J. Locher, surnamed Philomusus, regarding the reading of pagan works in schools, a dispute into which others were soon drawn; for instance, J. Wimpheling, who, though himself a humanist, found Locher's *Comparatio Mulae ad Musam* (1506) so outrageous, that he entered the lists on behalf of Theology. A more important conflict was that in which Reuchlin was involved. The learned humanist had opposed the demand of J. Pfefferkorn of Cologne that all Jewish books which either attacked Christianity or were at variance with the Jewish law should be burnt, and Pfefferkorn, enraged by some slighting remark in Reuchlin memorandum, assailed him with his ' Handspiegel ' (1511), to which Reuchlin replied by his ' Augenspiegel.' Reuchlin was now summoned by Jacob van Hoogstraaten to appear before the Cologne Inquisition, and the quarrel soon became general, humanists and scholastics everywhere taking up arms against each other. Reuchlin appealed to the bishop of Spires against Hoogstraaten, and the latter in his turn appealed against the bishop's judgment in favour of the ' Augenspiegel.' The matter was pursued still further in the courts, and the controversy held on till it was merged in the greater conflict soon to break out, and for which it was to a large extent accountable. Among the controversial tracts called forth by this dispute the first rank is occupied by the *Epistolae obscurorum virorum* (1515–17),[1] a collection of letters written in barbarous Latin, mostly addressed to Master Ortuinus Gratius of Deventer, and purporting to have been sent by Reuchlin's opponents ; they are really an amusing satire on monasticism and scholasticism, and were the work of Crotus Rubianus at Erfurt and Ulrich von Hutten.

[1] Ed. by BÖCKING, 2 vol. 1858–69 ; W. BRECHT, *Die Verfasser der Epistolae obscur. v.* 1904 (*Quellen u. Forschungen zur Sprach- u. Kulturgesch. der german. Völker*, vol. 93).

CHAPTER V

RELIGIOUS AND MORAL LIFE—CHRISTIAN ART [1]

§ 154

Worship, Prayer, Church Festivals

I. THE western practice of administering Holy Communion had assumed its modern form already in the previous period ; it was now the turn of **Baptism** [2] to undergo a similar change. The method of administering Baptism by infusion, which had even before been customary, especially in France, now became the practice more generally, and soon was adopted almost everywhere, Baptism by immersion surviving only in the Church of Milan. In another matter connected with Baptism a change occurred. The practice of only baptising on certain days was not to be reconciled without difficulty with that of infant-Baptism, and the old regulations had to be frequently enforced. There was also a superstition, widespread in both France and England, that Baptism administered on Holy Saturday or Whitsun-eve was harmful to the children.[3] Under the circumstances it was thought advisable to insist no more on the observance of certain days. The Council of Reading in 1279 (c. 4) demanded the observance of the fixed seasons only for those children born within eight days, and various councils of the fourteenth century (Olmütz, 1318, c. 19 ; Salamanca, 1335, c. 6) ordained quite generally that children should be baptised shortly after their birth.

II. **Communion** [4] continued to be approached but rarely,

---

[1] W. MAURENBRECHER, *Gesch. d. kath. Reformation*, I, 1880.
[2] FUNK, *A. u. U.* I, 478–83.
[3] Council of London, 1237, c. 3 ; 1268, c. 1 ; Worcester, 1240, c. 5.
[4] *St. a. ML.* 1890, vol. 38–39.

and Mass too was not so frequently said. The Council of Ravenna (1314, c. 13) bewailed the fact that many of the clergy never said Mass, and laid it down that each priest should celebrate Mass at least once a year. Councils held in Spain (Tarragona, 1317, c. 6; Toledo, 1324, c. 7) even made three or four Masses obligatory. The provincial Council of Aranda (1473, c. 12) was compelled to lay the same obligation on the bishops. A slight change in this respect was effected by the mystics, who often urged frequent Communion (*De imitat. Christi*, IV, c. 3), and whose voice was finally destined to prevail.

III. **Public penance**[1] as a general practice died out during this period. It had already ceased in the fourteenth century, so far as many Churches were concerned. After the sixteenth century it is found only in very few localities. This alteration must, without a doubt, be ascribed to the increase in indulgences, the indulgence of the **Jubilee**[2] being added to those already mentioned (§ 128). According to the ordinance of Boniface VIII (1300), the Jubilee was to be celebrated once only in the century, but by Clement VI the term was reduced to fifty years, by Urban VI to thirty-three, and lastly by Paul II to twenty-five years. This explains how the sixth general Jubilee was held in 1475, whilst the five previous were celebrated in 1300, 1350, 1390, 1423, and 1450 respectively. After the fifteenth century the gaining of the Jubilee indulgence was no longer made conditional on a visit to the Roman churches, but was rendered accessible even to those who were unable to undertake a pilgrimage to the Eternal City.

IV. The misfortunes of the age were accountable for the production of a new penitential practice. The **Flagellants**[3] were societies of men who marched from town to town, scourging themselves on the way, to expiate God's wrath, and to implore mercy and grace. Not that the practice was, however, entirely new. In 1260 a movement of this kind spread from Perugia, soon involved the whole of Italy, and extended even into Germany. To some extent it had been caused by

---

[1] *KL.* II, 1576 ff.
[2] F. X. KRAUS, *Essays*, II (1901), 217–336: *Das Anno santo*.
[3] Mg. by FÖRSTEMANN, 1828; COOPER, *Flagellation and the Flagellants*, 1896; F. UNGER, *Die Flagellanten*, 1902; FAGES, *Hist. de S. Vincent Ferrier*, 2 vol. 2nd ed. 1901.

the predictions of Joachim (§ 136), though the unhappy feuds between the Welfs and Ghibellines after the deposition of Frederick II were also partly responsible. A similar though more prominent movement was occasioned by the prevalence of the Black Death (1348–50). The Flagellants (*Flagellarii, Flagellatores*) journeyed through nearly the whole of Europe ; France alone was closed against them. As, however, these devotees were inclined to attach a superstitious value to their performances, which also not seldom led to excesses, the power of Church and State was soon arrayed against them on the initiative of Clement VI. Even so, they were to be met with later ; indeed, at the time of the Council of Constance one band was captained for a while by St. Vincent Ferrer.

V. The discipline of **Fasting** was alleviated to some extent through the dispensation granted in the fifteenth century by Rome, enabling inhabitants of the northern countries to partake of milk in its preparations. For instance, in the diocese of Augsburg milk and butter, though not cheese and eggs, were permitted during Lent, the dispensation being granted on condition that the natives should, on all the Fridays in the year, not only abstain, but also fast (1452). Similar indults, commonly known as ' butter-briefs,' were granted elsewhere. For the rest the old severity still prevailed.

VI. Among the **Festivals** which originated in this period was that of the Trinity ordered by John XXII (1334), and that of the Visitation established by Urban VI (1389) ; both these feasts, especially the former, had, however, long been kept by individual Churches.

The feast of **Our Lady's Conception** was known in the East, where it was kept as the Conception of Anna on the 9th December, as far back as the eighth century. The marble calendar at Naples witnesses that in the ninth century the feast was kept under the same name and on the same day in that portion of Italy which then depended on Constantinople. About 1100 we find it kept as the Conception of Mary in a few monasteries in England ; about 1140 it was known among the canons of Lyons ; and about 1170 at Rouen also, quite probably being observed not only at the metropolis but throughout the province, *i.e.* throughout Normandy. Fault was found by many with the innovation, both in England and in France, St. Bernard being among its opponents at Lyons (*Ep.* 174).

In spite of this the festival grew more and more popular ; in the fourteenth century, when the doctrine of the Immaculate Conception was already beginning to be generally held, the provincial Council of Canterbury (1328) and many German diocesan synods declared in its favour. The Council of Basel (Sess. XXXVI, an. 1439) even directed its celebration throughout the Church, though, owing to the council being then in opposition to the Pope, the enactment was not obeyed. When, however, Sixtus IV departed from the passive attitude hitherto maintained by Rome, indulgencing the feast, and introducing it into the diocese of Rome (1477), its cause was practically gained. In spite of this it was long before it was adopted as a real festival generally. Cp. *Z. f. k. Th.* 1904, pp. 676–78 ; H. KELLNER, *Heortology* (Engl. Trans. p. 239 ff.). The number of feasts was thereby slightly increased though it had already practically reached its full complement. Indeed the number was too great for the tastes of some. In the province of Canterbury, where, it is true, the ecclesiastical year was rather overstocked (§ 129), eleven festivals were struck off the list by archbishop Simon (1332). At the Council of Constance, Gerson and Peter d'Ailly proposed a reduction, which was, however, not accepted.

VII. A few new practices of devotion either came into being in this period, or spread more widely. The **Angelus** assumed its present form by three steps. The evening bell and prayer is first met with in the thirteenth century, and was encouraged by John XXII. In his time the morning bell was likewise known, at least in Italy. Lastly, Calixtus III ordained that the bell should be rung at midday to summon the faithful to pray for the discomfiture of the Turk (1456). The custom of ringing the bell three times a day became general in the seventeenth century, though the form of prayer with which we now connect it came into universal use only when Benedict XIII granted an indulgence to the performance of this devotion (1724). Previously to this various other prayers had served the purpose. *Hist. J.* 1902 ; THURSTON, in the *Month*, 1901 f.

VIII. The **Stations of the Cross,** which existed at Jerusalem at the time of the crusades, are heard of in the West in the fifteenth century. The sculptured Way of the Cross by Krafft at Nuremberg (1490) is especially remarkable for its artistic finish. In this case the Stations are seven in number, or eight if we reckon Mount Calvary (they are represented in Kraus's *Gesch. der christlichen Kunst*, II, 308) ; in other places they were more numerous. The present arrangement first appears towards the end of the sixteenth century, though minus the last two Stations, and gradually became the rule during the seventeenth century, when the last two Stations were added, and when the devotion received the official sanction of the Church (1686). A Way of the Cross comprising *seven* falls was long in vogue. Cp. KEPPLER, *Die 14 Stationen des hl. Kreuzwegs*, 2nd ed. 1892 ; *Kath.* 1895, I, 326–35 ; *St. a. ML.* 1897, II, 336–38. THURSTON, in the *Month*, 1900.

F 2

§ 155

Preaching—Instruction of the People [1]

Great attention was paid to the ministry of preaching. Again and again were the parochial clergy ordered to preach to the laity, and the laity commanded to attend the sermons. The Council of Lavaur (1368, c. 1) gave the fullest directions as to the manner in which the people were to be taught. Towards the end of the period special endowments were founded for preachers in nearly all the larger German towns. After the invention of the printing press (1450) the works of the more famous preachers—and other sermonaries—were published in numerous editions, a proof, if proof were needed, that the synodal enactments had not been issued in vain. Several homiletic handbooks enjoyed a wide circulation—for instance, the *Manuale Curatorum* of Ulrich Surgant, parish priest at Kleinbasel (1503). Most works of this character were written in Latin, and sermons delivered for the benefit of the clergy or of the monks, or again on special occasions, were usually couched in that language. As a general rule, however, sermons preached to the laity were in the vernacular.

The contents of the sermons were not always equally satisfactory. Frequently points debated in the schools were dealt with in the pulpit, and not seldom subtle distinctions, far-fetched allegories, and tasteless legends were all that the preachers were prepared to purvey. After the advent of humanism many preachers, especially in Italy, were wont to pay more attention to the classics than to Holy Writ. All the same, preachers of a better stamp never failed, being found more particularly among the mystics and among the more zealous of the monks. We must also mention John Geiler von Kaisersberg at Strasburg († 1510).[2]

---

[1] *Th. Qu.* 1868, p. 267 ff. ; J. GEFFCKEN, *Der Bilderkatechismus des 15 Jahrh.* 1855 ; V. HASAK, *Der christl. Glaube des deutschen Volkes beim Schlusse des MA.* 1868 ; JANSSEN (Engl. Trans. *History of the German People*, vol. I) ; THUREAU-DANGIN, *Un prédicateur populaire, S. Bernardin de Sienne*, 1896 (Engl. Trans., 1906, by G. VON HÜGEL) ; W. WALTHER, *Die deutsche Bibelübersetzung d. MA.* 1892 ; F. FALK, *Die Bibel am Ausgang d. MA.* 1905 ; F. LANDMANN, *Das Predigtwesen in Westfalen in den letzten Zeiten des MA.* 1900 ; *Festgabe für H. Finke*, 1904, pp. 420–80 ; *Z. f. k. Th.* 1906, pp. 470–91.

[2] DACHEUX, *Un réformateur cath. à la fin du XVe siècle, J. G. de K.* 1876.

Besides the sermons we must not forget that instruction was also given in confession to the faithful on their duties, and the abundant literature on the subject shows that this matter received great attention. Nor were the faithful unacquainted with Holy Scripture. Before 1500 not less than ninety-nine Latin editions had been printed, and probably even more, seeing that, of the twenty-five of doubtful date, some at least must belong to the fifteenth century. Before 1518 four Low German translations had been published, besides one in High German which had run through fourteen editions. Even more popular than the Bible were the so-called Postils and Plenaries, which originally contained only the Epistles and Gospels, but afterwards comprised the whole of the Mass in the vernacular ; of these more than a hundred editions had been published in Germany alone previous to the time of Luther. Yet other works existed for the instruction of the laity, works which may be considered as the first Catechisms ; among these the best-known were Gerson's *Opus tripartitum*, written in Latin and French, and translated into German by Geiler von Kaisersberg, and the ' Mirror of the Christian ' of the Franciscan Kölde of Münster (1470). Finally art, too, was made to serve for the edification and instruction of the people. In this connection we must mention the picture-catechisms, the Poor Man's Bible, and the Dance of Death.

§ 156

Witchcraft [1]

The belief in witchcraft and in compacts with the devil was an heirloom of paganism treasured throughout the Middle Ages. The weaker sex especially was suspected of being in league with the evil one, and of using his aid to the detriment of mankind. We already hear of such women in the *De eccles. discipl.* (II, 5, 45) of Regino of Prüm, and in the *Decretum*

---

[1] SOLDAN-HEPPE, *Gesch. d. Hexenprozesse*, 2 vol. 1880 ; JANSSEN, *Hist. of the German People*, vol. VIII (Engl. Trans. vol. XVI) ; RIEZLER, *Gesch. d. Hexenprozesse in Bayern*, 1896 ; J. HANSEN, *Zauberwahn, Inquisition u. Hexenprozess im MA. u. die Entstehung der grossen Hexenverfolgung*, 1900 ; *Quellen u. Unters. zur Gesch. d. . . . Hexenverfolgung im MA.* 1901.

(XIX, 5) of Burkhard of Worms (known after its inclusion in the *Decretum* of Gratian, c. 12, C. 26, qu. 5, as the canon *Episcopi*). In these documents the superstition in question is reproved, as it was often to be reproved later. Owing to this belief it was, however, difficult to eradicate the prevalent tendency to admit the possibility of intercourse with the demon, an inclination which is manifest not only in the history of the heresies, but also in that of Boniface VIII and the Templars. The superstition not only held its ground, but actually became more and more widespread during this period. It was in this age that the opinion gained ground that witches (*Sagae*) could enter into sexual intercourse with the devil. Under these circumstances the twenty-seven articles against sorcery, issued by the Sorbonne for the instruction of the people (1398), did but little good. Innocent VIII, by the Bull *Summis desiderantes* (1484), conferred full powers on the Dominicans Jakob Sprenger, Henry Institoris, and John Gremper to proceed against witches. To the two former worthies we owe the *Malleus maleficarum*, establishing the existence of witchcraft, and giving directions for self-protection, together with the method to be followed in dealing with those guilty of the practice (1487–88). The persecution of witches now became general, the Protestant Reformation only adding to its severity. As belief in witchcraft was then deemed an article of Faith, the various Christian denominations determined to vie with each other in stamping it out. The famous ' Witches' Hammer ' was frequently reprinted, even by the Protestants. Such was the senseless cruelty of the age, that confessions extorted by torture were utilised to demonstrate the fact of diabolical interference, and then made the basis of further prosecutions, reason and humanity alike being cast to the winds. To have attempted to withstand the movement would have involved death. Cornelius Loos, a professor at Treves, was compelled to formally retract his strictures (1592), and even the Jesuit Frederick von Spee was obliged to publish his *Cautio criminalis* (1631) under the discreet veil of anonymity. Only with the increase of enlightenment in the eighteenth century did reason regain its sway.

§ 157

Christian Art : Architecture, Sculpture, Painting

I. During this period the prevailing architecture was **Gothic.**[1] Whereas in the Romanesque style the main element of the building was in the walls, in the Gothic it was in the pillars and arches, the walls being practically reduced to mere accessories. The Gothic architects sought height before all else, whereas in the Basilica, and to a lesser extent in the Romanesque style, what was aimed at was rather breadth, this peculiarity of Gothic art being most evident in the lofty steeple. Other points which, in a Gothic building, strike the observer are the flying buttresses which strengthen the outer walls, the exclusive use of the pointed arch, and the great windows or lights divided by vertical shafts or mullions, and, in their upper portion, filled with fretwork wrought in stone. Besides this, all the pillars or columns served to support the vaulted roof. In the Romanesque churches the pillars were so arranged as to support alternately the vault or the wall of the nave, one square division of the vault overhead sufficing to cover the space of two arches below, whereas in the Gothic the division of the vaults as seen from below no longer presented the aspect of a series of squares, but of elongated rectangles placed transversally to the nave and rigorously equal in number to the spaces left open under the arches. In some cases the side-aisles were made as high as the nave, such churches being known in Germany as ' Hallenkirchen.' In France it was customary also to encircle the choir by a corridor, or deambulatory, around which chapels were built.

The style had its cradle in northern France. There it was in use as early as the second half of the twelfth century, and soon attained great perfection, as is attested by the superb cathedrals of Paris, Rheims, Chartres, and Amiens. In Germany it made its first appearance in the second quarter of the thirteenth century, and rapidly ousted the Romanesque or Transition style. The style there in vogue until the end of the century is known as Early Gothic, is remarkable for its simplicity and

---

[1] For literature see § 131 ; A. KUHN, *Allg. Kunstgesch.* 1891 ff. ; K. WÖRMANN, *Gesch. der Kunst*, II, 1905.

severity, and has left us its finest legacy in the church of St. Elizabeth at Marburg. In the fourteenth century, and in certain localities even earlier, we find German Gothic art at its best. To this period belongs a whole series of splendid edifices, built in accordance with the strictest requirements of this type of art. Towards the close of the century, new elements were, however, introduced at the expense of the older rules, and resulted in the debased Late Gothic style. The most remarkable churches built in true High Gothic style, most of which were commenced in the previous period to the one under consideration, are, in German countries, the cathedrals of Cologne (the choir was built in 1248–1322, the nave and towers were completed only in 1880), Ratisbon, Halberstadt, Freiburg and Strasburg, the church of St. Catherine at Oppenheim, St. Stephen's at Vienna, and the cathedral of Ulm.

During the best season of the Gothic art, the pillars were frequently grouped together in sheafs. The buttresses, which so far had been merely covered with an inclined slab or with a simple roof, were now adorned with turrets. Flying buttresses were frequently doubled and their backs, like the higher portion of the turrets, decorated with crockets. The arches surmounting the portals and windows were also crowned with pent-roofs, provided with crockets down the sides and with the usual floral cross at the topmost point. The stone fretwork or tracery in the windows consisted of a rich combination of trefoils, quatrefoils, and other similar devices. A gallery frequently ran round the nave, which, in addition, was pierced by the triforium. In Late Gothic the pointed arch was often replaced by the ogival arch, the simpler cross-vaulting of the roofs by star or net vaulting; for the tracery phantastic forms began to be preferred; the pillars lost their capitals, in lieu of which they were provided with decorated bases, &c., &c.

Gothic art produced in Italy several grand monuments such as the cathedrals of Milan, Florence, Siena, and Orvieto. Italian Gothic had, however, some peculiarities. The flying buttresses were always of very slight character, and the round arch was not seldom employed instead of the pointed over the portals. Nor did the Italians generally take at all kindly to the new art, and it is to them that it owes its name of Gothic (*i.e.* barbaric).

II. Graven images,[1] owing to the just and lasting horror of the ancient Church for things sullied by heathen practice, had been almost entirely banished from her buildings during the first thousand years of her existence. In the East the same prohibition exists to

[1] Lübke, *Gesch. der Plastik*, 3rd ed. 1880 (Engl. Trans., *Hist. of Sculpture*, 2nd ed. 1872); A. Weber, *Dill Riemenschneider*, 2nd ed. 1888.

this day. In the West, however, a change took place. Even in the Romanesque period the use of **sculpture** was not unknown. With the advent of Gothic architecture a much more copious use was made of this form of art. Not the portals alone, but also the pillars and walls were adorned with images, and the mediæval artists soon attained perfection in this line of work. Generally speaking, their aim may be said to have been at once ideal and ascetic. In Italy, however, they soon reverted to the antique. This change was brought about in the thirteenth century by Niccolo Pisano and his son Giovanni. To the former was due the pulpits in the baptistry of Pisa and in the cathedral of Siena, to the latter the pulpit in St. Andrew's at Pistoja, as for the famous sculptures on the front of the cathedral at Orvieto, they were not the latter's work but that of L. Maitani of Siena and of his sons. The artists were closely followed by Andrea Pisano and Lorenzo Ghiberti, the designers of the brazen door of the baptistry at Florence. This form of art was ultimately to reach its fullest expression in the works of Luca della Robbia († 1448), Donatello († 1466), and Michelangelo (1475–1564). The most famous German sculptors were Jörg Syrlin the elder at Ulm, Dill Riemenschneider at Würzburg, Adam Krafft, Veit Stoss, and the metal-caster Peter Vischer at Nuremberg.

III. It was in this period also that **painting** [1] assumed the status of a real art. From the earliest times it had been in use for the adornment of the churches and for other purposes, but its earlier productions all testified to the decay which had begun in Antiquity and which only deepened with the course of time. They were devoid of natural expression, lifeless in their conception, were incorrectly drawn and badly grouped, this being true of all the earlier mediæval paintings, though there are isolated instances in which the expression of the features was represented with greater accuracy. Painting was born anew in Italy in the fourteenth century. Cimabue of Florence and Duccio of Siena discovered the means of infusing a certain amount of charm and life into their creations, and they were followed by **Giotto**, the former's pupil († 1336), who laid down truth to nature as the artist's principle, and laboured with such success that, by the time of his death, Florentine art had changed completely. His masterpieces are the frescoes in St. Francis's at Assisi, in the chapel dell' Arena at Padua, and in that of St. John in the church of Santa Croce at Florence. Following in his footsteps, **Masaccio** († 1429), the painter of the frescoes in the Brancacci chapel inside the Carmelite church of Florence, outdid his model in his attention to nature, his pictures giving the impression of greater spatial depth, and his figures being endowed with both firmness and beauty. Florentine art was now at the eve of its

---

[1] Woltmann and Wörmann, *Gesch. d. Malerei*, 2 vol. 1879–88 (Engl. Trans., *Hist. of Painting*, 1880 ff.) ; E. Frantz, *Gesch. d. christ. Malerei*, 2 vol. 1887–94 ; *Kunstgesch.* 1900 ; Crowe and Cavalcaselle, *A History of Painting in Italy*, 1903 ff. ; M. G. Zimmermann, *Giotto u. d. Kunst Italiens im MA.* I, 1899.

triumph, its greatest exponents being the Carmelite, Fra Filippo Lippi, a pupil of Masaccio († 1469), Domenico Ghirlandajo († 1494), who painted the frescoes in the choir of Santa Maria Novella at Florence, Benozzo Gozzoli, to whom many of the paintings in the Campo santo at Pisa are due (1498), Filippino Lippi († 1504), Sandro Botticelli († 1510), and Lorenzo di Credi († 1537); all these men were devotees of realism, but religious idealism also had a representative in the person of the Dominican, Fra Giovanni Angelico da Fiesole († 1455). His work, especially the frescoes at St. Mark's, Florence, attains in some sense the high-water mark of religious art. Mg. by BEISSEL, 2nd ed. 1905.

Florence was, however, not alone in its devotion to art. Throughout central and northern Italy a like tendency made itself felt. Nearly everywhere, however, it was Giotto and his pupils who were followed. In the Tuscan and Umbrian schools, noted for their soft charm, there flourished Melozzo da Forli († 1484), Luca Signorelli of Cortona († 1523), Pietro Vanucchi, known as Perugino († 1524), and his disciple Bernardino di Betti, known as Pinturicchio († 1513); in the school of Bologna, allied to the previous, there was Francesco Raibolini, known as Francia († 1515); in that of Padua, renowned for the accuracy of its outlines, there was Mantegna († 1506); in that of Venice, celebrated for its colouring, the two brothers Gentile († 1507) and Giovanni († 1516) Bellini, who adopted from the Netherlands the practice of painting in oils. The school of Siena alone remained attached to the older style patronised by Duccio; it succeeded, however, in bringing this style to such great perfection, principally owing to the labours of Simone Martini († 1344) and the two brothers, Ambrogio and Pietro Lorenzetti, that it deserves a place by the side of the Florentine school.

Painting ultimately reached its prime, towards the end of the fifteenth and beginning of the sixteenth century, in the works of those great masters who united in themselves all the characteristics of the new art, truth to life, wealth of composition and colouring, and strength in expression with a dash of idealism. The first was **Leonardo da Vinci** († 1519),[1] renowned for the depth of his expression and for the airy lightness of his colouring. His masterpiece is the celebrated Last Supper, which he painted in S. Maria delle Grazie at Milan. The next was **Michelangelo Buonarroti,**[2] a great expert in anatomical knowledge and a master in the art of expressing nature in all its truth. His greatest work is the painting on the ceiling of the Sixtine chapel depicting the Creation and the Fall, and surrounded by the messengers of the Atonement, the prophets and sibyls and ancestors of the Redeemer (it was executed in 1508-12). The painting of the Last Judgment behind the altar is also by him,

---

[1] Mg. by E. MÜNTZ, 1899 (Engl. Trans., *L. da V., artist, thinker, and man of science*, 1898).

[2] Mg. by H. GRIMM, 2 vol. 5th ed. 1879; SPRINGER (*Raphael u. M.*), 2nd ed. 2 vol. 1883; E. STEINMANN, *Die sixtin. Kapelle*, 2 vol. 1902-5.

though the work is too realistic to be agreeable. The third was
Raphael Santi of Urbino (1483–1520),[1] son of the painter Giovanni
Santi, a pupil of Perugino's. He learnt much during his stay at
Florence, and spent the maturer years of his short life at Rome,
whither he migrated in 1508 ; in the complete harmony of his art
he outdid all his predecessors. His masterpieces, taking them in
practically their chronological order, are the Sposalizio or espousals
of the B.V.M., the Burial, the Stanze of the Vatican containing
among other frescoes the Disputa and the School of Athens,
sometimes known respectively as Theology and Philosophy, the
meeting of Leo I with Attila, and the Mass of Bolsena. We also
have his cartoons for the tapestry which was to adorn the lower
portion of the walls of the Sixtine chapel, representing scenes from
the lives of the apostles St. Peter and St. Paul, also the Madonna
della sedia, at Foligno, with the fish and with St. Sixtus, besides his
St. Cæcilia, his Carrying of the Cross (Lo spasimo), and his Transfigu-
ration, which is supposed to have been finished after his death by his
disciple Giulio Romano. This is also the place to mention two other
great masters, both of them Florentines : the Dominican, Fra
Bartolommeo († 1517), whose paintings are redolent of piety, and
Andrea del Sarto († 1530), who produced the frescoes in S. Annunziata
and in the Scalzo.

Northern Italy was not slow in following the good example set
by Florence. At Venice Giorgione founded a new school, which was
soon rendered illustrious by Palma Vecchio († 1528) and **Titian**
(1477–1576 ; his works include the Didrachma, an Assumption, and
the Death of St. Peter Martyr). This school remained true to
Venetian tradition and is not to be matched for its colours. In
Parma, finally, we meet Antonio Allegri, known after his birth-place
as **Correggio** († 1534).[2] He was an expert in chiaroscuro, but his
works, which comprise the frescoes in the cathedral and in the church
of St. John, and many canvasses (Holy Night, Madonna with St.
Jerome, or the Day, &c.), though they are technically perfect, are
deficient in religious feeling.

The Netherlands[3] occupy a place of honour immediately below
Italy. Art had been held in great esteem there since the fourteenth
century, and in the fifteenth century a new realism was born in which
the religious ideal was combined in quite a novel way with sordid
reality. The first famous masters were the brothers Hubert
(† 1426) and Jan († 1440) van Eyck, who may be considered to have
inaugurated the practice of painting in oils, for though it existed in
the Netherlands before their time, they perfected it to such a degree
that it soon ousted everywhere the older method. Their great work

---

[1] Mg. by PASSAVANT, 3 vol. 1839–56 (Engl. Trans. 1872) ; E. MÜNTZ,
1881 (Engl. Trans. 1882) ; GRUYER, 2 vol. 1881 ; CROWE-CAVALCASELLE,
Raphael, his Life and Works, 1882 ; H. GRIMM, 3rd ed. 1896 (Engl. Trans. 1889).

[2] Mg. by J. MEYER, 1871 ; C. RICCI, 1897.

[3] CROWE AND CAVALCASELLE, *Early Flemish Painters*, 1857.

is the altar at Ghent, which was conceived and begun by Hubert and completed by Jan. A little later we find Roger van der Weyden († 1464), and later still, Hans Memling († 1495), and Quinten Matsys († 1530).

In Germany Master Wilhelm of Cologne earned himself a great name towards the end of the fourteenth century. A little later we meet Stephen Lochner, who painted the picture of Cologne cathedral († 1457). He retained, indeed, though he also improved it, the older religious style of painting, but Realism was soon to find its way from the Netherlands into Germany. Its representatives in the latter country were Martin Schongauer at Colmar († 1488), Barth. Zeitbloom at Ulm, and Michael Wolgemut at Nuremberg (1519). It reached its highest with Albert Dürer[1] († 1528) and Hans Holbein the younger († 1543),[2] the two greatest of the German masters. The former was known also for his copper-work, and both were very clever at wood-carving. Finally a prominent place must be given to Luke Kranach († 1553), court-painter to the prince-elector of Saxony, though his life and artistic work belong to Protestantism rather than to Catholicism.

§ 158

Church-Reform [3]

As will have been sufficiently evident from the foregoing, religion and morality had by no means been entirely swamped during this period. Numerous churches and charitable foundations attest to this day the piety of the then laity. On the other hand, abuses were rampant especially among the clergy. As the higher preferments, particularly in Germany and France, were almost all in the possession of the nobles, whilst canonries were esteemed as mere conveniences for the benefit of the younger sons of genteel families, it is not surprising if the clerical state was often embraced without any vocation. One result of this was the repute for bad morality then enjoyed by the German cathedral chapters. The existence of such bad examples will not lead us to expect too much from the

---

[1] Mg. by M. THAUSING, 2 vol. 2nd ed. 1884 (Engl. Trans., *Albert Dürer, his life and works*, 1882); L. KAUFMANN, 1881; A. WEBER, 3rd ed. 1903.

[2] Mg. by WOLTMANN, 2nd ed. 1874. Cp. Engl. Adapt. *Hans Holbein*, by J. CUNDALL, 1879.

[3] J. HALLER, *Papsttum u. Kirchenreform*, I, 1904; W. KISKY, *Die Domkapitel der geistl. Kurfürsten (Quellen u. Studien zur Verfassungsgesch. des deutschen Reiches in MA. u. Neuzeit*, ed. by K. ZEUMER, I, 3 (1906)).

inferior clergy. To tell the truth the parish clergy were not in a temper to think of their own moral elevation, being in sad straits owing to the oppression practised by the monasteries and cathedral chapters, which, after having appropriated most of the parishes, refused to give their secular vicars more than the merest pittance. So widespread was concubinage that a French Council complained (Paris, or Sens, c. 23, 1429) of the general impression being prevalent that fornication was merely venial. At Constance and Basel the abrogation of clerical celibacy was proposed by no less a person than the emperor Sigismund. Even small towns in this age owned their public brothels. Faced by all these evils the heads of the Church made proof of astounding forbearance, preferring to leave things alone, so long as their own rights and claims and revenues were left untouched.

The period was deeply conscious of its own irregularities. Throughout it we have to listen to complaints, and demands for reform. Though this is of course a pleasing feature, yet the fact that, in spite of countless desires and efforts, two centuries did not suffice to purge the Church, is a sad witness to the deeply rooted character of the evils.

The Council of Vienne (1311–12) [1] was first in the field to debate upon a plan for ameliorating the general morality and the condition of the clergy, and, in conjunction with the Council, Clement V issued a number of decrees of reform. No effort was, however, made to put a stop to the abuse which was generally believed to lie at the root of much of the evil, namely the papal exemption of so many of the monasteries. During the Babylonian exile and the Great Schism of the West, as the abuses became more crying, so did the demand for reform in head and members become more imperative. The Council of Pisa even decided not to break up until it had given satisfaction to the reformists. As its task, however, proved no easy one, it was found necessary to leave its fulfil-ment to a later Council. In the meantime provincial and diocesan synods, as well as the monks in their general assemblies, were to discuss the reforms to be ultimately adopted. This plan does not, indeed, seem to have been carried out, but, on the

---

[1] HEBER, *Gutachten u. Reformvorschläge für das Vienner Generalkonzil*, 1897; *RHE*, 1905, pp. 319–26.

other hand, many private individuals now concentrated their attention on the matter. Among them were Peter d'Ailly, Gerson, Nicholas of Clemanges in his work *De corrupto ecclesiae statu seu de ruina ecclesiae*, the author of the twin tracts *De modis uniendi ac reformandi ecclesiam* and *Monita de necessitate reformationis ecclesiae* [1] (*i.e.* Dietrich of Nyem, or Nieheim, who was the author of at least one of these works, cp. § 146), and Henry of Langenstein, who soon after the outbreak of the Schism (1381) wrote his *Consilium pacis sive de unione ac reformatione ecclesiae in concilio universali quaerenda*.

As the next Council, held at Rome (1412–13), was productive of nothing, the matter was taken in hand by that of Constance.[2] Even this Council failed to find a solution of the difficulties. The question of reform was too much bound up with personal interests, and the fear of loss of privileges or revenues prevented the assembly from attacking the evil at its root. The proposals of the committee appointed to consider the reforms were in themselves insufficient, and this was the case still more with the actual decrees issued by the Council. The seven decrees of reform, published in the spring, 1418 (Sess. 43), confined themselves to (1) abolishing the exemptions granted since the beginning of the Schism and (2) the unlawful holding of a plurality of benefices; (3) requiring the Pope to abandon his claim to the revenues of vacant benefices; (4) interdicting and decreeing the punishment of simony; (5) obliging beneficiaries to take Orders, and recalling any dispensations which had been given them previously to this effect; (6) restricting the papal tithes and abolishing those of other dignitaries; and (7) renewing the old legislation regarding the dress, tonsure, and conduct of clerics, and forbidding the clergy to appear in secular apparel. The decisions agreed to in the Concordats with the various nations entered into by Martin V were of much the same character. The tenor of these understandings showed sufficiently that they were not expected to produce any lasting reformation. We must also add that the Concordats, with the one exception of that made with England, were only for five years.

---

[1] H. v. DER HARDT, *Conc. Const.* I, V, 68–142, 277–309.
[2] B. HÜBLER, *Die Konst. Reformation*, 1867; *Deutsche Z. f. G.* IV (1890), I–13.

By its decree *Frequens* the Council of Constance seemed
indeed to have hit on a plan by which a gradual reform would
surely be brought about. Any hopes founded on the decree
were, however, not destined to be fulfilled. At Pavia and
at Siena not a single decree of reform was issued, and those
which were published at Basel, owing to the Council's own
irregularity, were devoid of the requisite sanction. The
various legations dispatched by Nicholas V, though they
wrought some good, cardinal Nicholas of Cusa, for instance,
doing much as legate for the reform of the Religious Orders
in Germany (1451–52), had on the whole no remarkable nor
lasting result.

The task remained, therefore, unfulfilled, and towards
the end of the century it again came to the front, after having
been neglected for a few decades, owing to the menace of the
Turkish invasion. The Dominican Girolamo Savonarola [1]
of San Marco at Florence spoke with the voice of a prophet
of the approaching chastisement and renewal of the Church,
vehemently urged the deposition by a General Council of the
' simoniacal and unbelieving ' Alexander VI, and, other adverse
circumstances co-operating, paid for his temerity with his life
(1498). The popes of the time were forced at the conclave to
take an oath to assemble a general Council within two years of
their election for the reform of the Church. Julius II fulfilled
his promise by assembling a Council at the Lateran in 1512.
This Council, which sat for five years, published a few reforming
decrees concerning the manner of appointment to preferments,
the bettering of the life and conduct of clergy and laity
(Sess. IX), against the abuse of exemptions (Sess. X), and
on taxation (Sess. VIII). On the whole, however, the importance of the decrees was scarcely commensurate with
the length of the Council, nor were they at all sufficient
for the needs of the age, nor, lastly, were they earnestly
put into practice.

The long delay in effecting the reform was unfortunate
and not without grave danger. People finding that their

---

[1] Mg. by VILLARI, 2 vol. 2nd ed. 1887–88 (Engl. Trans. 1888) ; H. LUCAS,
1906 ; RANKE, *WW.* vol. XL–XLI (1877) ; PASTOR, *Zur Beurteilung Savon-
arolas,* 1898 ; G. BIERMANN, *Krit. Studie zur Gesch. des Fra Girolamo
Savonarola,* 1901 ; J. SCHNITZER, *Sav. u. die Feuerprobe,* 1904.

hopes were deceived, and that their efforts to secure a reform by lawful means were utterly disregarded, finally bethought themselves of other means, and the all but universal discontent, the growing conflict of rights and interests between clergy and laity, between monks and seculars, between higher and lower clergy, and between empire and papacy, conspired to increase the peril.

I. MODERN TIMES

FIRST PERIOD

FROM LUTHER TO THE FRENCH REVOLUTION (1517–1789)

CHAPTER I

THE PROTESTANT REFORMATION IN GERMANY AND
IN SWITZERLAND [1]

§ 159

Luther and the Indulgence Controversy

INSTEAD of the long-desired and long-delayed reform, there
came a revolution. Its main personal factor was Martin
Luther.[2] Born November 10, 1483, at Eisleben, he joined

---

[1] LUTHERI opp. edd. J. WALCH, 24 vol. (Halle), 1740–50 ; PLOCHMANN and
IRMISCHER, 67 vol. (Erlangen), 1826–57 ; KNAAKE (Weimar), 1883 ff.; *Opera
latina* ed. SCHMIDT, 7 vol. 1865–73 ; *Epistles*, &c. ed. DE WETTE, 5 vol.
1825–28; E. L. ENDERS, I–X, 1884–1903 ; *Archiv. für Reformationsgesch.*
ed. W. FRIEDENSBURG, 1904 ff ; *Deutsche Reichstagsakten unter K. Karl V*
(Gotha), 1893 ff. LAEMMER, *Monumenta Vaticana historiam ecclesiasticam
saeculi XVI illustrantia*, 1861 ; *Meletematum Romanorum mantissa*, 1875 ;
BALAN, *Monum. Reform. Lutheranae* (1521–25), 1884 ; *Monum. saec. XVI
hist. illustrantia*, I, 1885 ; *Nuntiaturberichte aus Deutschland* (ed. R. Prussian
Hist. Institute at Rome), 1892 ff. Catholic works : RIFFEL, *Christl. KG. der
neuesten Zeit*, 3 vol. 1844–46 ; DÖLLINGER, *Die Reformation, ihre Entwicklung
und ihre Wirkungen*, 3 vol. 1846–8 ; HEFELE-HERGENRÖTHER, *CG.* vol. IX,
1890; H. DENIFLE, *Luther u. Luthertum in der ersten Entwicklung*, I, 1904, 2nd
ed. 1904–6 ; supplementary vol. I : *Die abendländischen Schri/tausleger his
Luther über Iustitia Dei* (Rom. I, 17) *und Iustificatio*, 1905 ; II. *Lutherpsy-
chologie als Schlüssel zur Lutherlegende*, by A. M. WEISS, 1906 ; J. JANSSEN,
Hist. of the German People, 1899–1910 ; BUCHHOLTZ, *Gesch. Ferdinands I*, 8 vol.
1831–38 ; EVERS, *M. Luther*, 6 vol. 1883–92. Protestant works : K. A.
MENZEL, *Neuere Gesch. d. Deutschen*, 12 vol. 1826–48 ; 2nd ed. 6 vol. 1854–55 ;
L. RANKE, *Deutsche Gesch. im Zeitalter der Ref.* 6 vol. 4th ed. 1867–68 ; *WW.*
vol. I–VI ; BAUMGARTEN, *Gesch. Karls V*, 3 vol. 1885–92 ; F. v. BEZOLD,
Gesch. d. deutschen Re/ormation, 1890 ; Bg. of Luther by J. KÖSTLIN, 2 vol.
1875 ; 5th ed. by KAWERAU, 1903 ; KOLDE, 2 vol. 1884–93 ; A. BERGER,
I–II, 1895–97 ; A. HAUSRATH, 2 vol. 1904. See also J. KÖSTLIN, *Luthers
Theologie in ihrer geschichtl. Entwicklung*, 2 vol. 2nd ed. 1901 ; W. KÖHLER,
Katholizismus u. Reformation (giving an account of recent Catholic work
on the history of the Reformation), 1905.

[2] LÖSCHER, *Vollst. Reformationsakta der Jahre* 1517–19, 3 vol. 1720–23 ;
H. GRISAR, *Ein Grundproblem aus Luthers Seelenleben, Jahresbericht der
Görres-Gesellschaft*, 1905, pp. 30–45 ; K. BENRATH, *Luther im Kloster* (1505–25),
1905 ; DIECKHOFF, *Der Ablassstreit*, 1886.

the Augustinians whilst yet a student at Erfurt (1505), and after he had finished his studies was appointed professor at the newly-founded University of Wittenberg (1508). As he himself confesses (after 1530), finding that the penances which he was wont to practise in the cloister brought no peace to his soul, he gradually came to believe that good works are of no avail for salvation, that they are to be performed only because enjoined by God, but that man is justified by Faith alone by which Christ's merits are applied to sinners. Whether this was really the path he had followed in coming to his conclusion must remain a matter of doubt, seeing that elsewhere his explanation is different. However the conclusion was reached, this doctrine of his, which he himself modestly styled his Evangel and which afterwards was seen to be really the essential principle of Protestantism, had certainly been present in his mind since 1515. It was soon to be completed by a denial of human freedom. Man, as he stated in a thesis in August, 1517, having become an evil tree, could will nothing save evil. A few months after this he took the step which brought him into open conflict with the Church.

To obtain funds for the rebuilding of St. Peter's at Rome, an indulgence had, according to the custom of the time, been offered to all Christians in return for their gifts. Such a proceeding, accompanied as it often was by abuse, aroused the wrath of the pious Augustinian, and, on the arrival of the Dominican John Tetzel [1] to preach the indulgence, Luther nailed to the gate of the castle church a manifesto consisting of ninety-five Theses. This happened on All-Hallows Eve, 1517. Among other things it is there stated that the Pope can only remit such penalties as he has imposed, or as are prescribed by Canon Law (Thesis 5) ; that his forgiveness is merely a notification of the forgiveness bestowed by God (6) ; that indulgences are of no avail to the souls in purgatory (8–29) ; that any Christian who is truly sorry for his sins, even though he has no indulgence brief, receives full forgiveness of the sins and their penalties (36) ; that every true Christian, living or dead, has a part in Christ's and the Church's treasure, quite

---

[1] Mg. by GRÖNE, 1853 ; N. PAULUS, 1899 , J. MAY, *Der Kurfürst, Kardinal EB. Albrecht II v. Mainz u. Magdeburg*, 2 vol. 1865–75 ; A. SCHULTE, *Die Fugger in Rom*, 1495–1523, 2 vol. 1904.

independently of any indulgence (37) ; that the Church's treasure, from which indulgences derive their worth, does not consist of the merits of Christ and the saints, seeing that their grace has no connection with the Pope (58). On the other hand, it is admitted that the Pope's forgiveness, being a sign of that of God, is not to be made light of (38). Though it was not Luther's intention to do away altogether with indulgences, his Theses practically assailed them at their foundation.

The Theses attracted widespread attention, and were soon made the object of a host of confutations. At Frankfort on the Oder, Wimpina issued his Antitheses, and Tetzel, who published and defended them, also added fifty Theses of his own dealing with the power of the Pope and with heresy, and asserting the Pope's right to decide infallibly in matters of faith. The Roman Dominican, Silvester Prierias, composed his *Dialogus in praesumptuosas Martini Lutheri conclusiones de potestate papae.* Eck, a professor at Ingoldstadt, animadverted on the Theses in his *Obelisci.* Lastly, at Cologne they were attacked by the Dominican Hoogstraaten. Luther did not allow these contradictions to pass unanswered. His work against Eck is entitled *Asterisci.* He also wrote, in explanation and defence of his Theses, a work called *Resolutiones.*[1] A copy of this work he sent to the Pope.

That the Protestant reformation was truly a religious revolution scarcely admits of a doubt, and even the Protestants themselves are beginning to see it in this light. The only question is, where reform ends and revolution begins.

§ 160

Rome's Intervention and the Leipzig Disputation—Luther's Works [2]

I. In the meantime the Pope had interested himself in the movement. A summons was issued to Luther to present

[1] W. KÖHLER, *Luthers 95 Thesen samt s. Resolutionen und den Gegen-schriften von Wimpina-Tetzel, Eck und Prierias und den Antworten Luthers,* 1903. Cp. LÄMMER, *Die vortrid. kath. Theologie,* 1858, pp. 3–17.

[2] SEIDEMANN, *Die Leipziger Disputation im J.* 1519, 1843 ; O. SEITZ, *Der authentische Text der Leipz. Disp.* 1903; H. BARGE, *Andreas Bodenstein von Karlstadt,* 2 vol. 1905; TH. WIEDEMANN, *Joh. Eck,* 1865 ; D. F. STRAUSS, *Ulrich v. Hutten,* 2nd ed. 1871 ; KAWERAU, *H. Emser,* 1898 ; P. KALKHOFF, *Forschungen zu Luthers röm. Prozess,* 1905.

himself at Rome, but at the desire of his sovereign Frederick the Wise, prince-elector of Saxony, it was arranged that, instead of this, he should be examined before cardinal Cajetan (Thomas de Vio) at the Diet to be held at Augsburg in the autumn, 1518. He was then to be called upon to withdraw his Thesis fifty-eight and the opinion expressed in Resolution 7 : *non sacramentum, sed fides sacramenti iustificat.* Luther, however, refused to recant, urging that the Thesis was not even in contradiction with the papal decretals, and that the sacraments, seeing that Faith is the only condition of salvation, owe all their efficiency to Faith. All that he would consent to do was to keep silence so long as his opponents refrained from attacking him. At his departure, hearing that Rome had appointed his enemy Prierias to be his judge, he left behind him an appeal to the Pope, *a Leone male informato ad Leonem melius informandum.* Foreseeing, however, that he would soon be excommunicated, a week later he appealed to a General Council.

His fear was as yet without foundation. As Luther had justified his conduct by asserting that the Church had never yet authoritatively spoken her mind on the matter, the Pope decided to issue a special Bull on indulgences. This being done, Leo X sent into Saxony a papal dignitary, Carl von Miltitz, with the Golden Rose and an offer of indulgences, to solicit the elector's intervention. Again Luther promised to hold his peace on condition that others did likewise. He also vowed, in a public proclamation, to express regret for his actions and to urge the people to treat the Holy See with respect.

II. The excitement was, however, too great to admit of silence. Previous to the dissolution of the Augsburg Diet, a disputation had been arranged between Eck and Carlstadt of Wittenberg. This took place at Leipzig in the summer, 1519, and the Theses then advanced by Eck provoked Luther himself to enter into the controversy. The main point at issue concerned the primacy (Thesis 13), Luther denying that it was of Divine institution. He also rejected the infallibility of General Councils, alleging what had happened at Constance. By this time he had clearly become a convert to another great Protestant principle, viz. that that only which can be established by Holy Scripture is to be admitted as true in religion.

As the parties were too much opposed for a compromise

to be thought of, the controversy was allowed to continue by means of the press. A few new disputants were drawn into it, for instance, Jerome Emser of Ulm, secretary to duke George of Saxony, who took up the cudgels against Luther; his connection with the quarrel dated from the time of the Leipzig disputation. At Cologne and Louvain the theological faculties passed solemn censure on the reformer's works. In the spring, 1520, Rome, too, entered the lists with the Bull *Exsurge Domine*, in which forty-one of Luther's propositions were anathematised, he himself being threatened with excommunication should he not recant within sixty days. On the other hand, the number of his friends was also steadily growing. Many hoped that his action would really lead to a removal of the evils which oppressed the Church. Others, especially the humanists, joined him, because of their common detestation for the teaching of the schoolmen. Others again supported his cause out of hatred for Rome, among them Ulrich von Hutten, who, about this time, sent broadcast into the world his '*Vadiscus*, or the Triunity of the Roman Church,' and other similar seditious works.

III. Luther himself was busily engaged in writing. Probably at the request of his friends among the nobility, he composed, in the summer, 1520, his work addressed ' To the Christian nobles of the German Nation, on improving the condition of Christianity,' its title indicating sufficiently a manifesto against the crimes of Church and State, with proposals for their removal. Here we find for the first time the idea of a priesthood common to all the faithful, a denial of transubstantiation, and a demand for the abrogation of the law regarding celibacy. In the work *De captivitate babylonica*, published shortly after, he threw overboard the sacrificial character of the Mass, and all the sacraments save Baptism and the Last Supper, retaining, however, a portion of that of Penance, and requiring that Communion should be administered under both species. Now that the Holy See had pronounced judgment on him he had no reason to hesitate any longer, and his further mental evolution was rapid and constant. At the request of Miltitz he indeed consented to send another epistle to Leo X, but, though he therein affirmed that he had never attacked the Pope personally, he also made it known that he would never retract.   The treatise *De libertate christiana*, the reformer's third great work, contains the sum of his doctrine exposed for Leo's benefit.   Events now followed each other rapidly.   On the publication in Germany of the Pope's decision, he sent forth his ' Against the Bull of Antichrist,' and as the sentence had resulted in his books being burnt in many localities, he himself publicly committed to the flames the Bull together with the works on Canon law.

§ 161

The Diets of Worms, 1521, and Nuremberg, 1522–24— Melanchthon and the Anabaptists [1]

According to the directions of the papal Bull, proceedings were to be taken not only against the writings, but also against the person of Luther.   The question was debated at the Diet held at Worms in 1521.   The decision was, however, not arrived at soon enough to please Aleander, the papal legate present. The assembled princes submitted their own strictures on the Church, and prevailed on the young emperor **Charles V** (1519–56) to allow the condemned man a hearing.   Their intention was doubtless to give him an opportunity to recant, or to seek some honourable compromise, but any such hope was not to be fulfilled, for Luther remained obstinately true to his teaching. Even when the ban had been formally laid on him, the aim of his enemies was not gained, as his disciple the elector of Saxony hastened to bring him, disguised as the knight George, into safety at the Wartburg near Eisenach.   All the same he now lost the sympathy of a number of men who thus far had supported him, but who now began to see clearly that his object was to subvert, rather than reform, the Church.   Among these was Erasmus of Rotterdam.   Three years later the famous humanist was to oppose Luther with a work, *De libero arbitrio* (1524) ; on receiving Luther's answer, *De servo arbitrio* (1525), he retorted with the *Hyperaspistes diatribae adv. Servum arbitrium M. Lutheri* (1525–26).

---

[1] BRIEGER, *Aleander u. Luther,* 1521 (*Quellen u. Forschungen zur Gesch. der Ref. I*), 1884 ; HAUSRATH, *Aleander u. Luther auf d. Reichst. zu Worms,* 1897 ; *Nachr. Göttingen,* 1899, pp. 165–81; L. RUFFET, *Luther et la diète de Worms,* 1903.

In the solitude of his Patmos, as he called his new abode, Luther was assailed by doubts as to the righteousness of his cause. Convinced, however, that he had been raised up by God to be a religious reformer, he put away such doubts and qualms of conscience as mere temptations of Satan, and, full of confidence in himself, and of hatred for the papacy and the Catholic Church, he never deviated for a moment from the path he had selected. In the tract on the Abuse of Masses he describes the Mass as a creation of hell, and a scandalous piece of idolatry, whilst the clergy he terms priests of the devil. In the translation of the Bible which he then began (the New Testament appeared in 1522, the Old in 1523–32), he also showed that even Holy Scripture, on which so far he had based all his attacks, was not above criticism when it did not agree with his preconceived opinions. The epistle of St. James, for instance, because it so clearly teaches the necessity of good works for salvation, was denounced in the preface to the New Testament as an ' epistle of straw.'

At about this same time **Philip Melanchthon,**[1] born at Bretten in the Rhenish Palatinate (1497), and since the beginning of the Reformation (1518) professor at Wittenberg, produced his *Loci communes seu hypotyposes theologicae* (1521), the first text-book of dogmatic theology to embody the new doctrines. He was the second greatest of the German Reformers, and to some extent succeeded in infusing into Luther a little of his own peaceableness of disposition.

Melanchthon was, however, powerless to control the disturbances which broke out at Wittenberg during Luther's absence, and in which Carlstadt was the moving spirit. The new movement threatened to submerge everything in universal anarchy. The clergy began to marry, the monks, beginning with the Augustinians, quitted the cloister, Masses were abolished, Communion was administered under both species, and even without any preliminary confession. Even against study a war was declared. Artisans were to preach the Gospel and the students were to be set to learn trades. Matters became still worse when the Anabaptists, after an abortive attempt

---

[1] *Melanchth. opp.* ed. BRETSCHNEIDER et BINDSEIL, 28 vol. 1834–60 ; *Loci comm.* ed. PLITT, 1864, 3rd ed., ed. KOLDE, 1900. Mg. by C. SCHMIDT, 1861 ; R. SCHÄFER, 1897 ; G. ELLINGER, 1902,

to found a new kingdom at Zwickau, migrated in a body to Wittenberg. At the beginning of 1522 image-breaking became a regular frenzy. It was then that Luther made his appearance in the town and soon re-established order ; it was then, too, that he first began to carry out his doctrines in external worship. Private Masses were abolished, a sermon and prayers taking their place every week-day. Communion was distributed under both kinds, and certain alterations were made in the Mass, such words, for instance, as spoke of it as a sacrifice being omitted.

Adrian VI, who ascended the pontifical throne that same year, had some hope of putting a stop to the movement by reforming the Church and, above all, the Roman Curia, of which the conduct had of late been more than usually disgraceful. He accordingly proposed to the Diet of Nuremberg (1522–23) that a General Council should be held in Germany.[1] In his opinion the abuses in the Church were the source of all the trouble, but so suspicious were the assembled princes of the sincerity of the Pope's advances, that they received them with great coldness. When summoned to carry out the edict of Worms and take up arms against the Reformers, the Diet retorted by re-issuing the *Gravamina nationis Germanicae* ; ultimately it was settled that, until the Council, which was to meet within a year, the rulers should prevent Luther from taking any action, and see that the Gospel was preached according to the interpretation of the Church. These promises were, however, idle ones. Luther calmly continued his warfare against the Church, nor did the Council ever meet. Adrian died soon after, and his successor **Clement VII** allowed the matter to drop ; indeed, the plan had been rendered almost impracticable by the outbreak of a war between France and the emperor. The Reformation was, therefore, free to continue its progress. Only in southern Germany were any energetic steps taken against it. Although the Diet which met at Nuremberg in 1524 refused to sanction the rigorous application of the edict of Worms, the papal legate Campegio, in that same year, was successful in inducing the south German princes to declare themselves at Ratisbon in favour of the edict. All

---

[1] REDLICH, *Der Reichstag zu Nürnberg* 1522–23, 1887 ; *Hist. J.* 1895, pp. 70–91.

this hesitation enabled Luther to take, in 1525, the step by which he finally consummated the breach with Rome, marrying Catherine of Bora, a Cistercian nun, and thus setting the seal on his opposition to clerical celibacy and religious vows.[1]

§ 162

The Peasant War [2]

In the course of the last decades several revolts of the peasantry had occurred in south-west Germany. Being merely local they were put down before any great harm was done. A much more serious rising was now in preparation. The religious upheaval gave the peasants new cause for discontent and enabled the revolt to spread. Luther's declamations against the parish clergy and the monasteries, objects on which spite could so easily be vented, were not without their results. Some of his followers even preached open rebellion.

The demands of the rebels were not the same everywhere. In the Twelve Articles of the peasants of the Swabian highlands the right of the parish was asserted to elect and depose its own parson. The pure Gospel was to be preached without any human additions, tithes on cattle were to be abolished, an end was to be made of serfdom, the forests and the waters were to be common property which all should be free to use, taxes were to be diminished, &c. In other places these demands were greatly exceeded, and nearly everywhere the rebels went far beyond their original programme. The rebellion began in Hegau in the summer, 1524, and soon a large portion of Germany was involved in the movement (Swabia, Alsace, the Palatinate, the Rhenish province, Franconia, Thuringia, Hesse, Saxony, Brunswick, the Tyrol, Salzburg, Styria, Carinthia, and Carniolia). In the south the Bavarians only, owing to the strong action of the government, remained aloof from the coalition. In the spring, 1525, Luther, after giving his attention

---

[1] *Kath.* 1900, I (Melanchthon's epistle to Camerarius on Luther's marriage) ; *Z. f. KG.* 1900, IV.

[2] JANSSEN, *Hist. of the German People*, vol. iv. (Engl. Trans.) ; HARTFELDER, *Zur Gesch. d. Bauernk. in Südwestdeutschl.* 1884 ; F. L. BAUMANN, *Quellen zur Gesch des Bauernk.* 1876 ; *Die zwölf Artikel der oberschwäbischen Bauern,* 1896 ; *N. Jahrb. f. d. klass. Altert.* I (1904), 213–30 (on the origin of the Twelve Articles) ; *Hist. Vierteljahrsschrift,* 1904, pp. 53–58.

to the Twelve Articles, counselled peace. His warning was, however, not obeyed, which is no wonder, seeing that he himself had dwelt on the intolerable burdens laid on the peasants, and the oppression practised by the nobles. The rebellion only gained in strength, more than a thousand castles and cloisters perishing in the flames. Only violence could now suffice to keep the peasantry within bounds, and in his work ' Against the murderous and thieving mob of peasants,' the Reformer himself urged the princes to action and bade them cut down the peasants without mercy. His advice was followed, and the revolt was nearly everywhere crushed before the end of the year. The movement, which was in progress in Thuringia, and was led by the Anabaptist Thomas Münzer, came to an inglorious end with the battle near Frankenhausen (1525). Only in the district around Salzburg did the disturbances persist until the summer, 1526.

§ 163

The Diets of Spires, 1526-29—Progress of the Reformation and Beginning of the Lutheran Church [1]

After the death of Frederick, prince-elector of Saxony (1525), **Philip, Landgrave of Hesse,** was to be the mainstay of the Reformation among the German princes. One of his first public acts was a measure in favour of the Reformers. In the summer, 1525, several princes of North and Central Germany (the prince-elector Joachim of Brandenburg, duke George of Saxony, dukes Eric and Henry of Brunswick-Wolfenbüttel, and archbishop Albert of Mainz) had made an alliance at Dessau to guard against any attack from the Reformers. Following their example, Philip, in the subsequent spring, allied himself with Frederick's brother and successor, John the Constant, to uphold the Reformation, and they were joined a few weeks later by six other princes and by the city of Magdeburg. The results of this were felt even at the Diet of Spires in 1526. Though it was decreed that, according to the imperial message, no change was to be made in the Faith, the

---

[1] Mg. on the Diet of Spires, 1526, by FRIEDENSBURG, 1887; NEY, 1889; *Z. f. KG.* XII, 334–60 ; on that of 1529, NEY, 1880.

Estates of the Realm were informed that, with regard to the edict of Worms, and until a General Council should meet, they were at liberty to take what action they deemed most conformable with the interests of God and the emperor.

This concession was soon to be enlarged. At the Council of Homberg, summoned by the landgrave of Hesse that same autumn, the confiscation of all foundations and monasteries was decreed, and the old form of worship was abolished. In that portion of Saxony controlled by John, a special visitation was ordered, and everywhere the old worship was replaced by a new one (1527). The Mass was retained, though without the Canon. Much the same took place in the duchies of Brunswick-Lüneburg, Mecklenburg, Liegnitz, and Brieg in Silesia, in Brandenburg-Kulmbach (Ansbach-Bayreuth), in East-Friesland, and in a number of imperial cities.

An attempt was made at the Diet of Spires in 1529 to prevent the further progress of the Reformation, by enacting that it should be no longer pushed, and that, wherever it had already been introduced, nobody should be hindered from saying or hearing Mass. It thereby claimed not the extermination of the new Faith, but merely toleration for the old. Even so, the Reformers protested against the decree, and to this protest they owed their name of **Protestants.** To lend additional weight to their protest the princes of Saxony and Hesse, together with several imperial cities (Nuremberg, Ulm, Strasburg), entered into a defensive alliance. Philip was even anxious to secure the co-operation of that portion of Switzerland which had accepted the Reformation, and to bring about a compromise between the doctrines of Luther and of Zwingli, a conference was, at his instigation, arranged to take place at Marburg in the autumn, 1529. The attempt was, however, a failure, owing to the difference of opinion regarding the nature of the Last Supper (cp. § 191). All the while Philip was longing for a pretext to commence hostilities. Alleging that he had received from O. von Pack, one of the ducal councillors, a report that the Catholic princes had formed an alliance for the annihilation of the 'Evangel,' he banded himself with other adventurous spirits, and, though the report turned out to be a hoax, carried fire and sword into the possessions of the prince-bishops of Würzburg and Bamberg.

§ 164

The Diet of Augsburg, 1530, and the Religious Truce of Nuremberg, 1532 [1]

The protest of the Reformers at the last Diet had given open expression to the religious division existing in Germany   At the Diet of Augsburg (1530) the two parties were to be again both present, though from the beginning of the meeting it was perfectly clear that there was little hope of an understanding being reached.   The emperor's invitation to attend the Corpus Christi procession was emphatically declined by the Protestant princes.   It is true that in the *Confessio Augustana*, a tract submitted by these same princes in justification of their religious attitude, an attempt is made to describe the new doctrine as in accordance with the old, whilst allusion is made only to the more prominent points of divergence in discipline (Art. 22–28). Melanchthon, who drafted this document, was not unaverse to a compromise, and the same is true of others.   Luther, however, who, whilst the Diet was sitting, tarried at Coburg, refused to hear of any such agreement, and indeed so great was the divergency of views, that it is doubtful whether a settlement could have been made, even with his connivance.   The emperor's motion, that the *Confutatio*—representing the views of the Catholic theologians, Éck, Wimpina, Cochlæus, Faber, Dietenberger and others—should be adopted by the Diet, was opposed by the Protestants.   On the matter being referred to a committee for further discussion, the landgrave of Hesse ostentatiously left the assembly, thus protesting beforehand against any union that might be decided on.   The committee itself was unable to come to a decision on certain points, nor was a second and smaller committee one whit more successful.   The emperor's valedictory message to ponder until next spring on the method of reuniting the Church, and in the meantime

---

[1] PASTOR, *Die kirchl. Reunionsbestrebungen während der Regierung Karls V*, 1879 ; H. LENK, *Der Reichstag zu Augsburg im J.* 1530, 1894 ; P. TSCHACKERT, *Die unveränderte Augsb. Konfession*, 1901 ; TH. KOLDE, *Die älteste Redaktion der Augsb. Kon.* 1906 ; J. FICKER, *Die Konfutation des Augsb. Bekenntnisses*, 1891 ; A. PÄTZOLD, *Die Konfutation des Vierstädtebekenntnisses*, 1899 ; O. WINCKELMANN, *Der Schmalk. Bund*, 1530–32, *u. d. Nürnb. Religionsfriede*, 1892 ; *St. u. Kr.* 1893, 83–124 ;   1894, 339–62 (Wimpina) ; M. SPAHN, *J. Cochläus*, 1898.

not to introduce any new novelties, was answered by the presentation of the *Apologia Confessionis Augustanae*, a defence of the original Confession against the Catholic confutation. Negotiations which were entered into with the cities were equally abortive. Some proclaimed themselves in agreement with the Confession presented by the princes; four (Strasburg, Memmingen, Constance, and Lindau) presented a Confession of their own, based on Zwingli's tenets (*Confessio tetrapolitana*); whilst all unanimously refused to accept the emperor's parting message.

Nor had any change occurred in the minds of the Protestants when the time was ripe for the holding of the new Diet. On the contrary, in the spring, 1531, eight princes and eleven cities concluded at Schmalkalden a defensive alliance for six years. They even refused to furnish any levies for the Turkish war unless judicial proceedings against them were dropped. So great was the emperor's fear of the Turks, who had just gained the bloody victory of Mohacz (1526) at the expense of the Hungarians, whose capital Buda was now in the enemy's hands, that he consented to the demands formulated by the cities. The truce, which was agreed to at Nuremberg, 1532, was to hold good until the Council which the emperor was to summon within six months for the following year.

§ 165

Further Progress of the Reformation—Attempts at Reunion Previous to Luther's Death—The Conference at Ratisbon

To the great advantage of the Reformation, the truce lasted longer than had been expected. The emperor himself could not well summon a General Council, and Clement VII, whom he sought out with this object at Bologna (1532–33), could not be induced to go beyond the mere preliminaries. In the meantime Protestantism was establishing itself especially at Münster in Westphalia, where it had found a clever and determined advocate in Bernard Rothmann, a curate of the city. On the death of Eric the bishop (1532) there broke out a real revolt. The parish churches of the city were handed over to the preachers, and they remained in the possession of the

Reformers even after a settlement had been reached under the next bishop, Franz von Waldeck (1533). The following year the same town fell into the power of the Anabaptists, though on their expulsion (1535) the older faith was once more restored (cp. § 192). Whilst, however, Münster reverted to the Catholic Church, whole countries were being lost to her for ever. Duke Ulrich of Württemberg, who had been deposed in 1519 for his misgovernment, after the victory gained by the landgrave of Hesse near Lauffen on the Neckar (1534), was restored to his dukedom, and one of his first acts was to introduce the Reformation.[1] The same happened at about the same time in the duchy of Pomerania, at Zweibrücken in the Palatinate, in Nassau, and in several cities, namely Augsburg, Frankfort, and Hamburg.

The advent of a new Pope did not greatly facilitate the assembling of the promised Council. **Paul III** indeed summoned one to meet at Mantua at Whitsun, 1537, but as the king of France raised an objection to that town, whilst the duke of Mantua put forward conditions unacceptable to the Holy See, the place of meeting had to be transferred to Vicenza (1538). The Council, however, never assembled. The Protestants, meeting at Schmalkalden, as soon as it was announced (1537), roundly refused to take any part in it. They also, at the same time, drew up the Articles of Schmalkalden, clearly setting forth the difference between their doctrines and those of the Catholic Church. Previously to this they had renewed their military agreements and secured the adhesion of several new members. The emperor and his brother Ferdinand I for their part, in 1538 at Nuremberg, entered into a treaty with two of the bishops (Mainz and Salzburg) and with several dukes (Bavaria, Saxony, and Brunswick-Wolfenbüttel), and everything seemed ready for a war, till, in 1539, new proposals were made at the Diet of Frankfort for securing a truce founded on compromise. The main factor, however, which determined the Protestants to abstain from a declaration of war was the illness of the landgrave of Hesse. The religious conference,[2] after having been debated at

---

[1] STÄLIN, *Wirt. Gesch.* vol. IV. 1873 ; *Württembergische, KG.* 1893, p. 250 ff.

[2] DITTRICH, *Gasparo Contarini*, 1885, pp. 505-777 ; MOSES, *Die Religionsverhandlungen zu Hagenau u. Worms*, 1889 ; P. VETTER, *Die RV. zu Regensburg* (1541), 1889 ; W. v. GULIK, *Johannes Gropper* (1503-59), 1906.

Hagenau (1540) and Worms, took place at the Diet of Ratisbon in 1541. Agreement was then reached on the question of the original state of man, free-will, original sin, and justification, the doctrines being expressed in very general terms, and both the Catholic and the Protestant teaching being drawn upon. Further agreement was, however, not found possible, even the articles actually accepted being rejected or received with hesitation by the outer world, and the colloquy closed without any abiding result. To obtain speedy help against the Turks in Hungary, it was found necessary to renew and extend the truce of Nuremberg. This was done at Spires the following year, the truce being for five years.

During this time the cause of the Reformation had been steadily gaining ground. In 1539 duke George of Saxony died and was succeeded by his brother Henry, the duchy (Dresden) now falling wholly into the power of the Protestants. In the following year Protestantism was established by the prince-elector Joachim II in the Mark of Brandenburg, and by the margrave archbishop William of the same princely house it was introduced into the archdiocese of Riga. The conference of Ratisbon did not hinder its advance. To obtain funds to pay his debts, the count-palatine Otto Henry of Neuburg, following the example set by other Protestant princes, seized the church property and established a new order of divine worship (1543). Franz von Waldeck, who administered the dioceses of Münster, Minden, and Osnabrück, and who had for time past allowed the new teaching to be preached in his dioceses, now sought admittance into the confederation of Schmalkalden. Even Cologne seemed on the point of being lost to the Church. The archbishop count Hermann von Wied, in spite of the protest raised by his clergy, published a plan of reform composed by Bucer of Strasburg and Melanchthon (1543).[1] On the appointment of prince August of Saxony to be administrator of Merseburg, the Reformation secured a footing in this diocese also (1544).

The Catholic Church was oppressed by the Protestants even in localities where they were not supreme, and even at a time when the bigamy which Philip of Hesse had committed

---

[1] G. Drouven, *Die Reform. in der Köln. Kirchpr. u. H. v. Wied*, 1876; Varrentrapp, *H. v. Wied*, 1878.

with their consent (1540) [1] was beginning to cause them anxiety ; their impunity was however ensured by the danger of a Turkish invasion. On the election of the provost Julius von Pflug to the bishopric of Naumburg-Zeitz (1541), the elector of Saxony, alleging his rights as temporal protector of that Church, quashed the election and bestowed the See on the Lutheran Amsdorf. He also appropriated a portion of the diocese of Meissen, whilst duke Maurice of Saxony pushed forward in the other the Reformation which his father had begun. The Schmalkalden leaguers subjected the duchy of Brunswick-Wolfenbüttel to a somewhat similar treatment, expelling duke Henry and establishing Protestantism in the country (1542).

A Council was now promised at Trent, where it actually was to assemble, though only three years later. Again the Protestants at the Diet of Worms (1545) [2] declined the invitation, and the depth of their feelings against Rome may be gauged by the tract then issued by Luther: 'Against the Romish Papacy, founded by the devil.' Under such circumstances the effort of Charles V (agreeably with the parting message at the Diet of Spires, 1544) to secure a new conference at the Diet of Ratisbon in 1546 [3] was doomed to fail. Not only was the attempt a failure, but it also served to show that the breach was beyond repair. Only with difficulty were the Protestants prevailed on even to attend the meeting.

Luther did not live to see the issue of the negotiations. He died at his native place in the beginning of 1546 (February 18) of a stroke of apoplexy.[4]

§ 166

The Schmalkalden War and the Interim—The Treaty of Passau, 1552, and the Religious Truce of Augsburg, 1555 [5]

All attempts to secure a settlement by peaceful means having now failed, the emperor at last decided to make use

---

[1] W. ROCKWELL, *Die Doppelehe des Landgrafen Philipp v. H.* 1904 ; *Hist.-pol. Bl.* 35 (1905), 317–33 (on the seal of confession and the bigamy of Philip of Hesse).

[2] Mg. by P. KANNENGIESSER, 1891.   [3] Mg. by H. v. CÄMMERER, 1901.

[4] N. PAULUS, *Luthers Lebensende*, 1898.

[5] A. HASENCLEVER, *Die Politik der Schmalkaldener vor Ausbruch d. schmalk. Krieges*, 1901 (*Hist. Studien*, fasc. 23–25) ; G. BEUTEL, *Über den Ursprung des A. Interims*, 1889 ; *D. Z. f. G. N. F.* II, 39–88 (on the Interim) ;

of sterner methods, and laid the ban of the Empire on the elector of Saxony and the landgrave of Hesse (July 20, 1546). These had already prepared themselves for war and were assured of the support of their confederates, especially in the south of Germany. On the other hand, the emperor could count on the help of several Protestant princes, particularly on that of duke Maurice of Saxony, who had been won over by the promise of the electorate and a portion of his cousin's domains. The war was quickly over. The south German Protestants made their submission without delay. John Frederick of Saxony (1532–54) was defeated and captured near Mühlberg in the spring, 1547. The landgrave Philip soon after had to yield to superior might, and archbishop Hermann of Cologne was forced to resign ; Julius von Pflug was restored to his see of Naumburg-Zeitz, and Henry to his duchy of Brunswick-Wolfenbüttel, from which they had been unjustly expelled.

The vanquished were forced to promise recognition to, and attendance at, the Council of Trent. During the war a conflict had, however, broken out between the emperor and the Pope, with the result that the Council was transferred to Bologna. Under these circumstances Charles V decided to act independently. At the Diet of Augsburg (1548) an order of worship was proposed, which, though Catholic in the main, bore some resemblance to Protestantism, in that it admitted priestly marriage and the use of the cup for the laity. This decision was to hold throughout the Empire until the Council should have decided the question of religious discipline. As the Catholic Estates rejected the proposal as illegal, its observance was enforced only on the Protestants, a number of other decrees of reform being passed for the benefit of the Catholics. As for a lasting result there was none whatever. The **Interim,** as the arrangement came to be known, excited everywhere the deepest aversion. Throughout the North, save only in the Rhenish province and in Westphalia, it was vehemently opposed. Even Saxony could not abide it,

G. BOSSERT, *Das Interim in Württemberg*, 1895 ; F. HERRMANN, *Das I. in Hessen*, 1901 ; BARGE, *Die Verhandlungen zu Linz u. Passau*, 1893 ; G. WOLF, *Der Augsb. Religionsfriede*, 1890 ; BRANDI, item (text), 1896 ; THUDICHUM, *Die Einführung der Reform. u. die Religionsfrieden v.* 1552, 1555 *u.* 1648, 1896.

though it had been rendered somewhat more palatable to the Protestants of that country by the later Leipzig Interim obtained by Maurice.[1]   Only in South Germany did the inhabitants prove submissive, with this result, that Protestantism there received a set-back which lasted for several years.

The subsequent happenings were not at all in accordance with the emperor's expectations.   On the re-assembling of the Council at Trent (1551) the Protestants indeed sent their delegates.   But several of their princes, among them being Maurice of Saxony, had beforehand taken the precaution of entering into a treaty, and, to make more sure of their safety, had even allied themselves with France.   In the spring, 1552, they overran the Catholic provinces, and the position of the emperor, who, in addition, was at war with both the French and the Turks, became one of great danger.   Hence immediate redress was given to the Protestants by the **treaty of Passau,** which ensured the peace and promised that the Diet should be summoned within six months to evolve a new compromise.

The Diet met at **Augsburg** in 1555.   Again the question of a conference was raised.   At the same time, however, it was decided that the religious differences between the Catholics and the upholders of the Augsburg Confession were no pretext for conflict or war.   It was also agreed that the Protestants should retain all foundations, monasteries, and other church properties which were in their hands at the time of the treaty of Passau, so far as their retention involved no prejudice to the rights of the Estates of the Empire.   Henceforth two Confessions were to be permitted in the Empire, the Catholic one and that of Augsburg.   The choice between the two depended, however, on the Estates of the Empire, *i.e.* on the princes, imperial cities, and knights of the Empire, their decision being obligatory throughout their domains.   To use a later phrase, they had the *Ius reformandi* ; the principle which had been tacitly obeyed from the beginning of the Reformation : *Cuius regio, eius religio,* thus received formal approval.   The middle classes and other simple subjects had no right to practise freely what religion they chose, but were bound to follow the injunction of their lord, that is, unless they preferred to emigrate, a right which was ensured

[1] A. CHALYBÄUS, *Die Durchführung des L. Interims,* 1905.

them by the treaties. In the imperial cities, where both worships existed side by side, the same order of things was to continue. According to the proposal of the Protestants, prince-bishops, too, were to possess the *Ius reformandi*. Against this proposal the Catholics protested, and as an agreement was not reached regarding the matter, it was solved by Ferdinand, who, as the emperor's plenipotentiary, ordered that in future any cleric adopting Protestantism should lose his preferment, which was then to revert to the Catholic Church (*Reservatum ecclesiasticum*). On the other hand, he also permitted all knights, towns, and communes belonging to ecclesiastical princes to continue faithful to the Augsburg Confession, provided they were able to show that they accepted it long since. The latter declaration was not, however, like the former, embodied in the text of the treaty, but was published by special letter-patent.

This peace set the seal on the religious division of Germany, and showed how idle had been the hope of Charles V of restoring unity of faith. After this deception the emperor refused to attend the discussions personally ; this he left to his brother, abdicating in the following year, and retiring to the monastery of San Jeronimo de Yuste near Placencia in Estramadura, to spend the last days of his life praying for the unity of the Church († 1558).

§ 167

Zwingli and the Protestant Reformation in German Switzerland [1]

At about the time when the Reformation began in Germany, a portion of Switzerland, then as yet only recently (1499) separated from the Empire, also fell away from the Church. The birthplace

---

[1] Zwingli's works, ed. SCHULER and SCHULTHESS, 10 vol. 1828–42 ; *Suppl.* 1862 ; EGLI and FINSLER, 1905 ff. (*Corpus Reformatorum*, vol. 88 ff.) ; Mg. on Zwingli by MÖRIKOFER, 2 vol. 1867–69 ; A. BAUR (his theology), 2 vol. 1885–89 ; R. STÄHELIN, I–II, 1895–97 ; FINSLER (the bibliography), 1897 ; S. M. JACKSON, 1901 ; S. SIMPSON, 1903 ; B. FLEISCHLIN, 1903 ; *Archiv für d. schw. Reformationsgesch.* 3 vol. 1869–75 ; STRICKLER, *Aktensammlung schw. Reformationsgesch. in den J.* 1521–32, 5 vol. 1878–84 ; EGLI, *Aktens. z. Gesch. d. Züricher Ref.* 1879 ; *Analecta reform.* 1899–1901 ; RIFFEL, vol. III, 1846 ; R. SCHMIDLIN, *Bernhardin Sanson*, 1898 ; *Katholik*, 1899, II, 434–58 (on Sanson).

of the movement was Zürich. Ulrich Zwingli, born in 1484 at Wildhaus, in the district of Toggenburg, after having worked in Glarus (1506–16) and Einsiedeln, was appointed missionary priest (Plebanus) at the cathedral of Zürich (1518). Here he zealously preached against the abuses, real and imaginary, of the Church. On the arrival from Milan of the Franciscan quæstor Bernard Sanson to preach the St. Peter indulgence, he was fiercely opposed by Zwingli, who was now beginning to be strengthened by the example and writings of Luther. The first result of his preaching was the public neglect of the law concerning fasting (1522). To the remonstrances of Hugo von Landenberg, bishop of Constance, he replied with his tract 'Von Erkiesen und Freyheit der Spysen.' He also obtained from the city council an order that preachers should, in their sermons, confine themselves to Holy Scripture, and, alleging the difficulties he had himself experienced, he demanded the abolition of the law of celibacy. The ideas of the Reformer soon prevailed in the city. At the beginning of 1523 a great disputation was held at Zürich concerning the Mass, the priesthood, purgatory, the right of the Church to prescribe fasts and attendance at Mass, &c., and the magistrates of the town, who had arranged the debate at his request, proclaimed Zwingli the victor. A second conference on the Mass and on image-worship in the autumn of that same year ended likewise. In the course of the next year all images were removed from the churches, and in 1525 a new form of worship was introduced. Originally this consisted in a daily sermon and four communions yearly, Divine service being simplified to such an extent that even hymns and the organ were excluded. The Last Supper, which was partaken of under both kinds, was held to be merely a memorial of Christ's Passion, Baptism likewise being considered in the light of a mere sign of admittance into the Christian society. Catholic worship was sternly forbidden, attendance at a Catholic church outside the city's rule being punished by a fine (1529), and later on by banishment.

The other cantons were not disposed to stand idly by whilst Zürich was shuffling off the Faith. They warned their neighbour to desist, adopted various measures for their own reform (1525), and, to re-establish the unity of the Church, arranged for a conference to take place at Baden (1526). The latter indeed was a victory for the ancient faith, on behalf of which no less than eighty-two disputants appeared, against only ten for the opposition. In spite of this success, the new movement continued.

The next city taken possession of by Protestantism was that of Basel, where Œcolampadius of Weinsberg [1] had been labouring in its interests for several years. Here the Reformed religion, after having before received some minor privileges, was formally recognised in 1527 ; two years later the Protestants were in a majority sufficient to assume the offensive against the Catholics. Yet greater conquests awaited the Reformers in 1528, when Bern,[2] the most powerful of the cantons, besides St. Gall, the district of Toggenburg, the Rheinthal, and the free county of Biel (Bienne) declared in their favour. At Bern the painter and poet Nicholas Manuel and canon Berthold Haller of Aldingen near Rottweil, and at St. Gall the burgomaster Joachim von Watt (Vadian),[3] had been the principal exponents of the new doctrines. In 1529 Glarus, Schaffhausen, and Thurgau, and in 1530 the county of Neuchâtel also, joined the Reformers. Appenzell and the Grisons remained neutral, and left to each parish the choice of its religion (1524–25). The only cantons to remain entirely true to Catholicism were those which had formed the original Switzerland.

The religious divisions gave rise to much bitterness and animosity, and the cantons sought support in alliances. The chief subject of quarrel was furnished by the common districts, such as Thurgau, administered by agents appointed by several cantons alternatively ; owing to the Reformation, the religious interests of one canton were constantly being crossed by those of the other. In 1529 Zürich declared war on the older cantons, and though a peace was patched up, Zwingli's fanaticism, his efforts to repress Catholicism throughout Switzerland and to obtain for Zürich the leadership of the Confederation, again led to an outbreak of war (1531). At the battle of Cappel, where Zwingli himself was slain, and at that of Menzingen, victory remained with the Catholics. The peace which followed

---

[1] Mg. by HAGENBACH, 1859.
[2] M. v. STÜRLER, *Urkunden der Bern. Kirchenreform*, 1862–73 ; T. DE QUERVAIN. *Kirchl. u soz. Zustände in Bern*, 1528–36, 1906.
[3] Mg. by PRESSEL, 1861.

ensured to the cantons the right to practise their religion, whilst in common districts the choice was to be left to each parish. Under the protection of the older cantons, many churches in these districts were re-incorporated in the Catholic body, whilst the abbey of St. Gall received back its ancient princely privileges.

§ 168
The Reformation at Geneva—Calvin [1]

In the fifteenth century, with the help of Rome, the dukes of Savoy were at last successful in bringing the bishopric of Geneva into the hands of their family; of this the result was a long-lasting disagreement between bishops and citizens which contributed not a little to Geneva's apostasy. For protection against duke Charles III, the Genevese entered an alliance with Bern and Fribourg (1526), thus coming into contact with the Reformers. In 1530, when they formally joined the Swiss Confederation, and made an end of the temporal power of de la Baume, their bishop, the Protestant Bernese troops excited a frenzy of image-breaking in the city. After the departure of the allies the old worship was restored, only to be again repressed. Its greatest gainsayer was now William Farel. At a disputation arranged to be held in 1535 only two clerics, both of them Protestants at heart, could be found to undertake the Church's defence, and the larger churches of the city were accordingly appropriated by the Reformers, a war was declared on images, and the town council prevailed upon to prohibit the Mass.

The function of establishing a new form of church government was to fall to John Calvin of Noyon in Picardy (1509–64). Happening to visit Geneva (1536) after the publication of his great theological work, *Institutio religionis christianae*, he was prevailed upon by Farel to stay and devote himself to preaching. His uninterrupted work in the city, however, really dates from

---

[1] *Calvini opp.* 59 tom. 1863–1900 (*Corpus Reformatorum*, vol. 29–87); Mg. on Calvin by STÄHELIN, 2 vol. 1863; KAMPSCHULTE, 2 vol. 1869–99; SCHEIBE (his doctrine on predestination), 1897; DOUMERGUE, I–III, 1899–1905; CORNELIUS, *Hist. Arbeiten*, 1899; *Nachr. Göttingen*, 1905, pp. 188–255; *Z. f. KG.* XXVII (1906), 84–99 (on his conversion).

1541 ; the three previous years were spent in Germany, mainly at Strasburg, whither he retired when he and Farel were driven from Geneva owing to their intolerable severity (1538). The new constitution of the Church, *Ordonnances ecclésiastiques,* which he drew up on his return, was adopted after undergoing a few corrections. A kind of vigilance committee, styled the consistory, composed of both clergy and laity, was established on the model of the Inquisition and charged with the oversight of the religious and moral life of the whole community. To test the belief and conduct of the citizens all houses were searched annually. Those with whom fault was found were refused Communion, whilst grievous sinners, obstinate opponents of the new doctrine, blasphemers, adulterers, &c., were handed over to the secular arm to be punished, the penalty being not unfrequently death. The city was now compelled to accept the yoke of the Reformers. The church festivals disappeared with the exception of the Sundays, which alone were permitted by Calvin. Even social life was altered, all display and noisy rejoicings being strictly prohibited. Not that opposition was wanting ; people long accustomed to freedom were exasperated by the yoke, and there were many revolts. Calvin was, however, sure of his position. The difficulties with which he was faced, when Bolsec attacked his predestination doctrine (1551), and when the Spaniard Michael Servetus at his instigation had been condemned to perish at the stake on a charge of heresy (1553), ultimately turned out to his advantage. The opposition party was crushed (1555), and henceforth the Reformer was virtually ruler of the city. The Ordinances were now applied in all their rigour, and even rendered more severe, and to crown his work a new school was established (1559), comprising a faculty for teaching advanced students in Theology, besides an academy in which the ordinary branches of learning were taught. This college, of which the first rector was Theodore Beza, owing to the fact that, through its situation and language, Geneva was a centre for the Protestants of many nations, was largely responsible for the subsequent success of Calvinism. Not only did the latter oust Zwinglianism in Switzerland (§ 191), it also made its way into France, Great Britain, Holland, and even into Germany (§ 169). The two most remarkable of its tenets were a severe predestinarianism, and, concerning the Last Supper, a doctrine intermediate between that of Luther and that of Zwingli. Though Calvin considered the Bread and Wine to be mere signs of the Body and Blood of Christ, he also taught that Christ by His spirit or power is received in the Sacrament. He may be said, therefore, to have held the virtual presence of Christ in the Eucharist. At the same time, this being a consequence of his predestinarian doctrine, he maintained that only the predestined could receive Christ, the reprobate receiving merely bread and wine.

For Eucharistic purposes common broken bread was used instead of hosts, and the Bread and the chalice, instead of being tendered by the minister, were taken by the faithful.

§ 169

Germany after the Truce of Augsburg—Further Progress of the Reformation and Counter-Reformation [1]

Though under the circumstances nothing else could have been expected, the settlement arrived at at Augsburg was far from satisfactory. The emperor Ferdinand I (1556–64) continued accordingly to strive after the restoration of religious unity. At the Diet of Worms in 1557 the pre-arranged colloquy took place. A little later George Witzel and George Cassander, at the emperor's invitation, drafted tracts of a conciliatory character, that of the former being entitled *Via regia* (ed. 1650), that of the latter, *Consultatio de articulis religionis inter Catholicos et Protestantes controversis* (ed. 1573). At the Diet of Augsburg (1566), Maximilian II (1564–76) made a last effort to secure a compromise. At the request of the papal legate the matter was, however, dropped; the Protestants,

[1] Janssen, vol. VII–XVI (Engl. Trans.) ; M. Ritter, *Deutsche Gesch. im Zeitalter der Gegenreformation*, 1889 ff. ; G. Wolf, item, I, 1898 ; J. Loserth, *Reform. u. Gegenref. in den innerösterreich. Ländern*, 1898 ; *Akten u. Korrespondenzen zur Gesch. d. Gegenref. in Innerösterreich* (1590–1600), 1906 ; (*Fontes rer. Austriac.* vol. 58) ; V. Bibl, *Einführung der kath. Gegenref. in Niederösterreich durch K. Rudolf II* (1576–80), 1901 ; Ph. Knieb, *Gesch. der Reform. u. Gegenref. auf dem Eichsfelde*, 1900 ; W. E. Schwarz, *Briefe u. Akten zur Gesch. Maximilians II*, 1889–91 ; Hopfen, *K. Maximilian II u. der Kompromisskatholizismus*, 1895 ; R. Holtzmann, *K. Maximilian II bis zu s. Thronbesteigung*, 1903 ; M. Lossen, *Der Kölnische Krieg*, 2 vol. 1882–97.

too, were opposed to anything of the kind. This was the last time that the question was discussed at a Diet.

The respective strength of the two confessions had already greatly changed since 1555, and to the disadvantage of the Catholics. The peace of Augsburg, by giving the Estates the free choice of a religion, removed any fear of imperial reprisals which might attend the adoption of the Augsburg Confession, and thus, indirectly, assisted the Reformation. In point of fact, Protestantism was immediately introduced into the elector's portion of the Palatinate, and into the dominions of the margrave of Baden (1556); in Baden-Durlach it had come to stay, but in Baden-Baden the margrave Philip II again replaced it by the older worship (1570). At the death of Henry the Young, he was succeeded by his son Julius, who established Protestantism in the duchy of Brunswick-Wolfen-büttel (1568). The greatest conquests of the Reformation were, however, among the spiritual principalities. In spite of the *Reservatum*, the Church was soon to lose no less than fourteen dioceses in northern Germany, the two archdioceses of Magdeburg and Bremen, and twelve simple dioceses (those of Lübeck, Verden, Minden, Osnabrück (in part), Halberstadt, Meissen, Ratzeburg, Schwerin, Camin, Brandenburg, Havel-berg, and Lebus). The North-West alone remained faithful to Catholicism, and even there Protestantism sought to enter by violence. Gebhard von Waldburg, who had been elected archbishop of Cologne after the resignation of Salentin von Isenburg (1577), and whose election had been ratified after three years' negotiations with Rome, two years after his confirmation, declared in favour of Protestantism. He wedded a certain countess Agnes von Mansfeld, and on being deposed and the archbishopric coming into the hands of duke Ernest of Bavaria, he sought the help of the Protestant princes to regain his rights by force of arms. The conflict was, however, disastrous for him (1584) and, by the victory, peace was ensured not only to the Catholics of Cologne, but also to all the neigh-bouring dioceses. The division among the Protestants them-selves contributed not a little to this victory of the Catholics. Lutherism was now no longer the only reformed religion in the field. The elector Frederick III (1559–76) had already, in 1563, introduced into his portion of the Palatinate the

Calvinistic Heidelberg Catechism, and though Lewis VI
(1576–83) had suppressed the innovation, Calvinism was again
established by Frederick IV, or rather by his tutor John Casimir.
Calvinism was likewise adopted later on by Nassau (1578),
Bremen (1584), Zweibrücken (1588), Anhalt (1595), Hessen-
Cassell (1604), and several other states.

Progress was likewise made by the Reformation in the
dominions of the temporal princes, especially in those belonging
to the house of Habsburg. It had made its way into Silesia
during the reign of Ferdinand I. Maximilian II (1564–76),
who had long been secretly attached to it and who, even later,
in his efforts to secure reunion, took up a very independent
position, issued a permission to the Austrian nobility on either
side of the Enns to introduce the Augsburg Confession into
their churches (1568–71). His brother the archduke Charles
gave a like permission for Styria (1572), Carinthia, Carniolia, and
Goricia (1578). The disputes which afterwards broke out
between Rudolf II (1576–1612) and his brother Matthias also
helped on the Protestant cause. The Bohemian Brethren and
the Lutherans had already (1575) united on the basis of the
Bohemian Confession, and had received from Maximilian II a
verbal assurance of toleration ; Rudolf now, by a letter of
Majesty (1609), granted to all adherents of the Bohemian Confession liberty of conscience, and to all the Estates, lords,
knights, and royal cities freedom of worship for their churches
and subjects. A like right was also accorded to all inhabitants
of the royal dominions by a compromise made between the
Catholic and Protestant nobles. Simultaneously, Silesia was
awarded a letter of Majesty, assuring to all classes of subjects
full freedom of worship and of building churches.

Whilst political weakness and anxieties were here counselling
compliance with the demands of the Protestants, in other
localities the reforms of the Council of Trent and the activity
of the newly-founded Society of the Jesuits had stimulated
a strong Catholic reaction. Following the example of the
Protestants, the Catholic princes now began to exercise their
right of reform more severely. The result was what is now
known as the **Counter-Reformation.** This was commenced
by duke Albert V of Bavaria (1564). He was followed by the
prince-abbot Dernbach of Fulda (1570), archbishop Daniel

Brendel of Mainz in the Eichsfeld (1574), bishops Julius
Echter von Mespelbrunn at Würzburg (1582) and Theodore von
Fürstenberg at Paderborn (1585). Greater energy was also displayed in Austria. Rudolf II forbade Protestant worship at least
in the towns (1578), and his cousin the archduke Ferdinand
prohibited it entirely in Styria, Carinthia, and Carniolia (1598).

These proceedings of the temporal overlords were undoubt-
ably in perfect order according to the principles of law univer-
sally admitted. Nor was there any real ground for complaint
against the action of the spiritual princes. It is true that the
declaration of Ferdinand I might be urged against it, but the
Catholics for their part could also point to the far greater
violations of the right of reservation of which the Protestants
had been guilty. The Protestants were nevertheless very
wroth, and the hostility between the two Confessions soon
assumed a dangerous character. The impatience of the
Protestants in Donauwörth led to the banning of the city and
to its incorporation in Bavaria, and this action was followed
at the Diet of Ratisbon (1608) by a formal secession of the
Protestants. The link which thus far had, at least to a certain
extent, bound together the various Estates in spite of their
religious divergence was now broken, and separate confedera-
tions became the rule. In that same year, at Ahausen in
Ansbach, there came into being the Protestant Union, of which
the head was the elector Frederick IV of the Palatinate. In the
following year there was formed, under the leadership of duke
Maximilian of Bavaria (1598–1651), a Catholic confederation,
the so-called League, and the death of duke John William
of Julich-Cleve-Berg (1609), whose succession was disputed by
the houses of Bradenburg and Neuburg, brought the Union into
armed conflict with the League. This dispute was, it is true,
settled a few years later by a compromise. The duchy was
divided among the heirs, who, in the meanwhile, had both of
them changed their religion. The count palatinate Wolfgang
William wedded the sister of the duke of Bavaria, and together
with his country returned to the fold. The elector Sigismund,
on the other hand, accepted the tenets of Calvinism, though
he abstained from imposing them on his subjects. The two
confessions remained, however, very hostile, nor was it long
before war again broke out in dead earnest.

§ 170

The Thirty Years' War and the Peace of Westphalia [1]

In Bohemia the Protestants had gradually outnumbered the Catholics. The indefinite wording of the compromise of 1609 was to help on their cause yet more. Under the impression that church temporalities were comprised under the royal dominions, the subjects of the abbot of Braunau and the Protestants of the little town of Klostergrab, a dependency of the diocese of Osseg, set about erecting a church. The government was, however, disposed to interpret the law otherwise, and an order was issued for the closing of the churches (1614). The emperor Matthias (1612–19) next directed the introduction of Catholic reforms into all the royal domains. The letter of Majesty, which had been issued in favour of the Protestants by his brother Rudolf II (1609), was to be, moreover, interpreted strictly. His plan seems to have been to reduce little by little the concessions which had been wrung from his brother, a plan which quite agreed with the moral standards of the time. Everywhere the religious question was one of might rather than of right. So far as possible it was everywhere the practice to oppress those who dissented from the rulers. The prevalent conception of the State sanctioned and even required this practice ; the existence of several religions within a single state seemed incompatible with public order, and, as a matter of fact, was often a disturbing element. The Protestants were, however, much disappointed, and as no attention was paid to their remonstrances, their church at Klostergrab being, on the contrary, levelled with the ground (1617), at the instigation of count Thurn they rose in rebellion at Prague (1618). The governors, Martinitz and Slavata, and the secretary Fabricius were pitched out of the windows

---

[1] K. A. MENZEL, *Neuere Gesch. d. Deutschen*, 2nd ed. vol. III–IV, 1854–55 ; F. HURTER, *Ferdinand II*, 11 vol. 1850–64 ; O. KLOPP, *Der 30jähr. Krieg bis 1632*, 3 vol. 1891–96 ; GINDELY, *Gesch. d. 30j. Kr.* I–IV (to 1623), 1869–80 (Engl. Trans. *Hist. of the Thirty Years' War*, 1884) ; *Gesch. der Gegenreformation in Böhmen*, ed. TUPETZ, 1894 ; A. HUBER, *Gesch. Österreichs*, vol. V (1609–48), 1896 ; L. WINTERA, *Braunau u. der 30j. Kr.* 1903 ; M. RITTER, *Die pfälz. Politik u. die böhmische Königswahl im J.* 1619, 1897 (*Hist. Z.* 79, 239–83).

of the castle, and a new government was formed under thirty Directors. On the death of Matthias and the succession of **Ferdinand II** (1619–37), the Bohemian crown was bestowed on the elector-palatine Frederick V (1619). The rebellion, with which began the most deplorable period in German history, soon gained the neighbouring countries, Moravia, Silesia, and Lusatia, as well as the archduchy of Austria and the kingdom of Hungary. When the knell of the Habsburg monarchy and of the Catholic Church seemed already to have sounded, Ferdinand at last succeeded in obtaining the help of powerful allies. Banded with Spain, the League, and the elector of Saxony, he was victorious at the battle of the White Mountain near Prague (November 8, 1620), and at one blow secured the position of his house. The victory was of great importance from the Church's point of view. The right of reform was made a pretext for abolishing Protestantism in Bohemia, Moravia, in the archduchy of Austria, and in the hereditary principalities of Silesia, though not indeed in those parts of Silesia which were under their own princes, Brieg, Liegnitz, Münsterberg, and Öls, nor at the city of Breslau ; in lower Silesia, moreover, it was not found possible to make any great change. The same happened in the higher Palatinate (Amberg),[1] which was bestowed on Bavaria as its part in the indemnity of the war in Bohemia, and also in the Rhenish Palatinate, which came into the possession of the Spaniards and the Leaguers. On the banning of the ' Winter King ' the Palatine electorate was handed over to Bavaria, and the Catholics thereby again secured a majority in the college of electors. The war was, however, by no means at an end. The count of Mansfeld, Frederick's general, continued hostilities, pillaging the countries through which he passed. Similar raids were undertaken by the margrave George of Baden and duke Christian of Brunswick, though both of them were soon to be overthrown by Tilly (1622). In 1625, Christian IV of Denmark, with the support of England and Holland, declared war on behalf of the Palatinate, though without any conspicuous success. He was defeated by Tilly near Lutter on the Barenberg (1626), and a like fate befell Mansfeld at the hands of

---

[1] M. Högl, *Die Bekehrung der Oberpfalz durch Kurfürst Maximilian I*, 2 vol. 1903.

Wallenstein near Dessau. These defeats paved the way to the peace of Lübeck (1629).

Whereas the war now seemed over, the seed of a new conflict was already sown. Ferdinand, after the victory of 1620, had, in virtue of his rights, re-established Catholicism in his dominions, and now considered it his duty as emperor to reduce the frontiers of Protestantism to those which had been assigned to it by the treaties of Passau and Augsburg. He accordingly issued in 1629 (March 6) an edict, the so-called **edict of Restitution**,[1] dealing with the vacancies which had occurred within the Empire. The Protestants were summoned to restore all the church properties which they had seized since 1552, commissaries being immediately dispatched to attend to the execution of the decree. By the autumn, 1631, there had already been restored two archdioceses, five dioceses, two abbeys immediately subject to the Empire, 150 churches and monasteries, and about 200 parishes, all of them in towns and villages which had hitherto been Protestant. These proceedings, which resulted in Catholic worship being re-established for nearly twenty years throughout a great part of the Empire, were not without legal foundation. The Protestants were, however, not disposed to abandon their claim to the properties which, though illegally obtained, had long been in their possession, and without which the Protestant power would have been greatly weakened. Ferdinand's plan became all the more difficult to fulfil when the Leaguers, headed by Bavaria, had persuaded him to dispense with the services of Wallenstein and his army, and when France had promised the Swedes a yearly subvention to assist them in their war against the emperor. Fortune no longer smiled on the emperor's undertakings. Tilly, who had been able to boast of never having lost a battle, was, soon after the capture of Magdeburg, defeated by **Gustavus Adolfus** at Breitenfeld (1631). The conqueror was indeed slain at Lützen (1632), the battle of Nördlingen (1634) was a victory for the imperial troops, and the elector of Saxony was forced into the peace of Prague (1635). The

---

[1] Tupetz, *Der Streit um die geistl. Güter u. das Restitutionsedikt*, in *SB. Wien*, 1883, vol. 102, pp. 315–566 ; *Hist. Z.* 76 (1895), 62–102 (origin of the edict) ; H. Günter, *Das Restitutionsedikt v. 1629 u. die kathol. Restauration Altwirtembergs*, 1901.

emperor's position remained, however, one of great danger, and the edict of Restitution had to be withdrawn as a condition of the peace. It was agreed that the church properties, confiscated since the treaty of Passau and which were in the possession of the Protestants on November 12, 1627, should remain in their keeping for forty years more, and ever afterwards, should no agreement be reached before the expiry of the term, the emperor merely reserving to himself the right to assign disputed cases to the arbitration of an imperial court consisting of an equal number of Catholic and Protestant judges. The war, in which France now took open part, lasted yet thirteen years, during which Germany was overrun by troops eager only for blood and plunder, a large part of the Empire being turned into a wilderness. Peace was at last signed in 1648, at the Westphalian cities of Münster and Osnabrück, at the former with France, at the latter with Sweden. Historically the more important is the *Instrumentum pacis Osnabrugense*.

A general amnesty was proclaimed, and matters were henceforth to stand where they had stood in 1618. In consequence of this, the duke of Württemberg and the margrave of Baden, whose possessions had been much diminished during the war, received back their lands entire ; the Rhenish count Palatine obtained the lower Palatinate and the title of elector, an eighth electorship being established for his benefit in restitution for that which had been bestowed on Bavaria. The princes who had suffered at the hands of Sweden, for instance those of Brandenburg and Mecklenburg, were empowered to compensate themselves out of the church properties, which were, however, already to a large extent in the possession of the Protestants (*I.P.O.* art. II–IV). The treaties of Passau and Augsburg were confirmed (V, 1) and enlarged.

(1) Besides the Catholic and Augsburg confessions, Calvinism, or the Reformed Religion as it was styled, was to be tolerated and placed on the same footing as the other confession (Art. VIII).

(2) Church properties were to remain in the possession of those in whose hands they were on January 1, 1624 (V, 14), the *Reservatum ecclesiasticum* being made obligatory on Catholics and Protestants alike (V, 15).

(3) The form of worship in the imperial cities was also to depend on what it had been at the beginning of 1624, each city being henceforth obliged to remain Catholic, or Protestant, or mixed (V, 29). In the remaining states, any religion which could be proved to have been followed publicly or privately during the course of the year 1624 was to be permitted for all future time (V, 31). Apart from this, dissenters, whether Catholic or Protestant, were entitled to pray at home, to attend churches outside the limits of the district, to freely exercise their trade, and to dispose of their property should they elect to migrate elsewhere (V, 34–37). In Silesia and Lower Austria, no concessions were made to the Protestants on the basis of the *status quo ante* ; they were, however, to be permitted to attend church elsewhere and were not to be banished (V, 32).

(4) At the Diets, when religious matters—or any other questions in dealing with which the Estates would cease to form one corporation—came up for discussion (*Iura singulorum*), or whenever one of the Confessions declared a notion to be a party question, the two confessions were to divide into a *Corpus Catholicorum* and a *Corpus Evangelicorum* (*Itio in partes*), the question being decided, not by a majority of votes, but by arriving at a friendly understanding (V, 52).

(5) The *Ius reformandi* was to be a privilege of all the Estates, ecclesiastical as well as temporal (V, 30). In spite of this acknowledgment and enlargement of the privilege, the latter was much reduced by the introduction of the *status quo* of 1624 ; the privilege could now no longer be invoked save in cases of uncertainty as to what had prevailed in 1624. The measure ensured their religion to all subjects, this being even expressly stated. Among other matters it was decided that should a Lutheran prince pass over to Calvinism, or *vice versa*, he might establish at his court Divine worship suitable to his convictions, and also permit such worship for the benefit of those of his subjects as had likewise been converted, but that, otherwise, he was not to interfere with church matters in his country (Art. VII). As was only consistent, Catholics were to be bound by the same rules as the Protestants.

By the peace most of the property which had been restored

to the Church by the edict of Restitution was lost to her for ever. This explains why Pope Innocent X protested against the peace and declared it invalid (Bull, *Zelo domus Dei*, 1648). No heed was, however, paid to him. Considering all the changes which had occurred during the last century, the papal protest was a mere matter of form, and the signatory powers had already excluded it beforehand (XVII, 3).

CHAPTER II

THE REFORMATION IN THE REST OF EUROPE

§ 171

Prussia, Livonia, Curland, Poland, Hungary, and Transylvania

I. In dealing with the further progress of the Reformation, we must first speak of a territory which, though it still nominally formed a part of the Empire, grew more and more estranged from the remaining German States. This was the northern portion of the country controlled by the Teutonic Knights. The grand-master Albert of Brandenburg[1] had constituted the Baltic provinces into a **duchy of Prussia,** of which the suzerain was Poland. The Reformation which he then introduced into the country soon involved Samland and Pomerania, the two bishops George von Polentz and Eberhard von Queis making over their temporal sovereignty to the new duke, and themselves adopting Lutheranism. In 1612 the duchy came into the possession of the elector of Brandenburg, and at the demand of his overlord the king of Poland, the new sovereign promised to the Catholics freedom of worship, removed their disabilities to hold office in the State, allowed them to exercise the right of patronage, and gave permission for the erection of a church at the capital Königsberg. The concessions wrought, however, very little alteration, and the Augsburg Confession remained the prevalent religion. In consequence of this the headquarters of the Teutonic Knights was removed to Mergentheim.

II. Much the same happened in **Livonia.**[2] The army-master Walter von Plettenberg was favourable to the Reformation from the beginning, and as soon as the margrave William of Brandenburg, brother to the duke of Prussia, was made archbishop of Riga (1539), the older religion was doomed. The cession of Livonia to Poland by

---

[1] J. Rindfleisch, *Herzog A. von Hohenzollern, der letzte Hochm. u. d. Ref. in Preussen,* 1880; E. Joachim, *Die Politik des letzten Hochmeisters i. Pr. Albrecht v. Br.* 3 vol. 1892–95 (Publ. from the Prussian State Archives); J. Kolberg, *Einführung der Reformation im Ordenslande Preussen,* 1897 (*Kath.* 1897); F. Dittrich, *Gesch. des Katholizismus in Altpreussen,* I, 1901.

[2] Helmsing, *Reform.-Gesch. Livlands,* 1868.

the army-master Gotthard Kettler (1561) effected no change, as it was only made conditionally on the maintenance of the Protestant religion in that land. Far from losing ground, Lutheranism was soon to gain both **Curland** and **Semgallen.**[1] Following the example of Albert of Brandenburg, Kettler transformed this territory into an hereditary duchy under Polish suzerainty, and imposed the Augsburg Confession throughout his dominions.

III. In **Poland** in spite of the efforts of king Sigismund I (1506–48) to maintain his kingdom in the Catholic Faith, a certain number of Protestant communities established themselves at Danzig, Elbing, and Thorn. During the reign of Sigismund Augustus (1548–72), himself a Protestant, the Reformation, under both Lutheran and Calvinistic forms, was steadily pushed forward. The most prominent apostle of the new faith was John a Lasko ; its greatest opponent was Stanilaus Hosius, bishop of Ermeland. After the king's death, the Protestant nobility, when meeting for the election, carried through a motion by which Protestantism was explicitly recognised. According to the religious peace arranged at Warsaw (*Pax dissidentium*) in 1573, Catholics and Protestants were to enjoy the same rights, and to live henceforth at peace with each other. King Vladislaus (1632–48) indeed endeavoured to bring about a reunion, and a conference was held in 1645 at Thorn, though without any result. Cp. O. KONIECKI, *Gesch. der Ref. in Polen*, 3rd ed. 1904. Bg. of J. a Lasko by DALTON, 1881 ; PASCAL, 1894 ; JACOBI, *Das liebr. Rel.-Gespräch von Thorn*, 1895 ; *Z. f. KG.* XV, 1895.

IV. Lutheranism was at an early date preached in **Hungary,** and, favoured by the political troubles, it took firm root, in spite of the repressive measures enacted by the government. Later on Calvinism proved even more successful. The Reformers soon became so powerful that, at the peace of Vienna (1606), it was necessary to grant them full freedom of worship. Cp. J. BORBIS, *Die luth. K. Ungarns*, 1861.

V. **Transylvania** had, since the time of St. Stephen, been subject to Hungary, but had been given by Ferdinand I (1538) as an independent princedom to the woivode John Zapolya, a rival claimant to the Hungarian throne left vacant by the demise of Lewis (1526). Luther's works were introduced into the country by merchants from Hermannstadt (1521). In that town the Reformation made so many converts that the Catholics were soon after expelled (1529). A little later (1545), the entire nation of the Transylvanian Saxons adopted the Augsburg Confession. The movement also spread to the Hungarians and Seklers settled in the country, though they finally went over, not to Lutheranism, but to Calvinism. Cp. G. D. TEUTSCH, *Urkundenb. d. ev. Landesk. in Siebenbürgen*, 1862 ; *Die Ref. im siebenb. Sachsen*, 1876.

---

[1] TH. KALLMEYER, *Die Ref. in Kurland*, 1868.

§ 172

The Reformation in the Scandinavian Kingdoms

In **Denmark**[1] king Christian II (1513–23) had supported
the cause of the Reformation, his efforts being directed partly
to making an end of the abuses prevalent in the Church, partly
to breaking the might of the clergy and nobility. His tyranny
indeed brought about his deposition, but his uncle and successor
Frederick I (1523–33) was also a supporter of the movement,
though at his election he had bound himself to repress it.
He began by favouring it in the duchies of Schleswig and
Holstein, which had belonged to him previously, and as soon
as he had sufficiently established his power, he proceeded to do
the same in Denmark itself. Aided by the zeal of John Tausen,
Lutheranism now advanced rapidly. After having obtained
toleration at the parliament of Odense (1527), it was definitively
established by Christian III (1536). The bishops were cast
into prison to force them to surrender their dignities, and
Bugenhagen was summoned from Wittenberg to undertake the
organisation of the new Church. Not long after, the Catholics
were deprived of all political rights, and priests were forbidden
to enter the country on pain of death.

Norway and **Iceland,** owing to their connection with
Denmark, were infected with Lutheranism by Christian III. In
Iceland, however, the new religion did not gain the day until
after the execution of John Aresen II, the heroic bishop of
Holum (1550).

In **Sweden**[2] the two brothers Olaf and Lawrence Peterson
had been sowing the seeds of the Reformation since 1519.
The country, which ever since the union of Kalmar (1397) had,
like Norway, been under the suzerainty of Denmark, for
some time past had been seeking to free itself from the foreign
domination. In spite of the Stockholm massacre (1520), by

---

[1] F. MÜNTER, *KG. von Dänemark u. Norwegen*, vol. III, 1883 ; KARUP,
Gesch. d. kath K. in Dän. Germ. Trans. 1863 ; DAHLMANN-SCHÄFER, *Gesch.
von Dänemark*, I–V, 1840–1902 ; L. SCHMITT, *Der Karmeliter Paulus Heliä*,
1893 ; *Johann Tausen*, 1894 ; *Die Verteidigung der kath. K. in Dänemark
gegen die Religionsneuerung im 16 Jahrh.* 1899.

[2] GEIJER, Engl. Trans. *History of the Swedes*, 1845 ; THEINER, *Schweden
u. s. Stellung zum Hl. Stuhl unter Johann. III, Sigismund III und Karl IX,*
2 vol. 1838 ; J. MARTIN, *G. Vasa et la réforme en Suède*, 1906.

which Christian II fancied he had stamped out insubordination for ever, Gustavus Vasa succeeded in the following year in delivering his country, and two years later was elected its king. The new sovereign adopted Lutheranism, and within six years, by craft and violence, he had imposed it on all his subjects. One of his sons, Eric XIV (1560–68), sought to introduce Calvinism, but lost his crown in the attempt ; the other, John III (1568–92), attempted, though without success, to rejoin the Catholic Church. With the advent of Sigismund III, son of the latter, and at the same time king of Poland, the country again came under a Catholic sovereign. The difference of faith gave a pretext to the king's Protestant uncle to seize the crown ; on his ascending the throne in 1604 as Charles IX, an end was made of the prospect of restoring the Catholic religion in Sweden.

§ 173

The Reformation in England and Ireland [1]

I. Motives of the lowest character were responsible for the change of religion in England. **Henry VIII** [2] proved himself a zealous defender of the Catholic Faith. In his *Assertio septem sacramentorum* (1521) he even took up the pen against Luther, and was rewarded by the title of *Defensor fidei* conferred on him by the Holy See. His sensuality, however, involved him in a breach with Rome, and under his successors the schism grew ever deeper.

In his passion for Anne Boleyn, the king had been seeking, since 1526, for a divorce from Catherine of Aragon, the widow of his brother Arthur. On behalf of the project it was urged that the Levitical law (xviii. 16) forbade marriage

[1] J. LINGARD, *History of England*, copyright ed. 10 vol. 1888 ; RANKE, *Engl. Gesch. vorn. im 17 Jahrh*, 9 vol. 2nd ed. 1870–72, Engl. Trans. *History of England principally in the 17th century*, 6 vol. 1875 ; GASQUET, *Eve of the Reformation*, 1905 ; J. SPILLMANN, *Gesch. d. Katholikenverfolgung in England*, 1535–1681, 5 vol. 1899–1905.

[2] A. DU BOIS, *Catherine d'Aragon et les origines du schisme anglican*, 1880 ; *Hist. J.* 1888–92 ; *Hist. Taschenbuch*, 1889–90 ; EHSES, *Röm. Dokum. z. G. d. Ehescheidung Heinrichs VIII v. E.* 1893 ; GASQUET, *Henry VIII and the English Monasteries*, 1888–89 ; E. L. TAUNTON, *Th. Wolsey*, 1901 ; G. CAVENDISH, *Card. Wolsey*, 1905 ; A. HOPE, *The First Divorce of Henry VIII*, 1894.

with a brother's wife, a plea which appealed to many theologians of the time, who considered that the commandment in question was really obligatory. The majority were, however, of a different opinion, urging that even *Deuteronomy* (xxv. 5) admitted an exception to the rule. It was also pointed out that Arthur's marriage with Catherine had never been consummated. Under these circumstances, counsel for the king's ' private matter ' saw fit to question the validity of the dispensation which had been granted by the Holy See for the king's marriage, maintaining that it had been secured by false pretences and had never been demanded by Henry personally. This objection, considering that Henry and Catherine had long cohabited, was, of course, utterly puerile, but the king's heart was fixed on a divorce, and, as was to be expected, he found support in plenty. A court party, headed by the duke of Norfolk, Anne's uncle, seized the occasion as a pretext for involving in disgrace the Lord Chancellor, cardinal Wolsey. Wolsey himself, as soon as he realised that the king had made up his mind, sought to prove his loyalty and retain his position by using his influence to obtain the divorce. Clement VII gave a conditional dispensation from any impediments against the new marriage, should the previous one turn out to be invalid (December 17, 1527). At the imperative demand of Wolsey, the Pope even went further and declared in a Bull that a divorce was possible, apparently supporting the view that the command of *Leviticus* (xviii. 16) was a part of the Divine law, and as such could admit of no dispensation. The wording of the decretal is, however, unknown, for the document, after having been read to the king and Wolsey, was burnt. Cardinal Campegio, the papal legate, who brought over the Bull, proceeded to London with Wolsey in the autumn, 1528, to investigate and pass judgment on the matter. The legate strongly urged Catherine to take the veil, pointing out that by this means the matter would be more easily solved and great evil averted. The jurisdiction of the two legates was suspended by Catherine appealing to the Pope in 1529, and the trial was transferred to Rome. On this occasion not only the two English Universities, but also several Universities on the continent, whose support had been obtained by pressure or bribery, gave it as their opinion that no marriage between brother-in-law and sister-in-law was possible. On the other hand, Catherine could count on the help of Charles V, who was supreme in Italy, and whose wishes the Pope could not therefore neglect. As a matter of fact Clement VII gradually assumed an attitude of greater determination, in spite of the constant appeals which reached him from the English lords, both spiritual and temporal, who alleged that the dissolution of Catherine's marriage was desirable in the interests of the royal succession, seeing that the queen had only one daughter alive. The next step was taken by the king himself. Thomas Cromwell, who had come to power on the fall of Wolsey († 1530), pointed out to the king a way by which his plan could be carried through without any help from the Pope; this was to follow the example of the German princes, and cut himself loose from Rome. Soon after this, the king was actually proclaimed supreme head of the Church of the land by Convocation and Parliament (1531). It is true that the clause, added at the suggestion of Warham, archbishop of Canterbury, 'So far as the law of God permits,' involved a restriction, but even this was to disappear. Henry's passions were soon to lead to a complete breach with Rome. The new wedding was celebrated in 1533, Anne Boleyn being at the time already with child, and the previous marriage with Catherine was declared invalid by Thomas Cranmer, who, in the meantime, had been appointed archbishop of Canterbury. In 1534 the Act of Supremacy was passed, by which the king was declared sole and exclusive head of the Church of England, and received practically the same rights as had formerly been exercised by the Pope. Any refusal to admit the new order of things was to be construed as an act of high treason. Among the first victims of the new despotism were John Fisher, the worthy bishop of Rochester [1] and the famous chancellor Thomas More,[2] both of whom were beheaded in 1535. Other changes were soon to follow : the suppression of the monasteries, the destruction

---

[1] Bg. by KERKER, 1860; BAUMSTARK, 1879; VAN ORTROY, 1893; BRIDGETT, 1890.
[2] Bg. by RUDHART, 2nd ed. 1853; BRIDGETT, 1891.

of relics and of many images.   As for the rest, the older faith remained in possession, the king persecuting indiscriminately both Papists and Protestants from the continent.

In the six Articles of 1539, belief and acceptance of the following were made obligatory on pain of death : (1) Transubstantiation ; (2) Communion under one kind ; (3) the celibacy of the clergy ; (4) the binding force of the vow of chastity ; (5) masses for the dead ; (6) auricular confession.

Though Henry VIII had been content with establishing a schism, under his successor (his son by Jane Seymour), **Edward VI** (1547–53), the Reformation made great progress, mainly owing to the labours of Henry's own creature, archbishop Cranmer of Canterbury.   Images were removed altogether, celibacy was abolished, a new liturgy was created in the Book of Common Prayer,[1] Communion under both kinds was introduced, and a Calvinistic Confession of Faith was drafted in forty-two Articles.   Though the latter is founded mainly on the teaching of the Genevese reformer, the worship and constitution of the new Church was indebted more deeply to Catholicism than to either Luther or Calvin. Amongst other things the Church of England, or the Church as by law established, retained its old hierarchical form.   The English Reformation accordingly stands by itself side by side with the Lutheran and the Reformed Churches of Central Europe.   The Anglicans themselves even claim, in one or other of its meanings, the attribute of Catholicity.   As yet the work was not, however, firm.   Edward died an early death, and the new sovereign, **Mary I** (1553–58),[2] the daughter of Catherine of Aragon, with the help of her cousin, cardinal Reginald Pole,[3] though not without considerable bloodshed, restored the older worship.   Two hundred and ten Protestants, among them Cranmer, were put to death.   Not a few of these, however, were politically suspected, or had incurred the ruler's displeasure by deriding Catholic practices. In the next reign the country was to revert definitively to Protestantism.

[1] GASQUET-BISHOP, *Edward VI and the Book of Common Prayer*, 1890.
[2] A. ZIMMERMANN, *Maria d. Katholische*, 1890 ; *Kard. Pole*, 1893 ; J. M. STONE, *The History of Mary I*, 1901.
[3] Mg. by MARTIN HAILE, 1910.

Elizabeth (1558–1603),[1] during the reign of her half-sister, had embraced Catholicism, and at her coronation she took the oath to preserve the existing religion. As, however, she was a daughter of Anne Boleyn, and was accordingly accounted illegitimate by the Church, and incapable of succeeding to the throne, and as Paul IV, on being notified of her succession, had refused to acknowledge her rights, she soon found it advisable to return to her former Protestantism. The measures of Edward VI were re-enacted, and Matthew Parker, as archbishop of Canterbury, became the head of the reformed hierarchy (1559). The forty-two Articles were reduced to thirty-nine (1562), and a new step was taken to uproot Catholicism. The acknowledgment of the royal supremacy in Church matters had even previously been required as a condition of promotion to a royal fief, to any office in the State, to a benefice or to office at the Universities. The oath was now imposed on the members of the House of Commons, on all schoolmasters and solicitors, and on all persons suspected of leanings towards the older religion, a second refusal on the part of the last category entailing death. The measure was tantamount to suspending the sword of the headsman over every Catholic, and though, at first, the penalty usually consisted only of fines and imprisonment, increasing in severity when Pius V pronounced Elizabeth's excommunication and deposition (1570), ultimately recourse was also taken to the executioner. Among the Catholics who perished were the Jesuit Edmund Campion and nine other Catholics (1581). In 1587, when Philip II of Spain, husband of Mary I, made his famous attempt to invade England, with the aid of the Armada, over 100 persons died for their faith. The persecution was directed especially against the priests. It thus became necessary to educate them abroad. William Allen founded the English seminary at Douai (1568) [2] and Gregory XIII the English college at Rome (1579).

The Tudor dynasty having come to an end, King James

---

[1] F. G. LEE, *The Church under Queen Elizabeth*, 2 vol. 2nd ed. 1893; PROTHERO, *Select Statutes*, 1894; GASQUET, *Hampshire Recusants*, 1896; *Rquh.* 1895, II, 456–517; R. SIMPSON, *Edm. Campion*, 2nd ed. 1896.
[2] A. BELLESHEIM, *Allen u. die engl. Seminare auf d. Festlande*, 1885.

VI of Scotland, the son of Mary Stuart (Queen of Scots), became King of England under the title of **James I** (1603–25),[1] uniting the three kingdoms under a single sceptre, his accession also putting new hopes into the Catholics. As, however, the laws against them not only remained on the statute-book, but continued to be severely enforced, a few Catholics were led into a conspiracy against king and Parliament. The Gunpowder Plot (1605), which was discovered in time, made the situation of the Catholics yet worse ; they were now forced to take the oath of allegiance (or abjuration), in which the opinion that the Pope had the right to depose princes was declared a godless and damnable doctrine. Under **Charles II** (1660–85) two yet more stringent laws were passed. One, the so-called Test Acts (1673), by obliging all officials to take the oath of allegiance and of the Royal supremacy and to receive the Anglican Communion, precluded Catholics from assuming any office in the State. The other (1678) forbade them to sit in Parliament. The former Act was the outcome of the Fire of London (1666), which the Protestants with no more ado ascribed to the Catholics ; the other was the result of the Popish Plot which Titus Oates purported to have discovered. Charles, who died a Catholic, was succeeded by King **James II** (1685–88),[2] who had already joined the Church long before, and whose first endeavour it was to abolish the penal laws and the Tests. His plan led to his deposition, and the crown fell to his son-in-law **William of Orange**, who granted toleration to the dissenting Protestant sects, but during whose reign Catholics continued to be prosecuted. They were now no longer liable to the death penalty, but a law of William III (1700) declared them incapable of acquiring property (by inheritance or purchase), and adjudged such property to their nearest Protestant relatives. The saying of Mass and the keeping of schools were threatened with imprisonment for life, and informers against Catholic worship were to be well rewarded. Matters remained in this position until danger, threatened by America and France, induced the State to be more

---

[1] *Quellen u. Forschungen aus ital. Archiven u. Bibliotheken*, VII, 268–306 (Clement VIII and James I).
[2] *R. Qu.* 1903, pp. 56–80.

compassionate. In 1778 the laws of William of Orange were partly abolished and partly amended.

II. As the English rule extended over a portion of **Ireland** [1] the latter island was also touched by the Reformation. Under Henry VIII the Irish Parliament acknowledged the royal supremacy over the Church (1536), and under Elizabeth (1560) adopted the new worship. The decisions of Parliament did not, however, express the feelings of the nation, and Protestantism made but little headway. Henry had deprived the clergy of their right of voting, and many of the leading men were absent from the debates. Under Elizabeth, only a fourth of the nation was represented. The Irish as a nation remained true to the faith of their fathers. Their persistence furnished the English with a pretext for seizing the whole island, a plan which was accomplished in 1603, 600,000 acres of land being confiscated. Together with their sovereignty the English endeavoured to impose their Church. The Irish, however, stood firm by their belief, and as they were subjected to constant oppression and the confiscations continued, they rose in rebellion in 1641 against the tyrants. The result was that Cromwell again reduced the island (1652), and whatever remained of the population after the eleven years of warfare was pushed back into the deserts of Connaught, all the possessions which were still in Irish hands being seized by the English. The persecution was also made more severe. A price was set on the head of every priest. Under Charles II and William III there were new confiscations, so that ultimately only about one-eleventh of the arable land of the country was left to the natives. Under Queen Anne the Catholics even lost the right of purchasing land from a Protestant, or of acquiring it by inheritance or as a gift, or even of renting it on a lease of more than thirty years. They were also deprived of all civil rights, and discouraged from engaging in trade. Though the treaty of Limerick (1691) had assured them freedom of conscience, the oath of supremacy was again imposed, thus practically closing Parliament against them ; later on

[1] R. HASSENCAMP, *Gesch. Irlands von d. Ref. bis zu seiner Union mit England*, 1886 ; A. BELLESHEIM, *Gesch. d. k. K. in Irland*, vol. II–III, 1890 f.; CH. FIRTH, *Oliver Cromwell*, 1900.

still they were to lose even the suffrage (1727). Both in
education and in worship they laboured under great disabilities ; they were forbidden to establish schools, their
chapels were not to be provided either with steeples or
with bells, whilst on the other hand they were compelled to
pay tithes and stole-fees to the Church as by law established.
These intolerable laws remained in force till nearly the end
of the period ; only in the latter half of the eighteenth century
were they somewhat relaxed in practice, the more obnoxious
being ultimately repealed. Catholics then received the
right of renting on a lease of 999 years and of inheriting
landed estate (1778) ; the Tests were abolished and they
were thus enabled to hold office (1779) ; they were likewise
granted the right, conditional on the previous consent of the
Anglican bishop, of having schools, &c. (1782).

The question of the validity of Anglican Orders, which had of
late years been much discussed, was decided negatively by an
Apostolic Letter dated September 13, 1896.

§ 174

The Reformation in Scotland [1]

As is made evident by a decree of Parliament in 1525,
forbidding the importation of Lutheran books, or the preaching of Luther's doctrines, the continental Reformation had
made its way at an early date into far-off Scotland. In
the beginning it was rigorously persecuted, Patrick Hamilton,
a relative of the royal family, even paying for his zeal for
it with his life (1528). During the next few years a like
fate befell several members of Religious Orders who sym-
pathised with the Protestants, and ultimately also the
preacher George Wishart (1546). There was, however, a party
of the all-powerful nobility—headed by the earl of Arran,
who had been made regent on the death of James V (1542)—
which discreetly favoured the new movement, and enabled

[1] A. BELLESHEIM, Engl. Trans. see vol. I. p. 130 ; Mg. on Knox by P. H.
BROWN, 2 vol. 1895 ; M'CRIE, 1905 ; MACMILLAN, 1905 ; H. COWAN, 1905.
Mg. on Mary Stuart by KERVYN DE LETTENHOVE, 2 vol. 1889 ; PHILIPPSON,
3 vol. 1891–92 ; SKELTON, 1893.

it to establish itself in the land. Nor were there wanting
more determined partisans. Wishart's execution was
avenged by the murder of cardinal Beaton, archbishop of
St. Andrews. In the following years, indeed, to diminish the
crying abuses of the Church, several Councils were called
together, and the regentship came into the hands of Mary
of Guise, the queen-mother (1554). The attempt to carry
out a Catholic reform had, however, been made too late,
and the new government was also too weak to oppose the
new movement. Towards the end of 1557 the Protestants
joined forces as the 'Congregation of Christ' to fight the
'Congregation of Satan,' as they styled the Catholic Church.
Two years later John Knox, the zealous and fiery opponent
of Catholicism, who is often, and not unjustly, considered
the Reformer of Scotland, was able to return to his native
land after many years of absence. He was soon to make
his presence felt. At Perth and other localities the monasteries were sacked and images broken (1559). When the queen-
regent assumed a stronger attitude towards the Reformers,
the result was a civil war in which the Protestants were
supported by England. At her death peace was re-established, but Catholicism was doomed. The Parliament,
which met at Edinburgh after the conclusion of the peace,
abolished all papal jurisdiction in Scotland, recalled all
laws which had been previously passed in the interests of
the Catholic Church, and forbade the saying or hearing of
Mass on pain of deprivation of goods and banishment, or
of death in the case of a third conviction. The place of
the Catholic Church was now taken by the Reformed Church,
Calvinism being adopted in all its severity; the hierarchy
was abolished, a presbyterian form of government introduced, festivals were forbidden, &c.

Catholicism was now extinct as an ecclesiastical organisation, and though the sceptre was again to come into a Catholic
hand, it was already too late to effect any change. **Mary
Stuart**, on returning to her country (1561) after the death
of her husband Francis II of France, was compelled to acknowledge that the situation admitted of no remedy. So great
was the fanaticism stirred up by Knox's denunciation of
the Mass as idolatry, that only with difficulty was she able

to establish Catholic worship at the court chapel. The rebellious attitude of the nobility, headed by her half-brother, the earl of Murray, was rendered yet more intense by her marriage with Lord Darnley. By consenting to marry Bothwell, Darnley's murderer, she finally sealed her fate. She was compelled to abdicate in favour of her son James VI (1567), and on fleeing to England (1568), instead of the help she expected from Elizabeth her cousin, she was imprisoned, and finally died on the scaffold (1587).

The old faith was not indeed entirely dead. It continued to be cherished by a part of the people in spite of the law. The constant persecution which it had to endure lessened each year the number of its adherents; only in the eighteenth century did it begin to increase.

Mary Stuart was accused by her enemies of being Bothwell's accomplice in Darnley's murder. The charge is most probably unfounded. Of recent years even the Protestants have acknowledged her innocence. Cp. Mg. by TH. OPITZ, 2 vol. 1879–82; E. BEKKER, 1881; H. GERDES, I, 1885; STORM, 1891.

§ 175

The Reformation in France [1]

Owing to the vicinity of the countries in which the Reformation originated, France could not fail to be to some extent involved in the movement, and this happened in spite of the fact that Francis I (1515–47) and Henry II (1547–59) resolutely opposed the Reformation. The new religion recruited its adherents mainly in the south. Among the families of note which then embraced it, we may instance the Bourbons and the brothers Coligny of the house of Châtillon. Under Francis II (1559–60) one of the objects of the conspiracy of Amboise was to secure the recognition of Protestantism.

[1] L. RANKE, *Franz. Gesch. vornehmlich im* 16 u. 17 *Jahrh.* 6 vol. 1868–70; *WW.* vol. VIII–XIII; Engl. Trans. *Civil Wars and Monarchy in France in the* 16th *and* 17th *Centuries*, 2 vol. 1852; SOLDAN, *Gesch. d. Protestantismus in F. bis zum Tode Karls IX*, 2 vol. 1855; DE MEAUX, *Les Luttes relig. en Fr. au XVI*e *siècle*, 1879; *Hist. de France, publiée, sous la direction de* E. LAVISSE, V, 2–VI, 2 (1519–1643) 1904–5; H. DE L'EPINOIS, *La Ligue et les papes* (1585–95), 1886; AGUESSE, *Hist. de l'établissement du protestantisme en France*, 2 vol. 1891.

The plot, which was also to bring the power from the hands of the Guises into those of the Bourbons, was indeed a failure, but this did not materially hinder the spread of the Reformation. During the minority of Charles IX (1560–74), the regent and queen-mother, Catherine of Medici, summoned the king of Navarre, Anthony of Bourbon, to have a part in the government, and on his arrival an end was immediately made (December 13, 1560) of the legal persecution of the Huguenots, as the French Protestants came to be called. No success attended the efforts of the party which opposed this measure, consisting of Francis, duke of Guise, the constable Montmorency, and the marshal de St. André, generally known among their enemies as the Triumvirate. The regent, whilst allowing full liberty to Catholic worship, insisted on toleration being also accorded to the Protestants. After the failure of the religious conference at Poissy (autumn, 1561), which had been held in the hope of reuniting the Protestants to the Catholic Church, an edict was issued (January 1562) by which freedom of belief was granted to the whole kingdom and freedom of worship outside the towns pending the decision of a General Council.

This compliance did not appease the country. On both sides there reigned discontent and mistrust. Though their leaders contended for the due observance of the edict, the Huguenots were not disposed to be content. Their conviction that the Catholic Church was an idolatrous institution led them to demand its suppression. On the other hand the Triumvirate, who had now obtained the support of Anthony of Navarre, demanded the expulsion of the Protestant preachers. Between the two a conflict was inevitable, and was accelerated by the massacre of Vassy, in which a number of Huguenots were done to death by the followers of the duke of Guise. A civil war, in which both sides were guilty of much cruelty, broke out in 1562, but was concluded the following year, after the death of Navarre, St. André, and Guise. The edict of Amboise (1563) granted freedom of worship to the Huguenots on the estates of the higher nobility, at the residences of the inferior nobles, in one town in each province, and in all the strongholds which were in the power of the Protestants at the end of the war. Four years later the Protestants were responsible for a new outbreak of warfare, followed by another after the interval of a year ; yet a third war was due to the revocation of the freedom of worship which had been assured the Protestants by the peace of Longjumeau (1568). The peace which was re-established by the edict of St. Germain (1570) was very insecure. The king indeed was minded to observe it ; in 1572 he even gave his sister Margaret in marriage to Henry of Bourbon the head of the opposition. This wedding, which was intended to seal the peace, was really the signal for new hostilities. To preserve her influence over the government, the queen-mother, in conjunction with her son Henry of Anjou, determined to assassinate admiral Coligny, whose power over the king they thought too great. The plot miscarried, and a vaster conspiracy was planned to prevent the Protestants taking revenge on the king himself. It was decided to make away with all the chiefs of the party, not only at Paris but also in the provinces. The absence of due preparation, the rumours aggravated by falsehood which were rife, and the fact that the rabble, drawn by the hope of booty mingled with the soldiery, explains the extent of the subsequent massacre. The number of the victims may have amounted to 4,000 or 5,000, and some suppose it to have been much greater. St. Bartholomew's Day, as the slaughter is called, was of little use to the Catholic cause. The Huguenots were not stamped out, and soon new concessions had to be made to them. Henry III (1574–89) was compelled to grant them at the peace of Beaulieu (1576) freedom of worship throughout the realm, save at the capital, though the edict of Poitiers (1577) again restricted their privileges to those accorded by the peace of Amboise.

Nor was warfare yet at an end. As the king had no children, at the death of duke Francis of Anjou, the last of the house of Valois (1584), the succession seemed assured to Henry of Navarre. This was, however, by no means to the tastes of all, even foreign nations being interested in the question whether the French throne was to come into the power of a Protestant or remain in that of the Catholics. For the protection of the Catholic religion a powerful party called the League was formed under the leadership of Henry, duke of Guise, and the party, owing to the extent of its demands, soon came into conflict

with the king himself, thus exposing France to a great calamity.
After the king had rid himself by violence of the chief of the
League and of his brother cardinal Louis (1588), his own
unpopularity increased in the country, and being accounted
the tyrant of his people he was ultimately stabbed by Jacques
Clément, a Dominican friar. The crown now belonged by right
to **Henry IV** of Bourbon (1589–1610). Owing, however, to
the might of the League which was now allied with Spain,
he secured his throne only by fulfilling the promise which he
had originally made to the Catholic royalists, abjuring Protestantism (1593) and being absolved at Rome (1595). The
religious question was then settled by the **edict of Nantes**
(1598).[1] On the one hand, Catholic worship was again established wherever it had been abolished by the Huguenots, and
on the other, the Protestants received full freedom of conscience
and a large measure of freedom of worship—apart from the
castles and houses of the nobility, they were to have at least
two churches in each province, and similar liberties in every
town where their religion had been practised between 1596
and August 1597 ; they also received permission to hold
public offices, and, to defend their rights, were allowed representatives at Parliament and in the high courts. As a pledge of
peace the strongholds of which they had obtained possession
were left in their hands for some time after.

This last concession seemed necessary at the time, owing
to the excitement which prevailed. It involved, however, a
danger for the government, in that it constituted the Protestants as a State within the State, and was all the more
intolerable seeing that the Huguenots' conduct was by no
means above suspicion of treason. Lewis XIII, on the advice
of cardinal Richelieu, accordingly brought this arrangement
to an end. The obstinacy with which the Huguenots defended
their privilege proved how well founded was the suspicion.
To preserve their political position, they not only took up
arms under the duke of Rohan, but also besought assistance
of England and other powers against their own king. For
all this they were not subjected to any further loss of privilege.
The legal ground which had been re-established by Henry

---

[1] J. FAUREY, *Henri IV et l'édit de Nantes*, 1903.

IV was not, however, to endure long.   Lewis XIV,[1] after having a year previously curtailed the civil rights enjoyed by the Huguenots, revoked in 1685 the edict of Nantes and demanded of all Frenchmen the confession of the Catholic religion. The order was, of course, disobeyed.   In spite of a prohibition, thousands of Huguenots migrated to foreign lands, and in several places, especially in the Cévennes, revolts also occurred. Notwithstanding this the order was put into execution.   As all the greater States at that time admitted only the one religion of their choice, we can understand how Lewis XIV, whose consciousness of power was so great, could happen on such a plan.   Nor was the plan entirely successful, for Protestantism, in spite of the repressive measures, remained implanted in many hearts, and ultimately Lewis XVI was compelled to make terms with its adherents.   The edict of Versailles (1787) guaranteed them, not indeed full religious liberty, but at least a legal right to existence.

We must without a doubt seek the origin of the name of Huguenot at Geneva, where the defenders of the city's freedom against the duke of Savoy, on account of their connection with the 'Confederates' of Bern and Fribourg, were known as Eidgenot's (Eignot's), and as Huguenots after their leader Hugues.   The other suggested derivations are fabulous.

The St. Bartholomew's Day massacre can only be mentioned with reprobation.   It is, however, wrong to think, as some have recently done, that it was a long-premeditated deed.   Its motives were, moreover, originally of a political character, the religious element being introduced only after the failure of the attempt on Coligny's life.   The final responsibility of the action belonged to the French court, the Holy See, as recent research has clearly established, having had no part in it (*Th. Qu.* 1893, p. 527 f.)   It is true that on the arrival of the news a *Te Deum* was sung at Rome.   This jubilation, which has caused much comment, is perfectly comprehensible, whether it was the result of joy at the overthrow of the Protestants, or a thanksgiving for the deliverance of the French king from the conspiracy to which the French note to the foreign courts alludes.   In the then state of affairs the Pope will very likely have perceived in the massacre a victory of the Catholic cause, nor would he have made unusual inquiries as to the manner in which the victory was obtained.   In this and like matters, at that time, results, real or apparent, were apt to cast all other considerations into the back-

---

[1] DOUEN, *La révocation de l'édit de Nantes*, 3 vol. 1894 ; MICHELET, *Louis XIV et la révocation de l'édit de Nantes*, 1899.

ground. Of this Coligny himself, the first victim of the St. Bartholomew, is an instance in point. He had publicly hailed the death of
the duke of Guise as a stroke of fortune for France, though this
death was the result of murder; nor did he attempt to hinder the
crime, though he must have been aware beforehand of the plot that
was hatching. FRANQUEVILLE, *Étude sur la Saint-Barthélemy,*
1898; A. ELKAN, *Die Publizistik der Bartholomäusnacht,* 1905;
Heidelberger Abh. z. Gesch., ed. HAMPE, fasc. 9.

§ 176

The Reformation in the Netherlands [1]

The Netherlands, which had belonged to the house of
Habsburg since 1477, were invaded by the Reformation at an
early date, and though it was effectually repressed by Charles V,
its condition greatly improved under Philip II (1555–98).
This sovereign's encroachments on the privileges of the country,
his coldness and reserve, his choice of foreign ministers to the
exclusion of the natives, stirred up discontent. The malcontents
were headed by prince William of Orange and the two counts
Egmont and Horn, and as many of them were in favour of
Protestantism, the political unrest was soon complicated by a
religious one. Objection was made to the new division of
dioceses which had been undertaken by Paul IV at the king's
desire, a decrease of severity in the *Placata* or religious edicts
was demanded, and also the abolition of the Inquisition.
Towards the end of 1565 a confederation of nobles, known as
the Compromise of the Geuses, was formed to obtain these
demands, and was soon joined by a number of simple citizens.
No sooner had the regent Margaret of Parma, the king's half-
sister, allowed a slight relaxation in the execution of the
Placata than the supporters of the new movement emerged
from the darkness in which they had hidden themselves. Thirty
preachers were imported from Geneva, and in the summer,

[1] CRAMER ET PIJPER, *Bibliotheca Reform. Neerlandica*, I–III, 1903–5;
HOLZWARTH, *Der Abfall d. N.* 3 vol. 1865–72; WENZELBURGER, *Gesch. d. N.*
2 vol. 1879–86; NAMECHE, *Le règne de Philippe II et la lutte relig. dans les
Pays-Bas*, 4 vol. 1885–86; J. G. DE HOOP-SCHEFFER, *Gesch. d. Reformation
in den Niederlanden bis* 1531 (Germ. by GERLACH, 1886); HOFSTEDE DE
GROOT, *Hundert Jahre aus der Gesch. der Ref. in den N.*, Germ. Trans. by
GREEVEN, 1893; PUTNAM, *William the Silent*, 1896; E. MARX, *Studien zur
Gesch. des niederländ. Aufstandes*, 1902.

1566, the new Evangel began to be publicly preached. The result was a storm of image-breaking, which opened the eyes of many of the people. In the reaction which ensued, Egmont and Horn found it politic to change their views, whilst William of Orange fled back to Nassau in Germany, after having vainly endeavoured to prevail upon his friends to rise in rebellion. With this the trouble seemed at an end, and the time come to set public order on a firmer footing. The measures chosen by the king, who sent into the land, as plenipotentiary, the duke of Alba at the head of an army, with stringent orders to repress all manifestations of the popular will (1567), only succeeded in embittering the people yet more. Resistance continued and William returned with an army of his own. A few years later the Reformation was supreme in the provinces of Holland and Zealand (1574). By the treaty of Ghent (1576) all the provinces united to drive the foreign troops out of the land. When the country seemed on the point of being utterly lost to Spain, dissensions arising from political, national, and religious grounds again divided the allies. The Union of Utrecht (1579) comprised only the northern provinces—Holland, Zealand, Utrecht, Geldern, Groningen, Friesland, and Overyssel. The loss of the southern states did not dishearten the confederates ; two years later they formally cut themselves adrift from Spain and adopted a sort of Republican government. The offer of the crown to the duke of Anjou was an event of no significance, as he only survived by one month the murder of William of Orange (1584). Philip II indeed sought to maintain his sovereignty, and the war was continued ; the Republic was, however, able to hold its own, in 1609 obtaining a truce of twelve years, and finally receiving full recognition at the peace of Westphalia. Its loss to Spain was of importance from a religious point of view. Calvinism was made the religion of the State, entrance into public offices being made conditional on its acceptance. Catholics who remained true to their faith were only to retain the right of private worship.

CHAPTER III

THE CATHOLIC CHURCH

§ 177

The Council of Trent [1]

AT the very inception of the Reformation the popular
voice had called for a General Council as the only means of
solving the questions in debate. The Protestants indeed had
soon rejected its authority, but the Catholics never abandoned
their hope of restoring by its means the unity of the Church ;
by purging the Church it was expected that the Council would
gratify and reconcile the separatists.

There were, however, great hindrances in the way. Though
Paul III had set his heart on the convocation of a Council,
no less than ten years of his pontificate had slipped by before
it could be assembled. The appointments of the Council to
meet at Mantua, and then at Vicenza, were abortive (§ 165).
When Trent was assigned (1542), a like failure was again
threatened, for war having shortly before broken out between

---

[1] *Canones et decreta Conc. Trid.* Rom. 1564 ; Stereotype edd. Leipzig and
Ratisbon ; edd. RICHTER et SCHULTE, *cum declar. Conc. Trid. interpretum
et resol. thesauri S. Congreg. Conc.* 1853 ; LE PLAT, *Monumenta ad hist. Conc.
Trid. spect.* 7 vol. 1781–87 ; A. THEINER, *Acta genuina Conc. Trid.* 2 vol.
1874 ; DÖLLINGER, *Ungedruckte Berichte u. Tagebücher zur Gesch. d. K. v. Tr.*
2 vol. 1876 ; DRUFFEL-BRANDI, *Monum. Trid. Beiträge zur Gesch. d. K. v. Tr.*
I, 1884–99 ; *Conc. Trid. Diariorum, actorum, epistularum, tractatuum nova
collectio*, ed. Societas Goerresiana, 1901 ff. up to 1907 3 vol. have been issued,
ed. MERKLE et EHSES ; PIETRO SOAVE POLANO (PAOLO SARPI), *Hist. del Conc.
Trid.* 1619 (ed. DE DOMINIS) ; ed. 2ª rived. e corretta dall' autore, 1629 ;
French Trans. ed. COURAYER, 1736 ; SFORZA PALLAVICINO, *Istoria del Conc.
di Tr.* 3 vol. 1652 ff. Latin Trans. ed. GIATTINI, 1670 ; BRISCHAR, *Beurteilung
der Kontroversen Sarpis u. Pallavicinis*, 1843 ; MAYNIER, *Étude hist. sur le
Conc. de Tr.* 1874 ; *Hist. Taschenbuch*, 1886–87, 1890 ; VERMEULEN, *Das
XIX allg. Konzil in Bologna*, 1892 ; A. KORTE, *Die Konzilspolitik Karls V*,
1538–43, 1905 ; S. SUSTA, *Die röm. Kurie u. das Konzil v. Tr. unter Pius IV*,
I, 1904 ; S. MERKLE, *Das Konzil v. Tr. u. die Universitäten*, 1905.

the emperor and the king of France, the Council had to be again postponed. After the reconciliation of the two monarchs by the peace of Crespy (1544), as the outlook had improved, the bishops received the customary summons in the spring, 1545, and towards the end of the year the Council was formally opened. At first a new postponement seemed inevitable. The emperor, who was unwilling to cause premature annoyance to the Protestants against whom he was then meditating severe measures, wished the Council to be put off till the following spring, or at least desired it to refrain from discussing matters of Faith; the Pope, on the other hand, wished the Council to be transferred to Italy, or, at least, that the question of church reform should be postponed, and the matters of Faith be taken first. In spite of these difficulties, the Council was able to hold its first session on the third Sunday in Advent, 1545.

As the number of members in attendance was at first very small, the assembly began by discussing general and preparatory questions. Among other things the order in which the business was to be transacted was now settled. To meet the contradictory wishes of Pope and emperor, it was decided that doctrine and discipline should be discussed simultaneously. In doctrine the Council confined itself to defining such matters as had been denied by the Protestants, asserting that Tradition as well as Scripture is a source of Faith, that for the due understanding of Scripture the interpretation of the Church and the *unanimis consensus patrum* is the rule to be followed, and that among the Latin translations of the Bible the Vulgate is to be considered as authentic (Sess. IV). Having thus opposed the Catholic criterium to that of the Protestants, the next two sessions were devoted to the doctrines of original sin (Sess. V) and Justification (Sess. VI), the two main points of difference between the old and the new Faith. After this consideration was devoted to the sacraments, the Christian means of grace generally, and to Baptism and Confirmation in particular (Sess. VII). A few decrees of reform were also passed, and the Fathers separated for four years.

The seat of the Council was not Rome's choice, assent to its being held at Trent having been given only under pressure. The legates accordingly demanded that the assembly should either be translated or suspended, and on the outbreak of an epidemic in the town in the spring, 1547, the moment seemed come to adopt one of these alternatives. By the vote of the majority the Council was transferred to **Bologna** (Sess. VIII). The Italians and a few others, altogether about two-thirds of the whole, immediately proceeded thither, whilst the Spaniards remained at Trent. The translation was duly ratified by the Pope, but the emperor was exceedingly annoyed, as it spoilt his hopes of effecting a reconciliation with the Protestants. The latter had just been subdued, and his plan now was that the Council should win them over to the Church ; it was, however, manifestly hopeless to expect the Protestants to attend at a city within the Papal States. Hence the emperor strove with might and main to bring about the return of the Council to Trent, and succeeded at least in hindering the publication of the decrees passed at Bologna. The two sessions held there (IX, X) were devoted merely to discussing the postponement of the next publication, the difference of view between Pope and emperor finally leading to the suspension of the sittings (1549). The Pope died that same year, and though his demise caused the dispersal of the Fathers who had remained at Trent, it also facilitated a renewal of the negotiations. At the conclave the cardinals promised to hearken to the emperor, and in accordance with this promise the new Pope **Julius III**, del Monte, the former president of the Council, assented, though not with the best grace, to the assembly being again summoned to Trent.

The first, or rather the eleventh, session was held in the spring, 1551. The discussion regarding the sacraments was continued, and decrees were published concerning the Eucharist (Sess. XIII), Penance, and Extreme Unction (Sess. XIV). On account of the war which was proceeding between the Pope and the French king regarding the duchy of Parma (§ 179), no Fathers were in attendance from France. In spite of their absence, the number of members present had soon grown larger than in the earliest sessions. A few Protestant envoys also attended, though their mission had no success. It was, however, not found possible to bring the discussions to their normal ending. The Protestant princes having rebelled against the emperor, and Maurice of Saxony having descended on the Tyrol (§ 166), it became necessary in the spring, 1552, to prorogue again the Council.

The Fathers had hoped that at the end of the war, and at any rate before two years were over, it would be possible to resume their labours. Neither Julius III nor his two next successors were, however, to witness the resumption of the Council ; Marcellus II died three weeks after his election ; whilst Paul IV would not hear of a Council. Only under **Pius IV** (1559–65) was the matter again mooted. In spite of this Pope's willingness, two years of his pontificate had passed before any agreement could be reached. Not only did the question regarding the seat of the Council again come up for discussion, but the emperor and the French were also anxious that the Council should be an entirely new one instead of a continuation of the previous, and refused to be bound by the decrees so far issued.

On the re-opening of the synod at the beginning of 1562, the principal subjects to be decided concerned Communion under both kinds, the sacrifice of the Mass, Orders, and Marriage (Sess. XXI–XXIV), in a word the completion of the Church's doctrine regarding the sacraments. The debates were very lengthy, and occasionally stormy. Not a few of the Fathers were in favour of the use of the cup, but, as the Spaniards and the Italians were opposed to any such change of discipline, it was agreed that the matter should be referred to Rome. On the matter of Orders, there cropped up for renewed discussion the question of the relations between the episcopate and the Pope, whether the episcopate is a divine or an ecclesiastical institution, whether, in a word, the bishops receive their power from Christ or from the Pope. The Spaniards were strongly in favour of a definition in the former sense, the Italians, headed by the papal legates, were as strongly in favour of the opposite ; the French adopted a middle view. As the different parties were in no mood for compromise, the question was finally left unsettled. On the question of marriage, not only had the indissolubility of the tie to be defined against the view which had gained ground among the Protestants, but stringent disciplinary measures were also to be taken. To put an end to clandestine marriages it was decreed that such marriages should not only be illegal (this they were already by decree of the fourth Lateran Council, c. 51) but also invalid. Only such marriages should hereafter be accounted valid which were celebrated *praesente parocho et duobus vel tribus testibus*.[1] A number of important decrees of reform were passed at the same time. They dealt with the abolition of the office of indulgence preachers, or Quaestors, the duty of publishing indulgences now falling on the bishops,[2] increased the severity of the existing laws regarding episcopal residence,[3] insisted on the obligation of bishops and other dignitaries to receive consecration within three months of election,[4] decreed the erection of seminaries for the training of the clergy,[5] the annual and triennial holding of diocesan and provincial synods,[6] the more frequent visitation of the dioceses, of the chapels belonging to exempted monasteries or other foundations, and even of the institutions themselves when necessary,[7] the institution of a concursus for the appointment of parish-priests,[8] forbidding any *Cumulus beneficiorum*, and making no exception even for the cardinals,[9] abolishing provisions, expectancies, &c.[10] Finally, in the twenty-fifth session in December, 1563, the discussion bore on Purgatory, the invocation of the saints, the worship of relics and images, and indulgences. A certain number of reforms were also left to the Holy See to carry out. With this session the Council was able to end its labours. Its attendance then numbered 255 ; Germany was represented only by the imperial ambassadors and a few episcopal deputies having no right to a vote ; fear of the Protestants accounts for the absence of the German bishops. The decisions of the Council were ratified by Pius IV, and were accepted by the Catholic governments, and though in France the State refused to publish them, they were received by the provincial synods and thereby obtained practical recognition.

As cardinal Morone, the president, pointed out in his concluding discourse, there were many other matters of which a discussion would have been desirable. At the same time, the results actually obtained by the Council were sufficiently remarkable. The Church's doctrine was made clear on the

---

[1] Sess. XXIV, *de ref. matr.* c. 1.
[2] Sess. XXI, *de ref.* c. 9.
[3] Sess. XXIII, *de ref.* c. 1.
[4] *Ibid.* c. 2.
[5] *Ibid.* c. 18.
[6] Sess. XXIV, *de ref.* c. 2.
[7] Sess. XXI, *de ref.* c. 8 ; XXIV, c. 3.
[8] *Ibid.* c. 18.
[9] *Ibid.* c. 17.
[10] *Ibid.* c. 19.

points in which it had been threatened by the Reformers, the more crying scandals were removed, and the long-desired reform was, at least to some extent, accomplished. Its import-ance was immediately manifested by the deeper feeling of unity and greater self-reliance, which now took the place of the indecision and diffidence until then shown by the Church.

§ 178

Religious Orders in the Sixteenth Century—The Jesuits

Owing to the state of decay into which monasticism had fallen in the course of the Middle Ages, and which had recently issued in the wholesale apostasy of members of Religious Orders, a commission of cardinals and prelates, in 1538, had recom mended the abolition of all Orders, urging that their influence could only be for evil. The demand was too far-reaching to be accepted. There was also some hope of amending matters without having recourse to such extreme measures. At the Council of Trent a number of decrees were issued for the reform of monasticism (Sess. XXV, *de reg. et mon.*). The monks were forbidden to hold private property, the visitations of the monasteries were to be more regular, the rules for the enclosure of convents of women were made more stringent, the practice of bestowing monastic foundations on men who were not Regulars was prohibited, and, to obviate the evils which had arisen through the entry into religion of children, it was enacted that no youth should be allowed to make his profession before the age of sixteen, whilst girls, even in exceptional cases, were not to be professed until twelve years of age. Reforms were also undertaken on their own initiative by certain Orders. St. Theresia of Avila († 1582),[1] with the sanction of the Holy See, and the support of St. John of the Cross, success-fully laboured to introduce greater severity into the rule of the Carmelites, whilst a similar work was undertaken among the Cistercians by Jean de la Barrière, abbot of Feuillans († 1600), the founder of the Feuillantines. Especially noteworthy were

---

[1] St. Theresia's autobiography was turned into French by Bouin-Peyré (*Vie écrite par elle-même*), 1904, edited in English by B. Zimmerman, 1904 ; Bg. by Pösl, 2nd ed. 1856 ; E. D'Orves, 1890 ; Graham, 2 vol. 1894.

the attempts at reform made by the Franciscans. They resulted not only in the formation of a new division of the Order, the Capuchins, but also led to further developments among the Observants, whose rule was now imitated by the Reformed Friars, the Recollects, and the Discalced Franciscans —the latter founded by Peter of Alcantara († 1562)—so that henceforth this branch of the Franciscans comprised altogether four families, the older *Observantia regularis* and the three others of more recent creation, the four together being designated by the title of *Fratres minores strictioris observantiae.*

Even before these reforms had been carried out, several new Orders had come into existence, and a few were to follow somewhat later. The most important of all these was the **Society of Jesus.**[1] Its foundation was laid when Ignatius of Loyola and six friends, among them Francis Xavier, Laynez, and Lefèvre (Faber)—all of them Spaniards with the exception of the last, who hailed from Savoy—took a vow at Montmartre near Paris to observe poverty and chastity, and to undertake a spiritual crusade to the Holy Land, or, in the event of this proving impracticable, to offer their services to the head of the Church for any mission which he might assign (1534). According to the Bull *Regimini militantis ecclesiae* (1540) by which the Society was formally approved, its main task was to consist in preaching and in the education of youth, a task which could all the more easily be performed by its members, seeing that they were dispensed from service in choir and from similar monastic obligations. An additional vow, of unconditional obedience to the Holy See in all matters relating to the mission, was also imposed on them. In the event the whole strength of this powerful Order was devoted to education and preaching, the higher education of Catholic Europe soon being almost entirely in their hands. Ignatius himself founded the *Collegium Romanum* (1551), the greatest of the educational establishments

---

[1] CRÉTINEAU-JOLY, *Hist. rel. pol. et littér. de la compagnie de Jésus*, 6 vol. 1845–46 ; J. HUBER, *Der Jesuitenorden*, 1873 ; REUSCH, *Beiträge zur Gesch. des Jesuitenordens*, 1894 ; Bg. of Ignatius by POLANCO (in the *Monumenta hist. Societatis Iesu*, 4 vol. 1894–96) ; BARTOLI, 1650 (Engl. Trans. *Hist. of the Life and Institutes of St. Ig. of L.*, 2 vol. 1856) ; GOTHEIN, *Ign. von L. u. die Gegenreformation*, 1895 ; W. v. NIEUWENHOFF, 2 vol. 1900 ; GREFF, 1903 ; *Ratio Studiorum et institutiones schol. S. I. per Germaniam olim vigentes collectae per* PACHTLER, 4 vol. 1887–94 ; DUHR, *Die Studienordnung d. G. J.* 1896 ; *Jesuitenfabeln*, 4th ed. 1904.

controlled by the Society, comprising colleges for the teaching of Humanities, Philosophy, and Theology ; he also instituted the *Collegium Germanicum* at Rome (1552), a seminary for the formation of zealous German priests.[1] Besides this, the Order laboured with great success in the defence of the Church against the Reformers. The zeal and ability of the Jesuits were responsible for the expulsion of Protestantism from many localities, and for the retention of the older Faith in others. One of its members who deserved well in this connection was Peter Canisius († 1597),[2] whose catechisms were particularly valuable.

The *Monita privata Societatis Iesu* (Cracow, 1612), or *Monita secreta*, as the later and fuller edition was called, are spurious, and a mere satire on the Society (HUBER, pp. 104–108). It is now generally held that their compiler was the ex-Jesuit Jerome Zahorowski. Cp. *Z. f. k. Th.* 1890, p. 398 ; J. B. REIBER, *Monita secreta*, 1902.

The remaining Religious Orders may be divided, according to the field of their activity, into two classes, some concerning themselves with the education and improvement of the clergy, or with the instruction of the laity by means of missions, &c., others devoting themselves to the teaching of children or the nursing of the sick. Among the former we find : (1) The **Theatines,** an Order founded in 1524 by Cajetan of Thiene and Peter Caraffa, bishop of Theate (Chieti). Its members were bound to the severest poverty, were forbidden to beg, and had accordingly to subsist on free gifts. Cp. W. LÜBEN, *Der hl. Cajetan v. Th.* 1882 ; MAULDE DE LA CLAVIÈRE, *S. Gaëtan*, 1902.

(2) The **Capuchins** originated in 1528 through the efforts of Matteo di Bassi to bring back the Franciscans to their older observances. The rule was to be enforced more strictly, a pointed hood and the beard were also to be worn. The Capuchins became a distinct Order in 1619.

(3) The **Barnabites** were founded at Milan in 1530 by three high-born priests—Zaccaria, Ferrari and Morigia—and took their name from the monastery of St. Barnabas which was bestowed on them. Paul III gave them the title of ' clerks of St. Paul,' for which reasons they are sometimes termed Paulines. In their work with the opposite sex they were assisted by the ' Angelicals,' or *Sorores angelicae,* founded by the pious Luigia di Torelli, countess of Guastalla, a sisterhood which from the beginning had been under the direction of the Barnabites.

(4) The **Oratorians,** or congregation of the Oratory, founded at Rome by St. Philip Neri, and approved in 1574. Bg. of St. Philip

---

[1] STEINHUBER, *Gesch. d. Collegium Germanicum*, 2 vol. 1895.
[2] *Petri Canisii epistulae et acta*, ed. BRAUNSBERGER, I–IV, 1896–1905 ; F. RIESS, *P. Canisius*, 1865.

by Pösl, 1857; Reiching, 1859; Capecelatro, 1879; F. I. Antrobus, 1903.

(5) The **Oblates,** a congregation of secular priests established in 1578 by St. Charles Borromeo. Bg. of the founder by Dieringer, 1846; Sylvain, 3 vol. 1884.

(6) The **Regular Clerks minor** (*Clerici regulares minores*), established by Giovanni Adorno and Francis Carraccioli (1588).

The Orders belonging to the latter category are:

(1) The **Somaschans,** founded in 1528 by Jerome Æmilian for the care of orphans, and named after its mother-house at Somascha between Bergamo and Milan. W. E. Hubert, *Der hl. Hier Æmiliani*, 1895.

(2) The **Ursulines,** a sisterhood established in 1537 by St. Angela of Brescia for the education of girls, and for the care of the sick. Mg. by Postel, 2 vol. 1878; At, 1885; by an Ursuline (Innsbrück), 1893.

(3) The **Brothers of Mercy,** founded as an association of seculars for the care of the sick, having its headquarters in a hospital at Granada erected by St. John of God in 1540. After the founder's death (1550) they were constituted into an Order.

(4) The **Fathers of a Good Death,** a congregation of Clerks-regular for the nursing of the sick, founded at Rome by St. Camillus of Lellis (1584).

(5) The **Fathers of the Christian Doctrine** (*Pères de la doctrine chrétienne*), established in 1592 by César de Bus, and for a while (1616-47) united to the Somaschans.

(6) The **Piarists,** or *Patres piarum scholarum*, founded at Rome in 1597 by the Spaniard Joseph Calasancza for the education and instruction of boys. Bg. by W. E. Hubert, 1886.

§ 179

The Papacy to the Middle of the Seventeenth Century [1]

The first popes of the period were so closely connected with the Protestant Reformation, and with the Council by which it was to be opposed, that the main outlines of their history is already known to the reader. A few details may, however, be added.

---

[1] Reumont, *Gesch. d. St. Rom.* vol. III, 2; Ranke, *Die röm. Päpste im 16 u. 17 Jahrh.* 3 vol. 1838-39; 10th ed. 1900; *WW.* vol. 37-39 (Engl. Trans. *The Popes of Rome, their eccl. and polit. Hist. during the 16th and 17th centuries*, 3 vol. 1866); M. Brosch, *Gesch. d. Kirchenstaates*, 2 vol. 1880-82 (cp. the same author in the *Cambridge Modern History*, ed. by Lord Acton, vol. IV.); A. Pieper, *Die päpstlichen Legaten und Nuntien*, I, 1897; *RHE.* 1906 (*Origines des nonciatures permanentes*).

I. **Adrian VI** (1522–23) [1] was a native of Utrecht and was the last foreigner to sit on the throne of Peter ; henceforth the popes were to be Italians.

II. Under **Clement VII** (1523–34), a cousin of Leo X, the quarrels proceeding between the emperor and France, the two greatest of the European powers, had results unfortunate for Rome. As a cardinal the Pope had favoured the cause of Charles V, and even in the first period of his pontificate he had generally remained neutral. In 1526, however, fifteen months after the battle of Pavia in which Francis I had fallen into the hands of his enemies, Clement entered into the so-called Holy League with France, England, and several Italian States. It was the Pope who had to bear the brunt of the war. In May 1527 there occurred the famous Sacco di Roma,[2] the Eternal City being stormed and sacked by the imperial troops, and Clement himself being imprisoned in the castle of Sant' Angelo. After having been a captive for seven months, a peace was concluded at Cambrai in 1529. At the beginning of the next year Charles was crowned by Clement at Bologna. He was the last German king to receive from a Pope the imperial crown, a fact which is significant of the political and religious changes which were then being accomplished.

III. **Paul III** (1534–49),[3] of the house of Farnese, was undoubtedly a great prince of the Church. The loose morals of the later Middle Ages had, however, left their mark on him, and his earlier weaknesses were responsible for the misfortunes of his pontificate. Besides his concern in the affairs of the Church, he laboured with great zeal for the worldly advancement of his family. To his grandson Ottavio he gave Camerino and Nepi as fiefs (1540), and on the gift being withdrawn, his son Pietro Luigi Farnese, Ottavio's father, was appointed duke of Parma and Piacenza (1545). Two years later, the new duke was murdered and Parma was re-incorporated in the States of the Church, whilst Piacenza was occupied by the imperial governor of Milan. As the murdered man's son refused to relinquish his claims on Parma, the city was conferred on him by **Julius III** (1550–55). Ottavio, however, in order

---

[1] K. Höfler, *Papst Adrian VI*, 1880.
[2] H. Schulz, *Der Sacco di Roma*, 1894 ; D. Orano, *Il Sacco di Roma*, 1902.
[3] C. Capasso, *La politica di Papa Paolo III e l'Italia*, I, 1901.

to ward against a possible attack from the emperor, who claimed both cities for the duchy of Milan or the Empire, concluded an alliance with France, which resulted in the war which prevented the attendance of the French at the Council of Trent in 1551.

IV. After the brief pontificate of Marcellus II, formerly cardinal Marcello Cervino, Peter Caraffa ascended the pontifical throne under the title of **Paul IV** (1555–59).[1] Already seventy-nine years of age at his election, he was nevertheless still full of the vigour and zeal which he had already shown in founding the Theatines. His great concern was now to uphold the Faith and to abolish abuses. In the interests of the former he issued his Bull *Cum ex apostolatus officio* (1559), in which, giving as his grounds the *plenitudo potestatis super gentes et regna* possessed by the Pope, he withdrew from all apostates, clerical or lay, princes or subjects, all their dignities and rights, and conferred their properties on the first claimant. His harshness of character led him to hate the house of Habsburg, and through fear of the emperor's power he allied himself with France. The alliance soon embroiled the Pope in an unsuccessful war with the king of Naples, Philip II (1555–56). Partly on account of his distrust and partly on account of the peace of Augsburg, the Pope refused to recognise Ferdinand I as emperor. For all his zeal on behalf of the Church, the Pope did not forget his own family. His affection to his nephews was not, however, reciprocated, and he had finally to degrade and banish them. Under his successor they were compelled to stand their trial, cardinal Caraffa and the duke of Palliano being ultimately both condemned to death.[2]

V. The attention of **Pius IV** (1559–65), of the Milanese family of the Medici, was almost exclusively devoted to the Council of Trent, which largely owed to him the success of its concluding sessions. Having dissolved the Council, he occupied himself in putting the decrees into execution, and in completing the reforms which had been begun by the assembled Fathers, but had ultimately devolved on the Pope. No time was lost in drawing up a profession of Faith in accordance with the

[1] *MIŒ.* (1904), 470–89 (on the conflicts of Charles V, Philip II, and Paul IV).

[2] *Rev. Bénéd.* 1905, pp. 525–35.

decrees of the Council (*Professio fidei Tridentina*). At the earnest request of the emperor Ferdinand I and duke Albert of Bavaria, permission was given for the administration of Communion under both kinds in a portion of Germany, though the permission for priestly marriage which had also been requested was steadfastly refused.[1] A new and revised edition of the *Index librorum prohibitorum* was also issued (1564).[2] Further work was prevented by the Pope's death. A large share in the activity of this pontificate must also in justice be ascribed to the Pope's nephew, cardinal Charles Borromeo, archbishop of Milan.

VI. The next Pope, the Dominican Ghislieri, or **Pius V** (1565-72), was the last to be canonised. During his occupancy of the See the catechism, which had been designed to meet the needs of parish-priests (*Catechismus Romanus*), was completed (1566), and the correction of the Breviary (1568) and of the Missal (1570) were successfully achieved. The remainder of his pontificate was devoted to the upholding of the Faith and of discipline, and to the conflict with the Turks. The Bull *In coena Domini*, a list of the crimes and more grievous sins of which absolution was reserved by Rome, which it had been customary to read solemnly at Rome every Maundy Thursday since the time of Urban V (1364), was now made yet more stringent.[3] The Bull of Paul IV, to which allusion has already been made, was also renewed, and the penalties therein decreed against apostates and those suspected of heresy were actually enacted against Elizabeth of England (1570), though without any result, the Bull being already an anachronism. The Turks took Cyprus, but their further progress westwards was effectually barred by the great naval victory gained over them at Lepanto (1571).

VII. The reign of **Gregory XIII** (1572-85), a Buoncampagni, was remarkable for two things, the carrying out of the reform of the calendar, a reform the need of which had long been apparent (§ 4), and for the foundation and endowment of numerous ecclesiastical collegiate establishments. Colleges were founded by this Pope for Hungary (the institution was

---

[1] KNÖPFLER, *Die Kelchbewegung in Bayern*, 1891; *Hist. J.* 1892, pp. 144-57.
[2] Mg. by F. REUSCH, 2 vol. 1883-85; J. HILGERS, 1904; G. H. PUTNAM.
[3] HAUSMANN, *Gesch. d. päpstl. Reservatfälle*, 1868, p. 89 ff.

soon after incorporated in the German College), for England, for the Greeks, Armenians, and Maronites. The existence of the *Collegium Germanicum* was assured by endowments, and the *Collegium Romanum* was favoured to such an extent that it still venerates him as its second founder, and received the name of *Universitas Gregoriana* on being provided with the higher faculties of Philosophy and Theology.

VIII. Under **Sixtus V** (1585–90),[1] previously a Franciscan named Peretti, the emended edition of the Vulgate, which had been demanded by the Council of Trent, was at last published (1590),[2] though it turned out to be so faulty that before long a new edition had to be issued (1592). In other directions the Pope was more successful, and gave proof of quite uncommon administrative capacity. At the very commencement of his pontificate he took measures of extreme severity against the brigands who were disturbing the whole of Italy and were especially numerous in the States of the Church ; for a time, at least, brigandage was entirely suppressed within the papal territories. To assist in the business of governing the Church he also established fifteen congregations, of which those entrusted with the spiritualities survive to our own day. The city of Rome was enlarged and beautified. The dome of St. Peter's, a wonder among works of architecture, was completed, and the great obelisk which had thus far lain in the dust was erected in the Piazza di San Pietro. The Pope had also to face great trouble abroad. Owing to the civil war and the dispute concerning the succession which were raging in France, the Pope was subjected to constant pressure by the French parties and by Philip II of Spain, who were all desirous of obtaining his support, and the difficulties only grew with the progress of time. After the assassination of the duke of Guise and of the cardinal of Lorraine by Henry III (1588), and the latter's murder (1589), the claimant to the French throne who had the most right was Henry of Navarre, whom the Pope himself had excommunicated as a Huguenot at the beginning of his pontificate, and who still clung to Protestantism. For a time it seemed that the Pope would have to yield to the pressure of the Spaniards. Trusting, however, in the promised

---

[1] Mg. by HÜBNER, 2 vol. 1871 (Engl. Trans. 1872) ; CAPRANICA, 3 vol. 1884.
[2] KAULEN, *Gesch. d. V.* 1868.

conversion of the Bourbon, and dreading also any increase in
Spain's power, the Pope refused to be led into further action
against Henry IV.

IX. French affairs were to occupy the next popes also.
Urban VII indeed was unable to do anything, as he died before
his coronation.   On the other hand cardinal Sfondrato, as soon
as he had succeeded under the title of **Gregory XIV** (1590–91),
took a more determined line.   As the neutrality thus far
observed did not seem of any avail, he embraced the cause of the
League, sending them troops and bidding the Catholics forsake
Navarre.   The same policy was followed by Innocent IX
and by **Clement VIII** (1592–1605) of the house of Aldobrandini.
When, however, Navarre himself returned to the Church (1593)
and his cause began to gain ground, it became necessary in the
interests of peace and of the Church to adopt a different line
of conduct, and Henry IV was finally acknowledged (1595).
This step soon proved fortunate for the Papal States.   On the
death of duke Alfonso II of Este without issue (1597), the
Pope was able with the help of France to claim Ferrara as a
lapsed fief.

X. Leo XI, one of the Mediceans, reigned for only twenty-
six days, and was succeeded by cardinal Borghese as **Paul V**
(1605–21), who almost immediately entered into a violent
altercation with Venice.   The pretext for the quarrel was the
imprisonment of two criminal clerics by the Republic, and the
re-enactment of two laws forbidding the bestowal of landed
property on the clergy or the erection of new churches without
the consent of the government; the Republic had flatly refused
either to yield up the clerics to be tried by the Church, or to
repeal the laws in question.   Other complaints were also made
against Venice, and as the Republic, convinced by the arguments
of the Servite Paolo Sarpi that the exemption of the clergy and
the immunities of the Church rested on human and not on
Divine law, refused to reconsider its actions, it was laid under
excommunication and interdict (1606).   The only result of this
measure was to intensify the conflict.   The sentence was
rejected by the Republic as invalid, and the clergy, with the
exception of the Jesuits, Capuchins, and Theatines, continued
to hold the customary services.   When the parties were already
on the eve of war, the intervention of France led Venice to give

way, though only on such conditions as to make it impossible to speak of the event as a victory for the Pope. Nor was there anything really strange in this issue of the quarrel. The claims of Paul V were too mediæval in character to be made good. How circumstances had changed is also apparent from the fact that this was the last occasion on which a whole state was placed under an interdict.

XI. After the short reign of **Gregory XV** (1621–23) of the house of Ludovisi, a great patron of the Jesuits, who canonised Ignatius and Francis Xavier, there followed cardinal Barberini as **Urban VIII** (1623–44). His pontificate was rich in events. He corrected the Breviary, and practically gave the Bull *In coena Domini* its present form. To his time belongs the trial of Galileo [1] and the condemnation of the Copernican system by the Holy Office. The Papal States were enlarged by the addition of the duchy of Urbino, a papal fief which was occupied on the death of the last of the race of Rovere (1631). On the other hand, Urban was drawn into a lengthy war with the duke of Parma, which, after depleting the papal treasury, ended without any satisfactory result. In his foreign policy this Pope was too much inclined to favour France, and his conduct in this respect, as well as his concern for the promotion of his relatives, has often been made a subject of reproach, some even going so far as to allege that he rejoiced over the victory of the Swedes in Germany.[2]

XII. **Innocent X** (1644–55), a member of the house of Pamfili, soon after his accession was compelled to put his predecessor's nephews on their trial. On their fleeing to France their dignities and possessions were confiscated, though at France's request the trial was afterwards abandoned and the fugitives restored to their offices. A new quarrel now broke out with the duke of Parma. Not only did he refuse to fulfil his obligations, but he was also suspected of having murdered the bishop of Castro, in consequence of which this town was destroyed and the whole territory incorporated in the Papal States. In spite of Innocent's severity, at least for a time,

---

[1] Mg. by K. v. GEBLER, 1876–77 ; SCHANZ, 1878 ; REUSCH, 1879 ; GRISAR, 1882 ; FUNK, *A. u. U.* II, 444–76.

[2] *Hist. J.* 1895, pp. 336–341 ; *R. Qu.* 1899, pp. 151–262.

to the Barberini, he himself allowed his own relative, his sister-in-law Donna Olympia Maidalchini, an undue influence over the conduct of affairs. How unworthy she really was of his confidence was to be seen after his death, when she refused even to bear the costs of his funeral.

During this period a change had become apparent in the **election of the popes.** Since the end of the fifteenth century it had been the practice to retain permanent ambassadors at Rome, and at the conclaves the various States strove for the upper hand. In the first half of the sixteenth century it was France and the emperor who practically controlled the proceedings. Later on the cardinals were left to their own devices, with the result that there were usually two parties on the one hand, the creatures of the late Pope led by his nephews, and on the other, the remaining cardinals, the latter as a general rule being successful, the opposite party again coming into power only at the subsequent conclave. Since Julius III the election was almost invariably by ' Adoration ' ; the candidate was made to sit on the altar, and homage was rendered him, his supporters endeavouring to induce as many of the electors as possible to accomplish the action. This method was not one to safeguard the freedom of election, or to prevent outside influences, and accordingly Gregory XV, in his Bull *Aeterni Patris*, 1621, decreed that the election should in future be made by the *Scrutinium*, and that the vote should be secret. The method of compromise, or ' inspiration,' was only to be permitted when the cardinals were unanimously in its favour. In the many discussions respecting the reform of the election we frequently hear of the right of exclusion. Very little is known of the origin of the right of exclusion as claimed by the Catholic great powers (the emperor, France, and Spain), *i.e.* the right of each excluding one candidate at each conclave. SÄGMÜLLER (*Die Papstwahlen*, 1890 ; *die Papstwahlbullen*, 1892 ; *A. f. K. KR.* 1895, I, 193–256) traces it back to Charles V and Philip II. WAHRMUND (*Das Ausschliessungsrecht der kath. Staaten*, 1890 ; *A. f. K. KR.* 1894, II, 201–334) can find no certain use of it before the conclave in 1721. ' LECTOR ' (*Le conclave*, 1894) thinks it originated in 1691.

The famous **Predictions concerning the popes**, which were published by the Benedictine Wion in the *Lignum vitae*, 1595, as emanating from St. Malachy, archbishop of Armagh († 1148), and which deal with the popes from Celestine II (1143) till the end of the world (printed in GINZEL, *Kirchenhist. Schriften*, 1872, II, 83–90), were without a doubt composed shortly before their publication, under Urban VII, the last Pope to be clearly described, or during the conclave after his death (1590). J. MAÎTRE, *La prophétie des papes attribuée à saint Malachie*, 1901 (on their authenticity). *Festgabe für H. Finke*, 1904, pp. 1–40 ; *Th. Qu.* 1873, pp. 162–68.

§ 180

The Missions [1]

Whilst the Church was losing wide districts in the home-
lands, others were being won for her elsewhere. The dis-
coveries of the Spaniards and Portuguese in East and West
excited, particularly among the Jesuits and Capuchins, a
desire to convert these new countries. Missionaries departed
in every direction. The various missionary undertakings were
put by Gregory XV under the supreme direction of the *Congregatio de propaganda fide* [2] (1622). The *Collegium Urbanum*,
added by Urban VIII (1627), was a seminary in which young
men were to be trained to act as missionaries in every part
of the world. Later on, at Paris, similar institutions were
established—the College of Foreign Missions (1663) and the
College of the Holy Ghost (1703).

The Church's greatest conquests were made in the New
World. [3] All the countries taken possession of by the Spaniards,
the Portuguese, or the French were won over to the Faith.
It penetrated into the West Indies, or at least into Haiti, San
Domingo and Cuba, the largest of the islands, into South America,
Guiana, Venezuela, New Granada, and the kingdom of the Incas,
i.e. the modern States of Ecuador, Peru, Bolivia, and Chile
(conquered by Pizarro, 1532), into the lands of La Plata and
Brazil, into Mexico or New Spain (conquered by Cortez, 1519),
into California and Canada or New France (where Quebec was
erected into a bishopric in 1674). Owing to the cruelty frequently practised towards the natives by the conquerors, their
conversion was in many places a matter of much difficulty. In
spite of this, constant progress was made, here more slowly,
there more rapidly. The Indians soon discovered that the
missionaries were their best friends. One of the first to plead
on their behalf was Las Casas († 1566), whose life may be said
to have been devoted to the protection of the downtrodden

---

[1] HENRION, *Hist. gén. des missions cath. depuis le XIIIe siècle*, 2 vol. 1847 ;
H. HAHN, *Gesch. d. kath. M.* 5 vol. 1857-63 ; KALKAR, German Trans. from
the Danish *Gesch. d. röm. kath. M.* 1867 ; *Gesch. d. christl. M.* 2 vol. 1879-80;
O. WERNER, *Kath. Missionsatlas*, 2nd ed. 1885 ; *KL.* I, 711-40.
[2] Cp. PHILLIPS, *KR.* VI, 667 ff. ; O. MEJER, *Die Propaganda*, 2 vol. 1853.
[3] L. A. DUTTO, *The Life of Bartolomé de las Casas and the first Leaves of
American Ecclesiastical History*, 1902.

savages. The zeal, the kindness, the ability, and the persever-
ance of the missionaries met their due reward, and at the
present day only a small remnant of the population of those
countries remains heathen.

The same thing happened in the Philippines, when these
islands (discovered in 1521) were occupied by the Spaniards
(1571), in whose possession they were to remain till 1901. In
the course of nine years 250,000 natives were baptised, an
archbishopric with three suffragan sees being established at
Manila towards the end of the sixteenth century.

Missions were also sent to India, Japan, and China, though
their labours met with no permanent success.

In the **East Indies,** as soon as the Portuguese had firmly established their rule, a bishopric was erected at Goa (1534), and likewise
a seminary to educate the natives for the mission (1541).   The work
of conversion assumed greater dimensions when it came into the
hands of the Jesuits, headed by **St. Francis Xavier** (1542).   Such
was the success of his work that he obtained the name of the apostle
of the Indians.   He reclaimed the careless colonists of Goa, and led
them to a Christian life, completed the conversion of the already
baptised Paravians on the coasts at the south of the peninsula, and
baptised many others, besides converting thousands of pagans on
the coast of Travancore (Bg. by BOUHOURS, 1682 ; REITHMEIER, 1846 ;
N. GREFF, 1885 ; CROS, 2 vol. 1903).   His companions continued
his work, and, little by little, the pagans in and about Goa were won
over to the Faith.   Other missionary stations were established in
Cochin (a bishopric since 1557) and in Madura (1595).   A great
improvement occurred in the outlook of these last missions when
Robert Nobili (1606–56) proceeded to put a new project into
execution.   Until then converts had been required to quit their
caste, a demand which made conversion a matter of the greatest
difficulty.   Nobili, on the contrary, saw in the caste a mere social
institution, and he accordingly decided to tolerate the various caste-
marks and the solemnisation of certain festivals so far as they did
not assume a specifically religious or heathen character.   Becoming
himself a Brahmin he preached to the higher classes, whilst his
associate in religion, Fernandez, was appointed to teach the lower
castes.   He also took into account other prejudices of the natives ; for
instance, he omitted in Baptism ceremonies such as the breathing,
the use of the saliva and of salt, which were particularly obnoxious to
the Hindus.   He had not erred in supposing that thereby he would
facilitate conversions, but as the too great expectations which had
been built on his process of accommodation were not to be fulfilled,
only very few of the higher classes adopting Christianity, the
renewed complaints of the Capuchins led to his plans being

condemned at the beginning of the eighteenth century. Tournon, the patriarch of Antioch, as papal legate, forbade sixteen of the so-called Malabar customs (1704), and in spite of the opposition of the Jesuits, the sentence was ratified by Rome. The last and definitive prohibition is contained in the Bull *Omnium sollicitudinum* (1744). Cp. MÜLLBAUER, *Gesch. d. kath. Mission in Ostindien,* 1851.

The **Japan** mission was also a creation of St. Francis Xavier (1549), and here his success was very conspicuous. Thirty years later the Christians in the land of the Rising Sun numbered already 300,000, and their number was yet to increase, in spite of the severe persecution soon to break out (1596). Christianity even survived the great catastrophe of 1638. In consequence of the jealousy of the Bonzes towards the missionaries, of the official suspicion of all foreigners, and especially owing to the instigation of the Dutch, their bitter rivals in Asia, the Portuguese were banished from the kingdom. The missionaries were massacred and the native Christians were drowned in thousands. The Japanese Christians were now cut off from the rest of the Church, and their Faith was banned. In spite of this, Christianity was not extirpated, but survived to our day, though in many points obscured and disfigured ; of the sacraments, at least Baptism continued to be conferred. Cp. CRASSET, *Hist. de l'église du Japon,* 1715 ; PAGÈS, *Hist. de la rel. chrét. en J. depuis* 1598–1651, 1869 ff. ; H. HAAS, *Gesch. d. Christent. in Japan,* I–II (to 1570), 1902–4. Complaints were made against the Dutch of having pretended not to be Christians, in order to retain their trade with the Japanese, and of even having trampled on the crucifix. The charge cannot indeed be established, but it is certain that the Dutch were present when the crucifix was desecrated, and that they took at least a passive share in an action abhorrent to every Christian. Cp. A. v. HÜBNER, *Spaziergang um die Welt,* 3rd ed. (1875), II, 297 ff.

As the religious fortune of the whole of Asia rested, to some extent, on **China,** the Jesuits at an early date prepared themselves for a mission to this country by a thorough study of the language and of the arts and sciences which were expected to appeal to the Chinese. Three men especially were remarkable for their success : Matteo Ricci of Macerata, who proceeded to China in 1583 in the company of the Portuguese ambassador († 1610) ; Johann Adam Schall of Cologne († 1666) ; and Ferdinand Verbiest of Bruges in the Netherlands († 1688). In spite of the mandarins' opposition, they succeeded in ingratiating themselves with the emperor. Here, too, use was made of the process of accommodation, the missionaries permitting certain acts of homage to Confucius and to the departed (a kind of sacrifice offered before tablets inscribed with the names of the dead), seeing in it a mere political and social usage ; God was styled Tien (heaven) and Khangti (highest ruler). This toleration excited adverse comment here as well as in India, and the so-called Chinese rites were condemned by Innocent X (1645). The Jesuits again obtained their toleration from Alexander VII (1656), and continued their practice in spite of the prohibitions issued by the legate Tournon (1707), and Clement XI (1715). Ultimately they were, however, obliged to submit to the sentence of Benedict XIV, conveyed in the Bull *Ex quo singulari* (1742). These quarrels were naturally not to the advantage of the Christian cause, which, however, suffered yet more from the political changes then in progress The emperor Khangi (1662–1722), though he insisted on the observance of the Chinese usages, was not unkindly disposed to the missionaries, but his successor was of a different stamp, and allowed the nation to give full expression to its hatred of the foreigners. Henceforth the only certain refuge of the Jesuits was at the capital Peking, where they were employed by the court as mathematicians and artists. Cp. *Historica relatio de ortu et progr. fidei orth. in regno Chin. collecta ex litteris J. A. Schall*, Vien. 1665 ; Ratisbon, 1672 ; PRAY, *Hist. controversiarum de ritibus Sinicis*, 1789. On Schall's supposed marriage, cp. B. DUHR, *Jesuitenfabeln*, 3rd ed. p. 226 ff. ; *Z. f. k. Th.* 1901, p. 331 f.

In the seventeenth century Christianity took firm root in **Further India,** where the Gospel had previously been preached by isolated missionaries. Missions were established in Cochin China (in 1615 by the Jesuit Buzomi), in Tonking (in 1627 by another Jesuit, Alexander of Rhodes), in Cambodia (1617), Siam (1621), and other places. In the former countries the Christians soon numbered several hundred thousands, in the others their numbers remained small. Cp. PACHTLER, *Das Christentum in Tonkin und Cochinchina, dem heutigen Annamreiche*, 1861.

Of a very special character was the mission in **Paraguay.** To make an end of the evil influence of the Spanish colonists, Philip III handed over the government of the country to the Jesuits, the inhabitants being only required to admit his suzerainty and pay a small capitation-tax. This measure proved a great blessing to the land. The Indians were converted in great numbers, were then divided into ' reductions,' as the parishes were called, and taught the arts and crafts, so that, with Christianity, they received all the advantages of civilisation. Cp. MURATORI, *Il Christianesimo felice nelle missioni del Paraguai*, 1743 ; CHARLEVOIX, *Hist. de P.* 1757 ; PFOTENHAUER, *Die Missionen der Jesuiten in P.* 3 vol. 1891–93.

§ 181

Controversies regarding Grace [1]

The opposition of the Protestants moved Catholic theologians to devote especial attention to the doctrine of the original state of man and to Grace, their investigations leading to the renewal

[1] J. SCHWANE, *Dogmengesch. der neueren Zeit*, 1890 ; J. TURMEL, *Hist. de la théol. positive du concile de Trente au conc. du Vatican*, 1906.

of an old dispute. The questions then discussed, to tell the truth, do not admit of any entirely satisfactory answer, and will probably ever be solved differently. The theologians of the period were not, however, the men to settle down to a quiet exchange of ideas. The stringent Augustinian doctrine concerning sin and grace, now that it had been explained by the Protestants in an outrageously predestinarian sense, seemed to many of the Catholics more intolerable than ever. Others, however, full of confidence in the authority of the great bishop of Hippo, not only wished to retain his doctrine, but even went beyond him in the matter of severity. The first controversy started in the Netherlands, and was followed by others of a wider character in Spain and France.

A. BAIUS AND LESSIUS

In his attempt to refurbish the Augustinian doctrine, **Michael de Bay or Baius** of Louvain (1513–89) came to the following conclusions. Subsequently to the Fall, man by his own natural power is capable only of sin ; all the actions of unbelievers and the unrighteous are sinful and damnable. Man is therefore incapable of preparing himself for the reception of Grace, which is consequently always conferred on him, as it were, against his will. But though man is necessarily sinful, he remains free, freedom being indeed incompatible with external compulsion (*violentia*), but not with simple necessity (*necessitas*). These propositions were viewed with favour by many, though the number of their opponents was far greater. Among the latter the principal were the professors Tapper and Ravesteyn of Louvain, and the Belgian Franciscans at whose instigation the Sorbonne censured eighteen propositions extracted from Baius's lectures (1560), among which were the above. This was the signal for a general conflict, which continued for several years until Paul V, in his Bull *Ex omnibus afflictionibus*,[1] condemned seventy-nine theses advocated by Baius (1567), who, after some hesitation, submitted to the decree. Mg. by LINSENMANN, 1867.

Soon after this the Jesuit **Leonard Lessius** (1554–1623), also a Louvain professor, in opposition to Baius, extolled human freedom at the expense of Grace. His view was that God gives to all men sufficient Grace to render their conversion possible, and that this sufficient Grace has been from all eternity willed by God out of His entire good pleasure. On the other hand, man's will must be

---

[1] The Bull will be found in the Leipzig ed. of the *Canones et decr. Conc. Trid.*, which also contains the Bulls against Jansenius and Pasch. Quesnel. For the University censures see *Collectio iudiciorum de novis erroribus*, ed. D'ARGENTRÉ, 3 fol. 1724–36.

considered to be the only ground why in some cases the *gratia sufficiens* becomes *gratia efficax* and in others does not. Likewise Predestination to further means of Grace and ultimately to eternal happiness, depends on God's foreknowledge of man's merits (*praevisis meritis gratia [prima vel secunda] comparatis*). This doctrine, as it seemed to put Salvation in the power of man rather than of God, was vehemently assailed and was censured by the Faculties of Louvain (1587) and Douai (1588). It was also examined at Rome, though no decision was vouchsafed.

B. The Molinist Controversy [1]

Bañez, a Dominican professor at Salamanca, in order to explain the infallible efficaciousness of Grace, which had been taught by both Augustine and Thomas of Aquin, alleged a *physica praedeterminatio* or *praemotio* of the human will. At the other extreme, the Jesuit **Luis Molina** of Evora in Portugal considered that he had found in the theory of a *Scientia media*, or *Scientia conditionata*, the means of safeguarding both the infallibility of efficacious Grace and the freedom of the human will. His teaching was the following : God knows from all eternity what men will do under given circumstances, whether they occur or not, and He accordingly from all eternity bestows His efficacious Grace on those whom He foresees will co-operate with it, whereas on the others He merely bestows sufficient Grace. This view was brought before the public in the work *De liberi arbitrii cum gratiae donis &c. concordia* (1588), and was generally received with applause. It also found determined opponents. In the opinion of the Dominicans this view, like the doctrine of Lessius, involved a semi-pelagian exaggeration of human freedom at the expense of Divine Grace, disrespect for the authority of St. Augustine, St. Thomas, &c. So acute did the controversy become that Clement VIII was obliged to reserve to himself the decision of the question (1596), and to refer it to a special *Congregatio de auxiliis gratiae* (1598). In the two examinations which followed, the judgment of the congregation was adverse to Molina, but, as the judgment was

---

[1] Schneemann, S. J., *Entstehung u. Entwicklung der thomistisch-molinist. Kontroverse*, 1879–80; in Latin, 1881 ; Frins, S. J., *S. Thomae Aqu. doctrina de cooperatione Dei cum omni natura, &c.* 1893. On the opposite side : Dummermuth, O. P., *S. Thomas et doctrina praemotionis physicae*, 1886 ; *Defensio doctrinae S. Thomae de praemotione phys.* 1895.

not unanimous, the Pope refused to confirm it. Conferences were then arranged between the two parties, though with no result. Within the Congregation, however, the Molinists were gaining strength, and the number of Molina's propositions which had been reserved for censure was reduced from ninety to twenty, nor were the consulters unanimous even as to these. For the purpose of assuring himself of the position of matters, the Pope (1602) again had the whole question threshed out in his presence. His successor, Paul V, even ordered an inquiry into the Dominican theory of the Divine predetermina tion of the human will. The trial finally ended in 1607, either party being forbidden to incriminate the other of heresy, both opinions being thereby declared permissible. A few years later the publication of works dealing with this thorny question was made conditional on the permission of the Inquisition (1611).

The originator of the theory of the *Scientia media* was the Jesuit Peter Fonseca. It owes its name to the fact that it stands midway between the two kinds of Divine knowledge admitted by the Schoolmen, *i.e.* between the *Scientia visionis*, or knowledge of realities, and the *Scientia simplicis intellegentiae*, or knowledge of mere possibilities.

C. The Jansenist Controversy [1]

The occasion for the last of the disputes was furnished by **Cornelius Jansenius,** a Louvain professor, afterwards (1636–1638) bishop of Ypres. His great work on the Augustinian doctrine of Grace (*Augustinus, sive doctrina S. Augustini de humanae naturae sanitate, aegritudine, medicina adv. Pelagianos et Massilienses*) was published two years after his death, was hailed with great applause in the Netherlands, and found admirers even in France, where the ground had been prepared for it by the author's personal friend Verger de Hauranne, abbot of St. Cyran. The commotion was therefore all the greater when the book was attacked by the Jesuits and forbidden

[1] Leydecker, *Hist. Jansen.* 1695 ; Rapin, *Hist. du Jansénisme, publiée par l'abbé Domenech,* 1865 ; Reuchlin, *Gesch. von Port-Royal,* 2 vol. 1839–41 ; Saint-Beuve, *Port Royal,* 3rd ed. 7 vol. 1867–71 ; Séché, *Les derniers Jansénistes* (1710–1870), 2 vol. 1891.

by Urban VIII (1641–43).   Its great defender, the Sorbonnist
Antoine Arnauld, and the solitaries and nuns of Port Royal,
the latter headed by their abbess, Angélique Arnauld, refused
to see in the censure anything less than a condemnation of St.
Augustine, whose doctrines they therefore resolved to defend
in the person of Jansenius.   Other differences lent acrimony
to the quarrel.   The abbot of St. Cyran was an opponent of
the frequent Communions defended by the Jesuits, a practice
which was attacked by Arnauld in his work, *De la fréquente
communion* (1643).   This work was a success, but Arnauld
was soon to suffer defeat elsewhere.   The syndic Cornet laid
before the Sorbonne seven theses from the *Augustinus* (1649).
Eight-and-eighty bishops now demanded a condemnation of the
first five, whilst eleven bishops requested a delay, or at least
that the theses should receive due consideration.   The five
theses were ultimately condemned as heretical by Innocent X
in the Bull *Cum occasione.*

The five propositions read as follows :—
(1) Some of God's commandments, owing to the absence of the
needful Grace, cannot be fulfilled even by the just.
(2) Man is unable to withstand inward Grace.
(3) Merit and demerit presuppose freedom from physical compulsion, but not freedom from necessity.
(4) The Semi-Pelagians erred in teaching that the human will
is able either to resist or to follow Grace.
(5) It is Semi-Pelagian to hold that Christ died for all men.

It had been hoped that the Pope's decision would end the
controversy ; as a matter of fact it made it more acute.   The
Jansenists themselves, indeed, respected the judgment to the
extent of admitting the falsehood of the censured propositions,
but they did not hold themselves defeated.   Arnauld, for
instance, denied that the propositions really represented the
teaching of Jansenius; in other words, whilst admitting that
the *quaestio iuris* was definitively solved, he raised the *quaestio
facti,* justifying his conduct by the assertion that in questions
of fact the Church's decisions could lay no claim to inward
assent, but only to a respectful silence.   Simultaneously an
assault was led on the Jesuits' system of morality, to which
Pascal devoted the larger portion of his *Lettres provinciales*
(1656–57).   Alexander VII indeed rejected the subterfuge (1656),

but without bringing the controversy to an end. A formulary, which was offered for subscription by the General Assembly of the Clergy (1657), was rejected by many on the pretext that it was disapproved by Rome. Even the formulary drawn up by the Holy See (1665) was not accepted everywhere unconditionally, though the king had again threatened to withdraw their benefices from all who refused to sign it. Four bishops (of Alet, Angers, Beauvais, and Pamiers) issued pastoral letters in which they recommended the observance of a discreet silence on the question of fact. Their manifesto threatened further complications, but soon after the accession of Clement IX (1667–69) a compromise was reached. The four bishops signed the formulary, at the same time giving private expression to their own convictions in a separate protocol, and the Pope declared himself satisfied.

The peace was generally kept until the end of the century, though trifling conflicts were not wanting. The edition of the works of St. Augustine, undertaken by the Benedictines of St. Maur (1679–1700), was made a subject of severe strictures by the Jesuits and their allies, but the quarrel did not spread, for the attention of the French was then concentrated on the question of the Regalia (§ 182). New fuel was supplied to the controversy by the presentation in the summer, 1702, of the famous ' case of conscience ' in which the *quaestio facti* and the *silentium obsequiosum* again made their appearance. Forty doctors of the Sorbonne gave it as their opinion that the cherishing of this pet theory of the Jansenists could form no bar to absolution. This opinion was forthwith rejected by Rome and by several of the French episcopate. As the matter was not yet at an end, Clement XI, at the demand of Lewis XIV, issued his Bull *Vineam Domini* (1705). This did not improve matters, for not only was the Bull opposed by the bishop of St. Pons, but even the nuns of Port-Royal-des-Champs refused to accept it save under conditions ; their action resulted in the closing of the convent, which shortly afterwards (1710) was laid level with the ground. The independence of judgment claimed on this occasion by the General Assembly of the Clergy, even in questions already decided by the Pope, contributed to a lengthy misunderstanding which had not ceased when a yet greater controversy broke out.

The Oratorian **Paschase Quesnel** [1] had published several editions of the New Testament with moral reflections, and Noailles, bishop of Châlons, gave his approval, together with the highest commendations, to the edition published in 1693. As, however, the explanatory notes adopted the ideas of the irresistible efficaciousness of Grace, of God's particular Will to save, &c., the work found gainsayers, and was censured at Rome (1708). Two years later it was prohibited by the bishops of Luçon and La Rochelle, and upon these two bishops, through their pastoral letters, coming into conflict with Noailles, now cardinal-archbishop of Paris, the latter was challenged to withdraw the approbation which as bishop of Châlons he had granted to Quesnel's *Reflexions morales*. As he refused to comply, the book was again examined at Rome, and 101 propositions extracted from it were condemned by the Constitution **Unigenitus** in 1713. At about this time Noailles changed his mind with regard to the book, though this did not prevent him and other bishops from refusing to accept the Bull, alleging that many of the propositions condemned, as they stood and apart from their context, were open to a perfectly orthodox interpretation. On the death of Lewis XIV (1715), the new regent, duke Philip of Orleans, proved more compliant to the malcontents, and the conflict soon spread. The theological Faculties of Paris, Rheims, and Nantes, which had previously accepted the Bull, now withdrew their acceptance. Four bishops appealed against it to a General Council (1717), and their example was followed without delay by others of their colleagues and by hundreds of priests, secular and regular. The Bull *Pastoralis officii* (1718) indeed excommunicated the appellants, but only to be itself appealed against. Only in 1728 was it again possible to establish peace, when cardinal Noailles, a year before his death, consented to submit unconditionally to the Bull *Unigenitus*. The wonders which are said to have been wrought shortly afterwards, at the tomb of the deacon François de Paris in the cemetery of St. Médard at Paris, were of little avail, and the days of French Jansenism were numbered.

---

[1] A. SCHILL, *Die Konstitution Unigenitus*, 1876; Cp. *Th. Qu.* 1877, p. 150 ff.; BARTHÉLEMY, *Le Card. de Noailles*, 1888; LE ROY, *Le Gallicanisme au XVIIIᵉ siècle ; Hist. diplom. de la Bulle Unigenitus*, 1892; A. M. P. INGOLD, *Rome et la France : Fragment de l'histoire de la constitution Unigenitus de D. Vincent-Thuillier*, 1901.

D. THE SCHISM OF UTRECHT

Whereas in France the Jansenist dispute, whatever detriment it may have caused the Church, did not bring about a dissolution of the Church's unity, in the Netherlands, aided by other circumstances, it produced a schism. On the suspension of the vicar-apostolic Peter Kodde on suspicion of Jansenism and the nomination of Theodore van Kock to the succession (1702), a protest was made by both the States-General and a number of the clergy. In the conflict which ensued, Holland being without a bishop, the chapter of Utrecht, to bring this state of things to an end, elected the vicar-general Cornelius Steenoven (1723) to be their own archbishop. At a later date, to ensure the succession, suffragan bishoprics were established at Haarlem (1742) and Deventer (1757). All these bishoprics were schismatical, for the proceedings having been in several particulars contrary to the law of the Church, they were never recognised by Rome. Nor did the schism ever gain many adherents even in Holland. At the present day it can reckon only some 6,000 souls. Cp. *Th. Qu.* 1826.

§ 182

The French Regalia—The Gallican Liberties—Quietism [1]

I. During the pause in the Jansenist controversy which ensued after the intervention of Clement IX, France was disturbed by other conflicts. The occasion was furnished by the Royal rights, in virtue of which, ever since the twelfth century, the king had, during the vacancy of a see, appropriated its revenues, and himself bestowed the benefices belonging to its occupant, with the exception of the parishes. This was the practice throughout the larger portion of the realm, the exceptions being mostly in the south (the provinces of Bordeaux, Auch, and Narbonne, and the districts which had formerly belonged to the Empire, the Provence and Dauphiné, *i.e.* the provinces of Arles, Aix, Embrun, and Vienne). The institution had its origin in, and took its name from, the fiefs (regalia) which had formerly been granted to the dioceses in question.

---

[1] G. J. PHILLIPS, *Das Regalienrecht in Frankreich,* 1873 ; *Collect. Lac.* I, 793–846 ; LOYSON, *L'assemblée du clergé de 1682,* 1870 ; DE MOÜY, *Louis XIV et le Saint-Siège,* 1662–65, 2 vol. 1893 ; GÉRIN, *Louis XIV et le Saint-Siège,* 1894 ; MENTION, *Documents relatifs au rapport du clergé avec la royauté de 1682 à 1705,* 1893.

Subsequently to the fourteenth century, the name was no longer derived from the object which it concerned, but from the person of the sovereign, the regalia being considered in the light of a right inherent in the king. The new theory logically involved the extension of this right over the whole kingdom, and, in the event, repeated attempts were made in this direction. The Sainte Chapelle, to which the revenues in question were assigned, did not fail to demand them even of those dioceses which were not liable, and the Parliament at Paris supported its claims. For a long while the kings hearkened to the protests. The rights of the Sainte Chapelle were even abolished, the revenues of the vacant bishoprics being assured to the future bishops as gifts from the king. On the other hand, the right of nominating to the prebends in widowed dioceses the so-called *regalia spiritualis* was now more rigorously enforced throughout the kingdom, Lewis XIV giving the claim the force of a law (1673). The edict in question was even made retrospective ; all bishoprics, whose occupants refused to accept it, were to be considered vacant, and such of their benefices as fell under the regalia were to be filled by the king. The clergy submitted to the law, in spite of its injustice, realising that, in the then state of things, any protest would have been futile. Two bishops only ventured to reject it, Pavillon of Alet and Caulet of Pamiers. Pavillon's action was of little consequence, as he died soon after (1677), and his successor submitted to the new order, but that of Caulet had for its result a serious conflict. Both sides energetically strove to win the day, and the bishop's death (1680) only increased the trouble. The government now proceeded to deal severely with his supporters, one of his vicars-general being even condemned to death, a sentence which was, however, only carried out on his effigy. The two bishops on being condemned by their metropolitan appealed to Rome, and on being supported by Innocent XI, the quarrel became one between France and the Pope. In the meanwhile, the regalia retained the form which it had received, though with some slight amendment. The General Assembly of the Clergy (1681–82) requested the removal of certain hardships which it carried with it, suggesting that those on whom a benefice involving a cure of souls was bestowed, in virtue of the regalia, should receive the *missio canonica* from the ecclesiastical superiors; in other words, that, instead of such benefices being actually conferred by the sovereign, he should be content with presenting a candidate. To this the king acceded.

II. The dispute was, however, not at an end, as Rome, in spite of this modification, had rejected the increase of the regalia which had been sanctioned by France. The measures which had been taken by the Roman See were interpreted as an attack upon the liberties of the Gallican Church and a violation of certain articles (7, 8) of the Concordat of 1516. A portion of the clergy was therefore inclined to essay a defence, or a declaration of the limits of the papal power. The king was still more strongly in favour of the plan, having been greatly offended by Rome's conduct during the progress of the quarrel. The plan was put into execution by the General Assembly in 1682, when four articles were drafted by Bossuet, bishop of Meaux.

(*a*) The Popes have received from God only a spiritual power ; in temporal matters the princes are subject to no ecclesiastical power.

(*b*) The fulness of Apostolical power is limited by the decrees of Constance regarding the authority of General Councils.

(*c*) The execution of the papal power is determined by the canons of the Church ; the principles and usages of the Gallican Church must be respected.

(*d*) The Pope has the largest part in matters of faith, but his judgment, without the Church's consent, is not irreformable.

By an edict of Lewis XIV these articles were immediately imposed on the whole of France, professors of theology and all candidates for academic degrees being compelled to accept them. These proceedings aroused much wrath in Rome, where the opposite doctrines held the field. On certain deputies who had been present at the assembly of 1682 being presented to bishoprics, Rome refused to ratify the choice. As this was construed by the king as a breach of the Concordat of 1516 he took the course of forbidding any candidates nominated by himself, who had not signed the declaration, to seek their brief of confirmation from Rome. In consequence of all this, within six years no less than thirty-five sees were devoid of pastors, or rather were occupied by mere bishops-elect. A grievance of a different character now came to lend greater bitterness to the dispute. Innocent XI abolished the right of asylum possessed by the ambassadors at Rome ; this right had been extended by custom so as to cover the whole neighbourhood around the embassies, and had finally become an intolerable hindrance to the police in the performance of their duties. The measure was perfectly reasonable, and was submitted to with good grace by the other powers. Lewis, however, when the time came for changing his ambassador and for beginning the new arrangement, refused to forego the privilege (1687), and on the Pope laying a censure on the ambassador, he appealed to a General Council and took possession of Avignon and Venaissin. On a change occurring in the occupant of the Roman See, the king relented. He restored to Alexander VIII the two provinces and renounced the right of asylum. To the next Pope, Innocent XII, a promise was given to revoke the edict concerning the execution of the declaration of 1682, though the articles themselves were to remain in force. The bishops who had been nominated in the meantime now received permission to fetch their Briefs, and the conflict was practically at an end. The only other disturbing factor was the question of those candidates who had participated in the General Assembly. The difficulty had been in fact increased by a Bull published by Alexander VIII (*Inter multiplices*, 1691), in which the decisions of the Assembly were declared null and void, both as regards its consent to the extension of the regalia and its sanction of the four articles. Rome demanded an apology ; France was unwilling to give it. Ultimately, in 1693, an apology was so worded as to prove acceptable to both parties.

The four Articles agree in the main with the doctrines expressed by the Sorbonne in 1663. They will be found in PHILLIPS, pp. 358, 362 ; MENTION, p. 23 ; WALTER, *Fontes iuris eccles.* 1862, p. 127 ; *Coll. Lac.* I, 381 ; MIRBT, *Papsttum*, p. 300.

III. Whilst these disputes were in progress an ascetic controversy had broken out. **Miguel de Molinos,** a Spaniard living at Rome, was moved to teach that Christian perfection consists in entire quiet and passivity of the soul, and in such complete immolation of the self, that there remains no desire for the individual's salvation, for virtue, or for perfection ; in fact, no operation or effort whatever. This theory, commonly denominated Quietism, the author brought before the public in his *Spiritual Guide* (1675). The work was at first well received and was translated into several languages. Afterwards, however, it was seen to contain errors, and sixty-eight theses drawn from it were censured by Innocent XI (1687). Cp. DENZINGER, *Enchiridion. Th. Qu.* 1856 ; HEPPE, *Gesch. der quietistischen Mystik in der kath. K.* 1876 ; *Z. f. KG.* XVIII (1898), 572–95.

Similar views were advocated in France by the Barnabite La Combe (*Analysis orationis*) and the pious widow **de la Mothe Guyon.** They opined that a pure and disinterested love of God—in which He is loved wholly on His own account, and without any regard for reward or punishment—may exist as a permanent habit and not merely as a passing disposition. Their works accordingly fell under the Church's censure, and at the conference of Issy (1694–95), the genuine doctrine of the mystics, as distinct from theirs, was embodied in thirty-four Articles. Bossuet, bishop of Meaux, who had taken part in this conference, decided to pursue the aberration still further ; but through his work *Sur les états d'oraison* he came into conflict with Fénelon, archbishop of Cambrai, who answered him by his *Explication des maximes des Saints sur la vie intérieure* (1697). The quarrel, however, soon ended, Fénelon submitting when twenty-three theses from his book were condemned by Innocent XII (1699). Cp. Guyon's *Œuvres spirit.* 42 vol. Cologne, 1713 ff. ; C.T. UPHAM, *Madame Guyon*, 1905.

The General Assembly of the Clergy, which looms so large in French history during this period, was wont to meet in order to sanction by its vote the taxes or other support claimed of the clergy by the State. It also concerned itself with other matters affecting the Church. The Assembly was supposed to meet at intervals of ten years, though in point of fact it really met every five years in order to control the accounts of the Receiver-General. It consisted of four deputies from each province, two being bishops, and two representatives of the second Estate or lower clergy. Cp. MÉRIC, *Le clergé sous l'ancien régime,* 1890 ; L. SERBAT, *Les assemblées du clergé de France* (1561–1615), 1906.

§ 183

Festivals—The Fasting Discipline

I. During the Middle Ages the number of festivals had steadily increased ; even now it had not yet attained its limit, the feast of St. Joseph (1621) and that of the Immaculate Conception of our Lady (1708) being raised to the dignity of feasts of obligation. The latter had, however, been already ordered for the Austrian States by Ferdinand II (1629), and for Spain by Innocent X (1644) at the request of Philip IV.

On the other hand, during this period the conviction became more and more prevalent that the festivals were already too numerous, and repeated attempts were made to diminish them. So far as Germany and the adjacent eastern countries were concerned, by the statute of reform drafted by the legate, cardinal Campegio (c. 20), which received the force of law at the Assembly of the princes at Ratisbon (1524), the number of holidays was reduced to thirty-five, exclusive of the Sundays, manual labour being allowed after Mass on all the other festivals.[1] In France the Provincial Council of Bordeaux (1583, c. 7) also deemed it necessary to enact a reduction in the number of festivals.[2] Finally, Urban VIII intervened to settle the matter. As many bishops had complained that the numerous holidays prevented the poor from earning their living, and that the people spent their time in idleness instead of attending Divine worship, and as there was also a doubt as to which festivals precisely were of obligation, the Pope issued a Bull (*Universa*, 1642) in which the number of holidays—apart from the national festivals and patronal feasts of the church and diocese—was fixed at thirty-two, and the introduction of new church holidays was forbidden.

Though these measures did not modify things to any great extent—the primary object of Urban's Bull, for instance, having been not so much to reduce the number of festivals as to prevent their increase—more decisive legislation was soon to follow. On the advice of his minister Colbert, Lewis XIV recommended the bishops of the realm to abolish some of the less necessary festivals. Sixteen were accordingly struck off the list in 1666 by Harley, archbishop of Paris, whose example was followed by many of his French colleagues. More was to follow in the next century. In 1727 the Provincial Council of Tarragona addressed a petition to the Holy See asking that, apart from the Sundays, Easter Monday, and Whit Monday, the festivals to be strictly observed should comprise only the feasts of our Lord (Christmas, Circumcision, Epiphany, Ascension, and Corpus Christi) ; of our Lady (Candlemas, the Annunciation, Assumption, Nativity, and Immaculate Conception) ; and those of a few Saints (Saints Stephen, John the Baptist, Peter and Paul, James,

---

[1] HARDUIN, IX, 1915.   [2] *Ibid.* X, 1341.

besides All-Hallows and the patron of the church), and that on all other festivals previously kept the Faithful should, after having attended Mass, be allowed to work.[1] The request was granted by Benedict XIII (1728), and his successors were obliged to make similar concessions to other lands ; for instance to Austria, where the example of the Spaniards was followed in 1753 [2] and the festivals reduced by twenty-four. The introduction of half holidays proved to be a half measure, and under Clement XIV it was found necessary to convert the half holidays into whole workdays by abolishing the obligation to hear Mass. To replace the vigil-fasts of those festivals of the Apostles which now ceased to be of obligation, it was enacted that a fast should be observed on all the Wednesdays and Fridays in Advent.

II. To begin with, the fasting discipline remained the same as at the end of the Middle Ages. With the progress of time, however, indults grew more frequent. At the government's demand Rome at last granted a far-reaching dispensation to Austria. Meat was to be permitted during the whole of Lent save in Holy Week, and on Wednesdays, Fridays, and Saturdays (1781). [3]

§ 184

Febronius and the Memorandum or ' Punctation ' of Ems [4]

The relations between the German Church and Rome, as they had been settled by the Concordat of Vienna, soon proved unsatisfactory. At the commencement of the Reformation in the sixteenth century, we constantly hear of the complaints of the German nation against the Roman See. At the Diet of Nuremberg in 1522 the *Gravamina nationis Germanicae* were embodied in a document, and redress was demanded. As the demand was not granted,

---

[1] *Coll. Lac.* I, 786.
[2] ARNETH, *Maria Theresia*, IV, 56–61.
[3] WOLFSGRUBER, *Migazzi*, 1890, p. 462.
[4] HUTH, *KG. d. 18 Jahrh.* II (1809), 438 ff.; O. MEJER, *Febronius*, 2nd ed. 1885; *Th. Qu.* 1881, pp. 670–73 ; KÜNTZIGER, *Fébronius et le Fébronianisme*, 1891 (*Mémoires de l'Académie roy. de Belgique*, vol. 44) ; STIGLOHER, *Die Errichtung der päpstl. Nuntiatur in München u. d. Emser Kongress*, 1867.

the discontent remained, and again received public expression, though with moderation, in a memorandum drawn up by the bishops-elector in 1673.[1] In the next century it was to be voiced with much greater vehemence.

At the election of a new emperor in 1742, when the *Gravamina* again came up for discussion, Nicolaus von Hontheim, bishop-auxiliary of Treves, took the resolution to investigate more closely the relation of these grievances with the general constitution of the Church, ultimately committing his results to writing in a work, *De statu ecclesiae, &c.*, which he published in 1763 under the assumed name of Justinus Febronius. He therein follows the lead of the Gallicans in reducing the Church to the state in which she had existed in antiquity. The Pope is indeed acknowledged as head of the Church, on whom it devolves to supervise the observance of the canons, the preservation of the faith, and the rightful administration of the sacraments. It is also the Pope's duty to give judgment in cases of dispute regarding matters of faith or morals, and his decision is to be respected by all the faithful, provided the universal Church or a General Council be not of the contrary opinion. As for the other rights of the Pope, those, namely, which originated later, and are founded on the authority of the False Decretals, especially the right of confirming and of deposing bishops, they must be restored to the episcopate, or, if needs be, appropriated by the bishops.

The book caused a great commotion. A second and a third edition were soon called for (1765–70), and it was translated into German, French, Italian, Spanish, and Portuguese. Special works were also devoted to its confutation (BALLERINI, 1766–68 ; ZACCARIA, 1767–73). At Rome it was promptly placed on the Index (1764), and the German bishops were summoned to take action against it, an order to which very little attention was, however, paid. The work found many admirers. Deputies of the bishops-elector assembled at Coblence in 1769, under the presidency of Hontheim himself, drew up a list of thirty grievances against Rome,

---

[1] Printed in GÄRTNER, *Corpus iuris eccles.* 1799, vol. II, 322 ff. ; partly given by BUSS, *Urkundl. Gesch. d. Nat.- und Territorialkirchentums*, 1851, p. 702.

agreeing in their tenor with the principles of Febronius, and though the matter went no further, the proceeding itself throws a vivid light on the opinions then prevalent in Germany. Feeling himself secure, Hontheim refused to recant; on the contrary, the attacks of his opponents led him to continue his work, and though ultimately, when his own archbishop had joined his appeal to that of Rome, he consented to withdraw (1778), he steadfastly refused to abandon his principles. In the commentary which he published with his recantation (1781) he deplored indeed the aggressive tone of his work; the Gallican theory, however, he continued to cherish.

A few years later the Febronian ideas again came to the fore. On the occasion of the establishment of a papal nunciature at Munich (1785) the German archbishops, comprising the elector of Mainz (Carl von Erthal), the elector of Cologne (archduke Maximilian, brother of Joseph II), the elector of Treves (prince Clement Wenceslaus of Saxony), and the prince-bishop of Salzburg (Jerome, prince of Colloredo) again attempted to put into execution the plan of making the German Church less dependent on Rome. To this end they deputed delegates to attend at Ems and draw up a note to be presented at Rome (1786). The matter, however, never got beyond the preliminary stage. The proposals which, after a while, were made to Rome were peremptorily refused (1789), and the archbishops gradually changed their attitude. Complaints were indeed again heard when the time came to elect a new emperor (1790–92), but the matter was soon thrown into the background by the French invasion.

The most remarkable of the articles of the memorandum of Ems are the following: Recourse to Rome, save through the immediate superiors, is forbidden; the exemption of monasteries and all dependence on foreign superiors generally is abolished (1). Quinquennial faculties are suppressed; the powers of dispensing in matters of marriage, &c., conveyed by these faculties for a period of five years, in reality form a part of every bishop's jurisdiction, and dispensations obtained from abroad are invalid; papal Bulls and Briefs are not binding unless received by the bishops; nuncios have no jurisdiction (2–4). The decrees of Basel, having been accepted by the Diet of Mainz (1439), form the rule governing the relations

between Germany and the Holy See, the Concordat of Vienna forms
the exception (7). Disputes regarding church matters are to be
settled by the diocesan or metropolitan courts, and when an appeal
is made in the third instance to Rome, the Pope may only decide by
means of *Iudices in partibus* (22).

§ 185

The Reforms of Maria Theresia, Joseph II, and Leopold of Tuscany [1]

I. In her attempt to improve the whole system of government, the empress **Maria Theresia** (1740–80) introduced
also a number of ecclesiastical reforms into the Austrian
lands. Many of the existing institutions seemed at variance
with the habits of mind which had recently become general,
whilst in other matters changes were necessary in the interests
of the State, and of the souls of the people. A limit was
accordingly put to the further increase of monasteries and
of the properties of the Church, the administration of the
latter being placed under the control of the government;
it was also enacted that vows should not be taken before the
age of twenty-five, that the clergy should no longer be dispensed from taxes, that the papal Briefs should have no
force until they had been accorded the imperial *placet*. The
education department was reorganised under the direction
of Gerhard van Swieten, physician to the empress, and of
abbot Rautenstrauch of Braunau, the Church's influence
being considerably diminished. As, owing to the vastness
of some of the older dioceses, a careful supervision was
out of the question, several new bishoprics were created;
certain church holidays were abolished, &c. As far as
possible the consent of the Holy See was secured for these

[1] A. v. ARNETH, *M. Theresia*, 10 vol. 1863–79; K. RITTER, *K. Joseph II
u. s. kirchl. Reformen*, 1867; J. BEIDTEL, *Gesch. der österreich. Staatsverwaltung*,
1740–1848, 2 vol. 1896–98; S. BRUNNER, *Die theolog. Dienerschaft am Hofe
Josephs II*, 1868; *Die Mysterien der Aufklärung in Öst.* 1869; *Joseph II*,
2nd ed. 1886; WOLFSGRUBER, *Kard. Migazzi*, 1890; *Rquh.* 1894, I, 455–509;
ZSCHOKKE, *Die theol. Studien . . . in Österr.* 1894; H. SCHLITTER, *Die Regierung
Josephs II in den öst. Niederlanden*, I, 1900; LAENEN, *Étude sur la suppression des couvents par Joseph II dans les Pays-Bas autrichiens* (1783–94),
1905 (*Extr. des Annales de l'Académie roy. d'archéol. de Belgique*); F. GEIER,
Die Durchführung der k. Ref. Josephs II im vorderöst. Breisgau, 1905.

measures, and the reforms were accordingly carried through without any great disturbance.

II. The aspect of things was changed when, after his mother's death, the reins of government were taken by **Joseph II** (1765–90). Obedient to the counsels of prince Kaunitz, he not only went further than Maria Theresia, but also showed very little regard for the feelings of the other party. In a series of edicts following each other in rapid succession, he re-enacted the necessity of the *placet*, which he extended even to episcopal missives, abolished the special legal status of the clergy, informed the bishops that they were, in virtue of their own jurisdiction, and without seeking any papal faculties, to dispense in cases of consanguinity in the third and fourth degree, closed all the monasteries belonging to purely contemplative religious Orders, *i.e.* of Carthusians and Camaldulese monks, of Carmelite, Franciscan, and Capuchin nuns, doing the same with a number of the houses belonging to other congregations, especially with those of the Mendicants, in all, some 600 convents and monasteries, or about a third of the whole number in the Austrian dominions, and dissolving all the religious brotherhoods. The Protestants, or rather the Lutherans and Calvinists, and the non-uniate Greeks were granted full civil rights and the permission to practise their religion in private (*i.e.* without the ringing of bells, &c.). The dioceses were again reorganised so as to make them coterminous with the civil administrative districts, and new parishes were established out of the fortunes of the suppressed monasteries. Diocesan seminaries were supplanted by great central seminaries at Vienna, Buda-Pesth, Pavia, Freiburg, and Louvain, and certain smaller ones at Gratz, Olmütz, Prague, Innsbruck, and Luxemburg, care being taken to appoint as professors only such as were known to be favourable to the emperor's principles. Rules were even laid down for the details of public worship.

It would be idle to deny that Joseph in his ecclesiastical as well as in his political reforms was animated by the noblest intentions. Some of his measures, too, could not fail to win approval ; for instance, the increase in the number of parishes. Others, however, involved serious encroachments on the rights of the Church. It is, therefore, no wonder that the reforms, though accepted by a portion of the episcopate, encountered strong opposition. The archbishops of Vienna and Gran, cardinals Migazzi and Bathyani, frankly expressed their mind, whilst Pius VI undertook a journey to Vienna to endeavour to restrain the emperor's reforming zeal (1782). Still more energetic was the protest of the bishops of Belgium, headed by cardinal Frankenberg, archbishop of Mechlin, the whole province ultimately rising in revolt. The reforms were accordingly withdrawn so far as Belgium was concerned by Leopold II (1790–92). In the rest of the Empire, the central seminaries and certain limitations which had been laid on Divine worship were abolished. So far as all other matters were concerned, Joseph's reforms remained in force.[1]

III. Maria Theresia's zeal for the reform of the Church was inherited by her second as well as by her eldest son. Though the grand-duke **Leopold of Tuscany** (1765–90) was at first content with following his mother's example, he afterwards entered into the path chosen by his brother. Not only did he refrain from consulting Rome, but he allowed his activity to outstep the politico-ecclesiastical sphere, and to interfere in purely ecclesiastical matters. His end was to thoroughly reform the Church in his dominions. This he proposed to commence by diocesan synods, and to complete by a national council. Unfortunately, of the eighteen bishops belonging to the grand-duchy, only three were at all favourable to his plans, the most zealous of these being **Scipio Ricci** of Pistoja-Prato. The synod of Pistoja in 1786 passed a number of decrees according to Leopold's mind. In particular it accepted the four Gallican articles, and recommended the writings of Quesnel. The other bishops, on the contrary, more or less vigorously declined to have anything to do with the reforms which the grand-duke had recommended as necessary in a letter addressed to them. To bring the deadlock to an end, the bishops were summoned to a preparatory conference at the capital (1787). Perceiving that it would be useless to expect any reforms from a provincial council, Leopold determined to carry out the reforms himself, though this he was unable to do, being called soon after to the imperial throne (1790). On the prince's departure, the anger of his flock compelled Ricci to alter his demeanour, and soon after to lay down his office (1791). Most of the reforms were withdrawn, and eighty-five propositions of the synod of Pistoja were censured by Pius VI in the Bull *Auctorem fidei* (1794). Cp. POTTER, *Vie et mémoires de Scipion de Ricci*, 4 vol. 1826 ; GELLI, *Memorie di Sc. de Ricci*, 2 vol. 1865 ; REUMONT, *Gesch. Toskanas*, II (1877), 148 ff.

[1] *Z. f. k. Th.* 1880 ; VERHAEGEN, *Le Card. de Frankenberg*, 1890.

§ 186

Religious Orders in the Seventeenth and Eighteenth Century

A. New Religious Associations

Like the religious Orders of the sixteenth century, those of the two following centuries are mostly remarkable for their practical character.

Among the new congregations devoted to nursing the sick, to teaching children, and to the care of the female sex, were :

(1) The **Sisters of Charity,** *Filles de la charité*, divided into two branches, the more numerous being that founded at Paris in 1633 by St. Vincent of Paul [1] with the assistance of a pious widow Le Gras. The smaller branch is that of the Sisters of St. Charles Borromeo, established at Nancy in 1652.

(2) **The Brothers of the Christian Schools,** *Frères des écoles chrétiennes*, founded in 1680 at Rheims by one of the canons, J. B. de la Salle.[2]

(3) The **Visitandines**, or nuns of the Visitation, founded by St. Francis of Sales and St. J. Frances de Chantal at Annecy (1610). *Œuvres de St. François de S.* 14 vol. Paris, 1892–1906. Bg. of St. Francis by Hamon, 1866 ; Strowski, 1898 ; of St. Frances, by Bougaud, 1861.

(4) The **English Ladies,** who arose out of the remains of a Society of Jesuitesses, founded by Mary Ward at St. Omer for the education of girls (1609). The society was dissolved for certain irregularities (1631), but a few of its members, having obtained permission to fulfil their simple vows in the world under the supervision of the diocesan, again united themselves into a community. *KL.* IV, 572–80 ; Coleridge, *Mary Ward*, 1882 ; *Life of Mary Ward compiled from various sources*, ed. Gasquet, 1909.

(5) The **Sisters of Refuge**, founded by P. Eudes at

---

[1] Bg. by Stolberg, 1819 ; Maynard, 4 vol. 1860 ; Bougaud, 2 vol. 1889 ; Jeannin, 1889 ; E. de Margerie, *La societé de St. V. d. P.* 2 vol. 1874.
[2] Mg. by F. J. Knecht, 1879 ; J. B. Blain, 1887 ; J. Guibert, 1900 ; J. V. Bainvel, 1901 ; B. Dillinger, 1906.

Caen for the reclaiming of fallen women (1644).   D. Boulay, *Vie du vén. J. Eudes*, I, 1905.

Among the Orders established for mission work and the education of the clergy were :

(1) The **Lazarists,** or Priests of the Mission, founded in 1624 by St. Vincent of Paul, and called after the college of St. Lazare at Paris, which was bestowed on them soon after.

(2) The **Redemptorists,** or Congregation of the most holy Redeemer (*sanctissimi Redemptoris*), founded by St. Alphonsus of Liguori at Scala near Amalfi (1732).[1]

(3) The **Oratory of France,** founded at Paris in 1611 by Pierre de Bérulle, *KL.* II, 485–92.

(4) The **Passionists,** or Clerks of the Holy Cross and Passion of our Lord, founded at Orbitello in the kingdom of Naples (1737) by St. Paul of the Cross.

Two congregations of secular priests were also formed for the education of the clergy.   Of these one, the society of the Bartholomites, owed its origin to Bartholomew Holzhauser of Salzburg (1640). Mg. by Gaduel, 1861 ; *St. Bened.* 1902.   The other was founded at Paris by J. J. Olier, and called after the church and seminary of St. Sulpice (1641).   Mg. by G. Letourneau, 1906.

Two religious associations were especially conspicuous for their devotion to learning ; the Congregation of **St. Maur,** established in 1618, with a view to reforming the French Benedictine monasteries, as those of Lorraine and Alsace had been shortly before by the Congregations of St. Vannes and St. Hidulphe established by Didier de la Cour.   Dom d'Achery (1648) was mainly responsible for the love of learning which was to make this monastery famous (*Th. Qu.* 1833–34).   The Order of the **Mechitarists**, after having been established at the beginning of the eighteenth century by the Armenian Mechitar in Morea, was, owing to the persecution of the Turks, removed to the island of San Lazzaro, near Venice (1715).

Lastly, in the Order of the **Trappists** we find a revival of the spirit of mediæval monasticism.   It began when J. Bouthillier de Rancé re-established in his Cistercian Abbey of La Trappe in Normandy the old rule in all its severity, adding, moreover, to it the Carthusian practice of perpetual abstinence and of constant silence (1662). Learned work was not only discouraged, but declared incompatible with the true monastic spirit (*Traité de la sainteté et des devoirs de la vie monastique*, 1683), an opinion which Mabillon was at pains to confute (*Traité des études monastiques*, 1691).   Pfannenschmidt, *Gesch. d. Tr.* 1873 ; B. Schmid, *Bouthillier de R.* 1897.

---

[1] Bg. by Dilgskron, 2 vol. 1887 ; Capecelatro, 2 vol. 1895 ; Saintrain-Schepers, 2nd ed., ed. Krebs, 1898 ; Berthe, 2 vol. 1900.

B. The Suppression of the Jesuits [1]

As we have already had occasion to see (§§ 178–80), the Society of Jesus had done great service in the cause of the Church. In the course of time, however, when nearly all the schools of the Catholic world had come under its control, and when its members were everywhere in demand as confessors and confidential advisers to the princes, it attained a position not devoid of danger. The Society soon acquired a strong spirit of independence, which it did not hesitate to display even towards the Holy See. In effect, the determination with which the Jesuits adhered to their rites and usages in Malabar and China, in spite of their condemnation by Rome, can only with difficulty be reconciled with their vow of obedience, even though all allowances be made for their being convinced of the necessity of their methods. Their conduct was repeatedly made a subject of complaint by Benedict XIV. In his Bull *Immensa pastorum* (December 20, 1741), he was compelled to recall to the Jesuits and to other Orders the precepts of Christian charity, and to forbid them to hinder the progress of the Gospel among the Indians by trading in slaves and by other inhuman practices. In this matter he was indeed obeyed, but in other directions the proceedings of the Society remained open to criticism. The great influence which the Jesuits had obtained by assuming the direction of the consciences of those in power had made them many enemies, and little by little the antipathy to the Society took possession even of the rulers, becoming so strong in the latter half of the eighteenth century that in many countries a regular war of extermination was proclaimed against the Jesuits. It cannot be said that the Society had deserved this fate, especially as the character of its opponents was not such as to excite our confidence, whilst sovereigns such as those of Prussia

---

[1] [Le Bret] *Sammlung der merkwürdigsten Schriften die Aufhebung des Jes.-Ordens betr.* 4 vol. 1773 ; A. Theiner, *Gesch. d. Pontifikates Klemens XIV*, 2 vol. 1852 ; [Reinerding] *Klemens XIV und die Aufhebung der Gesellschaft J.* 1854 (a critique of Theiner) ; Crétineau-Joly, *Le pape Clément XIV*, 1862 ; Ginzel, *Kirchenhist. Schriften*, II (1872), 205–82 ; Döllinger, *Beiträge*, III (1882), 1–74 (on the work of the Jesuit T. Cordara, 1740–73) ; Masson, *Le card de Bernis*, 1884 ; Crousaz-Crétet, *L'église et l'état au XVIIIe siécle*, 1893 ; *Z. f. k. Th.* 1898, pp. 432–54, 689–708 ; Duhr, *Jesuiten-Fabeln*, 4th ed. 1904 ; *Th. Qu.* 1891, pp. 627–37 ; 1901, pp. 374–88 (decision of Benedict XIV).

and Russia would certainly not have taken the Order under their protection had it been guilty of outrageous crimes.   On the other hand, we can perfectly well understand how the storm arose.   A position of power, such as the Order had obtained in Catholic countries, was not one to be long borne with.

Hostilities began in **Portugal.**[1]   As the Jesuits were unfriendly to his interests and his politics, the minister Pombal had recourse to measures against them.   The opposition raised against the new rulers by the inhabitants of the seven reductions of Paraguay, which Spain had exchanged with Portugal in return for the colony of San Sagramento (1750), furnished him with an occasion to forbid the Jesuits to visit the court and to complain to Benedict XIV.   In consequence of this complaint, Saldanha, patriarch of Lisbon, was appointed visitor to the Order, and suspended from the ministry of the pulpit and confessional all the Jesuits living under his jurisdiction (1758).   The attempt which was shortly afterwards made on the king Joseph's life gave Pombal an opportunity for going yet further.   The Jesuits were charged with having been privy to the conspiracy, and were, some of them, imprisoned, and the rest embarked on ships and landed on the coast of the Papal States (1759).

Shortly after this clouds began to gather in **France** also. Here the Jesuits were opposed not only by the encyclopædists, who hoped to strike the Church through them, but also by the Jansenists, by the minister Choiseul, and by Madame de Pompadour, the mistress of Lewis XV, the last because père Périsseau, the king's confessor, had urged her removal from the court. The occasion for the persecution was, however, provided by the insolvency of père Lavalette, procurator-general of the island of Martinique, or rather by the refusal of the Society to pay the sum of 2,400,000 francs owed by him to a business house at Marseilles.   The first adverse measures were taken in the very year (1761) in which the Society was condemned by the courts to make good its debt.   Some time after (1763) the parliament at Paris decreed the abolition of the Order.   Finally (1764), the king gave his assent to the law, after his petition for a

[1] DUHR, *Pombal*, 1891 ; *Revue hist.* 60 (1896), 272–306.

change in the constitution of the Society had been declined at Rome with the words : *Sint ut sunt aut non sint.* As a result of the law the Society as such was dissolved, though its members were not forced to leave the country ; on the contrary, they were henceforth to work as secular priests under the jurisdiction of the bishops.

The Order having now lost two of its most important branches, Clement XIII thought it his duty to come to its assistance, and in his Bull *Apostolicum pascendi* (1765) he again bestowed on it the papal approbation and repelled the spiteful calumnies which had been made against it. His action was, however, of little real help to the Society, for simultaneously the aggressive was assumed by **Spain.** At first, restraints were placed on the activity of the Jesuits, and their pupils and admirers were removed from the higher offices of the State. Two years later, following the example of Portugal, the Spanish Jesuits were granted a small pension and dismissed to the Papal States (1767). Ferdinand of Naples, being a son of Charles III of Spain, the latter's proceedings were forthwith imitated in the kingdom of **Sicily.** A conflict with the Holy See regarding the question of church reform afforded a pretext to the duke of **Parma,** grandson of Lewis XV and nephew of Charles III, to abolish the Order in his country also (1768). The *Monitorium* addressed by Clement XIII to these sovereigns even moved the Bourbon courts to attack the Pope himself ; France seized Avignon and Venaissin, and Naples Pontecorvo and Benevento.

The Bourbons were, however, not content with expelling the Jesuits from their States. Their plan was to obtain the utter suppression of the Society, and, on the death of Clement XIII, France and Spain exerted every nerve to secure the election of a Pope who might be expected to meet their wishes. The votes of the cardinals fell on a Franciscan, Lorenzo Ganganelli, who assumed the name of **Clement XIV** (1769–74). Till then he had observed an attitude of reserve on the burning question, but it was his opinion that, now that things had gone so far, the Society should be sacrificed for the peace of the Church. At the conclave he handed a note to the Spanish cardinal de Solis declaring that, in his view, the suppression would not be contrary to the rules of canon law, of prudence, or of justice.

To the French cardinal de Bernis he even expressed his intention
of putting the project into execution.   Soon after his election
he gave still clearer assurances to the sovereigns of France
and Spain.   In spite of this, the actual decision was postponed,
the matter being more difficult than he had at first supposed.
For a time he endeavoured to conciliate the courts by offering
to reform the Society.   As this offer was declined, and as the
suppression seemed the only means of securing peace and of
preventing the irrevocable loss to the Church of the provinces
which had been seized, he reluctantly issued the Brief of
suppression, *Dominus ac redemptor* (1773).   The members of the
Society received permission to join other Orders, to remain
in their own houses, though without exercising any functions,
their obedience being transferred to the bishop, or to offer their
services to the ordinaries for parish work.   Ricci, the general,
his assistants, and a few other fathers were put on their trial,
and at the request of the sovereigns, and in order to prevent any
attempt to restore the Order, were long kept in prison.   In the
event a portion of the Society was very loath to submit ;
in Russian Poland, and for three years in Prussian Silesia,
the Order continued to subsist under the protection of Catherine
II of Russia and of Frederick II of Prussia, in spite of the papal
enactment.   This it was enabled to do, owing to the fact that
Clement XIV had died within a year, whilst his successor
Pius VI, so far as considerations of policy allowed, was favourably disposed to the Jesuits.   The trial of the general and of his
companions came to an end with Ricci's death (1775).

The abolition of the Society of Jesus was the beginning of further
reductions.   In France all Orders were forbidden to occupy more
than two houses at Paris, or more than one in any city in the provinces.   The taking of vows before the age of twenty-one in the case
of men, or of eighteen in the case of women, was prohibited.   Every
conventual establishment was to have a certain minimum number of
inmates, failing which it was to be closed, or forbidden to receive
new novices.   The consequence of these enactments was that in
twelve years nine religious associations had been wiped out, among
them the Order of Grandmont, the Servites, Celestines, Bridgittines,
and Antonines, whilst in twenty years 386 monasteries had been
closed.   Cp. GUETTÉE, *Hist. de l'Église de France*, vol. XII.   We have
already spoken (§ 185) of the similar regulations adopted in Austria.
Two Orders, the Humiliati (1571) and the Jesuats (1668), had already
been dissolved by the Holy See on account of their irregularities.

§ 187

The Papacy in the Second Half of the Seventeenth Century [1]

I. On the death of Innocent X, cardinal Chigi was elected as **Alexander VII** (1655–67). Animated by the best intentions, he, at the beginning of his reign, was minded to put an end to the nepotism so commonly practised. He was, however, persuaded to relent, and in the second year of his pontificate summoned his relatives from Siena to Rome, where they settled down in princely estate. As for the rest, he was a well-meaning ruler, a friend of learning and of scholars, and not devoid of a certain zeal for reform. The most remarkable event of his pontificate was the conversion of queen Christina of Sweden, daughter of Gustavus Adolfus. In the year of his election she had visited Rome and been received with every honour ; after having spent several years in France and at Hamburg, she returned and took up her permanent residence in the Eternal City (1669–89). On the other hand the Pope had to suffer much from France. The pretensions of the duke of Créqui, the French ambassador (1662), might even have led to further complications had not Alexander, being left without support by the other powers, submitted to the demands of the French at the peace of Pisa (1664).

II. He was succeeded by his Secretary of State, Rospigliosi under the name of **Clement IX** (1667–69),[2] a worthy ruler and a man of education, whose pontificate was, however, all too short. He was instrumental in making with the Jansenists the peace which bears his name, and actively supported the Venetians in their war with the Turks, without, however, being able to prevent the capture of Crete.

III. After a vacancy of nearly five months, cardinal Altieri mounted the papal throne as **Clement X** (1670–76).[3] Being already eighty years of age, he left the conduct of affairs in the hands of his favourite cardinal, Paluzzo Altieri. No event of importance marked this pontificate.

IV. **Innocent XI** (1676–89),[4] of the Odescalchi family,

---

[1] Literature as above, § 179.
[2] CH. TERLINDEN, *Le pape Clément IX et la guerre de Candie*, 1904.
[3] C. N. D. BILDT, *Christine de Suède et le conclave de Clément X*, 1906.
[4] *Innocentii PP. XI epistolae ad principes*, 1890 ; IMMICH, *Papst Innocenz*

had to encounter difficulties with France. To the dispute already pending about the regalia there was now added the conflict concerning the Gallican freedoms, and the right of asylum of the French ambassador at Rome. Owing to the determination with which Lewis XIV made use of all the power at his disposal, the quarrel soon assumed dangerous dimensions (cp. § 182). At the same time the new incursions of the Turks also caused the Pope great concern. To the pretensions of the French monarch the Pope was only able to oppose his steadfast resolution not to abandon the Church's cause, but in the East he had, at least, the consolation of learning of the deliverance of Vienna (1683), and of the capture of Buda-Pesth by the Christians (1686), by which the arch-enemy of Christianity was not only deprived of its power of further conquest, but actually driven out of a portion of the countries which it had vanquished. Among his reforms was the abolition of the college of the twenty-four Apostolic notaries, which had been in existence since the time of Calixtus III, and of which the appointments were regularly bought and sold.

V. Under **Alexander VIII** (1689–91),[1] formerly an Otto-boni, the relations with France were improved. The pontificate, which lasted only sixteen months, is remarkable only for the promotion of the Pope's family, and the securing for the Vatican Library of the precious collection of books left by Queen Christina.

VI. To **Innocent XII** (1691–1700),[2] whose family name was Pignatelli, the Church owes a great debt for the strong action which he took against papal nepotism. The Bull which he issued in the second year of his reign made an end of this deplorable abuse, at least as a regular system, though it did not prevent its recurrence in isolated cases.

VII. Five weeks after this Pope's demise, died Charles II, and with him, the male line of the Spanish Habsburgs. War was imminent between France and Austria regarding the right of succession, the difficulty of the situation being felt even at the Conclave, and being to a large extent accountable for the

XI, 1899 ; W. FRAKNÓI, *Papst Innocenz XI und Ungarns Befreiung von der Türkenherrschaft* (from the Hungarian by P. JEKEL, 1902).

[1] S. v. BISCHOFSHAUSEN, *Papst Alexander VIII und der Wiener Hof*, 1900.

[2] *Internation. theol. Z.* 1904, pp. 1–22 (on his election).

election of cardinal Albani as the man most likely to prove equal to his task. **Clement XI** (1700–21),[1] as he named himself, did not deceive the hopes which had been built on him, but it was impossible to dissociate himself from the Spanish war of succession, seeing that he was, as Pope, the suzerain of a portion of the heritage concerning which the quarrel raged. In effect he was immediately approached by both sides, each demanding to be invested with the crown of Sicily, the Pope being faced, whichever alternative he chose, with the certainty that the slighted party would take its revenge.' To begin with, he favoured the Bourbons, whereupon the emperor Joseph I advanced on the States of the Church. Later on, when he acknowledged the emperor's brother Charles III as king of Spain (1709),[2] Philip V, who was already in possession of the country, promptly broke off his relations with Rome. When, by the truce of Utrecht (1713), it had finally been settled that the kingdom of Sicily should be conferred on duke Victor Amadeus II of Savoy, a prince whose ecclesiastical pretensions had already brought him into conflict with the Holy See, a still more violent dispute broke out concerning the so-called *Monarchia Sicula*, a certain right of intervention in matters ecclesiastical which had originated in a privilege granted by Urban II to count Roger, but which had been unduly enlarged by his successors.[3] Matters were not put to rest until the treaty of London, in 1720, had settled that Savoy should be content with Sardinia, and had assigned the kingdom of the Two Sicilies to Charles III, after which peace prevailed for rather more than a decade. Clement was to die soon after. At the beginning of his reign he had protested against the election of the elector of Branden- burg to the kingdom of Prussia (1701),[4] a protest which, needless to say, was futile, as it was founded on a state of things which had long ceased to exist. In the truce and the subsequent peace, the change of things was also apparent. Without seeking the assent of the Holy See, the Powers disposed of countries over which it had possessed suzerain rights.

---

[1] *Archivio della R. Società Romana*, XXI (1898), 279–457; XXII, 109–179; XXIII, 449–515.
[2] M. LANDAU, *Gesch. K. Karls VI als König von Spanien*, 1889.
[3] SENTIS, *Die Monarchia Sicula*, 1869; E. CASPAR, *Die Legatengewalt der normannisch-siz. Herrscher in 12 Jahrh.* 1904.
[4] *Hist. Z.* 87 (1901), 407–28.

VIII. The pontificates of **Innocent XIII** (1721–24),[1] a former Conti, and of **Benedict XIII** (1724–30), an Orsini, passed without any event of note. Both were worthy men, but the latter's government was unsatisfactory. As archbishop of Benevento he had proved an excellent administrator, but as Pope he allowed far too much power to unworthy favourites, especially to Coscia, his former menial and secretary, whom he now created a cardinal. So great was the vexation excited by their proceedings that, after the Pope's death, a revolt broke out. Coscia was ultimately condemned to ten years' imprisonment in the Castle of Sant' Angelo and to other penalties (1733).

IX. The reign of **Clement XII** (1730–40), of the Florentine family Corsini, falls within a period during which Italy was again thrown into commotion. The question of the Polish succession issued in a war in which France, Spain, and Sardinia were pitted against Austria. The political situation in Italy was thereby changed anew. The ruling families of the Farnese (1731) and of the Medici (1737) having shortly before died out, the peace of Vienna (1738) assigned Naples, by the rule of secundogeniture, to the Spanish Bourbons, Tuscany to the duke Francis Stephen of Lorraine, husband of Maria Theresia, Parma and Piacenza to the emperor. Clement, though already seventy-nine years of age at his election, in spite of his sickly disposition and of the blindness which overtook him, gave proof throughout these negotiations both of a strong will and of discretion. Rome also owes to him many public buildings.

X. After a six months' vacancy, the Roman See fell to cardinal Prosper Lambertini, archbishop of Bologna, or **Benedict XIV** (1740–58), the most learned of the popes, equally noted for his simplicity and courtesy in private life, and for the cautiousness and moderation which characterised his public actions. In the Austrian war of succession which occupied the first half of his pontificate, and which largely affected Italy—the peace of Aachen (1748) handed Parma, Piacenza and Guastalla to the Spanish Infante Philip— he maintained strict neutrality. In ecclesiastico-political questions he showed a wise spirit of compromise, and abandoned many rights which he perceived could no longer be maintained under the new state of things. Concordats were signed with

---

[1] *Internat. theol. Z.* 1897, pp. 42–61.

Sicily (1741), Sardinia (1742–50), Spain (1753), and Milan (1757). The king of Portugal received the right of nominating to all bishoprics and abbeys in his realm, and the title of *Rex fidelissimus*. At Rome a new delimitation of the regions of the city was undertaken, and the aristocracy was brought under better control.

XI. The pontificates of **Clement XIII** (1758–69), of the Venetian family Rezzonico, and of **Clement XIV** (1769–74) were wholly taken up with the disputes concerning the Jesuits (cp. § 186). Clement XIV was the first Pope to omit the customary publication of the Bull *In coena Domini* (§ 179, VI).

XII. A lengthy conclave ended in the election of cardinal Braschi of Cesena, as **Pius VI** (1775–99).[1] A man of good education, of noble birth and yet eminently affable, he was to taste both magnificence and misfortune in far more than the common measure. The Papal States owed to him the draining of a portion of the Pontine marshes, and the improvement of the government. He also erected many buildings at Rome, among them the *Museum Pio-Clementinum*. Surrounded by his treasures of art he received the visit of many a king and prince. In his pontificate also fell, on the other hand, the downfall of public order, both civil and religious, in France, a catastrophe which resulted in the loss of the Papal States and in his being himself led into exile.

The papal elections in this period, owing to political opposition and to the intrigues of the cardinals, were frequently—even apart from the instances mentioned—delayed very considerably. Cp. *KL.* IX, 1441.

§ 188

Church Literature [2]

The period just dealt with was rich in learning. The clergy secular and religious rivalled each other in mental work. France was especially prominent, where, in the Congregation

---

[1] Mg. by Artaud, 1847 ; Wolf (*Gesch. d. röm.-kath. K. unter P. VI*), 7 vol. 1793–1802 ; *KL.* X, 55–60.

[2] Hurter, *Nomenclator lit. rec. theologiae cath.* 3 vol. 2nd ed. 1892–95 ; Backer, *Biblioth. des écrivains de la comp. de Jésus*, 7 vol. 1853–61 ; ed. Sommervogel, 8 vol. 1890–98 ; K. Werner, *Gesch. d. kath. Theologie seit dem Tr. Konzil*, 1866 ; 2nd ed. 1889.

of St. Maur, there had been established a religious association of which the primary object was scholarship.[1] Owing to confessional differences, the literary productions were at first, and to a certain extent even later, mostly of a polemical character, though the other branches of Theology soon came in for their share of interest.

The most famous names are the following :—

(1) Among the **Apologists** and polemics the first rank was taken by cardinal Bellarmine with his *Disputationes de controversiis christ. fidei adv. huius temporis haereticos* (3 fol. 1581), and the two bishops, Bossuet of Meaux (*Histoire des variations des églises protestantes*, 1688), and Huet of Avranches (Mg. by J. N. ESPENBERGER, 1905).

(2) **Dogmatics** were well represented from the standpoint of the Schoolmen by the Dominican Bañez († 1604), and the Jesuits Vasquez († 1604), Suarez († 1617) (mg. by WERNER, 1861), and Ruiz de Montoya († 1632). On the other hand, the *Loci theologici* of the Dominican Melchior Canus († 1560), a work on the fundamentals of Theology directed against the Protestants, is of a more Biblical and patristic character. Still more weight was laid on the teaching of Scripture, of the Fathers and of the Councils, in the *Opus de theologicis dogmatibus* of the Jesuit Petavius († 1652), the founder of the History of Dogma (Mg. by STANONIK, 1876). Tournely († 1729) and Billuart († 1757) were also to earn themselves a repute as dogmatic theologians.

(3) Among the many **Moralists** a few merit notice : Bartholomew de Medina († 1572) as the founder of Probabilism ; Concina († 1756) and Patuzzi († 1769) as exponents of rigorous Tutiorism ; Alphonsus Liguori and Eusebius Amort († 1775) as mediators between the extremes ; also Azor († 1607), Laymann († 1635), J. Lugo († 1660), Busenbaum († 1668), and Lacroix († 1714).

(4) Among the more distinguished **Canonists** were Pr. Fagnani, an interpreter of the Decretals (3 fol. 1661), Reiffenstuhl († 1703), Schmalzgruber († 1735), van Espen († 1782), and Prosper Lambertini (*De servorum Dei beatificatione et beatorum canonizatione*, 1734–38 ; *De synodo dioecesana*, 1748). Thomassin by his *Ancienne et nouvelle discipline de l'Église touchant les Bénéfices et les Bénéficiers* (3 fol. 1678–81 ; Lat. 1686, and often since) has a claim to be ranked among the Canonists, though the work also gives him a place among Archæologists.

(5) The best-known **Exegetists** were the Jesuits Maldonatus († 1583) and Toletus (1596), Estius at Douai († 1613), Cornelius a Lapide at Louvain († 1637), and Dom Calmet of the Congregation of St. Vannes († 1757). The Bible critic of the period was the Oratorian Richard Simon († 1712).

---

[1] [TASSIN] *Hist. littéraire de la Congrégation de St. Maur*, 1770 ; *Th. Qu.* 1833–34 ; E. DE BROGLIE, *Mabillon et la Société de l'Abbaye de St. Germain des Prés*, 1888 ; *Bernard de Montfaucon*, 2 vol. 1891.

(6) The famous **Preachers** of the time were the Jesuit Bour-
daloue († 1704 ; mg. by PAUTHE, 1900 ; CASTETS, 1900) ; Bossuet
(† 1704 ; mg. by BAUSSET, 4 vol. 1819 ; LANSON, 1891) ; Fénelon,
archbishop of Cambrai († 1715 ; mg. by BAUSSET, 3 vol. 1809 ;
MAHRENHOLTZ, 1896) ; Fléchier, bishop of Nîmes († 1710) ; Massil-
lon, bishop of Clermont († 1742 ; mg. by SANVERT, 1891).

VII. Historical Theology, which had been so utterly
neglected during the Middle Ages, now began to be cultivated with
great success. The literature of the past was put within the reach
of all by superb editions, comprising, some of them separate works,
others whole collections. Nor did the editors confine their work
to mere editing. in most instances the editions of the Fathers contain
a critical account of their life and works. Other aspects of the
Church's life, and, in fact, the whole domain of Church History were
carefully studied. The sciences which are now considered necessary
auxiliaries of Church History were practically an invention of the
period, and many of the works then devoted to them retain their
value even now. Several of these works have already been alluded
to in the present Manual (§§ 2–5 ; 36–40 ; 74–78, &c.), and it is,
therefore, unnecessary to mention them again. Among the other
capable editors were D'Achery (*Spicilegium veterum scriptorum*, 13
vol. 1655–77) ; Martène and Durand (*Thesaurus novus Anecdotorum*,
5 fol. 1717 ; *Veterum scriptorum et monumentorum amplissima
collectio*, 9 fol. 1724–33) ; B. Pez (*Thesaurus Anecdotorum novissimus*,
6 fol. 1721–29). Among the archæologists : A. Bosio, the first to
compose a *Roma Sotteranea* (1632), and Pellicia (*De christ. eccl.
politia*, 3 vol. 1777 ; ed. RITTER et BRAUN, 1829 ; Engl. Trans.
The Polity of the Christian Church, 1883). Among the critics :
Jean de Launoy (Opp. 5 fol. 1731). Conspicuous for his mastery
of the whole field of historical Theology was Gerbert, prince-abbot
of St. Blasien († 1793 ; mg. by C. KRIEG, 1897). Among those who
occupied themselves with the history of national Churches were
Ughelli (*Italia sacra*, 9 fol. 1644–62 ; ed. COLETI, 10 fol. 1717–22),
Sainte-Marthe and others (*Gallia christiana*, 15 fol. 1715–1860),
Hansiz (*Germania sacra*, 3 fol. 1727–54), and Florez, &c. (*España
sagrada*, 51 vol. 1747–1879).

§ 189

Christian Art : Music, Architecture, Painting [1]

I. The introduction of harmony into the Church's chant
was an improvement due to the Middle Ages,[2] but music of

---

[1] Literature, §§ 131, 157 ; BURKHARDT-HOLZINGER, *Gesch. der Renaissance
in Italien*, 3rd ed. 1891 ; FABRICZY, *Fil. Brunnelleschi*, 1892.

[2] W. BÄUMKER, *Palestrina*, 1877 ; *Orlandus de Lassus*, 1878 ; KATSCH-
THALER, *Gesch. der Kirchenmusik*, 1893 ; H. A. KÖSTLIN, *Gesch. der Musik*,
5th ed. 1899.

this kind soon came to involve unnatural interruptions of the text, the curtailment of words through the use of counterpoint, the adoption of secular melodies, &c., so that even as far back as the time of John XXII it was found necessary to denounce these excesses (*Extrav. commun.* III, 1). As the abuse nevertheless persisted, the prohibition was re-enacted by the Council of Trent (Sess. XXII). The question even arose whether polyphonic music should be permitted at all, and whether a return to simple Gregorian chant should not be enforced. **Palestrina** († 1594), by his *Missa papae Marcelli*, was, however, able to show that the art as such was not responsible for the faults complained of, and that good music could perfectly well convey the words ; he thus became in some sort the saviour and reformer of Church music. Among his other compositions his *Missa Assunta*, his *Improperia* and *Stabat mater* are especially remarkable. At about the same time **Orlandus Lassus** († 1594) was also creating his masterpieces at Munich. Born in the Netherlands (at Mons), which during the last centuries had retained the first place as a musical country, and which, ever since the Babylonian Exile, had provided the singers for the papal chapel, he brought the art of his native land to its highest pitch, and carried it with him into South Germany when he entered the service of the dukes of Bavaria (1557).

Not only were the works of Palestrina of a nature to excite imitation, but he himself also laboured as a master to propagate his form of the art. Among those who followed him must be reckoned Allegri († 1652), the composer of a striking *Miserere* for two choirs ; also Vittoria. The severe style did not, however, continue in vogue everywhere, and, though it was still long after to be represented by Lotti († 1740), the rise and development of oratorios and operas again brought a worldly spirit into the Church's music. Violins and other instruments, which about this time made their entrance into the Church, soon took a leading part instead of serving as a mere accompaniment, and so great was the influence exerted by the new current that even masters such as Mozart († 1791), Joseph Haydn († 1809), and Beethoven († 1827) were not able to escape it.

II. Whilst north of the Alps the mediæval architecture survived into the sixteenth century and even later, in Italy a style of completely different character had made its appearance

c. 1420. As it was essentially nothing else than a revival of the
old Roman style, and as its origin coincided with the new
birth of classicism, it received the name of **Renaissance Style.**
Its foundation is usually ascribed to the Florentines Brunellesco
and Alberti.   Its peculiarities are mainly in the decorations.
The walls were adorned in antique fashion with leaf-work,
fruits, scrolls, wreaths, garlands, and other designs, with statues
and high reliefs, the cornices were formed on the ancient system,
and the lintels of the doors and windows assumed the shape
of an obtuse triangle or of a segment of a circle.

During the fifteenth century the style remained in its infancy,
being now known as Early Renaissance. A kind of uncertainty prevailed, the architects being still gingerly feeling
their way, and as yet not willing to abandon entirely the
mediæval principles. The masterpiece of the period is the front
of the Certosa near Pavia. By the beginning of the sixteenth
century uncertainty had ceased, and the style had already
spread from Italy over the rest of Europe. Its greatest
monument is St. Peter's at Rome, the largest church in the
world, in shape a Latin cross, with a dome rising above the
point of intersection. Its erection occupied 120 years (1506–
1626). Among the architects who had a part in the building
we must mention Bramante, the draughtsman of the earliest
plan, Michelangelo, whose creation was the huge dome, Maderno,
who built most of the nave and the front, and, finally, Bernini,
who planned the superb colonnade enclosing the court, which,
however, was not finished until forty years after the completion
of the Basilica. The Renaissance Style did not long survive
in its purity, the decay beginning even before the close of the
sixteenth century. Caprice now took the place of order and
rule, the columns were twisted, the pediments interrupted, and
the ornamental details tastelessly multiplied, the result being
the debased style termed Rococo.

III. The lives of some of the Italian **Painters** already enumerated
(§ 157) partially belong to the present period.   Paolo Caliari, generally known after his birth-place as Veronese († 1588), a painter of
the Venetian school, belongs entirely to this period.   For a while
the Italian school retained its eminence, though it soon degenerated
into mannerism.   Two artists, however, merit a passing mention,
Vasari († 1574), whose ' Lives of the best Painters, Sculptors, and

Architects ' is one of the main sources of the History of Art, and Baroccio († 1612). Towards the end of the sixteenth century there occurred a sort of second spring. Two new schools were established. Of these, one, cultivating a noble eclecticism, was represented at Bologna by Ludovico Caracci († 1619) and his two nephews Agostino and Annibale. Domenichino († 1641), Guido Reni († 1642), and Carlo Dolci († 1686) belonged to the same school. The other was noted for its, often crude, naturalism. It was founded by Caravaggio († 1609).

In the seventeenth century painting rose to great eminence in the Low Countries and in Spain. **Rubens** († 1640) was a first-rate master. Some of his works, such as the Crucifixion and the Descent from the Cross, at the cathedral of Antwerp, are among the finest creations of Art ; other works of his are, however, too naturalistic to satisfy the claims of healthy idealism. The greatest of his pupils was Sir Anthony Van Dyck († 1641). In Spain two stars of the first magnitude blazed out : **Velasquez** at Madrid († 1600), court painter to Philip IV, a realist, whose paintings are mostly of a worldly character, and **Murillo** at Sevilla († 1682), an idealist, who so ably combined his rare use of colour with the deepest feeling and devotion that he is numbered among the greatest of religious painters (Mg. by K. JUSTI, 2nd ed. 1904).

§ 190

The Græco-Russian Church [1]

The capture of Constantinop'e by the Turks, and their further progress westwards had not for Christianity the same unhappy results as the invasions of the Saracens in the seventh and eighth century. The policy of the conquerors was not to oppress their new subjects in the practice of their religion, the consequence being that, though a few apostates were not wanting, the mass of the p ople remained true to their Faith. Not only did the Greeks resist the allurements of the Mohammedans, but they also stood firm against the attempts made to introduce Protestantism into their midst. The proselytising efforts of Melanchthon (1559), of the Tübingen professors M. Crusius and J. Andreae (1573–81), and of Cyril Lucaris, patriarch of Constantinople († 1638), who had embraced Calvinism as a

[1] D. KYRIAKOS, *Gesch. der orientalischen Kirchen von* 1453–1898, German Trans. by E. RAUSCH, 1902 ; LEROY-BEAULIEU, *L'empire des Tsars et les Russes*, 3 vol. 3rd ed. 1898 ; *Z. f. k. Th.* 1894, pp. 417–56 ; KATTENBUSCH, *Vergleichende Konfessionskunde*, I, 1892 ; J. GEHRING, *Die Sekten der russ. Kirche* (1003–1897), 1898.

student at Geneva, were utterly fruitless. On the questions of Justification, of the sacraments, of the sacrifice of the Mass, &c., the Greeks persisted in opposing the Catholic doctrine to the Reformers. In other respects, however, the situation of the eastern Church was eminently unsatisfactory. Great corruption reigned amongst the clergy, especially in the appointment to the patriarchate, which was often made a matter of barter.

The **Russian Church**—of which the metropolis was originally Kief, but, subsequently to the middle of the fourteenth century, Moscow, the capital of the realm—remained throughout the Middle Ages dependent on the Church of Constantinople. The political alterations of the time were, however, soon to break the link by which the two Churches were joined. Whilst the Byzantine Empire was being slowly occupied by the Turks, the Russians were engaged in delivering themselves from the yoke of the Tartars or Mongols, under which they had been since 1250. Under Ivan IV, who in 1547 was crowned czar of all the Russias, the Russians at last obtained complete independence (1550). No sooner was this done than they sought to secure the independence of their Church also, their wish being fulfilled without delay. Jeremias II of Constantinople, with the consent of his eastern colleagues, bestowed on the patriarch Job the title of metropolitan (1589), thus creating a new independent province. The new patriarchate of Moscow was, however, not to retain its dignity. In spite of the patriarch being wholly in the emperor's power, his position appeared too high, and likely to prove a hindrance to the autocracy, and accordingly, after the patriarch Adrian's death (1702), a great alteration was made in the government of the Church. The patriarchate remained unoccupied for near twenty years, only an administrator being appointed, and was then formally abolished, the supreme direction of Church matters being assigned to the Holy Synod (1721), a college consisting of bishops and others of the higher clergy, together with a procurator-general representing the State. Simultaneously the dignities of the metropolitans and archbishops, with the exception of those of Kief and Novgorod, were extinguished, their positions being afterwards taken by simple bishops. They were to exist henceforth merely as titles of honour which the czar might bestow as he pleased. In instituting a Synod the

Russians were following the lead of Constantinople, where the patriarch was also assisted by a Holy Synod, the only difference being that in Russia the place of the patriarch was taken by the czar.

Though by these reforms the Russian Church was centralised, and made utterly subservient to the secular ruler, this did not prevent the rise of numerous sects. The first rank among these is taken by the **Raskolniky** (separatists) or **Starovertzy** (Old Believers), to use the name they apply to themselves. They parted from the Church in the latter half of the seventeenth century. The patriarch Nikon having (1652–58) undertaken a revision of the liturgical books, which had been much corrupted, the Old Believers refused to accept his alterations. With their intense attachment to the older rites and usages they combine a horror for all new-fangled customs such as shaving, smoking, and the use of coffee, &c. At the present day they number over 10,000,000 and are split into two bodies, those having priests (Popovtzy) and those without priests (Bespopovtzy), the latter holding that the priesthood lost its power through Nikon's heresy ; instead of priests they are ministered to by elders whom they elect. Other sects either originated or first came into notice during the eighteenth century. Two of these are remarkable for their semi-gnostic fanaticism, the Chlyssty or flagellants, and the Skoptzy or eunuchs. Two others hold peculiar views, partaking at once of spiritualism and rationalism, and reject all external worship : the Molokans or milk-drinkers, so named because they do not scruple to break the law of the Orthodox Church and use milk during the fasting season, and the Dukhobortzy or spiritual combatants, who, after the habit of the nearly allied Quakers, hold both oaths and military service to be unchristian. Cp. *Z. f. k. Th.* 1890, pp. 416–46 ; K. K. GRASS, *Die russ. Sekten*, 1905 ff.

CHAPTER IV

THE PROTESTANT CHURCH

§ 191

Doctrinal Controversies to the Middle of the Seventeenth Century [1]

THOUGH the Reformers were unanimous in their rejection of one portion of the doctrines and institutions of the Catholic Church, they were far from agreeing among themselves when the time came for them to state their own attitude. Even within one and the same denomination there existed many divergences, especially in Germany, where Luther's followers were not all of them inclined to give to their master's views the unconditional assent which he demanded. In consequence of this, numerous controversies broke out in the Protestant body, two of which are of special importance.

I. **The Eucharistic Controversy.** Owing to his belief in the bodily ubiquity of Christ, Luther taught that, when the consecrated Bread is received, Christ is present in, with, and beneath the Bread (Impanation theory). On the other hand, Carlstadt and the Swiss, possibly owing to the influence exerted by an epistle of the Netherlander Honius which had circulated widely, not only denied Transubstantiation, but any real presence, though they did not all justify their denial in the same way. Instead of connecting the words *hoc est corpus meum* with the previous words *accipite et manducate*, Carlstadt, at the expense of the text, applied them to the suffering of Christ. The Swiss interpreted the words of consecration figuratively, Zwingli, for instance, taking 'is' to mean

---

[1] DÖLLINGER, *Die Reformation*, vol. III. 1848; HEPPE, *Gesch. des deutschen Protestantismus in den J.* 1555–81, 4 vol. 1852–59; DORNER, *Gesch. d. prot. Th.* 1868.

'signifies,' and Œcolampadius the word ' body ' to mean
' sign of the Body.' The divergency led to a conflict.   Carlstadt, whose actions had long been a source of annoyance to
Luther, and who had at last been banished by him from
Saxony, revenged himself by publishing a tract, ' On the
Antichristian Abuse of the Bread and Chalice of the Lord '
(1524).   Luther replied in 1525 by his work ' Against the
Heavenly Prophets.'   As in the same year Zwingli (*Comm. de
vera et falsa religione*) and Œcolampadius (*De genuina verborum
Domini, Hoc est corpus meum iuxta vetust. auctores expositione*)
both appeared in the field with their doctrine concerning the
Eucharist, Luther attacked them, his first tract being followed
by others of even more violent character.   At the religious
conference held at Marburg (1529) [1] the disputants indeed
promised to desist from insult, and in the following years
attempts were repeatedly made to come to some understanding,
a temporary one being actually arrived at by the Concord of
Wittenberg (1536).   The peace was not long kept, the signal
for the renewal of hostilities being given by Luther's work,
' A Short Avowal concerning the Blessed Sacrament, against
Fanatics ' (1544).   For the rest, the Zwinglians did not uphold
their doctrine long.   Zürich, by the *Consensus Tigurinus* (1549),
accepted Calvin's teaching on the subject, and its example was
followed by the other Protestant cantons ;   a little later the
union was still further cemented by the *Confessio Helvetica
posterior* (1564), a profession of faith drawn up by Bullinger,
Zwingli's successor, for the elector-palatine Frederick III.

II. Cryptocalvinism and the Formula of Concord.
Melanchthon, though little inclined to countenance Zwingli's
Eucharistic doctrine, was in later life drawn to favour that
of Calvin as opposed to that of Luther.   Owing to the esteem
in which Melanchthon was held, this doctrine, especially after
Luther's death, won many adherents at Wittenberg and in
Saxony generally.   Subsequently to Melanchthon's demise (1560)
it was defended by his son-in-law, Caspar Peucer, who, being the
elector's medical attendant, wielded considerable influence.
In 1564 a collection of Melanchthon's doctrinal confessions of
Faith and other works, the *Corpus doctrinae Philippicum seu*

---

[1] Erichson, *Das M. Religionsgespr.* 1880 ;   *Th. Z. aus d. Schweiz*, 1884.

Misnicum (1560), was declared the rule of Faith throughout the land. The elector Augustus (1553–86), on assuming the regency over the duchy of Saxony, banished from the country the two most zealous of Luther's supporters, Hesshus and Wiegand of Jena, and withdrew their preferences from many of their friends (1573). A change was, however, not long in coming. A work, *Exegesis perspicua de coena Domini* (1574), caused the institution of an inquiry, and an intercepted letter assisted to make clear the real state of affairs. The result was that the Cryptocalvinists, or Philippists, were either imprisoned or banished. For the consolidation of Lutheranism, Jakob Andreae, chancellor of the University of Tübingen, M. Chemnitz, superintendent of Brunswick, and other theologians met at Torgau and drew up a new profession of Faith (1576), which was further revised at the monastery of Bergen near Magdeburg (1577), and ultimately, in 1580, together with the Confession of Augsburg and its Apology, the Schmalkalden Articles, and the two Catechisms issued by Luther in 1529, was published as a formula of concord (*Formula concordiae*).[1] As it was not accepted by several of the States, it became, in the event, a *Formula discordiae*. Under the next elector, Christian I (1586–91), Philippism was resuscitated, though only to sink again at his death. Against his prime minister and chancellor, Nicholas Krell, the feeling of the opposition was so strong that, after having lingered ten years in prison, he at last perished on the scaffold (1601).

Other similar disputes were :

III. The **Antinomist** controversy (1537–41). Melanchthon in his visitation-instructions issued in 1527 had ordered the clergy to urge the people to repentance by preaching the Law. This order was contravened by John Agricola, a preacher at Eisleben, who opined that repentance could not be the outcome of a dead Law, but only of the Gospel. As, however, he thereby came into conflict with Luther's doctrine regarding the mere consolatory character of the Gospel, he was (after 1537) opposed by the other Lutherans as an antinomist. Cp. KAWERAU, *J. Agricola*, 1881 ; *Beiträge zur Reformationsgesch. zu Köstlins 70 Geburtstag*, 1896 ; *N. k. Z.* 1904.

IV. The **Adiaphorist** controversy (1548–55) arose through the Leipzig Interim, Matthias Flacius, and other fanatics finding fault

---

[1] Cp. *Libri symb. eccl. evang. sive Concordia rec. C. A. Hase*, ed. 3ª, 1846.

with Melanchthon and the more moderate Lutherans for having sanctioned during the interval as adiaphora (*i.e.* indifferent) the old rites and usages of the Church.   Cp. W. PREGER, *M. Flacius Ill. u. s. Zeit,* 1859.

V. The **Osiandrist** controversy (1549–56) began when Andrew Osiander, first at Nuremberg and then at Königsberg (1548–52), ventured to express the opinion that God does not merely cover sin, as Luther taught, but that He also sanctifies the sinner, in other words that Justification depends on the indwelling of God in man, and not merely in the fact that God is pleased to account sin as nothing out of regard for Christ's merits.

VI. The **Majorist** controversy (1551–62) was excited by the theory put forward by George Major, a Wittenberg professor, that works are necessary for Salvation ; he was opposed by Nicholas Amsdorf, who maintained the thesis that good works are hurtful to Salvation.

VII. The **Synergist** controversy (1555–67) arose through John Pfeffinger, a Leipzig professor, teaching that man is obliged to co-operate (συνεργεῖν) with Grace in the work of Justification.

VIII. The **Syncretist** controversy.   Duke Julius of Brunswick, having soon after his accession rejected the Formula of Concord, orthodox Lutheranism was unable to take firm footing at the University of Helmstädt, which he had founded.   The result was that the teaching there was of a more independent character than elsewhere, especially after the staff had been joined by the scholar and traveller George Calixt (1614).   Calixt, whose attention was riveted on the underlying common principles of Christianity, to the exclusion of the points of difference, yearned for the union of Christendom. To the Lutheran zealots of Wittenberg and Leipzig his intentions seemed, however, to involve a syncretism or confusion of religions, and they accordingly led on him an attack (1640) which threw nearly the whole of Germany into a commotion, which was prolonged even after his death (1656).   Mg. on Calixt by GASS, 1846 ; HENKE, 2 vol. 1853–60.

§ 192

Protestant Sects to the Middle of the Seventeenth Century [1]

I. The **Anabaptists** and **Mennonites.**   At the very inception of the Reformation, certain fanatics had proposed the abolition of infant baptism, and expressed their belief in Millenarianism and other similar fancies.   After the battle of Frankenhausen and the death of Münzer (1525), this form of

---

[1] ERBKAM, *Gesch. d. prot. Sekten im Zeitalter der Reformation,* 1848.

fanaticism spread far and wide. For a time it was absolutely supreme at Münster in Westphalia.[1] B. Rothmann, a priest of the town, who had at first withstood the Anabaptists, soon changed his mind and joined their party, and on the arrival at Münster of the two chiefs of the sect in the Netherlands—Jan Mathys, a baker of Haarlem, and Jan Bockelson, a tailor of Leyden—the ' reign of God upon earth ' was formally proclaimed. Property was to be held in common, even polygamy being tolerated, and whoever refused to be rebaptised was banished. After the reconquest of the city by the bishop (1535) the guilty parties were indeed executed ; nor were the Anabaptists treated more kindly elsewhere, though they contrived to survive the persecution. Menno Simonis, parish priest of Wittmarsum in Frieseland, who joined them in 1536, was successful in mitigating the practices of these sectarians, who in consequence are now sometimes called, after him, Mennonites. Besides infant baptism, they rejected also the taking of oaths, military and civil service, the use of courts of justice, and divorce, save only in the case of adultery. The membership of the sect was numerous, especially in Holland, Germany, and North America.

II. The **Baptists**[2] were nearly related to the previous. Beginning as a small and obscure English sect, they now reckon in America, where they are first found in 1633, some 4,000,000 communicants, and about 12,000,000 adherents, split up into thirteen denominations. They are also found both in Germany and elsewhere.

III. The **Puritans.**[3] By the Act of Uniformity (1559) the form of worship to be used in all English Churches was settled by Parliament. This form did not, however, prove to the liking of everyone. Not a few found that it contained far too many Catholic elements, this being especially the case with those who were acquainted with the much simpler ritual in use in Switzerland and Scotland. Their opposition was at first directed

---

[1] H. A. KERSSENBROCH, *Anabaptistici furoris Monasterium evertentis hist. narratio*, ed. H. DETMER, 1899–1900 (*Die Geschichtsquellen des Bistums Münster*, vol. V–VI) ; C. A. CORNELIUS, *Gesch. des Münst. Aufruhrs*, 2 vol. 1855–60 ; L. KELLER, *Gesch. d. Wiedertäufer und ihres Reiches zu M.* 1880 ; *Hist. Z.* 1882, pp. 429–56.
[2] M. G. BRUMBAUGH, *Hist. of the Germ. Baptist Brethren in Europe and America*, 1900 ; J. C. CARLILE, *Story of the English Baptists*, 1905.
[3] Mg. by HOPKINS, 3 vol. 1860 ; CAMPBELL, 2 vol. 1892 ; BYINGTON, 1896.

against the practice of singing, or playing the organ, against the sign of the cross, against godparents, priestly vestments (other than the gown), church festivals, and a host of other points of discipline. Their ideal was a thoroughly pure and scriptural Christianity, whence their name of Puritans, their opposition to the Act of Uniformity earning them also the name of Nonconformists or Dissenters. As their demands were rejected, and they themselves subjected to persecution, they began, in 1567, to form themselves into a separate body on a wholly Presbyterian basis. This, however, did not tend to ameliorate their position ; on the contrary, the persecution became each year more severe, driving many of the Puritans to seek greater independence beyond the seas. On the outbreak of the politico-ecclesiastical quarrels under Charles I, the Episcopal Church was indeed abolished (1643) and a form of Presbyterianism introduced (1646), but the old order of things was again established by Charles II soon after his return (1660), and the Puritans were again in trouble. Two thousand clergymen chose to lose their preferences rather than submit to the Act of Uniformity. Toleration was ultimately granted to all Protestant Dissenters by the edict of toleration issued by William of Orange (1689).

IV. The **Schwenkfeldians.** Soon after making common cause with Luther, Caspar von Schwenkfeld of Ossig in Silesia († 1561) proceeded to lay such stress on the inner union between God and man that the necessity for external worship almost disappeared. Among other things he also denied the presence of Christ in the Eucharist, urging that our Lord did not wish to imply that the Bread and the Wine were His Body and His Blood, but that His Body and His Blood were Bread and Wine, *i.e.* a food to nourish and strengthen the soul. Expelled from his native country, he betook himself to South Germany, where, in spite of persecution, he made some converts. Mg. by KADELBACH, 1860 ; F. HOFFMANN, I, 1897.

V. The **Antitrinitarians** and **Socinians.** Shortly after the outbreak of the Reformation the doctrine of the Trinity was denied, among others, by the Spanish physician Michael Servetus (cp. § 168), and by Laelius and Faustus Socinus of Siena. The latter († 1604), after a short sojourn in Switzerland (whither he had been preceded by his uncle Laelius, 1547), went on to Transylvania, and thence to Poland, where he settled at Rakov. Here there were already many who professed Unitarianism conjointly with Anabaptism, and Socinus was soon able to gather together a band of followers. The

Rakov catechism (1605) provided the sect's creed. Later on it was driven from Poland, but it retained its ground in Transylvania, where antitrinitarianism had prevailed even before the advent of Socinus, and in other localities also. Mg. by O. FOCK, 2 vol. 1847 ; *Th. Jahrb.* 1848, pp. 371–98 ; LECLERC, *F. Sicine*, 1886 ; BURNET, *L. Socin*, 1894.

VI. The **Independents** or **Congregationalists.** Robert Brown, who, for a time, had belonged to the Puritan party, in 1580 departed from the latter's principles by rejecting not only the episcopate, but even the presbyterian or synodal method of government. His wish was to establish the various parishes on the broadest democratic basis, and to secure to each complete independence. He himself finally reverted to Anglicanism, but his ideas remained popular, their supporters being named Congregationalists, on account of the stress they laid on the will of the congregation, and Independents, because they rejected the control not only of the State, but even of any common synod of their own. FLETCHER, *Hist. of Ind. in England*, 4 vol. 1862 ; WADDINGTON, *Congreg. Hist.* 1874.

VII. The **Remonstrants** or **Arminians.** Scarcely had the Reformation proved victorious in Holland than conflicts broke out between the Calvinists themselves. The exaggerated doctrine of predestination excited some opposition, and in the controversy which ensued, a split occurred among the stricter sort of Calvinists. The Supralapsarians held that predestination was independent of sin, whilst this was denied by the Infralapsarians. In so doing, the latter were departing to some extent from the severity of the original doctrine ; Arminius, an Amsterdam preacher († 1608), was, however, to go much further. He abandoned the Calvinistic doctrine, and on being summoned to the University of Leyden (1603) he made many disciples. His adherents were known after him as Arminians, and occasionally as Remonstrants, on account of the document entitled *Remonstrantia*, which, in 1610, they addressed to the States of Holland and West-Frieseland. Therein they declared that God reprobates or predestines, only on the ground of His foreknowledge, that Christ died for all men, and that Grace is not irresistible ; they, moreover, affirmed that Faith alone is insufficient for Justification, and that, for this, charity operating through Faith is requisite. Their opponents were known as Contra-remonstrants, or as Gomarists, after Francis Gomar, a Leyden theologian. The latter were at first successful, the stadtholder Maurice of Orange supporting them for political motives. The synod of Dordrecht (1618–19) removed from their offices some 200 Arminian-minded preachers, and even expelled some of them from the country, among these being Episcopius the leader of the party. Under the next stadtholder, however, the Remonstrants not only secured toleration, but were soon allowed to worship publicly (1630). Mg. by D. DE BRAY, 1835 ; C. FLOUR, 1889 ; J. H. MARONIER, *J. Arminius*, 1905.

§ 193

The Pietists [1]

The attitude which the Reformers had assumed towards the Catholic Church led to their laying great stress on Faith. This proceeding was, however, not without danger for morality. The doctrine of Justification by Faith alone was in itself of a nature to be misunderstood by the mass of the people, and sayings such as Luther's *Fortiter pecca, sed fortius crede*, &c. were more likely to give rise to false impressions than to check them. The doctrinal controversies, which early broke out among the Protestants, also contributed to enhance unduly the value of mere orthodoxy. Hence it is no wonder that the Reformed Churches soon found themselves sadly in need of a moral reformation. The task of introducing into them more practical Christianity was undertaken by the Pietists.

They are first met with in the Reformed Churches of the Netherlands and Switzerland. In the first half of the seventeenth century, associations were formed to cultivate virtue and piety. The leaders of the movement were Gisbert Voet († 1676), a professor, and Jodocus van Lodensteyn († 1677), a preacher of Utrecht, and, at Altona, John de Labadie († 1676), the originator of Separatism in the Reformed Church.

Ph. J. Spener was responsible for the introduction of the movement into Lutheran Germany. As he realised the impossibility of imposing on the whole of the Church the perfection which he sought, he determined to attempt it only on a few, in the hope that the *ecclesiola in ecclesia* would, in time, act as a ferment on the whole. The best means to secure his end appeared to him to be the *Collegia pietatis*, select gatherings held for the purpose of mutual edification and for Bible-reading. He began his work at Frankfort in 1670, and in 1675 issued his *Pia desideria*, a treatise on the evils prevailing in the Church with proposals for their betterment, in which he acquainted the public with his scheme. In the event his example was widely

---

[1] A. RITSCHL, *Gesch. d. Piet.* 1880–86; E. SACHSSE, *Ursprung und Wesen d. P.* 1884; P. GRÜNBERG, *Spener*, 2 vol. 1893–1905.

imitated. At Leipzig a similar work was started with the *Collegium philobiblicum* (1686), established by two young masters, Hermann Francke and Paul Anton. These proceedings did not fail to excite indignation ; the *Collegium philobiblicum* was dissolved (1690) ; but the movement answered too well to the needs of the Protestant Church to be so easily checked. Banished from the Saxon Electorate, Pietism found a new home at Berlin, where Spener had been appointed provost (1691), and also at the new University of Halle, whither both Francke and Anton had been summoned to teach. The quarrel, however, continued, especially when it became known that the Pietists professed to be recipients of visions and predictions, and that they favoured separatist tendencies. In spite of this the movement persisted, the headquarters of its propaganda being the great orphanage established by Francke at Halle, an institution comprising several schools and educational departments.

§ 194

The Quakers, Herrnhuters, Methodists, and Swedenborgians [1]

I. The **Quakers** [2] originated in England in 1649, when George Fox (1623–91), as a protest against the formalism prevailing in the Church, laid the foundation of his ' Society of Friends,' a band of enthusiasts, strong in Faith, and simple and sober in life. They soon became numerous in spite of the persecutions which they incurred for their interference in public worship, and finally were granted toleration by William's Toleration Act (1689). Even stronger than in England were they in North America, where William Penn, in quittance for a debt due to him, had obtained from the British government a grant of land on the Delaware (1681). Here was established the State of Pennsylvania, of which nearly half the population consisted of Quakers. The Friends did not, however, long retain either their numerical strength or their original severity, and soon split into the parties known as ' damp ' and ' fighting ' or ' free Friends.'

[1] H. WEINGARTEN, *Die Revolutionskirchen Englands*, 1868.
[2] CUNNINGHAM, *The Quakers*, 1868 ; *KL.* X, 656–67.

To the Quakers the source of religious knowledge is the immediate enlightenment produced by Christ, the light within. Holy Scripture itself can only be understood by means of this light, which, as ' the true light which enlighteneth every man that cometh into this world ' (*John* i. 9), has ever assisted man both before and after the advent of Christ. The worship in use in the sect agrees with its belief. Prayer and preaching are made to depend on immediate inspiration. The sacraments they either rejected or reduced to mere unnecessary symbols. Military service, oaths, tithes, theatres, dances, and other frivolities they refused to countenance. In the beginning the office of preaching devolved on anyone who felt moved by the Spirit, though, later on, the more capable members in each community were granted a permanent right of addressing the Friends. Their place of meeting was a simple house of prayer, devoid of bell, altar, or pulpit, and the severity of their tenets was similarly evinced by the peculiar garb the Quakers affected, the men wearing dark coats minus any buttons, and wide-awake hats, and the women green aprons and black bonnets. They were also accustomed to use the familiar ' thou,' and refused to uncover the head to anyone. Owing to their theory of the light within, the sect had very little by way of dogma, though it has always held by its principal theologian Robert Barclay († 1690), who cast the Quakers' teachings into a sort of system.

II. The founder of the **Herrnhuters** was count L. von Zinzendorf (1700–60).[1] He had been educated among the followers of Spener, and even in his tender youth had endeavoured to work for the *ecclesiola in ecclesia*. At last, in 1722, an opportunity presented itself for carrying out the idea on a larger scale, and he gave permission to a small colony of Moravian Brethren to establish themselves on his estate on the Hutberg near Berthelsdorf in Upper Lusatia. This settlement, which was the cradle of the village of Herrnhut, increased very fast, and, in spite of the differences prevailing between its members, Zinzendorf, by dint of work and self-sacrifice, and thanks to his power of organisation, succeeded in keeping the community together and in transforming it into a Brotherhood (1727). Its members, to prevent friction, were divided, according to the sect to which they had previously belonged, into three categories, those of the Lutherans, of the Calvinists, and of the Moravians.

[1] Mg. by A. G. SPANGENBERG (the sect's most influential leader after Zinzendorf), 1772–75; G. BURKHARDT, 1866; B. BECKER, 1886, 2nd ed. 1901 ; G. REICHEL, *A. G. Spangenberg*, 1906.

Generally speaking, they considered Christianity to consist essentially in the belief in the Redemption by Christ's
death on the Cross and in a childlike surrender of the Christian
to the Saviour, with whom, in 1741, a kind of alliance was
entered, and whose will was invariably sought by means
of lots in cases of elections, marriages, &c. New communities
were soon formed on the same model both in the Old and in
the New World. The direction of the whole is in the hands
of a conference of elders, elected by the general synod, and
which has its residence at Berthelsdorf. Each community has
a like constitution, being divided into choirs according to
sex, age, and conjugal state. Worship consists in sermons,
prayers, hymns, and in a communion service which follows
an Agape once every four weeks. Private devotions consist
in the daily drawing of lots (for a passage from the Old
Testament) and in certain readings from the New Testament.

III. **Methodism** [1] grew out of a society of students
formed at Oxford in 1729 for the promotion of virtue and
piety, and known at the University as the pious club, or the
' Methodists,' owing to the severe method of life followed
by its members. The society's founder was Charles Wesley,
but its head and soul was his elder brother, John Wesley
(1703–91), a fellow of Lincoln College. Another well-known
member, who joined in 1732, was George Whitefield. The
aim of these young men, who for a time worked in conjunction
with the Herrnhuters, was to infuse a higher life into the
Church of England. In spite of their own intentions,
Wesley's followers, gradually and against their will, soon
found themselves drifting away from the established
Church. On being forbidden to hold their meetings in the
churches, Wesley and Whitefield proceeded to preach in
the open air (1739), and when this too was prohibited,
they erected chapels of their own. As the clergy thereupon
declined to have any more to do with the movement, laymen
were appointed to preach, and as, finally, the English bishops
refused to confer ordination on the lay preachers, Wesley
himself undertook to confer it. The society was to grow

[1] Bg. of Wesley by SOUTHEY, 3rd ed. 1846 ; TYERMAN, 3 vol. 1870–71 ; R.
GREEN, 1905 ; WINCHESTER, 1906 ; A. STEVENS, *Hist. of Method.* 3 vol. 1868 ;
ATKINSON, *The Beginnings of the Wesleyan Movement in America,* 1896 ;
J. JUNGST, *Der Meth. in Deutschland,* 3rd ed. 1906.

vastly, and counts at the present day over 20,000,000 members. The parishes are divided into classes under lay stewards, whose importance is all the greater owing to the custom prevailing of changing the preacher every two years. The supreme direction is in the hands of a conference, meeting annually (in America every four years).

The Wesleyans severed their connection with the Herrnhuters (1740) owing to a disagreement regarding re-birth. According to Wesley this consists in a violent break with sin and self-seeking, the moment of conversion being consequently perfectly well known to the person who has experienced it. On the other hand, Zinzendorf conceived of the action of the Spirit as something milder. This schism was soon followed by one between Wesley and Whitefield (1741), the pretext in this case being a difference regarding Grace, on which Wesley was inclined to follow Arminius, and Whitefield Calvin. The two friends were soon reconciled, though the quarrel again broke out on the death of Whitefield (1770). At a later date other divergencies resulted in the formation of many new Denominations, especially in North America, where the sect is most strongly represented.

IV. The **New Jerusalem Church,** or the sect of the **Swedenborgians,** owes its origin to Emanuel Swedenborg, assessor at the College of Mines at Stockholm. Believing himself to have been called by God to expound the inner spiritual sense of the Scriptures (1743), he maintained a perpetual intercourse with the spirit-world, and wrote many books, of which the principal is the *Vera christiana religio* (1770). On the day following the completion of this work, the New Jerusalem, or the New Church, was to be made manifest. Outside of Sweden he found followers, more especially in England, where he spent the last days of his life, in North America, and in Württemberg. He believed that God is one in person, but is manifested in three revelations as Creator, Redeemer, and Regenerator of the world. TAFEL, *Swed. und s. Gegner*, 1841 ; *Documents concerning the Life and Character of E.S.* 2 vol. 1875–77.

§ 195

Learning and Art among the Protestants [1]

I. The Protestants, relying as they did on Holy Scripture, were led to devote great attention to Biblical studies. Nor were they forgetful of the claims of the other branches of

---

[1] J. A. DORNER, *Gesch. d. prot. Theologie, besonders in Deutschland*, 1867 ; G. FRANK, *Gesch. d. prot. Theologie*, 4 vol. 1862–1905.

Theology, and though their literature for a time was sadly shackled by a strong spirit of denominationalism and creedal orthodoxy, at a later date much greater freedom obtained. The change was in large part due to the advent of Deism and Rationalism, though Protestant scholars, in discarding their too narrow creeds, not unfrequently went the length of altogether rejecting the Divine character of Christianity.

Apart from the Reformers themselves and a few men whose names have already been mentioned in speaking of the controversies of the day, the principal exponents of Protestant learning were the following :—

Exegetists and Biblical Philologists. The two orientalists (father and son) Buxtorf of Basel (*Concordantiae Bibliorum Hebraicae*, 1632 ; *Lexicon Chaldaicum, Talmudicum et Rabbinicum*, 1639) ; Walton, editor of the London Polyglot (6 fol. 1657) ; J. Lightfoot of Cambridge (*Horae Hebraicae et Talmudicae in quatuor Evangelistas*, 1658–79) ; J. A. Bengel (*Gnomon N. T.* 1742).

Historical Theologians (see §5). D. Blondel (cp. §99) ; J. d'Aillé (Dallaeus : *De pseudepigraphis apostolicis*, 1653 ; *De scriptis Dionysii Areopagitae, &c.*, 1666) ; J. Usher (*Polycarpi et Ignatii epistolae*, 1644) ; J. Pearson (*Vindiciae Ignatianae*, 1672) ; H. Dodwell (*Dissertationes Cyprianicae*, 1684, *in Irenaeum, &c.*) ; W. Cave (*Scriptorum eccles. hist. literaria*, 1693) ; C. Oudin (*Commentarius de scriptoribus ecclesiasticis*, 2 fol. 1722) ; J. Bingham (*Origines ecclesiae, or the Antiquities of the Christian Church*, 8 vol. 1708–22 ; Lat. ed. by GRISCHOVIUS, 10 vol. 1724–38) ; Ch. W. F. Walch (*Historie der Ketzereien*, 11 vol. 1762–85) ; J. Planck (*Gesch. der Entstehung, Veränderungen und Bildung unseres protest. Lehrbegriffs*, 6 vol. 1781–1800 ; *Gesch. d. christl. Gesellschaftsverfassung*, 5 vol. 1803–9).

Apologists and **Dogmatic Theologians.** Hugo Grotius (*De veritate religionis christianae*, 1627) ; N. Lardner (cp. § 196) ; M. Chemnitz (*Examen decretorum concilii Tridentini*, 1565–73 ; *Loci theologici*, 1591) ; J. Gerhard (*Loci theologici*, 9 vol. 1610–22) ; J. A. Quenstedt (*Theologia didactico-polemica seu systema theologicum*, 4 fol. 1696) ; J. Cocceius or Koch (*Summa doctrinae de foedere et testamento Dei*, 1648) ; S. J. Baumgarten (*Glaubenslehre*, 3 vol. 1759).

II. **Painting** during this period flourished in the northern as well as in the southern Netherlands. It was in the former that Rembrandt († 1669) produced his finest works. The art was, however, exclusively concerned with nature, religious painting not being encouraged by the Protestants. **Poetry** and **Music,** on the other hand, were zealously fostered, especially by the Lutherans. A large number of men occupied themselves with the composition of hymns.

The first place, after Luther himself, must be assigned to the Berlin preacher Paul Gerhardt († 1676) and the Breslau physician Johann Scheffler, or Angelus Silesius, who afterwards became a convert to Catholicism († 1677).   Among the great composers were J. Sebastian Bach, head of St. Thomas' School at Leipzig († 1723), who composed many pieces for the organ, and Passions, and G. F. Händel of Halle, who spent the latter years of his life in England († 1759), and is renowned for his oratorios.

CHAPTER V

THE OUTBREAK OF RATIONALISM [1]

§ 196

England and France

IN spite of occasional outbursts of unbelief, the Middle Ages, on the whole, may be said to have been ruled by Faith, the same being true of the first half of the period now under discussion. In the seventeenth century, however, a change is noticeable, many of the better classes then abandoning their beliefs and either falling into materialism or embracing a mere religion of reason. Though at first blush this may seem extraordinary, it may to some extent be explained as a natural development of events which had preceded. The division of Western Christendom into a number of warring denominations, and the still further lack of unanimity prevailing within the Protestant body, served not a little to excite religious doubts, and to lead some to discard the supernatural. Though the change, in so far as it involved the loss and destruction of positive beliefs, is to be deplored, we must not close our eyes to the fact that it was also productive of much good. Growing enlightenment was largely responsible for the cessation of the belief in witchcraft, besides destroying many other superstitious notions and practices, and thereby was eminently serviceable in purifying religion. It also prepared the way for religious tolerance and freedom of conscience, which, whatever we may think of it in itself,

---

[1] J. A. von STARK, *Triumph d. Philos. im 18 Jahrh.* 2 vol. 1803; re-edited by BUCHFELNER, 1834); W. BINDER, *Gesch. des philos. u. revol. Jahrhunderts mit Rücks. auf d. kirchl. Zustände,* 2 vol. 1844–45; F. A. LANGE, *Gesch. d. Materialismus,* 4th ed. 1882 (Engl. Trans. *Hist. of Materialism,* 1877 ff.); LECKY, *Hist. of the Rise and Influence of the Spirit of Rationalism in Europe,* 2 vol. 3rd ed. 1866.

owing to the divisions prevailing among Christians, had become a necessity.

England was the first to experience the change.[1] Lord Herbert of Cherbury († 1648) suggested the establishment of a purely natural religion, consisting of the following elements : (1) Belief in God ; (2) worship of the deity by means (3) of virtue and piety ; (4) sorrow for sin and improvement of conduct ; (5) belief in a reward in this life and hereafter. His suggestion was favourably received by many, though, as they were at variance as to details, the matter gave rise to several controversies. In one thing, however, they all agreed, and that was in depriving Christianity of its supernatural character, and in bringing it down to the level of a mere religion of reason. Their proposals and their writings were not allowed to remain unchallenged, and the conflict continued until the middle of the eighteenth century. Nor were their opponents' efforts spent in vain, for belief in a revelation gradually regained the ground it seemed to have lost. Its main supporter in this controversy was Nathaniel Lardner, whose work, *The Credibility of the Gospel History* (12 vol. 1727–55), was translated into many languages.

Among the other seventeenth-century representatives of Deism, or Free-Thought as the movement was sometimes called, were Thomas Hobbes († 1679), who subordinated the Church to the State to such an extent that he was willing even to permit blasphemy on the latter's responsibility, Th. Brown, and Ch. Blount. In the eighteenth century they were followed by the earl of Shaftesbury († 1713), Toland, Collins, Woolston, Tindal (*Christianity as old as the Creation*, 1720), Morgan, Chubb, and lord Bolingbroke († 1751). The philosophers John Locke († 1704) and David Hume († 1776) also have a right to be mentioned here, the former because the sensist theory which he founded was in itself hostile to Christianity, even though the author personally was not inclined to be unfriendly, the latter because he maintains that doubt is the only result to be attained by investigating religion.

A rallying point for all the freethinkers was provided by the **Freemasons.** After the completion of St. Paul's, the remaining members of the masonic guilds, which had taken a prominent part in the work of reconstruction subsequent to the Fire of London, united at the capital (1717) and formed themselves into a grand Lodge. The institution soon spread, and its attitude is sufficiently

---

[1] LECHLER, *Gesch. d. engl. Deismus*, 1841 ; GÜTTLER, *Eduard Lord Herbert von Cherbury*, 1897.

evident from the thoroughly deistic constitution drawn up for it by the English clergyman Anderson. Cp. FINDEL, *Gesch. d. Fr.* 7th ed. 1900 (Engl. Trans. *Hist. of Freemasonry*, 2nd ed. 1869).

In **France** a way was opened for rationalism by the sceptic Pierre Bayle († 1706). The corruption, which pre-vailed at the court and throughout the higher classes, greatly aided its progress, and it was soon represented by a whole band of men. Owing to the esteem in which the writings of some of these were held, unbelief soon found its way into every class of society, at a time, too, when in England a movement in the contrary direction had already set in. Its main instrument was the Encyclopædia,[1] edited by Diderot and d'Alembert. In its beginning the new enlighten-ment had showed a certain amount of consideration for the old beliefs, for instance in the *Lettres persanes* (1721) of Montesquieu, a satire on the state of the Church penned by the famous author of the *Esprit des lois*. Later on, however, it did not hesitate to give open expression to its hatred of both Church and Christianity. The motto of Voltaire († 1777),[2] the head of the so-called philosophers, was *Ecrasez l'infâme*. Not a few, such as Helvetius (*De l'esprit*), de la Mettrie (*L'homme plante, l'homme machine*), Condillac, and Baron de Holbach (*Système de la nature*), preached more or less overtly the crassest materialism. J. J. Rousseau († 1778) was, on the whole, less hostile to Revelation, but by his natural religion (*Émile*, 1761; *Confessions*, 1770) and his assertion of the sovereignty of the people (*Contrat social*, 1762) he contributed as much as any other man to the destruction of Christianity and to the overthrow of political and social order.[3]

§ 197

Germany

In Germany the first to lead an assault on Christianity, and on Scripture, the Christian Koran as he called it, was

---

[1] *Encyclopédie ou dictionnaire raisonné des sciences, des arts, et des métiers,* 28 fol. (7 supplementary vol.), 1751–80.

[2] Mg. by STRAUSS, 2nd ed. 1878.

[3] BERSOT, *Étude sur les philosophes du XVIIIᵉ siècle*, 1878; LANFREY, *L'église et les philosophes au XVIIIᵉ siècle*, 1879; CHARAUX, *Critique idéale et cath. : l'Esprit de Montesquieu, sa vie et ses princ. ouvrages*, 1885.

the Holsteiner Matthias Knutzen, who endeavoured (c. 1672) to form a party known as the *Conscientiarii*.[1] In the eighteenth century rationalism was more successful. In 1735 was published the first part of the Wertheim translation of the Bible, a work of L. Schmidt, unfavourable to revelation. In the same year began the literary activity of J. Chr. Edelmann († 1767),[2] who attacked both Christianity and the Church as products of ignorance and priestcraft.

Shortly afterwards, Reimarus wrote at Hamburg († 1768) the *Wolfenbüttel Fragments*, to be later on published by Lessing, in which revelation in general and Christ's resurrection in particular were denied. As, at this same time, Frederick II of Prussia (1740–86) had made his court the asylum of French freethinkers, and as the greatest German writers of the day, Lessing, Goethe, and Schiller, were likewise infected with the same spirit, it is no wonder that rationalism won ground. It was mainly furthered by the 'General German Library,' founded by the Berlin bookseller Nikolai (1765). Even theologians were carried away by the current, rationalism being proclaimed both from the professor's chair and from the preacher's pulpit. It had as its representatives among the exegetists, J. A. Ernesti at Leipzig († 1781) and J. D. Michaelis at Göttingen († 1791), and among Church historians, J. S. Semler at Halle († 1791). The movement was spread still further through their pupils, such as the notorious K. F. Bahrdt († 1792). The edict of Wöllner (1788) indeed insisted that teaching and preaching should be conformable to the creeds, but so deep was the contrary feeling that it had to be revoked ten years later.

The movement of ideas was not confined to Protestant Germany, but even invaded the Catholic provinces.[3] In Austria the premature reforms undertaken by Joseph II had

---

[1] *St. u. Kr.* 1844.

[2] His autobiography (in German), 1752; ed. W. KLOSE, 1849.

[3] RULAND, *Series et vitae Professorum SS. Theologiae qui Wirceburgi usque ad annum 1834 docuerunt*, 1835; H. BRÜCK, *Die ration. Bestreb. im kath. Deutschland*, 1867; SCHWAB, *Franz Berg*, 1869. Mg. on Eul. Schneider by L. EHRHARD, 1894; E. MÜHLENBECK, 1895; TAUTE, *Die kath. Geistlichkeit und die Freimaurerei*, 2nd ed. 1895 (*Kath.* 1895, I, 509–27); L. WOLFRAM, *Die Illuminaten in Bayern und ihre Verfolgung*, 1898–1900, Erlangen, Programm. *Altbayer. Monatsschrift*, 1900; A. F. LUDWIG, *Weihbischof Zirkel von Würzburg*, 2 vol. 1904–6; J. B. SÄGMÜLLER, *Die k. Aufklärung am Hofe d. H. Karl Eugen von Württemberg* (1744–93), 1906.

prepared the way for it. At Ingolstadt in Bavaria, the professor A. Weishaupt founded the Order of the ' Illuminati ' (1775), of which the tendency is sufficiently indicated by its name, and though the society was soon (1784) suppressed by the government, the spirit which had directed its formation still survived. In the remainder of Germany, the new enlightenment made itself felt more especially at the Universities of the three Rhenish archdioceses, and also at Würzburg. Its best known supporters among the theologians were Lorenz Isenbiehl and F. A. Blau, at Mainz ; at Bonn, Ph. Hedderich and Eulogius Schneider, who afterwards entered the service of the constitutional bishop of Strasburg, then flung himself into the revolution, and finally ended his life on the scaffold at Paris (1794) ; and at Würzburg, the dog- matic theologian F. Oberthür, author of many works and editor of the *Opera polemica sanctorum patrum*, and the Church historian Franz Berg.

II. MODERN TIMES

SECOND PERIOD

FROM THE FRENCH REVOLUTION TO THE PRESENT DAY,
1789–1906 [1]

CHAPTER I

THE CATHOLIC CHURCH

§ 198

The French Church in the Age of the Revolution (1789–1800) and Pius VI [2]

IN the spring, 1789, the Estates-General were summoned to meet at Versailles to discuss the measures to be taken to relieve the financial depression in which France had involved herself in the course of the eighteenth century. Many other abuses also claimed consideration. The condition of the finances was really a result of a more deeply-seated evil. The absolute monarchy and feudalism had outlived their time, and it was now the intention of the rulers to bestow on the people a share in the government of the State, and to distribute more evenly the burden of taxation, which had so far been almost exclusively borne by the Third Estate. In the event no sooner had the Estates met as the 'Constituent Assembly' than they began to discuss the establishment of a new order of things.

[1] B. GAMS, *Gesch. der Kirche Christi im* 19 *Jahrh.* 3 vol. 1854–56; F. NIPPOLD, *Handb. d. neuesten KG.* 3rd ed. 5 vol. 1889 ff.; J. SILBERNAGL, *Die kirchenpolit. u. relig. Zustände im* 19 *Jahrh.* 1901.

[2] Mg. on the French Revolution by BUCHEZ et ROUX (*Hist. parlementaire*), 40 vol. 1834–38; THIERS, 10 vol. 4th ed. 1836 (Leipzig. 6 vol. 1846) (Engl. Trans. last illustrated ed. 1895); SYBEL, 4 vol. 1877 ff.; JAGER, *Hist. de l'église de France pendant la révolution*, vol. 1852; KL. X, 1122–60; A. WAHL, *Vorgesch. der franz. Revolution*, I, 1905; ANGLADE, *De la sécularisation des biens du clergé sous la révolution*, 1901; W. M. SLOANE, *The French Revolution and Religious Reform* (1789–1804), 1901; G. GIOBBIO, *La Chiesa e lo Stato in Francia durante la Rivoluzione* (1789–99), 1905.

The deliberations soon degenerated into disorder, the government completely losing control of the proceedings. At the time the people's heads were too full of the abstract ideas of the *Contrat social* to make sufficient account either of the laws of life or of history. Instead of the constitution being amended it was overthrown, a change which was pregnant in misfortunes for the Church, all the more so because she was then in sad need of reform, because her clergy belonged to the hated privileged class, and because the power was now wholly in the hands of the Voltairean party who had vowed the destruction of Christianity.

The Assembly first abolished feudal rights and the class privilege of the tithes, and in the Declaration of the Rights of Man proclaimed freedom of worship. All superfluous treasures of the Church were confiscated for the good of the country, and as still greater financial resources were needed, the whole of the church property was, on the motion of Talleyrand, bishop of Autun, placed at the disposal of the nation. In 1790 the religious Orders were dissolved, with the exception of those which devoted themselves to education, to the care of their neighbours, or to the progress of learning, and, in the *Constitution civile du clergé*, a new constitution, totally at variance with existing institutions, was given to the French Church. The 134 sees which the kingdom (including Corsica) then possessed were reduced to the number of the new departments, *i.e.* to eighty-three: the parish priests and bishops were to be elected by those qualified to vote in the election of district and departmental assemblies, canonical institution was to be undertaken by the bishops and metropolitans, and all sinecures, such as canonries, prebends, and chaplaincies were abolished. In accordance with a further enactment, no one could be appointed to any office in the Church who had not previously subscribed to this law. In the event only about a third of the clergy consented to take the oath, the first to do so among the clerical deputies being abbé Grégoire. The rest of the clergy, some 46,000 in number, refused to have anything to do with it, and were supported in their resistance by the mass of the people. France was therefore, from a religious point of view, split into two camps, the Church of the Jurors, or constitutional party, and the Church of the Non-Jurors. The Constitution was also rejected by Pius VI (April 13, 1791), who, however, paid for his action with the loss of the counties of Avignon and Venaissin.

The movement was, however, by no means at an end. The Legislative Assembly which replaced the Constituent Assembly in the autumn, 1791, took a new step. Under threat of the loss of pension, of the right of exercising their ministry, and of other penalties, it summoned all the clergy to take the civil oath, and to promise to uphold the Constitution in the measure of their power. In many of the departments the law was rigorously enforced. In the spring, 1792, all religious corporations which had survived were abolished, the wearing of the cassock was prohibited, and every ' suspect,' *i.e.* non-juror, was condemned to banishment, a measure which soon drove some 40,000 persons out of the country. There were also many deeds of violence. In the revolutionary massacre, which cost the lives of over 1,200 people at Paris in the first week of September, there perished some 300 of the clergy, and the example of the capital was followed in many parts of the provinces. The completion of the work of demolition, ecclesiastical and civil, was left to the Convention (1792–95). The monarchy was abolished, the Republic proclaimed (September 21), and Lewis XVI was sent to the scaffold (January 21, 1793). The law of celibacy, which had already been largely transgressed, was annulled in the autumn, 1793, the Christian method of reckoning time and the Sundays were replaced by the Republican calendar and the Decadis, and finally Christ anity itself was laid aside, atheism being proclaimed amidst outrageous ceremonials. Gobel, archbishop of Paris, and others of the constitutional clergy, timidly laid down their charges and professed the worship of ' freedom and equality,' and a girl from the opera was enthroned as ' goddess of reason ' on the altar of the country in the cathedral of Notre Dame.

The supremacy of utter atheism did not, however, last long. The power of the Hébertists and Dantonists, representing the extreme wing of the Convention, was broken early the next year, and on the motion of Robespierre, who at least held that belief in Providence was the basis of virtue and probity, a decree was passed acknowledging a Supreme Being and the immortality of the soul, and introducing a new worship comprising thirty-nine feasts, inclusive of the thirty-six decadis of the Republican calendar. On Robespierre's fall the ardour of the Republicans was still further moderated. In 1795 Christian worship again received toleration; at first it was only to take place at private dwellings, but, soon after, all the churches which had been in the possession of the parishes on the first day of the second year of the Republic (September 22, 1793), and which had not yet been alienated, were restored to their owners. The non-juring clergy also received permission to hold services, provided they submitted to the Republic and its laws, of which the civil constitution now no longer formed a part. Those who refused remained objects of the old-standing hatred. Under these circumstances, even under the Directory (1795–99), the clergy had much to suffer; there were some executions, and after a momentary lull in the persecution, hundreds were transported to Guiana and to the islands of Ré and Oléron (1797). The anti-Christian spirit also made itself felt in other directions. The Deistic sect of the ' Théophilanthropes,' [1] a creation of the age, was for a time in high favour with the government, chiefly because it was thought that it would rival the Church. The constantly renewed attempts of the government, to enforce its calendar with the national feasts, were so many covert attacks on the Christian worship and the observance of the Sunday, nor were they to cease entirely until the establishment of the Consulate.

For the Holy See the loss of its French possessions was not the only result of the Revolution. On the conquest of Lombardy by general Napoleon Bonaparte (1796), the Papal States in Italy were also attacked, and at the peace of Tolentino (February 19, 1797) the Pope was compelled to cede to France not only Avignon and Venaissin, but also the legations of Ferrara, Bologna, and Ravenna. In 1798 the death of general Duphot, in a tumult at Rome late in the previous year, was seized as a pretext for proclaiming a Republic at the Eternal City itself, and Pius VI was brought as a prisoner, by way of Siena and the Certosa or Charterhouse near Florence, to Valence where he died in 1799.

The Republican Era began September 22, 1792, the first day of the Republic. The Republican year also commenced that

[1] A. MATHIEZ, *La théophilanthropie et le culte décadaire* (1796–1801), 1904.

same day, the autumnal equinox, and was divided into twelve months each of thirty days, and thirty-six weeks each of ten days, known as Decadis, and five (in leap years, six) supplementary days. The formal revocation of the new calendar took place in 1805. The Christian Sunday had, however, been already recognised in 1802, when, as a result of the Concordat entered into with the Holy See, it was again made a day of rest for the official classes.

§ 199

Pius VII and Napoleon I [1]

When the cardinals met in conclave at Venice, the French had already been driven out of Italy, hence the new Pope, **Pius VII** (1800–23), formerly cardinal Chiaramonti, bishop of Imola, was able to take up his residence at Rome. His primary concern was to be the French. By the battle of Marengo (1800) they had begun their re-conquest of Higher Italy, and their victorious leader, **Napoleon Bonaparte,** who since 1799 had been First Consul, was already evolving a plan by which the French Church should be reconciled with Rome. In the summer, 1801, the plan took shape and form in a Concordat. It was settled that the Church should be re-organised (under ten metropolitans and fifty bishops), that the First Consul should have the right of nominating to the Sees, the Pope that of canonically instituting the bishops, &c. The negotiations, to further which Consalvi the cardinal secretary of State had betaken himself to Paris, were not easy, but still greater were the difficulties due to Napoleon's arbitrariness, which were encountered in putting the compact into execution. In spite of the promise which had been given of not nominating to the new sees any of the episcopate who had taken the civil oath, no less than ten were actually proposed for canonical

[1] ARTAUD, *Hist. du pape Pie VII*, 2 vol. 2nd ed. 1837 ; *Mémoires du card. Consalvi*, ed. CRÉTINEAU-JOLY, 1864 ; RANCE-BOURREY, 1896 ; DUERM, *Le conclave de Venise*, 1896 ; D'HAUSSONVILLE, *L'église romaine et l'empire*, 5 vol. 3rd ed. 1870 ; BOULAY DE LA MEURTHE, *Documents sur la négociation du Concordat, &c.* 1800–1, 6 vol. 1891–1905 ; SÉCHÉ, *Les Origines du Concordat*, 2 vol. 1894 ; P. J. RINIERI, *La diplomazia pontificia nel secolo XIX. Il concordato tra Pio VII e il primo console*, 1902 ; *Napoleone e Pio VII* (1804–13), 1906 ; MATHIEU, *Le Concordat de 1801*, 1903 ; H. WELSCHINGER, *Le pape et l'empereur* (1804–15), 1905 ; RICARD, *Le concile national de 1811*, 1894 ; *MICE.* 1898, pp. 92–156 (on Napoleon's second marriage) ; *Historical Memoirs of Cardinal Pacca*, 2 vol. 1850.

institution ; nor was this all.   The Concordat was published (1802) only after the addition of the so-called Organic Articles,[1] which are in several respects at variance with the Concordat itself, besides being opposed to the principles of the Holy See. By these Articles the Pope's decrees and those of foreign Councils were to be subject to the Placet of the State, synods and similar assemblies were forbidden save by express permission of the government, the *Recursus ab abusu* was allowed, the Gallican Articles of 1682 were enforced as the common teaching, a distinction was made between parish priests, *i.e.* head priests serving a cantonal or greater parish, and ' des-servants,' serving supplementary parishes, the latter—who numbered about 20,000 against only 3,500 of the former category—were not only assigned a smaller income, but informed that they might be removed at will (*i.e.* without any canonical reason).   The Pope was therefore compelled to protest, especially as the Articles had been so published as to create the impression that they had been approved by the Holy See.   The tyrant's ambitions were, however, soon to lead to yet graver issues.

Napoleon, on being elected emperor of the French (1804), invited Pius to attend at Paris for the coronation, and so strongly was the invitation urged that, after much hesitation, it was accepted by the Pope.   He hoped for some return for his own services, and even ventured to formulate his desires, though without going so far as to ask for the evacuation of the provinces of the Papal States which had been occupied by the French.   The Pope had, however, reckoned without his host. The new emperor, though willing enough to receive, was not disposed to give.   In the event he made new demands, and as some of them were quite incapable of fulfilment, it came to a new rupture.

Pius VII had scarcely reached Rome before he received an application for the dissolution of the marriage which Jerome Bonaparte had contracted at Baltimore with Miss Patterson (1803).   The emperor's next step was to seize Ancona in violation of all law, the Pope being rudely given to understand that in future he was to consider the emperor's foes as his own, particularly the Russians, English, and Swedes, was to expel

---

[1] E. Münch, *Sammlung aller Konkordate*, 2 vol. 1830–31.

them from his States, and close his harbours to their shipping. When Joseph Bonaparte took possession of the throne of Naples, and Pius, on being informed of the fact, ventured to remind him of the right of suzerainty which the Apostolic See had exercised from time immemorial over the kingdom of the Two Sicilies, he was threatened with the loss of his own sovereignty (1806). On Candlemas Day, 1808, the French actually made their entry into Rome; two months later several of the papal provinces, and in 1809 the whole of the States of the Church were brought under France, or rather annexed to the new kingdom of Italy. The Pope, after having retorted by a decree of excommunication, was carried off a prisoner to Savona; cardinal Pacca, his secretary of State, was shut up in the fortress of Fenestrelle in Piedmont; and the remaining cardinals, excepting those who were too old or feeble to travel, were brought to Paris. When the emperor had secured a dissolution of his marriage with Josephine Tascher, the widow of the marquis of Beauharnais, and thirteen cardinals refused to attend his new marriage with the archduchess Maria Louisa, urging that the divorce had been granted, not by the Pope, who alone has the right of settling questions of royal marriages, but only by a judgment of the French Church, they were declared to have forfeited their positions, and were banished in twos to various French towns (1810). Pius, too, had yet more misfortunes to experience. Owing to the absence of his counsellors, he refused to ratify the election of the bishops presented to him, and, to punish him, his intercourse with the outer world was further curtailed, the pension assigned him for his support was reduced to a sum altogether insufficient, and in other ways also he was made to feel the weight of the imperial displeasure.

As the number of widowed sees was growing ever larger owing to the continuance of the conflict, Napoleon determined to fill the vacancies independently of the Holy See, and to this end summoned a national Council to meet at Paris (1811). This assembly, after having first declared itself incompetent to take any action, at last yielded to the pressure brought to bear on it by the monarch, and in a supplementary session decided that the metropolitans should have the right of confirming the candidates should the Pope not have given them canonical institution within six months. Through his ignorance of the real state of affairs the Pope himself actually gave his consent to the decision. At Fontainebleau, whither he was brought in the summer, 1812, during the Russian campaign, it was proposed to wring new concessions from him, Napoleon personally entering into negotiations with him in 1813. According to the preliminaries of a new Concordat which were then discussed, the Pope was to receive a yearly income of 2,000,000 francs, and take up his residence in France or in the kingdom of Italy ; the emperor was to have the right of nominating to all the bishoprics of both countries, the Pope retaining the full rights of nomination only in the case of the six suburban bishoprics and ten others. The emperor furthermore demanded approval of the four Gallican Articles, the appointment of Paris to be the seat of the Apostolic See, the nomination of two-thirds of the cardinals by the Christian princes, and that the ' black ' cardinals should be severely reprimanded for their conduct at his wedding. To these latter demands the Pope, however, steadfastly refused to submit, and even the other reforms decided on were never to be carried into effect. Whilst Napoleon, in order to ratify in all haste the concessions he had succeeded in wringing from the pontiff, ordered a solemn *Te Deum* to be sung in all the churches in thanksgiving for the peace, at the same time notifying the Senate of the Articles which had been agreed upon, Pius was already regretting at leisure the renouncement of the Papal States which was implicitly contained in the extension of the right of nomination which he had granted the emperor. As, moreover, the majority of the cardinals who now surrounded him were opposed to the whole measure, he formally revoked his consent. In notifying his decision he, however, requested the opening anew of the negotiations. As in that same year Napoleon's power was broken, the Pope demanded that, before all else, he should be restored to freedom. His request was finally granted in the spring, 1814, the Pope having already shortly before been brought back to Savona. Negotiations were, however, never to be again opened with the emperor, for, whilst Pius was on his way to Rome, Napoleon had already signed his abdication at Fontainebleau. After having again seized the reins of government in 1815, he was, after the lapse of only a few months, again overthrown, and this time for ever.

The so-called 'Little Church,' a sect with a small following in the diocese of Lyons and in that of Poitiers, originated through the refusal of a certain number of the Faithful to accept the Concordat of 1801. In thus refusing, they were following the example set by a portion of the episcopate. Cp. *Internat. theol. Z.* 1905, pp. 121–24.

§ 200

Secularisation and Reorganisation of the Church in Germany [1]

In Germany, which then consisted of well-nigh 300 states, the Revolution produced political and ecclesiastical changes scarcely less decisive than those in France. The decree of the French National Assembly (August 4, 1789) having made an end of the feudal rights, not only of the French landed proprietors, but also of those of the many German princes who possessed property in Alsace and Lorraine, a conflict between the two nations was opened. The antipathy shown by the German powers for the Revolution adding to the misunderstanding, there broke out in 1792 a regular war, the cost of which was to be borne mainly by the German Church. After preliminary discussions at the peace of Basel between Prussia and France (1795), and at the peace of Campo Formio (1797) between France and the German emperor, the whole left bank of the Rhine, by the peace of Lunéville (1801), was definitively ceded to France on the understanding (Art. VII) that the hereditary princes, whose provinces were confiscated, should receive compensation out of the imperial lands. In the event, however, the decision was carried out in a spirit contrary to the tenor of the article in question. By decree of the Imperial Deputation meeting at Ratisbon in 1803 (35), ' all properties belonging to pious foundations, abbeys, and monasteries were

---

[1] H. Brück, *Gesch. der kath. Kirche im* 19 *Jahrh.* 4 vol. 2nd ed. 1901 ff. ; O. Mejer, *Zur Gesch. d. römisch-deutschen Frage*, 3 vol. 2nd ed. 1885 ; L. König, *Die Säkularisation und das Reichskonkordat*, 1904 ; J. Rinieri, *Il congresso di Vienna e la S. Sede* (1813–15), 1904 ; *Civiltà cattolica*, 1905 ; G. Goyau, *L'Allemagne religieuse ; Le Catholicisme* (1800–48), 2 vol. 1905. The Bulls and decrees spoken of in this and following section will be found in Münch (cp. § 199) ; Phillips, *KR.* vol. III. ; Walter, *Fontes iuris eccles.* 1862 ; Nussi, *Conventiones*, 1870 ; Ph. Schneider, *Die partik. Kirchenrechtsquellen in Deutschland u. Österreich*, 1898.

placed at the free disposal of their respective princes, for them to use either for maintenance of public worship, for the support of educational or other establishments of public utility, or for the relief of their finances.' [1]   A result of this measure was that all the spiritual principalities were abolished, with the exception of two which, on personal grounds, were allowed to survive, though they, too, were overtaken by the fate of the others a few years later; the two in question were the territories belonging to the Teutonic knights, the grand master being at the time the archduke Anton Victor, and the diocese of Ratisbon, which was erected into an archdiocese and bestowed on the arch-chancellor Dalberg in compensation for the archbishopric of Mainz (1805).   The domains of the bishops and the properties of the chapters and monasteries were everywhere seized, save only in Austria, where the emperor Francis II refused to take advantage of the right conferred by the Imperial Deputation, and contented himself with uniting to his hereditary domains properties possessed by the mediatised archbishoprics of Trent and Brixen.   The loss to the Church on both sides of the Rhine has been reckoned as amounting to 1719 square (German) miles, with 3,162,576 inhabitants, and a revenue (exclusive of that of the monasteries) of 21,026,000 florins.[2]   On the other hand, the princes undertook to provide for the support of the injured parties and for the ecclesiastical needs of their states.

Now that the Church throughout Germany had lost all her possessions, save those belonging to the parishes and lower offices, now, too, that vast changes had occurred in the territorial division of the country, a reorganisation of the Church had become a pressing need.   Bavaria, which under Maximilian Joseph (1799–1825) and the minister Montgelas had forsaken mediæval methods of government and adopted the constitution of a modern state, was the first, soon after the peace of Lunéville, to open negotiations in view of a Concordat. Rome preferred, however, to await overtures from the Empire rather than enter into agreements with the separate states. On the downfall of the German Empire in 1806, Napoleon,

---

[1] WALTER, *Fontes*, pp. 138–86.
[2] KLÜBER, *Übersicht der diplom. Verhandlungen des Wiener Kongresses*, 1816, p. 404.

moreover, conceived the idea of obtaining a Concordat for the whole Confederation of the Rhine. Under these circumstances neither Bavaria nor Württemberg, which, in 1807, had likewise opened negotiations with Rome, were able to secure what they desired. In the event neither Rome's project nor the French emperor's was to be realised, the Pope's captivity bringing the proceedings to a lengthy standstill. As new territorial changes were, moreover, constantly being made, for instance, by the peace of Pressburg (1806) and the peace of Vienna (1809), the time was not yet come for a definitive arrangement.

At the **Congress of Vienna** (1814–15), at which finally the political relations of Europe were settled anew, the re-establishment of the previous state of things, so far as church property was concerned, was advocated by cardinal Consalvi and the representatives of the former ecclesiastical princes. Their efforts were, however, in vain owing to the lands being already in the possession of others. Another motion which failed to find approval was that of Dalberg, or rather of his representative, the vicar-general of Constance, baron von Wessenberg, that a Concordat should be entered into for the whole of Germany. The only decision of the Congress touching religious matters was contained in Article XVI of the Act of Alliance, by which the civil equality, which had already been secured by several of the German States either through the free-will of their princes, or the pressure of Napoleon, was given to all religious denominations throughout the German confederation.

This being so, it only remained for each State to regulate its own church matters. **Bavaria** [1] was the first to come to an arrangement with Rome. The Concordat of 1817 ensured to the Catholic Church throughout the kingdom the retention of all the rights and prerogatives founded on its Divine constitution and on Canon Law (Art. I). The country was divided into two church provinces, Augsburg, Ratisbon, and Passau being assigned as suffragan sees to the archbishopric of Munich-Freising, and those of Würzburg, Eichstätt, and Spires to that of Bamberg (Art. II). The king, Max Joseph I, and his Catholic successors were to have the right of nominating the bishops, and the Holy See that of conferring canonical institution (Art. IX),

---

[1] H. von Sicherer, *Staat u. K. in Bayern*, 1799–1821, 1874.

the bishops being granted freedom in the government of their dioceses so far as spiritualities were concerned (Art. XII). The agreement was published in the form of an appendix to the religious Edict of 1818, which supplemented the constitution of the kingdom, this plan being adopted, both to safeguard the sovereignty of the State and to spare the susceptibilities of the Protestants, who fancied that their rights were endangered by Article I. The matter was, however, not yet over. As the Edict, conformably with the new condition of things, but contrary to the demands of Canon Law, granted general freedom of conscience (1), political and civil equality to the three chief Christian denominations of the country (24), besides asking of them that they should treat each other with mutual consideration (80), &c., great discontent was excited at Rome, whilst in Bavaria many of the clergy refused to take unconditionally the constitutional oath. In process of time the Apostolic See decided not indeed to approve, but at least to tolerate the measures adopted, and peace was finally restored to the country by the royal declaration made at Tegernsee (1821) ; that the constitution was not intended to do violence to the conscience of anyone, that the constitutional oath concerned only civil matters, and that the Concordat was part of the law of the State and was accordingly to be considered and executed as such.

With **Prussia,** which through the conquest of Silesia and the division of Poland had already some time before gained several Catholic provinces to the East, and which had since through the new treaties increased its Catholic population to the West also, negotiations were opened by Pius VII. The result was a convention between the Pope and Frederick William III, which was published by the Bull *De salute animarum* (1821). It sanctioned the establishment of the church provinces of Cologne, with the bishoprics of Treves, Münster, and Paderborn, and of Gnesen-Posen, with that of Kulm, as well as the two exempt bishoprics of Breslau and Ermeland. The election of the bishops was to devolve on the cathedral chapters, the latter being warned in the Brief *Quod de fidelium* to elect only such as were pleasing to the king.

In the kingdom of Hanover, afterwards to be incorporated (1866) with Prussia, the Bull *Impensa Romanorum* (1824) re-established the old bishoprics of Hildesheim and Osnabrück and declared them exempt. The crown also obtained the so-called Irish veto, *i.e.* the right of removing from the list of candidates any persons obnoxious to the government, provided always that a sufficient number of candidates was left to render a choice possible.

The Catholics of south-western Germany, *i.e.* of Württemberg, Baden, and Hessen-Darmstadt, as well as of the former States of Hesse, Nassau, Hohenzollern-Sigmaringen, Hechingen, and Frankfort, were constituted by the Bull of circumscription, *Provida solersque* (1821), into the church province of the Upper Rhine,[1] having its metropolis at Freiburg, with bishoprics at Mainz, Rottenburg, Fulda and Limburg. The condition of the Church in these regions was further regulated by the Bull *Ad dominici gregis custodiam* of 1827 and a Brief *Re sacra* published at the same time. The latter gives the canons the same instructions as those conveyed to the Prussians by the Brief *Quod de fidelium*, whilst the Bull itself grants the governments the Irish veto.

Catholics dwelling in the other states were either placed under the administration of neighbouring dioceses, or under the jurisdiction of Vicars-Apostolic. The grand-duchy of Oldenburg, for instance, was placed, in 1831, under the bishop of Münster, though a special vicariate was established at Vechta. A Vicariate-Apostolic was established for the kingdom of Saxony in 1816. Upper Lusatia was governed by the dean of Bautzen, a dependency of Prague. Subsequently to 1830 it became the rule to nominate to this position the Vicar-Apostolic of Dresden, the ecclesiastical control of the whole of the country thus coming into the hand of one person.

§ 201

Church Matters in Germany and Austria-Hungary, 1830-70 [2]

The arrangements detailed in the previous section by no means served to settle church matters in Germany to the satisfaction of all concerned. In the province of the Upper

---

[1] J. Longner, *Beiträge zur Gesch. d. Oberrhein. Kirchenprovinz*, 1863; Brück, *Die Oberrhein. Kirchenprov.* 1868.

[2] Brück, *Gesch. d. k. K. im* 19 *J.* § 200; H. Maas, *Gesch. d. k. K. im Grossherzogtum Baden*, 1891; Pfülf, *Kardinal von Geissel*, 2 vol. 1895-96; *Bischof v. Ketteler*, 1899; Golther, *Der Staat u. d. k. K. in Württemberg*, 1874; H. A. Krose, *Konfessionsstatistik Deutschlands . . . im 19 Jahrh.* 1904.

Rhine, the states were bent on governing the Church themselves instead of allowing it to be governed by its lawful superiors, and, even in opening negotiations with Rome, their aim was not so much to come to real understanding as to hoodwink the Holy See. They accordingly refused to ratify the last two (V–VI) Articles of the Bull *Ad dominici gregis custodiam*—which dealt with the training of the clergy according to the prescriptions of the Council of Trent, with freedom of intercourse with Rome, and episcopal jurisdiction *iuxta canones nunc vigentes et praesentem ecclesiae disciplinam*—and in 1830 they published a decree in thirty-nine Articles, much of which was at variance with the Bull. Among other things it was enacted that all ecclesiastical ordinances, even those dealing with matters which concerned the Church only, were to be subject to the Placet of the State, and that the presentation to livings, whether the sees were vacant or occupied, was to devolve on the sovereigns as a part of their right of majesty. Proceedings such as these could not be allowed to pass unchallenged, and the Holy See accordingly rejected the thirty-nine Articles by the Brief *Pervenerat* (1830). From time to time, in Parliament and elsewhere, zealous Catholics raised their voices in protest against the state of subjection in which the Church was kept, though with very little result. The governments were all the less disposed to change their methods, seeing that a large portion of the clergy were on their side, and that most of the bishops were apathetic. Only in the electorate of Hesse, where both bishop and cathedral chapter assumed a more energetic attitude, was some account made of the Church's claims.

Especially disagreeable to the Church were the encroachments of the State in the matter of mixed marriages, which was soon to excite a great conflict in Prussia. According to the declaration of 1803 ' legitimate children were to be invariably brought up in the religion of the father,' and neither party was ' to oblige the other to depart from this enactment as by law established.' The law was first enforced in the eastern provinces, and mixed marriages were accordingly celebrated there unconditionally. When, however, the decree was extended to the western provinces (1825), it encountered great opposition. The clergy in the Rhinelands and Westphalia refused to bless mixed marriages except on the condition that the children were brought up in the Catholic Faith, and their conduct found approval at Rome. The Brief *Litteris altero abhinc* (1830) gave the decision that, in mixed marriages where the parties refused to educate their offspring in the Catholic Faith, the priest could only assist passively, *i.e.* was in other words to refuse the nuptial blessing. Even so, the Prussian government refused to withdraw its decree, and as the bishops were disposed to yield, it seemed for a time that the government would have its own way. Count Spiegel, archbishop of Cologne, was persuaded by von Bunsen, the Prussian minister at Rome, to issue a Convention (1834), which, while purporting to explain the Brief, really twisted it into an approval of the practice which had been condemned ; and this Convention received the approbation of his suffragans also. A change was not, however, long in coming. Spiegel's successor, archbishop Clement Augustus von Droste-Vischering (1835–45), took the Brief for his line of conduct, and the constancy with which, in spite of all cajolements and threats, he refused to execute the Convention and continued to manifest when he was accused of treason (1837) and carried off to the fortress of Minden, did much to put heart into the Catholics. Not only did the suffragans recall their subscriptions to the Convention, but even the bishops of the eastern provinces pronounced in favour of the Brief. The only exception was the prince-bishop of Breslau, count Sedlnitzky, who was, however, soon compelled to resign (1840) and afterwards became a convert to Protestantism (1863). Among other bishops who had to suffer persecution was the archbishop of Gnesen-Posen, Martin von Dunin, who was also condemned to imprisonment at a fortress. The government soon proved more amenable. Frederick William III himself gave way to some extent. The clergy were permitted to make private inquiries beforehand regarding the education proposed for the children, and the decision as to the wedding was to be reserved to the judgment of the bishop. His son and successor, Frederick William IV (1840–61), being a more religious-minded man than his father, and being animated by kindlier feelings towards Catholicism, went still further on the path of conciliation. He not only withdrew the decrees which grieved the

consciences of his Catholic subjects, but he restored one of
the banished archbishops to his fold, and appointed Clement
Augustus († 1845) a coadjutor, with right of succession in the
person of John Geissel, bishop of Spires. Justice was also
done to the Church in other respects. Episcopal intercourse
with Rome, which up to then had always taken place through
the intermediate of the State, was now set free of this restraint
(1841), and to advise the government in church matters a
Catholic as well as a Protestant department was created at
the ministry of public worship. Finally, by the constitution
of 1848 (1850) independence of government was assured to
both Catholic and Evangelical Churches (§ 15).

Whilst in Prussia matters were already mending, in central
and southern Germany they continued as they were, the
marriage question causing trouble here also. The motion
which was brought in at the Württemberg house of representatives by Keller, bishop of Rottenburg (1841), and which
demanded for the Church the exercise of that autonomy
which had been granted by the constitution, was of little avail.
Measures of a more energetic character were required to free
the Church from the thraldom of the State. So far the bishops
had fought their cause singly, now they determined on united
action, the determination coinciding with the revolutionary
year of 1848. In the autumn of that year the whole German
episcopate met in conference at Würzburg, under the presidency of archbishop Geissel of Cologne. Soon after (1850)
the bishops of the province of the Upper Rhine assembled at
Freiburg, and drew up a memorandum to the governments in
which was asserted, among other things, the right of the bishops
to educate and appoint their clergy, to take their own disciplinary measures, to erect schools, to control the conduct of
their flocks, and to administer the belongings of the Church
(1851). As the reply of the governments was considered
unsatisfactory, a new meeting was held at Freiburg and a new
memorandum presented (1853). At the same time the bishops
began to take the law into their own hands and to make use
in practice of the rights withheld from them. As the governments were, however, in no mood to make concessions, the
bishops' action only sharpened the conflict. The archbishop
of Freiburg was placed under police supervision, and finally

imprisoned.   At the same time the protests of the Catholics had made some impression on the governments, and soon after they consented to come to terms.   Württemberg and Baden concluded Conventions with Rome in 1857 and 1859 respectively, whilst in 1854 Hessen-Darmstadt, and in 1861 Nassau made their arrangements directly with the bishops of Mainz and Limburg.   The two Conventions were, however, rejected by the Estates, and the matter had ultimately to be decided by ministerial decree,[1] though with very different results in either country.   In Württemberg so great was the success of the new measure (1862) that the country has enjoyed religious peace ever since.   In Baden, on the other hand, new conflicts broke out.   The death of H. von Vicari (1868), archbishop of Freiburg, was even followed by an interregnum of fourteen years.   In Hesse the Convention was so violently opposed that it was voluntarily withdrawn by W. E. von Ketteler, bishop of Mainz (1866).

Bavaria had at first followed the bad example set by her neighbours, and, contrary to the Concordat of 1817, had greatly interfered with the government of the Church. Ludwig I (1825–48) [2] showed, however, greater friendliness. He allowed the bishops free access to Rome (1841), erected a few monasteries, and manifested his religious dispositions and his love of art in a series of ecclesiastical buildings, some of them restorations and others entirely new.   After his abdication the episcopate appealed on two occasions to his son Maximilian II (1848–64), and some, though not all, of its demands were ultimately accorded.[3]

In Austria [4] the fetters which had been fixed on the Church in the eighteenth century were, in the main, burst only in 1848. A few of the Josephite enactments had, however, been withdrawn previously, Leopold II (1790–92), for instance, having again established diocesan seminaries instead of the hated central seminaries.   In 1850 the Placet was abolished by the emperor Francis Joseph, the bishops also receiving freedom

---

[1] Brück, *Oberrhein. Kirchenprov.* p. 561 ff.

[2] Mg. by Sepp, 1869 ; 2nd ed. 1903 ; Heigel, 1872.

[3] *Systematische Zusammenstellung des Verhandlungen des bayrischen Episkopats mit der k. b. Staatsregierung von 1850 bis 1889 über den Vollzug des Konkordats*, Freiburg, 1905.

[4] J. Beidtel, *Unters. über die kirchl. Zustände in den k. österreichischen Staaten*, 1849.

of intercourse with Rome, and the acknowledgment of their right to control discipline and to regulate the public worship. On the other hand, the Concordat entered into with Rome, in 1855, was not of long duration. After it had been to some extent damaged by legislation in 1868, it was, on account of the Vatican decrees (1870), formally revoked and replaced by a special law governing the external relations of Church and State (May 7, 1874).[1]

The population of the German Empire in 1900 (December 1) was 56,367,178 ; of these 35,231,104 were Evangelicals, 20,321,441 Roman Catholics, and 586,833 were Jews. Cp. *Statistik des Deutschen Reiches*, vol. 150 (1903), p. 105. Austria, in 1900, on a total population of 26½ millions, had 20,661,000 Latin Catholics, 3,134,000 Uniate Greeks, 607,000 non-Uniates, 494,000 Protestants, 1,225,000 Jews. In Hungary, in 1902, the population of 19½ millions was divided into 10,179,035 Latin Catholics, 1,893,410 Uniates, 2,863,095 non-Uniates, 3,796,881 Protestants, 69,499 Unitarians, 875,431 Jews, &c. Cp. O. HÜBNER, *Geogr. Tabellen*, 1904, pp. 33–36.

§ 202

The Church in Switzerland [2]

The French Revolution was not without consequences in Switzerland. The temporary annexation of Geneva to France led to the restoration of Catholic worship in Calvin's own city after an interruption of more than two centuries and a half. By the congress of Vienna the same city was granted some twenty Catholic rural parishes, with the result that the Catholic population of the canton was notably increased. The changes occurring in Germany also had an effect on Switzerland. The Swiss portion of the diocese of Constance was detached (1814) from the German, that it might escape the reforms of the vicar-general von Wessenberg, and the separation was soon consummated by the abolition of the bishopric

---

[1] On the present relations between State and Church in Austria-Hungary, see VERING, *KR.* 2nd ed. pp. 106–56.

[2] RHEINWALD, *Acta hist. eccl. saec. XIX* (1835–37) ; *Kath. Schweizer Blätter*, 1885, p. 27 ff. ; ROLFUS-SICKINGER, *Kirchengeschichtliches in chronologischer Reihenfolge*, 3 vol. 1877–82 ; WOESTE, *Hist. du Culturkampf en Suisse*, 1887 ; PERI, *La questione diocesana Ticenese*, 1892 ; A. BÜCHI, *Die kath. Kirche in der Schweiz*, 1902.

itself. The Swiss portion of the territory was first placed under a Vicar-Apostolic and, later on, was divided between the sees of Chur (1823), Basel-Solothurn, and the newly erected diocese of St. Gall (1845). According to the new arrangement (1828), the diocese of Basel was to comprise the cantons of Basel, Bern, Solothurn, Lucern, Zug, Aargau, and Thurgau.

Though, to begin with, the Church enjoyed peace, this state of things did not last long. In the canton of Aargau (1841) she lost all her religious houses with the exception of three convents of women, which were re-established owing to the displeasure of the people at the arbitrary measure. No sooner had Lucern (1844) allowed the Jesuits to establish a settlement in the canton than it was invaded by a Free Corps, and, on the Catholic cantons forming a defensive alliance, there broke out the Sonderbund war in which the Catholics were utterly defeated (1847). Marilley, bishop of Lausanne, having ventured to protest against the laws of the cantons which formed his diocese, was banished for nearly eight years (1848). The Vatican Council furnished an occasion for new persecutions, particularly at Geneva and in the diocese of Basel. When the former canton was separated from the diocese of Lausanne and erected into a Vicariate-Apostolic (1873), bishop Mermillod, the occupant of the new see, was forthwith driven into exile, and the Catholic churches were handed over to the Old Catholics. For having threatened censure to those of his clergy who refused to subscribe to the Vatican doctrine, bishop Lachat of Basel was, that same year, deposed by all the cantons belonging to his jurisdiction, with the exception of Lucern and Zug, and banished from Solothurn, his chapter being likewise dissolved the next year. The same fate befell all the clergy who stood by their bishop. The measures taken in the Catholic Jura were particularly far-reaching. All the churches were assigned by the Bernese government to the Old Catholics, and the clergy were not only deprived of their offices, but also banished. Three years later the decree of expulsion was indeed revoked (1876), but, even so, Catholic worship could only be performed in barns and under great disadvantages. Only some years later did the government consent to restore the churches, and then only by degrees. The reinstatement of the bishop of Basel followed in the autumn, 1884. In this case the conclusion of peace was facilitated by what had taken place in the canton of Ticino. The latter had been severed from the dioceses of Milan and Como, assigned to Basel, and constituted as an Apostolic Administratorship, the first administrator being bishop Lachat himself. At his death (1888) the collegiate church of St. Lawrence at Lugano was created the cathedral. Geneva, as soon as a vacancy occurred (1883), was re-united to Lausanne. As, however, Mermillod was appointed to the united sees, the government maintained its attitude of hostility. His successor ultimately received official recognition (1891).

The population of Switzerland in 1900 comprised 1,918,197 Protestants, 1,383,135 Catholics, 12,551 Jews, and 13,453 of various denominations.

§ 203

The Church in France after the Fall of Napoleon I [1]

As soon as the Bourbons had again settled themselves on the French throne, new overtures were made to the Holy See. The fruit of the negotiations was the Concordat of 1817, by which that of 1801 was abrogated, and that of 1516 renewed. The new Concordat was, however, rejected by the French Parliament, and withdrawn by Lewis XVIII (1814–24), the consequence being that Napoleon's settlement continued to be observed. Certain changes were, however, made. The number of dioceses was increased to eighty, among which there were fourteen archdioceses (1822), two other archdioceses, that of Cambrai (1842) and that of Rennes (1859), being of later creation. The stipends of the clergy were also raised, some religious Orders were recognised by law, and yet others on settling in the country were granted toleration.

---

[1] NETTEMENT, *Hist. de la Restauration*, 8 vol. 1860–72 ; THUREAU-DANGIN, *L'église et l'état sous la monarchie de Juillet*, 1880 ; *Hist. de la monarchie de Juillet*, 7 vol. 1884–92 ; P. DE LA GORCE, *Hist. du second Empire*, 1894–1901 ; ZEVORT, *Hist. de la troisième République*, 4 vol. 1896–1901 ; A. DEBIDOUR, *L'église cath. et l'état sous la troisième République*, I, 1906 ; BAUNARD, *Un siècle de l'église de France* (1800–1900), 1901 ; BOURGAIN, *L'église de France et l'état au XIXᵉ siècle*, 2 vol. 1901 ; LECANUET, *Montalembert*, 3 vol. 2nd ed. 1902.

The Restoration did not succeed in restoring to the country a settled government. The next two sovereigns, Charles X (1824–30), brother of Lewis, and the citizen-king, Louis - Philippe of Orleans (1830–48), were displaced by revolutions. The Republic which followed the last king's fall (1848–52) ended in the empire of Napoleon III (1852–70), and the latter's overthrow, after the unsuccessful Franco-German war, was in turn followed by the proclamation of the third and last Republic.

Changes so frequent point to deep-seated political differences. In religious matters, likewise, the nation had been divided ever since the Revolution. Belief and unbelief existed side by side, and as, in spite of all that was done to check it, unbelief, mainly owing to the State's monopoly of education, was steadily gaining ground, the Catholics, more particularly Montalembert and Falloux, resolved to secure freedom of education. In this they were, broadly speaking, successful. Liberty to establish elementary schools was granted in 1833, a like concession being made for secondary schools in 1850; finally, the present Republic made it possible to establish Catholic academies, from which, however, it soon withdrew the right of styling themselves Universities, and of conferring degrees (1879). All these concessions, obtained at the cost of so much toil, were to be finally lost. To the Radicals the Christian schools were a rock of scandal, and the aversion to the Republic shown by many of the Catholics, and especially by the religious Orders who controlled so many of the schools, helped not a little to bring about the consummation. In 1880 the schools of the Jesuits were closed and their settlements dissolved. At the same time a like fate was threatened all other unauthorised congregations, should they not within three months seek recognition of the State and the ratification of their statutes. This decree, which resulted in many establishments being dissolved, was extended by the law of July 1, 1903, so as to involve the closing of all secondary schools which had remained in the hands of unauthorised congregations. Finally, in 1904 it was enacted that all congregations, whether unauthorised or not, should lose their right of teaching, and that all teaching Orders and their schools should be abolished within ten years. In all this the aim of the legislator was to laicise education, and as far as possible to banish religion from society. In accordance with this plan, it was ordered that the crucifix, the sign of Christianity, should be removed from all courts of justice. For years the Radicals had been demanding the denunciation of the Concordat, and the separation of Church and State, and though the proposal was long refused by the government, besides being defeated in Parliament, it was ultimately to be adopted by the majority. The pretext was afforded by the attitude of the Roman Curia on the occasion of the visit of the president of the French Republic to the king of Italy, and also by the action taken by the same Curia against two French bishops. The government first recalled its minister at the Vatican (1904), and then presented a Bill for the abolition of the Concordat and the disestablishment of the churches, its proposals being, with a few slight modifications, accepted by the Lower House (341 votes against 233) and by the Senate (179 against 103).

The law of December 9, 1905, assures freedom of conscience and of worship; forbids the support of any form of worship by either State or public local authority (Art. 1–2); ordains the establishment within a year of ' associations of worship ' (18–22); assigns to these associations the administration of the church funds (4); attributes also to them, free of cost, all buildings used for public worship, episcopal residences, presbyteries, and seminaries belonging to the State, the departments, or to the local authorities (13, 14); assigns a pension to all the clergy at present holding office (11); theological students are to be obliged as formerly to merely one year of military service, on the condition, however, that before the age of twenty-six they have obtained a salaried position under an association of worship (39); the Concordat of 1801 and the Organic Articles are abrogated (44). A portion of the French Catholics were of opinion that it would be politic to submit to the law, and make their arrangements accordingly. Pius X condemned, however, as uncanonical, the proposed associations of worship, and left it to the bishops to choose their own organisation (August 10, 1906). Further developments are a secret of the future.

In 1830 the *Église catholique française* was founded by abbé Châtel. The sect was not a success, and in 1841 Châtel's church was closed by the government.

In 1901, in a total population of 38·9 millions, there were in France 36·1 millions who professed Catholicism, and 0·6 million Protestants.

§ 204

The Church in Italy, Spain, and Portugal [1]

I. The subjection of **Italy** by the French resulted in changes similar to those which had occurred in France. The dioceses were curtailed in number, and those of the monasteries which had not already been closed were suppressed in 1810. The Italian Republic, comprising Lombardy and the three northern legations of the Papal States, in 1803 were granted a Concordat similar to that of France. On the Corsican's fall and the reinstatement of the previous sovereigns, new arrangements had to be made. The kings of Sardinia and Naples concluded Conventions with the Holy See on behalf of their respective states (1817–18), and these agreements were soon followed by others. On the whole, perfect harmony prevailed between the Church and the various states. The year 1848 and the accession of Victor Emanuel († 1878) to the throne of Piedmont brought about a great change. The clergy were deprived of their exempted courts of justice ; tithes and the right of asylum were abolished (1850) ; a little later all religious Orders, save those concerned with the nursing of the sick or with education, were suppressed (1855). These measures were not, indeed, of any great importance, as similar laws had already long ago been adopted elsewhere. New violations of the Church's rights were, however, to follow. Victor Emanuel, on beginning in 1859 the subjection of the whole of Italy, not only extended the new laws to the newly won provinces, but, in order to replenish his treasury, which was being sadly depleted by the war, in 1866 confiscated the whole of the church property, the clergy being assigned stipends by the State. All the existing

---

[1] La Fuente, *Hist. ecles. de España*, 6 vol. 2nd ed. 1873–75 ; Brück, *Die geh. Gesellschaften in Spanien bis Ferdinand VII*, 1881 ; Fehr, *Gesch. d. 19 Jahrh*. I–IV.

monasteries disappeared with a few exceptions, though permission was not refused to erect new ones.   Finally, in 1870,
Rome became the capital of the new kingdom, and the
conflict between the papacy and the Italian kingdom, which
had been growing more and more acute since the first attack
on the Papal States, now reached its height (cp. § 208).

The census of February 10, 1901, showed that, in a population
of 32,475,298, there were 31,539,863 Catholics, 65,595 Protestants,
inclusive of the Waldensians, 35,617 Jews, 36,096 unbelievers,
and 795,276 whose religion was unknown.   Cp. P. M. BAUMGARTEN,
Kirchl. Statistik, 1904, p. 66.

II. After the five-year reign of Joseph Bonaparte
(1808–13), the throne of **Spain** came into the possession of
Ferdinand VII, who quashed the laws passed by his predecessor suppressing the Inquisition, the monasteries, &c.
The Spanish government, however, proved as unstable
as the French.   In 1820 a revolution of a character hostile
to the Church broke out.   The monasteries were again
largely abolished, church property was confiscated, and the
clergy who refused the constitutional oath of 1812 were
punished by imprisonment, banishment, and death.   On a
French army coming to the king's help in 1823, the acts of
the constitutional government were indeed again cancelled.
Ferdinand himself was, however, responsible for new trouble,
by contracting a third marriage with his niece, Maria Christina
of Naples (1829), and by abrogating the Salic Law and
reverting to the ancient Spanish rule of succession (1830).
After his death (1833), the three-year-old Isabella was
indeed proclaimed queen, but the Basque provinces and
Aragon were loyal to Don Carlos, and civil war was the
only result.   Under Isabella's reign there was a new persecution of the Church, the monasteries and church property
being the greatest sufferers.   All monasteries of men were
suppressed in 1837, only a few of the convents of women,
those, namely, belonging to charitable and teaching Orders,
were allowed to survive, and the number of bishops sank
finally to six (1841).   Only in 1843, when the regent Espartero
was compelled to hand the reins of government to duke
Narvaez of Valencia, did more cheerful days begin to dawn.

Espartero indeed returned to power (1854–56), and the persecution was renewed, but he was soon again forced into retirement. The reorganisation of the Church and its relations with the State were settled anew by Conventions with the Holy See in 1851 and 1859.

In 1901 the population of Spain amounted to 18,250,000, of whom about 50,000 were non-Catholics.

III. The recent history of **Portugal,** like that of its neighbour, has been one of many vicissitudes. The invasion of the French (1808) was followed by the flight of the royal family to Brazil. In 1822 Brazil dissolved its union with the mother country and became an empire under Dom Pedro. Finally, at home the royal succession was the subject of endless disputes after the death of Joao VI (1826), the majority of the people favouring the candidature of his second son Dom Miguel, whilst Dom Pedro claimed the Portuguese crown for his own daughter, Maria da Gloria, and ultimately succeeded in snatching it from his brother (1833). As for the Church, she had to undergo a violent persecution which, after lasting seven years, was mitigated in 1840.

The population in 1900 numbered 5,428,659, of whom about 500 were Protestants, and a few hundred Jews.

§ 205

The Church in the Netherlands, in Great Britain, and in Scandinavia [1]

I. On Holland being transformed by the French in 1795 into the Batavian Republic, freedom of worship was proclaimed. The rights which the Catholics thereby secured were ratified by the constitution of 1815, when Holland and Belgium had been already united by the Congress of Vienna into the United Kingdom of the Netherlands.[2] In spite of the fact that the Catholics were now legally on an equal

---

[1] GAMS, *Gesch. d. K. im* 19 *Jahrh.* III, 200–308.

[2] CH. TERLINDEN, *Guillaume I, roi des Pays-Bas, et l'église cath. en Belgique,* I (1814–26), 1906.

footing with the Protestants, whom they also outnumbered by three to two, they were systematically oppressed and neglected. The Convention concluded by the government with the Holy See in 1827 was of little avail, as it was never put into execution; and though some improvement occurred in 1827, a real reconciliation between races who differed not only in religion, but also in character and manners, was scarcely to be hoped for. The July Revolution at Paris (1830) was accordingly seized by the Belgians as a pretext for separating from Holland and forming themselves into a distinct kingdom.

The separation resulted in the removal of most of the old disabilities. As the constitution of 1831 granted freedom both of worship and of education, the Church of **Belgium** obtained complete independence of action. Free Catholic universities were established at Mechlin (1834) and Louvain (1835). These liberties have, however, been retained only at the cost of great energy, owing to the opposition of the freethinking Liberals.

In **Holland** the situation of the Catholics underwent an improvement on the accession of William II (1840–49). They again received a guarantee of religious freedom by the revised constitution of 1848, and in 1853 the hierarchy was re-established by Pius IX, with an archbishopric at Utrecht and four suffragan bishops.

The population of Belgium amounted in 1902 to 6,896,079. There were then about 20,000 Protestants and 4,000 Jews. Holland in the same year reckoned 5,347,182 inhabitants, of whom 1,790,000 were Catholic. O. Hübner, *Geogr. stat. Tab.* 1904.

II. The emancipatory movement which had spread abroad from France, and the dangers which threatened the kingdom, had been instrumental in obtaining some relief for the Catholics of **Great Britain,**[1] even before the

---

[1] Theiner, *Aktenstücke z. Gesch. d. Emanzipation der Kath. in England*, 1835; Amherst, *Hist. of Catholic Emancipation* (1771–1820), 2 vol. 1886; J. Blötzer, *Die Katholikenemanzipation in Grossbritannien und Irland*, 1905 (B. Ward, *The Dawn of the Catholic Revival in England*, 1781–1803, 1909); Lilly-Wallis, *Manual of the Law affecting Catholics*, 1893; W. Ward, *Life and times of Card. Wiseman*, 2 vol. 1897; *W. G. Ward and the Catholic Revival*, 1893; Purcell, *Life of Card. Manning*, 2 vol. 1895; Hemmer, *Vie du cardinal Manning*, 1898; other Biographies by Gasquet, 1895, A. W. Hutton, 1892, Pressensé, Engl. Trans. 1897; Thureau-Dangin, *La Renaissance cath. en Angleterre au XIXe siècle*, 1899–1906.

close of the eighteenth century. In England they received the right of practising their religion without fear of penalty, of erecting schools, of becoming barristers, and of taking low offices (1791). In Ireland, besides these rights (1792), they were soon to receive the suffrage, and that of advancing in the military service to the rank of colonel (1793). The first Relief Bill for the Scotch Catholics was passed at about the same time. On the union of the Irish Parliament with the English (1800) new concessions were offered, and the mighty agitation directed by O'Connell finally led to the Catholics being granted equal rights with others throughout the realm. In 1828 O'Connell was returned to Parliament, from which, for the last 150 years, Catholics had been excluded by the oath of supremacy, and the next year the Bill of Emancipation passed into law. The Catholics were to be admitted to all offices and dignities of the State, save to the positions of Lord Chancellor of England and Lord Lieutenant of Ireland. By the Bill of Tithes (1838) the Irish were also dispensed from paying tithes to the Protestant clergy. Later still, the Lord Chancellorship of Ireland was opened to Catholics, and the oath exacted from members of Parliament was again modified for the benefit of the Catholics. Lastly, in 1869, the Protestant Church of Ireland was disestablished, a part of its property falling to the Catholics.

The year 1829 marks the commencement of a new period for the Church in England. Hitherto it had been steadily decreasing; now, however, the number of Catholics rose by leaps and bounds. Though this is to a large extent to be explained by Irish immigration, it must also in part be assigned to the new courage which was infused into the Catholics by the relief from their old disabilities. The conversions must also be reckoned. The Oxford Movement (§ 216) brought into the Church hundreds of the noblest and most learned of England's sons, clergy as well as laity. Owing to the progress of Catholicism in the region, Pius IX finally determined to re-establish the Catholic hierarchy in England, erecting Westminster into an archbishopric, with twelve suffragan bishops (1850). Leo XIII did the same for Scotland, creating two archbishoprics (St. Andrews and Glasgow) and four simple bishoprics (1878).[1]

---

[1] BELLESHEIM, *Hist. of the Church in Scotland.*

The first archbishop of Westminster, Wiseman, was succeeded
by Manning in 1865 († 1892).

In Great Britain and Ireland in 1903 there were 42,522,926
inhabitants, of whom a little over $5\frac{1}{4}$ millions were Catholics,
distributed as follows : 1·5 million in England, 433,000 in Scotland,
and the remainder in Ireland.

III. Among the Scandinavian States, Denmark was the first to
break with the old ecclesiastical traditions of tyranny. The penal
laws enacted against the Catholics were repealed in 1847. The
fundamental State law of 1849 proclaimed freedom of religion,
and put the Catholics on the same footing as the Protestants. In
Sweden and Norway the Church secured her freedom only in 1873.
The number of Catholics in the states in question is, however, very
small. In Denmark (1901) there were 5,000 ; Sweden and Norway
have each about 1,500.

§ 206

The Church in Poland and Russia [1]

The partition of Poland (1772, 1793, 1795) was not only the
first step towards the breaking up of a mighty kingdom, but
was also an event pregnant in consequences for religion. It
is true that Russia, to whom the greater portion of the country
fell, undertook to maintain the religion of the Roman Catholics
of both rites, *i.e.* of the Latins and of the Ruthenians, who had
been amalgamated with Rome by the Union of Brest (1596).
What the value of the promise was became apparent when
Catherine II (1762–96) separated nearly eight millions of
Uniates from the Apostolic See and incorporated them in
the Russian Church. The czar Paul I indeed desisted from the
persecution, and even reorganised both the Uniate and the
Latin Churches of his kingdom. The old sees were re-erected
(Poloczk, Luck, and Brest for the Uniates, and the arch-
bishopric of Mohilev and five suffragan bishoprics for the
Latins), and a few new ones established, one being at Warsaw

---

[1] THEINER, *Vetera monum. Poloniae et Lithuaniae*, 1863 ; THEINER,
Neueste Gesch. d. kath. K. in R. und P. 1841 ; PELESZ, *Gesch. d. Union d.
ruthen. K. mit Rom.* vol. II, 1880 ; LIKOWSKI, *Gesch. d. allm. Verfalls d.
unierten ruthen. Kirche im 18 und 19 Jahrh.* (German Trans. by TLOCZYNSKY),
2 vol. 1885–86 ; *Die ruthenisch-römische Kirchenvereinigung gen. Union zu
Brest* (German Trans. by JEDZINK), 1904.

(promoted to an archbishopric in 1817). He also established at St. Petersburg a special department, the 'Roman Catholic College,' charged with the care of all the Catholics of the realm. Alexander I (1801–25) also dealt very fairly with the Catholics. On the other hand, Nicholas I (1825–55) reverted to Catherine's policy. He determined to subject the Uniates to the State Church, and, by dint of craft and coercion, he succeeded to a large extent. The bishops of Lithuania (Jos. Siemazko), Brest, and White Russia, together with many of their priests, announced their secession in 1839. The Polish rising in 1830 led to severe measures being taken against the Latins also. On the occasion of the czar's visit to Rome in 1845, and in consequence of the representations then made to him by Gregory XVI, Nicholas indeed promised to ameliorate the situation of his Catholic subjects, and two years later a Concordat was arranged. This agreement, however, remained a dead letter; it was not even published in Russia until a year after the advent of Alexander II (1855–81), and even then its execution left much to be desired. Another rising in Poland (1863) brought new misfortunes on the Catholics. The suppression of the union was now pushed forward with all energy, and Chelm, the last of the Uniate dioceses in Russia, was incorporated in the State Church (1875). As for the Latin Church, a new understanding was arrived at between Alexander III (1881–94) and Rome (1882); even so, the burden imposed by the State religion was exceedingly heavy. To pass from the Orthodox Church to any other was forbidden under penalty; children of mixed marriages, in which one of the parties belonged to the State Church, were to be educated in that religion, a rule which was, however, modified by Alexander II and again by Nicholas II (1897), sons being brought up in their fathers', and daughters in their mothers' religion; even the civil rights of the non-Orthodox were curtailed. Only after the unhappy war against Japan (1903), and as a result of the internal state of Russia, did the principle of religious equality contrive to assert itself. In the spring, 1905, the penalties decreed against departure from the Orthodox fold, and the administration of the sacraments to converts, were abolished, and a few of the disabilities of the Poles— those, namely, which concerned the acquirement of landed property—were also removed. In consequence of these measures it is said that several hundred thousand Uniates have returned to the Church in the district of the Vistula.

Including Finland, Russia in Europe, in 1897, possessed 102,000,000 inhabitants, 11,326,804 being Catholics, 6,273,679 Protestants, and 5,000,000 Jews.

§ 207

The Church in America

I. So vast has been the growth of Catholicism in North America, especially during the nineteenth century and owing to the influx of Europeans, that, though it is still reckoned a missionary country (1909), it deserves a separate section.

From the end of the seventeenth century Canada had possessed its own bishop, the episcopal see being Quebec (§ 180). By the beginning of the nineteenth century the number of Catholics had increased to such an extent that Quebec was erected into an archbishopric (1819), and the existing Vicariates-Apostolic into dioceses, to which yet others were added. Of these dioceses not a few were afterwards to be promoted to the metropolitan status (Halifax, 1852, Toronto, 1870, St. Boniface, 1871, Montreal and Ottawa, 1886, Kingston, 1889).

Still greater was the Church's growth in the United States.[1] The persecutions to which Catholics were liable in England induced lord Baltimore to seek a new home beyond the ocean, and to found the colony of Maryland (1634) ; similar colonies were founded elsewhere. The Catholics were, however, long in the minority, and though in Maryland, on their motion, an Act of Toleration was passed ensuring freedom of worship to all forms of Christianity, they had many hardships to experience. Nearly everywhere the Protestants—the only exception being the Quakers of Pennsylvania—took advantage

---

[1] BANCROFT, *Hist. of the United States of America*, 6 vol. last ed. 1885 ; J. G. SHEA, *Hist. of the Catholic Church within the limits of the United States*, 1886 ff. ; O'GORMAN, *A History of the Roman Catholic Church in the United States*, 1895 ; *A. f. k. KR.*, pp. 522–30 (the Brief *Testem benevolentiae*) ; *Kath.* 1902, I, 494–512 ; A. HOUTIN, *L'Américanisme*, 1904 ; K. BRAUN, *Amerikanismus, Fortschritt, Reform*, 1904.

of their greater number to issue new penal laws. The War of Independence (1776–83), in which Protestants and Catholics fought side by side, finally brought the latter their freedom. At the time they numbered only some 30,000, and were administered by the Vicar-Apostolic of the London district. This arrangement came to an end with the proclamation of independence, and the country was placed under the immediate control of the Holy See ; J. Carroll was created Vicar-Apostolic (1784), and soon after bishop of Baltimore (1789). The subsequent progress of Catholicism was as remarkable as that of the country itself. Twenty years later four new dioceses were established at Boston, New York, Philadelphia, and Bardstown, Baltimore now becoming an archdiocese (1808). As the Union was constantly growing by the incorporation of new territories and states, and as the population was likewise being constantly augmented by immigrants, new dioceses were soon called for. In the middle of the nineteenth century there were six provinces, which by the end of the century had grown to fourteen with seventy-three sees. The bishop of Baltimore, the occupant of the oldest see, received the title of Primate in 1858. Seminaries were also established for the training of a native clergy, the first being that of Baltimore, the direction of which was taken by Sulpicians who had been driven from Paris by the Revolution in 1791. A Catholic university was also erected at Washington (1889). The number of Catholics now amounts to about ten millions (by O'Gorman it is estimated at twelve millions) on a total population of 86,900,000 (1904).

The creating of so huge an organisation demanded both hard work and united action, especially as the Catholic missioners had to reckon on themselves alone, the State, beyond guaranteeing freedom of conscience, doing nothing for their support. Hence it is no wonder that recourse was frequently taken to Councils. Carroll, soon after his appointment, commenced the practice of holding diocesan synods (1791), and some time after it also became customary to hold Provincial Councils (1829) and Plenary Councils (1852). The object of the missioners was ever to adjust matters in such wise as to bring them into harmony with the peculiar conditions of the people among whom their lot was cast. That here and there the adjustments ultimately proved to some extent inconformable with the Church's teaching, cannot be a matter of surprise to those who know how one-sided in its developments human nature is prone to be. Americanism, as the complexus of these errors came to be known, was condemned by Leo XIII in his Brief *Testem benevolentiae* (1899).

The bishops are nominated by Rome. The provinces have, however, the right of recommending persons fit for the posts, and according to the last two Plenary Councils (1866–84) their commendation takes place in this wise. The councillors and immovable rectors of the widowed diocese assemble, summoned by and presided over by the metropolitan—or by the senior bishop of the province should the vacancy be in the metropolis itself—and by secret vote draw up a list of three candidates, which is afterwards examined by the bishops of the province, who under certain circumstances have the right of adding other names.

II. Following the example set by the North, Central and South America,[1] which hitherto had been under the domination of Spain and Portugal, severed their connection with their respective motherlands (1818–24). The consequence was the creation of a number of new independent states: Mexico; in Central America, Guatemala, Honduras, Salvador, Nicaragua, and Costa Rica; in South America, Venezuela, Colombia, Ecuador, Peru, Bolivia, Chile, Brazil, &c. Nearly all these states, on separating from Europe, adopted a republican constitution. In Mexico Augustine Iturbide had at first been proclaimed emperor (1822), but was forced to abdicate within a year; a subsequent attempt to establish an empire under the archduke Maximilian of Austria (1864–67) was also a failure. On the other hand, republicanism was ultimately to triumph even in Brazil (1890), which had formed itself into an empire under Dom Pedro on separating from Portugal. The changes in these two great states show the existence of deep political animosities. The same uncertainty, however, prevailed in the other states, which for a number of years were torn by incessant civil wars, through the struggles of the different parties for mastery. Only by degrees did they reach a position of stable equilibrium. Under such circumstances

---

[1] J. FEHR, *Gesch. des* 19 *Jahrh.* I (CANTU, *Weltgesch.* XIV), 1262–1305; IV (XVII), 5109–95; *St. a. ML.* 1906, I, 531–47 (Brazil).

the condition of the Church could not be one of much security. Under Pius IX Conventions were made with most of the states. In Mexico, in 1875, the Church was disestablished, religion was banished from the schools, and sisters who busied themselves in teaching and in the care of the sick were expelled the country. In Brazil, where Catholicism had been so far the religion of the State, the proclamation of the Republic (February 24, 1891) was made the occasion for introducing freedom of worship and disestablishing the Church.

§ 208

The Papacy and the Vatican Council [1]

Enough has a'ready been said concerning the relations of the papacy with the various states. Here we shall confine ourselves to supplying such details as have been omitted.

I. **Pius VII,**[2] on assuming the tiara, found himself faced by the task of establishing order anew in his States, which the political upheaval which had occurred during the latter years of his predecessor's pontificate, the shameful exactions and thefts of the French, and the constant wars had reduced to a condition of chaos. Returning to Rome after five years of exile in France, he had to commence the same task anew. Many of the reforms which had been introduced by the French were retained, particularly such as tended to centralise and simplify the administration. The Pope's attention was also claimed by church matters in other lands. Save for a few years (1806–14), during which Napoleon had his own way, the Pope's chief adviser was his secretary of State, cardinal Ercole Consalvi.

II. He was succeeded by cardinal Annibale della Genga as **Leo XII** (1823–29), whose pontificate was taken up with the reorganisation of the Church.

---

[1] ARTAUD DE MONTOR, *Hist. du pape Pie VII*, 3rd ed. 1839; *de Léon XII*, 1843; *de Pie VIII*, 1844; DUERM, *Vicissitudes politiques du pouvoir temporel des papes, de 1790 à nos jours*, 2nd ed. 1896; NÜRNBERGER, *Papsttum u. Kirchenstaat*, 3 vol. 1897–1900.

[2] Mg. by PISTOLESI, 1824 f.; GIUCI, 1864; RANKE, *Kard. Consalvi u. s. Staatsverwaltung*, in *WW*. vol. 40; E. FISCHER, *Kard. Consalvi*, 1899; DUERM, *Correspondance du Card. H. Consalvi avec Cl. de Metternich*, 1899.

III. The reign of **Pius VIII** (1829–30), of the Castiglione family, was too short, lasting only twenty months, to allow of his putting any plans he may have had into execution.

IV. The pontificate of **Gregory XVI** (1831–46),[1] formerly a Camaldulese monk, by name Capellari, was disturbed by repeated rebellions. The backwash of the July Revolution was felt even in the States of the Church, and the movement, beginning at Bologna, soon involved the larger portion of the country. On the arrival of the Austrians, the papal government was indeed again set up, and, at the demand of the Powers, the Pope consented to introduce a few reforms. These, however, proved insufficient, and the opposition continued, resulting in Bologna and Ancona being occupied by Austrian and French troops for nearly seven years (1832–38). A rising also took place at Rimini, but was suppressed by the papal troops (1845). Disturbances so persistent prove the difficulty there was in maintaining the old order of things, and the need of far-reaching alterations.

V. **Pius IX** (1846–78),[2] formerly cardinal Mastai Ferretti, bishop of Imola, determined to adopt a more conciliatory attitude. He began by publishing a general amnesty to those who had been condemned for political reasons during the previous pontificate, allowed the laity to enter several of the State Departments, and finally (1848) published a Constitution in which he appointed the establishment of two Chambers, the first of members nominated by the Pope, the second of representatives of the people, both of which should, however, be subject to the college of cardinals. These reforms were hailed with joy. Amidst the revolutionary movements which involved the whole of Europe in 1848, such reforms were not, however, sufficient to establish public order. The excited populace demanded further concessions, and on the Pope's flight to Gaeta a Republic was proclaimed, at the head of which was Mazzini with two others (1849). The papal domination was soon again restored by the intervention of the Catholic Powers, and in the spring, 1850, Pius returned, bent on healing

---

[1] *Acta Gregorii XVI*, ed. A. M. BERNASCONI, 4 vol. 1901–5.
[2] Mg. by STEPISCHNEGG, 2 vol. 1879; POUGEOIS, 6 vol. 1877–86; J. G SHEA.

the wounds which had been caused to his country by the Revolution. The old constitution existing prior to 1848 was again renewed, though the laity were assured a place in the administration. Under these circumstances a real conciliation was out of the question : the French were compelled to remain at Rome and the Austrians in the Legations, and how necessary their presence was was seen when they retired. In 1859 Victor Emanuel, backed by France, commenced his attack on the Austrian provinces of northern Italy, and Austria, in obedience to the Pope's requests, withdrew her troops from the Papal States. No sooner was this done than risings occurred in the evacuated Legations, the papal domination was declared at an end, and the people clamoured for incorporation in the new kingdom of Italy, which was then in the first stage of its formation, the duchies of Modena, Parma, and Tuscany having just then thrown in their lot with the Piedmontese. Ferrara, Bologna, and Ravenna were lost to the Pope immediately, the province of Umbria and the mark of Ancona following suit the next year (1860), the Papal States being thereby reduced by two-thirds. The remainder of the States was in the occupation of the French. The attack made on the latter by Garibaldi and his band was successfully repelled at Mentana (1867). On the outbreak of the Franco-German war (1870) the French troops were, however, withdrawn, and the whole country was at the mercy of the Italians, who accordingly marched on Rome. To the Pope there now remained only the palace of the Vatican and the villa Gandolfo. The law of Guarantee (May 15, 1871) acknowledged the Pope's person as sacred and inviolable, and granted him an annual pension of 3,250,000 francs.[1] The offer was, however, declined, lest it should be interpreted as conveying an indirect approval of an act of injustice, and in the confidence that the gifts of the Faithful would make good the losses of revenue incurred by the Pope through being deprived of his States.

From an ecclesiastical standpoint the pontificate was not less eventful than from the point of view of politics. After having consulted with the episcopate throughout the world, Pius, in his Bull *Ineffabilis* (1854), in virtue of the *Iudicium supremum* of the Apostolic See (or *supremo suo atque infallibili*

---

[1] F. GEIGEL, *Das ital. Staatskirchenrecht*, 1886 (*A. f. k. KR.* vols. 54, 55).

oraculo, to use the words of the new Office, lect. VI) raised the doctrine of the Immaculate Conception of Mary to the status of a dogma. He also issued the Syllabus,[1] a list of eighty errors which had already previously been condemned by him in detail. Finally, in the late autumn, 1869, he summoned a General Council to meet at the **Vatican** [2] for the definition of Papal Infallibility. The proposal caused great excitement everywhere ; it was also opposed with much vehemence by not a few of the Council which assembled, 747 strong, some holding that the doctrine was without foundation, others that its definition was inopportune, *i.e.* would only engender new hatred and new difficulties for the Church. The majority was, however, in its favour, and it was passed by the Council, the actual definition following at the fourth session in the Constitution *Pastor aeternus* (July 18, 1870). As only one decree had been previously issued by the Council, the *Decretum de fide* (Sess. III), its labours had scarcely begun, and other debates and decrees were to have followed, but, in the event, the fourth session proved to be the last. On the following day, France declared war against Germany ; two months later Rome became the capital of the kingdom of Italy, and on October 20 the Council was formally adjourned.

The commotion which had preceded and accompanied the Council did not cease even when the assembly had dissolved. The bishops of the minority, indeed, all submitted to the ruling of the majority and published the new dogma in their dioceses. Their action was not, however, well received everywhere. Numerous lay folk and not a few of the clergy, particularly in Germany, refused to accept the doctrine, and, as the clergy, in spite of the excommunication which they incurred by their protests, were maintained at their posts by the governments, new conflicts became the order of the day. In many places the dogma disturbed the relations between Church and State. Austria denounced its Concordat in the very year of the Council, and other states, such as Prussia, took their measures against the Church. The pontificate of Pius was sufficiently

---

[1] F. HEINER, *Der Syllabus*, 1905.
[2] *Acta et decreta,* in *Coll. Lacensis*, vol. VII, 1890 ; *Constitutiones dogmaticae,* ed. Trevir. 1901 ; Mg. by CECCONI, 1873–79 ; J. FRIEDRICH, 3 vol. 1877–87 ; TH. GRANDERATH, ed. by KIRCH, 3 vol. 1903–6.

long to discredit the old saying that no Pope shall see the (twenty-five) years of Peter.

VI. At his death the Church was in many countries in an unsatisfactory situation. To cardinal Pecci, bishop of Perugia, who assumed the name of **Leo XIII** (1878–1903),[1] it was reserved to improve matters. His wisdom and innate sense of justice found wide appreciation. In the conflict over the Caroline island of Yap he was chosen to arbitrate between Germany and Spain (1885). On the occasion of his golden and diamond jubilees he was the recipient of congratulations and gifts from nearly all the sovereigns and states of the world (1887–97). Learning also owes him a debt for having thrown open the Vatican archives and made their treasures accessible to historians. In a series of encyclicals he sought to promote religious life in all its manifestations, and to apply the principles of Christianity to every department of life.

VII. He was followed by cardinal Giuseppe Sarto, patriarch of Venice, as **Pius X** (1903).[2] Whilst maintaining with regard to the Roman Question the attitude adopted by his two predecessors, he soon showed that he was disposed to make some account of the changes which had occurred, and, without abolishing the *Non expedit*, he granted permission to his countrymen, by way of dispensation and under certain conditions, to take a part in the political and parliamentary life of United Italy (1905).

The principal clause of the Constitution *Pastor aeternus* touching infallibility runs as follows : *Romanum pontificem cum ex cathedra loquitur, id est, cum omnium Christianorum pastoris et doctoris munere fungens, pro suprema sua apostolica auctoritate doctrinam de fide vel moribus ab universa ecclesia tenendam definit, per assistentiam divinam, ipsi in beato Petro promissam, ea infallibilitate pollere, qua divinus redemptor ecclesiam suam in definienda doctrina de fide vel moribus instructam esse voluit, ideoque eiusmodi Romani pontificis definitiones ex sese, non autem ex consensu ecclesiae irreformabiles esse.* For a fuller explanation of the definition see LÄMMER, *Institutionen des k. KR.* 2nd ed. 1892, pp. 155–59.

[1] Bg. by WEINAND, 1892 ; NORBERT, 1894 ; T'SERCLAES, 1894 ; RICARD, 1895 ; McCARTHY, 1896 ; DOMENICO, 1896 ; L. K. GÖTZ, 1899 ; DE CESARE (*Dal conclavee di Leone XIII al ultimo Consistoro*), 1899 ; O'REILLY, 1903 ; *Die kath. Kirche unserer Zeit*, ed. the Leo-Gesellschaft, Vienna, 3 vol. 1898–1902 ; Encyclicals, published by Herder; S. VON SMOLKA, *Erinnerung an Leo XIII*, 1906.

[2] A. MARCHESAN, *P. Pius X* (German Trans. 1905–6).

§ 209

The Kulturkampf in Germany [1]

Since 1848 the Church in Prussia had enjoyed the fullest freedom of action, nor had the State had the slightest cause for complaint. As late as 1866, king William I spoke with satisfaction of the admirable order of the Church in his lands. The victorious war against France and the foundation of the German Empire (January 18, 1871) was, however, the signal for a change of policy on the part of the State. The Church was now to be robbed of the liberties she had been accorded, and made wholly subject to the State. The war against her, which was described by one of her enemies as a Kulturkampf (*i.e.* as a war of culture against the cramping influence of Catholic dogma), and has ever since been generally known by that name, was, without a doubt, the doing of the chancellor, prince Bismarck, though its immediate conduct was left to the minister of public worship. The Catholics, indeed, defended themselves with a will, in Parliament, in the press, and elsewhere, and were supported by a portion of the Protestants, who saw that the arbitrary proceedings of the government threatened even the freedom of their own Church. As, however, the majority of the nation—partly out of hostility to Christianity, partly out of hatred of Catholicism, partly, too, because of the uneasiness caused by the Syllabus and Vatican decrees—willingly followed the government's lead, the enactment of oppressive laws was made possible. The aim of the legislators was not attained. After nearly ten years of warfare, the government was compelled to withdraw one by one the more obnoxious of its new laws. The same also happened in the grand-duchy of Hesse, which had at first followed Prussia's example and issued similar laws (1875), only to follow suit again and withdraw them in 1887.

The progress of the Prussian Kulturkampf was as follows: To begin with, the two denominational departments at the ministry

---

[1] Mg. by N. Siegfried, 1882; F. X. Schulte, 1882; Wiermann, 1885; P. Majunke, 2nd ed. 1902; J. Falter, 1900; H. Brück, 2 vol. 1901–5 (*Gesch. d. k. K. im 19 Jahrh.* IV, 1–2). Also V. Rintelen, 1887 (3rd ed. 1903), and G. Wendt, 1887; J. N. Knopp, *Ludwig Windthorst*, 1898.

of public worship, of which the object was to advise the ministry in matters of religion, were abolished (1871). Education was put exclusively into the hands of the State, and the Jesuits were expelled the country (1873), the last measure extending not to Prussia only, but to the whole Empire. A year later a like expulsion was decreed against Redemptorists, Lazarists, Priests of the Holy Ghost, and nuns of the Sacred Heart, as being religious associations allied to the Jesuits. There followed the May Laws of 1873 dealing with the training and nomination of the clergy, the disciplinary powers of ecclesiastical superiors, establishing a secular court for deciding church matters, and bestowing on it the right, under certain circumstances, of dismissing the clergy from their posts, setting a limit to the Church's power of punishing, and laying down rules for those who desired to leave the Church. So much were these laws at variance with the constitution, that the two paragraphs (15, 18) guaranteeing the independence and self-government of the Church had first to be amended (1873), and finally, together with another (16), entirely abrogated (1875). Some of these laws were not absolutely unacceptable. In some of them Prussia was merely claiming rights which had already been granted to other states by the Holy See by means of special conventions. The Prussian episcopate, fearing, however, to acknowledge the competence of the State to interfere in Church matters, elected to reject the laws as a whole. First and foremost, they refused to present to the government the candidates for nomination. As, however, the government was determined to execute its laws by all the means at its command, a violent conflict was not long in breaking out. The bishops and many of the clergy were fined and imprisoned, some were even removed from their posts, and the May Laws were made more severe. By the military law Divinity students were deprived of the privilege which they had so far enjoyed in the matter of military service (1874). Salaries due from the State to bishops and episcopal administrators were to remain unpaid until they had made their written submission to the laws of the State. All religious Orders and similar religious associations were dissolved, save only those who devoted themselves to the care of the sick (1875). A law was passed for the whole Empire enacting that any of the clergy who refused to submit when ejected from their office by the secular court might be expelled either from a determined locality, or even from the whole territory of the Empire (1874). It was not long before most of the sees and hundreds of parishes were deprived of their occupants, with results which may well be imagined, as no strange priest was allowed to enter the 'closed' parishes, not even for the purpose of administering the last sacraments. Great as were the efforts of the government to execute its laws, they were in vain. The great majority of both clergy and laity remained loyal to the episcopate, and their power of resistance grew with the progress of the conflict. The Catholic fraction, the so-called Centre, at the next elections was returned both to the Prussian Diet and to the Imperial Parliament in greatly increased numbers, in one case the number rising from fifty-two to ninety, and in the other from sixty-three to ninety-one. Led by Ludwig Windthorst († 1891), it became each year more powerful, and the government, however unwilling to acknowledge defeat, was at last compelled to retreat. The death of Pius IX and the accession of Leo XIII (1878) helped the cause of peace. A twofold attempt on the life of the emperor William, which followed soon after, demonstrated that by oppressing the Church, religion, the basis of social order, had suffered. Three 'novels' (1880, 1882, 1883) were issued dealing with the re-establishment of a more regular diocesan administration, and with the provisional relief of the more crying needs of the Catholic parishes. The sees were gradually provided with pastors, the last to be filled being Cologne (1885) and Posen (1886). Two of the former bishops, in spite of having been deposed by the State, were allowed to return to their dioceses. The law on the 'closure' of parishes, the so-called 'Bread-basket Law,' was recalled, though it continued to be applied in the archdiocese of Posen, where, for nationalist reasons, the government had throughout acted with greater severity than elsewhere. Diplomatic intercourse between Berlin and Rome was resumed. Finally, the State renounced its claim to a voice in the nomination of assistant priests. So far the May Laws remained practically intact, but a few years later, when the Holy See had elected to meet half-way the government's demands regarding the nomination of the clergy, and probably also on account of the clouds which were gathering on the political horizon, the laws were to be strikingly amended. In a fourth 'novel' (1886) the secular court for the judgment of church matters was abolished, together with the so-called 'Culture examination' which Divinity students had been obliged to undergo under State super-vision, whilst under certain conditions church students were to be allowed to perform their studies at the seminaries. Yet another 'novel' (1887) readmitted some of the religious Orders, per-mitted all priests, save those belonging to Orders not tolerated in the Empire, to say Mass and to administer the sacraments. It also enacted that the State should have a right to intervene only in cases of nominations to permanent cures of souls, and that, even then, its intervention should be governed by rule.

Under the emperor William II, Catholic church students again received exemption from military service in time of peace (1890), the accumulated funds of the dioceses were restored to their owners (1891), and the Redemptorists were readmitted (1894).

§ 210

The Missions [1]

After having fallen off in the eighteenth century, missionary activity again became very great in the present period. The various religious Orders, the Propaganda at Rome, the College of Foreign Missions and that of the Holy Ghost at Paris continued to send forth bands of missionaries, and in the course of time these establishments were joined by yet others. Such were the seminaries at Milan (1850) and at Lyons (1856), the societies of the Black Fathers, or Fathers of the Holy Ghost (1848), of the congregation of the Immaculate Heart of Mary in Belgium (1863), of Mill-Hill in England (1866), founded by cardinal Vaughan (†1903), of the White Fathers (1868), founded by cardinal Lavigerie, archbishop of Algiers (†1892), of the Divine Word at Steyl in Holland (1875), and of St. Ottilien in Bavaria (1884). To collect the funds many missionary associations were also formed, such as the Association for the Propagation of the Faith at Lyons (1822), similar associations being The Xaveriusverein at Aachen, (1832), the Leopoldsverein in Austria (1839), the Ludwigsverein in Bavaria (1839), the Association of the Holy Child Jesus at Paris (1843), and the Bonifatiusverein at Paderborn (1849). Missionary zeal was displayed in every quarter of the world, nor were the usual difficulties absent. Missionaries and converts in great numbers were found ready to lay down their lives for the Faith.

In the **East Indies**, where the Portuguese had been gradually ousted by the English, the old dioceses had fallen into decay, and a reorganisation of the Church had become imperative. For the care of the English provinces, Vicariates-Apostolic were established by Rome. In 1838 a certain number of the old sees were abolished, and as Portugal refused to recognise the change, whilst also declining to perform its obligations with respect to the bishops, a long-drawn conflict was the result. The Convention of 1857 again settled matters on a better footing. In 1886, when the number of Catholics in India amounted to some 1,600,000, the archbishopric of Goa was

---

[1] O. WERNER, *Kath. Missionsatlas*, 2nd ed. 1885; *Orbis terr. catholicus*, 1890; LOUVET, *Les missions cath. au XIXᵉ siècle*, 1898; PIOLET, *Les miss. cath. franç. au XIXᵉ siècle*, 6 vol. 1901–3; P. M. BAUMGARTEN, *Die kath. Kirche*, III : *das Wirken der k. K. auf dem Erdenrund*, 1902; *Kath. Missionen*, Freiburg, 1874 ff. ; KLEFFNER-WOKER, *Der Bonifatiusverein*, 1899.

granted the dignity of a patriarchate, its metropolitan rights being reaffirmed over the suffragan sees of Damaun-Cranganor, Cochin, and St. Thomas-Meliapur ; the Vicariates-Apostolic of Agra, Bombay, Verapoly, Calcutta, Madras, Pondichery, and Colombo (Ceylon) were erected into archbishoprics, thus establishing a hierarchy independent of that of Portuguese India. Cp. *Archiv. f. KR.* 58 (1887), 3–25. In **Further India,** *i.e.* in the kingdom of Annam, which was established in 1802 by the union of Tonking and Cochinchina, many persecutions had to be undergone. As late as 1885–86 thousands of Christians fell victims to the pagans' hatred.

In **China** the Christians had much to suffer under the emperor Kia-King (1795–1820). This was, however, the last organised persecution. The mission at this time was rather unfortunately situated, owing to the lack of workers. Better days dawned after the treaty of Tien-tsin (1858) and the peace of Peking (1860), the missioners thereby securing the right of entry into the Celestial Empire. Of a total population of about 380 millions, the number of the Christians soon reached 1,155,000. The Chinese continued, however, to cherish their old hatred of foreigners and Christianity, and as late as 1900 the lives of many missioners and of thousands of native Christians were sacrificed by the pagans.

In **Corea,** the peninsula lying to the north-east of China, Christianity, after having already previously been preached from Japan, again entered by way of China towards the end of the last period. It was forthwith subjected to severe persecution, and in forty years (1800–39), of a Christian population of only 10,000, no less than 300 died martyrs.

Japan, after having remained closed against Christianity for more than 200 years, again opened its doors to the missioners, at about the same time as China. By treaties with England and France (1858) foreigners, *i.e.* Christians, were to have admittance to a few ports. In 1862 a church was erected at Yokohama, in 1884 religious freedom was proclaimed throughout the land, and in 1891 an archbishopric, with three suffragan sees, was established at Tokio. Of a population of about 50,000,000, Catholics now number about 60,000.

A new period opened in **North Africa** with the conquest of Algiers by the French (1830). Though the Mohammedans have so far resisted the appeals of Christianity, nevertheless the country, owing to immigration, has obtained a considerable Christian population. Algiers was erected into a bishopric in 1838, and in 1867 became an archbishopric with two suffragan sees. The proclamation of the French protectorate over Tunis (1881) was soon followed by the re-establishment of St. Cyprian's venerable see at Carthage.

In the Soudan a Vicariate-Apostolic was established in 1846 at the request of the Polish Jesuit Ryllo. Many missions were also founded at this time and later, on the west, south, and east coasts of Africa, and on the neighbouring islands. Here the missioners had

to face a double difficulty—an unhealthy climate and a besotten population—in spite of which they were not discouraged.   These regions
form the especial field of work of the associations mentioned at the
commencement of this section.

Australia was discovered by the French as far back as the
sixteenth century, but only in the nineteenth century did it attain
the dignity of an ecclesiastical government of its own.   After having
been, since 1818, governed by the Vicariate of Mauritius, the whole
country was placed under a Vicar-Apostolic of its own in 1835.   The
Catholic population soon grew ; in 1842 Sidney became an archbishopric with simple sees at Adelaide and Hobart (in Tasmania).
These two were later on erected into metropolitan churches, together with Melbourne, Brisbane, and in New Zealand, Wellington.
In 1844 the first Provincial Council was held, Plenary Councils also
being held in 1885 and 1895.   MORAN, *Hist. of the Cath. Church in
Australasia*, 1896.

§ 211

Relations with the State—Discipline and Worship [1]

I. The Revolution and the subsequent secularisation of
her property were heavy blows to the Church.   In France
she lost all, and in Germany a great part of, her wealth.   This
wholesale robbery was, however, to conduce to a new birth.
Many a reform which had previously been impossible, owing
to the Church's possessions and to the greed which wealth
ever entails, was now accomplished with scarcely an effort.

The confiscation of monastic property made an end of
commendams and of the abuse, which, in spite of its condemnation by the Council of Trent, had prevailed more particularly in France, of bestowing abbacies and priories on seculars.
In France, too, the cessation of the political privileges of the
clergy involved also the cessation of the ecclesiastical privileges
of the nobility.   The episcopate was now thrown open to all
without distinction of birth, whereas hitherto only five French
bishoprics were open to commoners.   The same happened
with the canonries, which had previously been largely reserved
for the nobles.   Little by little the highest classes withdrew
from the Church's service, a fact which shows that they had
hitherto entered the ranks of the Church's ministry, less through

---

[1] KOPP, *Die k. Kirche im 19 Jahrh.* 1830 ; B. SCHÄFER, *Einheit in Liturgie
und Disziplin für Deutschland*, 1891.

vocation than from worldly motives. A like change occurred in Germany, and was here even more noticeable than in France, for whereas the French bishops at most could only dispose *in commendam* of some one or two abbacies, in Germany it was no rare thing for a bishop to possess two or three bishoprics.

The clergy also lost their privileges as a class apart. In France they consented from the beginning to lose their exemption from taxes. Little by little tithes were abolished, or rather redeemed, nearly everywhere. The privilege of possessing its own special courts of justice was also suppressed, the clergy everywhere being placed under the common law of the land, a change which was recognised by the Holy See, not indeed unconditionally, but *temporum ratione habita*, to use the expression of the Austrian Concordat (1855) and of the Conventions with Württemberg and Baden (1857, 1859).

In the trial of ecclesiastical cases, more care now began to be taken to observe the rules as to appeals, the Roman See frequently deciding the cases referred to it by means of *Iudices in partibus*. Thereby justice was done to one of the demands which had been raised in the memorandum of Ems.

II. With regard to worship, the Concordat of 1801 merely stated that in France the Catholic religion might be freely practised, and that Catholic worship should also be free so far as was not detrimental to public order (Art. I). Beyond this an understanding was also arrived at regarding the number of festivals, which it was found advisable to diminish yet more. Besides the Sundays only four festivals were to be observed as holidays : Christmas, the Ascension, the Assumption, and All Saints. Some of the others were to be allowed to drop, whilst the solemnisation of the remainder was to be transferred to the following Sunday, this being the case with the Epiphany, Corpus Christi, SS. Peter and Paul, and the patronal feast (1802).[1] This order was to apply throughout the French Empire as it then existed, in consequence of which it continued to form the rule not only in France, but also in several countries then belonging to it, for instance, in Belgium, Luxemburg, and Dutch Limburg. In the Palatinate and in Hessen-Darmstadt, *i.e.* in the dioceses of Spires and in part of that of Mainz,

---

[1] Decree of the papal legate cardinal Caprara, April 9, 1802 ; *Bullarium Magn.* contin., ed. Rom. XI (1846), 323 ff.

where for a time it prevailed, it had an after-effect, in that only five more festivals were re-established (New Year, Corpus Christi, Easter Monday, Whit-Monday, and Boxing-day). In other countries similar reductions were undertaken, but as account was made in each case of special circumstances, the result was a considerable variety of usage. The suggestion of the Plenary Council of Baltimore (1852), that in the United States of North America only the four French festivals should be observed, was not accepted by Rome, which insisted on the observance of New Year's Day and of the Immaculate Conception (1868).[1]

III. The fasting discipline was subjected to great alterations, principally owing to the intermingling of Catholics and Protestants. The Advent fast, which had been ordered at the time when the festivals were reduced in the eighteenth century (§ 183, I), does not seem to have secured general obedience. In the Church province of the Upper Rhine it was abolished in 1900. In Germany abstinence came to be observed only on all Fridays throughout the year, on Ash-Wednesday, and on the last three days of Holy Week. In the dioceses of Fulda and Hildesheim (as in Spain) even the Friday abstinence has been abolished. In other places abstinence, or even fasting, continues to be practised on the Ember-days, on the Wednesdays and Saturdays of Lent, and on the vigils of certain festivals.

IV. Whereas the above reforms issued in great divergencies of practice, in the matter of the liturgy far greater uniformity was secured. Though in the Middle Ages, save in a few Churches, the Roman Liturgy was everywhere followed (§ 100), in minor details much diversity prevailed. When, in accordance with the decree of Trent, the Breviary and Missal were revised at Rome (1568–70), this diversity was recognised, and though the new Office was imposed generally, an exception was made for those Churches which, for at least two centuries, had been in possession of a rite of their own. The reforms undertaken by many bishops, especially in France, during the seventeenth and eighteenth centuries, made the differences still greater. Since the Revolution, however, a strong tendency to unity of rite has made itself felt, and the war on local liturgies, preached

---

[1] KELLNER, *Heortology, a Hist. of the Christian Festivals*, p. 423 ff.

by abbot Guéranger in his *Institutions liturgiques* (1840–51), led to the Roman Liturgy being nearly everywhere rigorously imposed. In France Lyons was the only locality to preserve its ancient rite.

§ 212

Christian Life and Christian Art

I. For a time Christian life continued to feel the numbing influence of the shallow so-called enlightenment of the eighteenth century, but, with the passing of the revolutionary storm, a deeper religious consciousness and also a deeper attachment to the Church began to take possession of men's hearts. This change was made apparent in several ways ; for instance, in the increase of zeal both among the clergy and laity, in greater loyalty to the Church's superiors, in the more frequent reception of the sacraments, in the wider support of the work of the propagation of the Faith, and in an increase of interest in the temporal and eternal good of the lower classes. And, as great results can be obtained only by the united action of many individuals, Christian associations were everywhere called into being. Besides the missionary societies already spoken of (§ 210), the following deserve to be named : the Society of St. Vincent of Paul, for the support of the poor, founded by eight students at Paris in 1833 ; the Society of St. Elizabeth, an association of women and girls, having the same object ; the Gesellenverein, founded by Kolping at Cologne (1845) ; the Borromäusverein, for the distribution of good books (1845) ; the Piusverein, founded by provost Lennig at Mainz (1848) to secure freedom for the Church, and to promote a Christian spirit ; this association soon spread far and wide through Germany, and is now the main prop of the Katholikentag, a general annual congress of all the German Catholic clubs and associations. From Germany the custom of holding such meetings has now spread to other lands.

II. The strong upward movement was felt more particularly in the Arts.[1] At the end of the Renaissance, true art had sunk into a sad state of decay, but in the course of the nineteenth century a new enthusiasm was awakened for the Christian

---

[1] For literature, see §§ 157, 189.

art of the past, and with prodigious results in every department of the beautiful. Numerous ancient churches (for instance, the cathedral at Cologne) were restored or completed in accordance with their style. Many of the new churches were also of great artistic merit. Painting and sculpture were also practised with great success. Among the greatest modern masters of the former must be reckoned Fr. Overbeck of Lübeck († 1869), and P. Cornelius of Düsseldorf († 1867). In the plastic arts the Venetian Canova († 1822) earned great fame, but was surpassed by the Dane Thorwaldsen († 1844). Music also was much improved. K. Ett at Munich († 1847) and K. Proske at Ratisbon († 1861) did much to turn Catholics against the soft and worldly works of the eighteenth century and to recall them to the masterpieces of earlier times. This reform was introduced throughout Germany by the Society of St. Cæcilia, founded in 1868 by F. Witt († 1888). The restoration of Plain Chant was commenced (1840) and pushed forward by abbot Guéranger of Solesmes († 1875).

§ 213

Religious Orders and Congregations [1]

No small part in the religious restoration was taken by the religious Orders, which in their turn profited greatly by the new awakening of Christian life. The Revolution and the subsequent secularisation made a clean sweep of the monasteries and convents, which were then appropriated for other uses, and in some cases even demolished. As soon as the storm was over juster counsels and a better appreciation of their work came to prevail. The Sisters of Charity were readmitted into France by Napoleon (1807), and thence soon spread throughout the world. The Society of Jesus was re-established by Pius VII, first in Russia (1801) and in the kingdom of the Two Sicilies (1805), and then throughout the Church by the Bull *Sollicitudo omnium ecclesiarum* (1814). Many of the Orders succeeded in again obtaining possession of the houses which they had been forced to quit. Several reforms were also

---

[1] Heimbucher, *Die Orden und Kongregationen*, 1896–97 ; O. Brauns-berger, *Rückblick auf das kath. Ordenswesen im 19 Jahrh.* 1901.

introduced. Numerous new Benedictine congregations were formed, and the nomination of an abbot primate (1893) ensured the whole Order a greater unity. Most of the Cistercians adopted the reform of La Trappe, and the monasteries of the strict observance were formed into a special Order of Reformed Cistercians or Trappists (1892). The four groups of Franciscan Observantines (§ 178) were reunited into a single society (1897). Several entirely new religious associations also came into being, most of them devoted to the mission or to education.

The better known foundations of the period are.—

I. The Congregation of **Picpus** or of the Sacred Hearts of Jesus and Mary, founded by P. J. Coudrin at Paris (1801), and confirmed by Pius VII (1817).

II. The Congregation of the **Oblates of Mary Immaculate,** by Eugène Mazenod at Marseilles (1816).

III. The **Marists** (priests), by abbé Colin at Lyons (1816).

IV. The **Dames du Sacré-cœur,** founded in 1800 by Sophie Barat at Paris ; eighty years later the Congregation possessed 101 houses in the Old and New World.

V. The community of the **Good Shepherd,** which arose through the union of the houses of the Sisters of Refuge (§ 186), effected by Marie Pelletier at Angers in 1835. In 1887 it counted 158 various settlements in every part of the world.

VI. The **Little Sisters of the Poor,** founded by J. Jugan at St. Servan in Brittany (1840) and now very widespread.

VII. The **Assumptionists** or Augustinians of the Assumption, a Congregation following the rule of St. Augustine, founded in 1840 by J. d'Alzon, vicar-general of Nîmes. The members devote themselves especially to the apostolate of the press. Leo XIII also entrusted them with several missions in the East and with the task of promoting the reunion of the Eastern Churches.

VIII. The **Salesians** or Oratory of St. Francis of Sales, founded at Turin by Don Bosco for the moral and religious education of boys (1868), but also devoted to missionary work. The Salesians have many houses in both Europe and America.

§ 214

Literature and Controversies [1]

I. To repair the disasters wrought by philosophism and the Revolution, it was before all else necessary to enliven the

---

[1] K. WERNER, *Gesch. d. k. Th. in Deutschland,* 1866 ; 2nd ed. 1889 ; J. BELLAMY, *La théologie au XIXᵉ siècle,* 1904. We refrain from mentioning the scholars who are still engaged in active work.

religious consciousness. Especially was this the case in France, where indifferentism and unbelief had pervaded the whole of society, and was, even later on, to be mightily furthered by Renan († 1892) with his many works, and particularly his *Life of Jesus* (1863). Here quite a series of men, endowed with both zeal and ability, devoted themselves to the task, similar work being also done in Germany. In the latter country a great improvement was also manifested throughout the field of Theology. The centres of this movement were the theological faculties of the universities, which were afterwards joined by certain other educational establishments. The Protestant opposition and its scholarship proved an incentive to Catholic work, and though the contact between the two was attended by some evil consequences, on the whole its results were much to the advantage of both Faith and learning. The Romance nations, which in the previous period were far ahead in learning, had now to yield their primacy to the Germans. The religious Orders and other institutes, which had formerly been the mainstay of scholarship, had been mostly sacrificed by the Revolution. The theological faculties, which have proved so successful in Germany, are scarcely known there, the clergy being almost in its entirety educated at seminaries, which, when deprived of competition, are notoriously unfavourable to original work and research. Since the establishment of the Catholic Institutes great progress has, however, been made in France.

We append a list of the best known writers of the period.

1. **Apologists :** Vicomte de Chateaubriand (*Génie du Christianisme*, 1802 ; [Engl. Trans. 1854, 1858] ; † 1848) ; count J. de Maistre (*Du pape*, 1817 [Engl. Trans. 1850] ; *Les soirées de St. Pétersbourg*, 1821 ; † 1821) ; the Dominican Lacordaire († 1861) and the Jesuit Félix (conferences at Notre Dame, Paris) ; J. A. Möhler (*Symbolism or Exposition of the Doctrinal Differences between Catholics and Protestants as evidenced by their Symbolical Writings* (Engl. Trans. by ROBERTSON, 5th ed. 1906; † 1838); Bg. by KIHN, 1885 ; KNÖPFLER, 1896 ; G. GOYAU, 1905 ; J. S. Drey (*Apologetik*, 3 vol. 1834–47; † 1853) ; F. Staudenmaier (*Der Geist des Christentums, dargestellt in den heiligen Zeiten, in den h. Handlungen u. in der h. Kunst*, 1835, 8th ed. 1880; † 1856 ; Bg. by F. LAUCHERT, 1901) ; F. Hettinger (*Apologie des Christentums*, 1863; 9th ed. 3 vol., ed. E. MÜLLER, 1906 [Engl. Trans. by H. S. BOWDEN, *Nat. Rel.* 1890; *Revealed Rel.*

1895]; † 1890); P. Schanz (*Apologie d. Chr.* 3 vol. 3rd ed. 1903-6 [Engl. Trans. *A Christian Apology*, 1891]; † 1905); H. Schell (*Apol. d. Chr.* 2 vol. 1901-5; † 1906).

2. **Dogmatic Theologians and Historians of Dogma :** H. Klee (*Kath. Dogm.* 3 vol. 1834-35 ; *Dogmengesch.* 2 vol. 1837-38 ; † 1840); A. Berlage (*Kath. Dogm.* 7 vol. 1839-64 ; † 1881); J. Perrone, S.J. (*Praelectiones theolog.* 9 vol. 1835-42 ; † 1876); J. B. Franzelin, S.J. (*Tractatus de sacram. &c.*, 6 vol. 1868-70 ; † 1886); J. Kuhn (*Kath. Dogmatik*, 3 vol. 1846-68 ; † 1887); J. Scheeben (*Dogmatik*, 3 vol. 1873-87; Engl., *Manual of Catholic Theology based on Scheeben's Dogmatik*, ed. WILHELM AND SCANNELL, 4th ed. 1909; † 1889); J. B. Heinrich (*Dogm. Th.* 6 vol. 1873-87; † 1891); J. Schwane (*Dogmengesch.* 4 vol. 1862-90; † 1892).

3. **Moralists and Pastoral Theologians :** J. M. Sailer, a very successful professor who died bishop of Ratisbon († 1832 ; *WW.* 40 vol. 1830-41); J. B. Hirscher (*Moral*, 3 vol. 1835; † 1865); K. Werner (*Ethik*, 3 vol. 1850; † 1888); F. X. Linsenmann (*MTh.* 1878; † 1898).

4. **Canonists :** F. Walter (*Kirchenrecht*, 1822 ; † 1879); G. Phillips (*KR.* 7 vol. 1845-69; † 1872); F. Vering (*KR.* 3rd ed. 1893 ; † 1896); F. Kober († 1897); F. Maassen († 1900).

5. **Exegetists :** L. Hug (*Einleitung ins N.T.* 2 vol. 1808 ; 4th ed. 1847 [Engl. Trans. 2 vol. 1827]; † 1846); J. G. Herbst († 1836), and B. Welte († 1885 ; *Einleitung ins A. T.* 2 vol. 1840-42); D. B. Haneberg, O.S.B., bishop of Spires (*Gesch. der biblischen Offenbarung*, 1850 ; *Die religiösen Altertümer der Bibel*, 1869; † 1876); P. Schegg (*Leben Jesu*, 3 vol. 1874-75 ; *Evangelienkommentar*, 1856 ff.; † 1885); P. Vetter († 1906).

Church Historians and Patrologists : F. L. count zu Stolberg (cp. § 5; † 1819); Bg. by J. JANSSEN, 1882; J. I. Döllinger (§§ 6-8); K. J. Hefele, from 1869 bishop of Rottenburg (*Konziliengesch.* 1855 ff. cp. § 3 ; † 1893); K. Höfler (§§ 143; 161; † 1897); the cardinals A. Mai (*Scriptorum veterum nova collectio*, 10 vol. 1825-38 ; *Spicilegium Romanum*, 1839-44 ; *Nova patrum bibliotheca*, 7 vol. 1844-54 ; vol. VIII add. COZZA, 1871 ; † 1854); J. B. Pitra (*Spicilegium Solesmense*, 4 vol. 1852-54 ; *Analecta sacra*, 6 vol. 1876-88 ; *Anal. novissima*, 2 vol. 1885-88 ; † 1889); the explorer of the catacombs G. B. de Rossi, § 3, I (*Roma sotterranea*, 3 fol. 1864-77 (Engl. Abridgment by NORTHCOTE and BROWNLOW, 1869); *Bulletino di Archeologia cristiana*, 1863-94; † 1894); J. Hergenröther (*Photius*, 3 vol. 1867-69; † 1890); J. Janssen (§ 159; † 1891); H. Brück (cp. §§ 200-9 ; † 1903); H. Denifle (§§ 133-59 ; † 1905 ; Bg. by M. GRABMANN, 1905, H. GRAUERT, 1906, 2nd ed.).

Among the best means of cultivating and furthering learning must be reckoned **Periodicals** and **Encyclopædias.** The nineteenth century produced a rich crop of learned reviews and magazines, of which we give a list of the principal. For German-speaking countries : The *Theologische Quartalschrift*, published by the Catholic theological faculty at Tübingen since 1819 ; the *Katholik*; published at Mainz since 1821 ; the *Archiv für katholisches Kirchenrecht* (1857), the *Zeitschrift für kath. Theologie*, published by the Jesuits at Innsbrück since 1877 ; the *Historisches Jahrbuch*, published since 1880 under the auspices of the Görres Society (1876) for the promotion of learning ; the *Studien und Mitteilungen aus dem Benediktiner-und Cisterzienser-Orden* (1880) ; other similar reviews are no longer published.

In other countries : The Maredsous, *Revue Bénédictine* (1884) ; the *Revue d'histoire ecclésiastique* (Louvain, 1899) ; the *Revue d'histoire et de littérature religieuses* (Paris, 1896–1908) ; the *Bessarione* (Rome, 1896) ; the *Dublin Review* (London, 1836 ff.) ; the *Irish Ecclesiastical Record* (Dublin, 1864 ff.) ; the *Irish Theological Quarterly* (Dublin, 1906 ff.), and the *American Ecclesiastical Review* (Philadelphia, 1889 ff.).

The greatest and only complete Encyclopædia yet published is the *Kirchen-Lexikon*, edited by H. J. WETZER and B. WELTE, aided by a number of other scholars (12 vol. 1847–56 ; 2nd ed., ed. F. KAULEN, 1882–1901). The *Dictionnaire de théologie catholique*, edited by A. VACANT and E. MANGENOT, is still in course of publication. On Christian archæology there is the *Real-Encyklopädie der christlichen Altertümer*, edited by KRAUS (2 vol. 1882–86), and a promising *Dictionnaire d'archéologie chrétienne et de liturgie*, edited by abbot CABROL, and now in the course of publication, 1903 ff. [A *Catholic Encyclopædia* is now appearing in America (ed. C. G. HERBERMANN, &c., 1907 ff.).]

II. Among the **controversies** of the time, that connected with the name of G. Hermes (of Münster and Bonn) must be given the first place. Generalising his own experience in life, he took doubt as the starting-point of his speculation, and the rigorous demonstration of Christianity as its end. His theory exaggerated the force of reason, mistook the nature of mystery and the meaning of Faith, and caused some scandal even during his lifetime. After his death (1831) it was strongly controverted, and was finally censured by Gregory XVI (1835).

The philosophy of Günther, a Viennese professor († 1863 ; bg. by KNOODT, 2 vol. 1881), shared the same failing, its author maintaining that the mysteries of Faith can be reached by reason alone. His view also was censured.

On the other hand, the Traditionalists fell into the opposite error, denying that human reason is able to attain even to the knowledge of God, and reducing all knowledge to revelation transmitted by tradition. The theory, first forged by de Bonald († 1840), was supported chiefly by Bautain at Strasburg. On action being taken by the bishop of that city he recanted (1840). Cp. RHEINWALD, *Acta hist. eccles. saec. XIX*, Jahrg. 1835, pp. 305–59 ; 1837, pp. 68–79.

§ 215
'German Catholics' and Old Catholics

I. In 1844 the Holy Coat of Treves,[1] which had long lain neglected, was again exposed for the veneration of the Faithful, who came in their thousands to visit the relic. This occasion was seized by Johann Ronge, a priest at Laurahütte in Silesia, who had been suspended since the previous year, for making a violent demonstration against Arnoldi, bishop of Treves. His open letter caused great commotion throughout Germany, and many Catholics who had fallen away from the Church declared for Ronge. Simultaneously, Johann Czerski, also a suspended priest, established a ' Christian Catholic Church ' at Schneidemühl in the province of Posen, his example being also followed in other places. In the spring, 1845, the ' German Catholics,' as they called themselves, were already numerous enough to hold a synod at Leipzig, at which the papal primacy, auricular confession, celibacy, and the veneration of saints were rejected, and a German liturgy introduced, minus the Canon. The following summer they numbered 170 different communities, some of which were, however, very small. Thanks to the support which they received from the Protestants, and thanks also to the disorders which prevailed in 1848, they were able to make yet further progress. The hopes which had been built on them were, however, never destined to be fulfilled, and the movement soon began to fail. The governments were opposed to them for their conduct in 1848, whilst the rationalism favoured by Ronge, and manifested in the general terms of the profession of Faith published at Leipzig, proved a strong disintegrating element.

Whilst this movement was gradually being deprived of its vitality, another one had been occasioned by the Vatican Council.[2] For a time the Old Catholics or opponents of the new dogma were satisfied with a protest, but in the autumn,

---

[1] Mg. by S. BEISSEL ; C. WILLEMS, 1891.

[2] E. FRIEDBERG, *Aktenstücke d. altkath. Bewegung betreffend mit einem Grundriss d. Gesch. ders.* 1876 ; J. F. SCHULTE, *Der Altkatholizismus, Gesch. s. Entwicklung, inneren Gestaltung, u. rechtl. Stellung,* 1887 ; MICHAEL, *J. v. Döllinger,* 3rd ed. 1894 ; J. FRIEDRICH, item, 3 vol. 1899–1901 ; P. GSCHWIND, *Gesch. der Entstehung der christkath. K. in der Schweiz,* I, 1904 ; J. M. REINKENS, *Jos. Hub. Reinkens,* 1906 ; *Internat. theolog. Z.* 1906, pp. 205–19 (bishop Weber).

1871, at a congress held at Munich, in spite of the warning given by Döllinger († 1890), the leading spirit of the opposition, it was decided to form a separate Church. Parishes were established in many places, and after the episcopal functions had been performed for a time by Loos, Jansenist archbishop of Utrecht, a bishop of their own was chosen in the person of J. H. Reinkens, a Breslau professor (1873). He was recognised by the governments in Prussia, Baden, and Hesse as a 'Catholic bishop,' and in Prussia and Baden the Old Catholics were promised the partial use of the Catholic churches, and support out of the funds provided for Catholic worship (1874). Rome, fearing disorder or possible apostasy, having moreover forbidden the Catholics to make use of the Simultaneum, *i.e.* to worship in churches where the Old Catholics had a right of entry (1875), the result was that wherever the Old Catholics were sufficiently numerous to claim their right of entry, the churches practically became their exclusive property. The movement soon changed its character, reforms similar to those adopted by the 'German Catholics' being introduced. Obligatory confession was abolished in 1874, celibacy in 1878, and a vernacular liturgy was adopted in 1880. These reforms, especially the abolition of celibacy, were opposed by many partisans of the movement, particularly by the better elements. Reinkens († 1896) was succeeded by Th. Weber († 1906), and the latter by Demmel.

In Switzerland, too,[1] the opposition to the Vatican Council was responsible for the establishment of a separate, so-called 'Christian Catholic' Church. Here the movement was patronised by the Bernese government. An Old Catholic Faculty of Theology was erected at the University of Bern (1874), and E. Herzog, one of its members, was elected bishop (1876).

---

[1] G. VERMOT, *Le Vieux-catholicisme en Suisse, Revue de Fribourg*, Sept. 1902.

CHAPTER II

PROTESTANTISM [1]

§ 216

Alliances, Tendencies, and Sects

I. THE Protestant denominations, which thus far had been anything but amiably disposed to each other, now began to draw together. In comparison with the profound differences of opinion excited by the progress of rationalism between members of one and the same confession, the old differences prevailing between the two great Protestant bodies began to appear petty. As a consequence, in **Germany** at least, the outlook of reunion began to appear more promising. In the event, a Union [2] was realised, so far as a large portion of the country was concerned, first by a General Synod at Nassau in the summer, 1817, and then, at a summons of Frederick William III, throughout Prussia and other states. The old separatist spirit was not, however, yet dead. On the introduction into Prussia of a new mode of worship conformable with the Union, there was, particularly in Silesia, an outburst of the old Lutheran spirit, and so little disposed were the natives to compromise, even when subjected to persecution, that Frederick William IV (1841) was at last compelled to allow the so-called Old Lutherans to erect themselves into a special denomination, with its centre at Breslau. As certain differences of opinion continued to prevail even among

---

[1] E. JÖRG, *Gesch. d. Protest. in seiner neuesten Entwicklung*, 2 vol. 1858 ; DÖLLINGER, *Kirche und Kirchen*, 1861 (Engl. Trans. *The Church and the Churches, or the Papacy and the Temporal Power*, 1862) ; CHR. TISCHHAUSER, *Gesch. der evangel. K. Deutschlands in der ersten Hälfte des 19 Jahrh.* 1900 ; K. MATTHES, *Allg. k. Chronik*, 1855 ff.

[2] J. G. SCHEIBEL, *Aktenmäss. Gesch. d. Union*, 2 vol. 1834 ; TH. WANGEMANN, *Sieben Bücher preuss. KG.* 3 vol. 1859.

the friends of the Union, the same sovereign also summoned
a General Synod to meet at Berlin (1846) to decide the matters
at issue.   The attempt was, however, a failure.   The formula
of ordination which was drafted by the synod, by its generality
made too great concessions to unbelief to be ratified by the
pious king.

Whilst doctrinal differences between the two sects were
on the wane, they were threatened by a new danger.   Ever
since the birth of rationalism, the Protestant world, particularly in Germany, was split into two camps, that of belief and
that of unbelief, this being true not only of the laity—for
even in Catholic countries great masses of the laity were
infected with freethought—but also of the clergy.   This
division of minds was soon to be outwardly manifest.   The
Evangelical Alliance, founded by the Scot, Robert Chalmers,
in London (1846), was to comprise in a kind of federation
all believing Protestants throughout the world.   The more
orthodox German Protestants also formed their Evangelical
Kirchenbund, meeting in annual congress (1848).   On the
other hand, the freethinking party, led by a lawyer Bluntschli
at Heidelberg, and by the court-preacher Schwarz at Gotha,
established a Protestantenverein (1863), of which the aim was
to reform the Protestant Church in the spirit of Evangelical
freedom and in accordance with modern progress.   The
latter association assumed so strong an attitude in denying
the supernatural character of Christianity, that the official
Church was several times compelled to take action against
its members, and to displace and otherwise penalise those
clergymen connected with it.

In spite of the differences prevailing between the Protestants
themselves being far greater than those between Protestantism
and Catholicism, when it became a question of opposing the
Catholics, the Protestants were all of one mind and one heart.
This was proved at the celebrations in honour of Luther in
1817 and 1883.   The Gustav-Adolf-Verein, founded in 1832 at
Leipzig, and now widespread in the land, is a federation of
Protestants of every shade of opinion, of which the main
task is to support necessitous communities in Catholic
parts.   The Evangelischer Bund, which owed its origin to the
dissatisfaction caused by the upshot of the Kulturkampf,

and to dread of the growth in both numbers and importance of the Catholic Church (1887), is even more explicitly hostile.

II. **England,**[1] after the power of the Established Church had been curtailed, and both Dissenters (1828) and Catholics (1829) had secured the right of admittance to Parliament, and to hold office, was greatly excited by what is variously known as Puseyism, Tractarianism, or the Oxford Movement. In their dissatisfaction with the Church of England, numerous persons felt drawn to Catholicism. The centre of the movement was at Oxford, the chiefs of the party were Pusey († 1882) and Newman,[2] and their principal instrument the 'Tracts for the Times' (beginning in 1833), by which they were able to reach a far wider circle. To some extent the supporters of the movement differed. Whereas some considered it their first duty to lay stress on the primitive faith and obedience, others, the Ritualists, saw salvation in the restoration of Catholic ceremonial, in fine churches, richly decorated altars, and added solemnity of ritual. Nor was opposition to the movement wanting, especially in the ranks of the Low Churchmen, so strongly represented among the middle classes. The rigorous Protestant party, far from desiring an increase of ceremonial, would have preferred the abolition even of those elements of Catholic worship which had been retained in the Church of England. Still more vehement did the opposition become when the Tractarians, in considerable numbers, went further, and became converts to the Church, particularly when Newman, one of the most striking English writers of the century, took the same step († 1890). Not long after, the Church of England was disturbed by a totally different current of opinion. The Broad Church party was the embodiment of a movement which aimed at a greater measure of freedom of thought, and which received fitting expression in the Oxford *Essays and Reviews* (1866). Though this work called forth thousands of protests, the deep-seated difference which it revealed was not thereby removed.

---

[1] R. W. Church, *The Oxford Movement*, 1835–45, 1891 ; W. Ward, *W. G. Ward and the Oxford Movement*, 1889.
[2] Bg. by R. H. Hutton, 1891 ; L. Faure, 1901 ; Barry, 1904 ; H. Bremond, 1906 ; W. Meynell, 1907.

III. Among the sects of the time, nearly all of which hold millenarian hopes, the most remarkable are :—

(*a*) The **Irvingites,** or the Catholic Apostolic Church, as they style themselves, a modern form of Montanism, their founder, E. Irving, a Presbyterian minister in London († 1834), having preached the renewal of the charismata of the early Church, and the near return of the Lord to establish the kingdom of a thousand years. Outside of England they found followers, more particularly in Germany, where they even secured a convert of some distinction in the theologian Thiersch at Marburg. Cp. OLIPHANT, *The Life of E. Irving*, 3rd ed. 1865 ; TH. KOLDE, *Edward Irving*, 1901 ; E. MILLER, *Hist. and Doctrine of Irvingism*, 2 vol. 1878 ; G. SEESEMANN, *Die Lehre der Irvingianer*, 1881.

(*b*) The **Mormons,** or Latter-Day Saints, were founded by Joseph Smith. Their principal sacred book is the *Book of Mormon* (published by Smith in 1830), purporting to have been written on plates of gold by Mormon—a prophet of the Israelites who had settled in America after the Confusion of Tongues—and by his son Moroni (A.D. 424). After having been forced to quit the States of Ohio, Missouri, and Illinois—Smith himself and his brother Hyram being shot dead by the populace (1844)—they spent two years wandering through the mountains (the so-called Wanderings of the Desert), and finally settled in the West in the valley of the Great Salt Lake in Utah, where their new chief, the carpenter Brigham Young († 1877), established a kind of theocratic state. They consider polygamy in the light of a religious duty, and share with the Irvingites the belief in a renewal of the Apostolic gifts and in the near Coming of the Lord. As for the rest, their religion is an odd medley of superstitions borrowed from every source. Polygamy was ultimately prohibited in the United States by a decree of Congress (1884). This the Mormon president Taylor (1877–87) evaded by retiring to an unknown place. In 1890 the president of the Mormons publicly pronounced against polygamy. Mg. by TH. OLSHAUSEN, 1856 ; M. BUSCH, 1869 ; R. VON SCHLAGINTWEIT, 1874 ; W. LINN, 1902.

(*c*) The German **Templars** (or Templists), founded by Christopher Hoffmann († 1885), were to unite the Faithful in a nation of God's own. The first settlement was established at Kirschenhardthof, near Marbach in Württemberg, and since 1868 several colonies have settled in Palestine. Cp. PALMER, *Die Gemeinschaften und Sekten Württembergs*, 1877.

(*d*) The **Salvation Army,** a form of Methodism with a military organisation, founded in London by W. Booth (1865), with the object of winning over the lower classes. Of late, divisions of the Army have been sent to effect the conquest of North America, France, and other countries. Cp. *KL.* V, 1632–47 ; J. FEHR, *Die Heilsarmee*, 1891 ; TH. KOLDE, item, 2nd ed. 1899.

§ 217

Home and Foreign Missions [1]

In the previous period the conversion of the heathen world had been left almost wholly to the goodwill of the Catholics. The only Protestant efforts deserving mention were the foundation of the missionary college at Copenhagen by Frederick IV of Denmark (1714) and the zeal shown by the Herrnhuters, who, not long after their first establishment, sent missioners into various lands, particularly to Greenland, to effect the conversion of the Eskimos, among whom, even previously, the Norwegian Hans Egede (1721) had worked with the licence and support of the Danish Missionary Society.[2]

In the present period, however, the missionary activity shown by the Protestants has been enormous. No less than seventy different missionary societies have come into being, forty-five in Great Britain and North America and twenty-five on the European continent.

Of these the most important are the English Baptist Society (1792), the London Missionary Society (1795), the Wesleyan Methodist Missionary Society (1814), the American Board of Foreign Missions (Boston, 1810), and the societies of Basel (1816), Berlin (1823), and Barmen (1829). The total annual subscriptions in 1881 amounted to £1,120,000 and have greatly increased since. The number of neophytes then being cared for was estimated at about two millions. These missions are spread over the whole world, but they have met with especial success in Polynesia, or the islands of the Pacific Ocean, especially in the Sandwich (Hawai), Society (Tahiti), and Friendly Islands, and also in South and West Africa, and in the African islands, especially in Madagascar, where, in 1869, Queen Ranavalona adopted the Evangelical tenets. Notwithstanding this, it may be questioned whether results

---

[1] KALKAR, *Gesch. d. chr. M.* (from the Danish), 2 vol. 1879–80 ; WARNECK, *Abriss einer Gesch. d. prot. M.* 3rd ed. 1905 ; EPPLER, *Gesch. der Basler Mission* 1815–99, 1900 ; TH. SCHÄFER, *Die weibl. Diakonie*, 3 vol. 1879–83, *KL.* III, 1678–92.

[2] To the above may be added the English Society for the Promotion of Christianity among the Indians (of North America), 1649, and the Society for the Propagation of the Gospel in Foreign Parts (1698), now represented by the S.P.C.K. (Trans.).

have been commensurate with the vast expense. However this may be, and though in this respect the Protestants have failed to be as successful as the Catholics, the great efforts which they have displayed deserve a word of praise, particularly as it would be unjust to make the measure of success a mere matter of finance. It can, however, only be regretted that the rivalry prevailing between Catholics and Protestants, and between the different Protestant sects, should have to a large extent neutralised the efforts made, instead of proving an incentive to either side to work more earnestly for their common aim, the conversion of the heathen.

Owing to the reliance placed by Protestantism on the written word, it has ever sought to effect conversions through the Bible. For the diffusion of Holy Writ there was established in London in 1804 the great British and Foreign Bible Society, which was soon joined by numerous smaller associations. Similar societies were founded at Berlin in 1814 and at New York in 1817. In the course of the nineteenth century it is said that altogether some 180,000,000 Bibles, in 324 various languages, were distributed. In this case, again, it can scarcely be claimed that results have corresponded with the outlay. The very fact that the Bibles thus distributed are unaccompanied by any explanations, proves the small use of the practice, seeing that those very classes which the Bible Societies are anxious to reach, are the least likely to understand Scripture without additional help.

In spite of this it was the societies' intention by distributing Bibles, not only to convert the heathen, but to promote the Faith among those already Christians, *i.e.* to serve the cause not only of the foreign, but also of the home missions. It was this latter object which also inspired the labours of J. H. Wichern († 1881), the founder of the Rauhes Haus at Horn near Hamburg, a house of rescue which became a model of many similar foundations both in and out of Germany. The Institute of Deaconesses, founded by Pastor Fliedner at Kaiserswerth near Düsseldorf (1836), has also done much good work, in nursing the sick and performing other services. This institute, nevertheless, stands far behind its Catholic model, the Sisters of Charity, not only as regards its membership, but even in the self-sacrifice and devotion to duty of its members.

§ 218

Protestant Theology [1]

Throughout this period, and particularly in Germany, great zest was shown in the prosecution of theological studies. To a great extent this was the result of the altered conditions of Protestantism. Rationalism had destroyed the faith of many and had brought to the fore the principle of free-research, in itself a great stimulus to learning. On the other hand, the opposition of old and new also proved an incentive to study. One party took for its task the search for new truth, the other the defence of the Faith against its modern opponents. The consequence of this diversity of attitude was that, whilst some theologians continued to abide by the creeds and to uphold at least the supernatural character of Christianity and the Divine Nature of its Founder, others pushed denial to its furthest limits, whilst yet others strove to find a *via media*.

The first man of importance, and in a sense the founder of modern Protestant theology, was **F. C. D. Schleiermacher** at Berlin († 1834). Though he had begun by sacrificing all the doctrines which contemporary rationalism denounced as untenable, even to doubting God's personality and the immortality of the soul, and though, even later, he never really succeeded in rising above the standpoint of Naturalism, yet his influence in an age of unbelief was very great. With great eloquence and persuasion he insisted that religion is the immediate sentiment of the infinite and eternal, and as such praiseworthy; he also consented to acknowledge in Christ the Redeemer of mankind, seeing that consciousness of the Divine had reached its highest point in Him, and that, owing to it, He had contributed to the freeing of the human race. Schleiermacher's chief works were the *Reden über die Religion an die Gebildeten unter ihren Verächtern* (1799) and *Der christliche Glaube* (1821–22). *WW.* 30 vol. 1835–65. Mg. by DILTHEY, 1870; W. BENDER, 2 vol. 1876–78.

At about this same time **Hegel** (†1831) was at the height of his popularity. Owing to the esteem in which his philosophy was

---

[1] O. PFLEIDERER, *Die Entwicklung der protest. Theologie in Deutschland seit Kant und in Grossbrit. seit* 1825, 1891 (Engl. Trans. *Development of Theol. in Germany since Kant and its progress in Great Britain since* 1825, 1890); F. H. R. VON FRANK, *Gesch. und Kritik der neueren Theologie*, 3rd ed. 1898; F. HETTINGER, *Die ' Krisis des Christentums,' Protestantismus und kath. Kirche*, 1881.

held, not a few theologians embraced it under the impression that no real opposition existed between it and the Faith. The dogmatic writings of Marheinecke († 1846) are wholly impregnated with Hegelianism.

How unfounded this impression was became evident on the publication by **D. Fr. Strauss** of his *Life of Jesus* (1835–36), in which the history of Christ was explained as a myth which had originated among the early Christians. His work, which within five years passed through four more editions, and was later on to be again published in a popular edition (1864), threw the whole theological world into confusion. Many took up the cudgels on behalf of the Faith, but, on the other hand, new supporters of Naturalism also took the field, among whom the name of one is epoch-making in the history of Protestant Theology.

F. Chr. Baur of Tübingen († 1860 ; cp. *KL*. II, 64–75) indeed did not scruple to blame Strauss for having attempted to write a history of Christ without having first devoted himself to the criticism of the Gospels. In the rejection of supernaturalism he was, however, in thorough agreement with his predecessor, and by his criticism of the canon of the New Testament he, more than anyone else, promoted the spread of unbelief. It is true that before him Schleiermacher and de Wette († 1849) had denied or questioned the authenticity of certain biblical writings. Baur, however, went further, and rejected nearly the whole of the New Testament, granting an apostolic origin only to the four great Pauline Epistles and to the Apocalypse. The master's disciples and adherents modified this theory in many details, increasing the number of Apostolic works, or, at least, pushing further back their date of composition. On the whole, nevertheless, the influence of the theory was both widespread and lasting. It now forms the scientific basis of the Free Protestant Theology, to give its new name to the movement which was formerly known as Rationalism. Among its adepts were R. Rothe († 1867), D. Schenkel († 1885), K. Schwarz († 1885), A. Schweizer († 1888), K. Hase († 1890), R. A. Lipsius († 1892), K. Weizsäcker († 1899).

Confident as the critics were of having already won the battle against Faith, the latter was by no means dead. Romanticism and the soul-stirring political events which had introduced the period predisposed people to belief, nor was there ever a failure of learned and determined advocates of Christianity. They were now, however, no longer unanimous, being divided into Old and New Lutherans, the latter acknowledging only the word of God as represented in Holy Writ, the former also cherishing the authority of the Protestant Creeds. The best-known names are those of A. Neander—the father of modern enlightened Pietism († 1850)—and E. W. Hengstenberg († 1869) at Berlin, A. Tholuck at Halle († 1877), J. Chr. K. Hofmann at Erlangen († 1877), and J. T. Beck at Tübingen († 1878 ; bg. by Riggenbach, 1888).

As for the intermediate school of Theology, it indeed refuses to acknowledge fully the supernatural character of Christianity, whilst, however, refraining from dogmatic denial. It seeks to give Christ as high a place as possible, agreeing to describe him as a prophet sent by God and filled with the Divine spirit. Of the Gospel miracles it also retains at least the cures. The chief representatives of this movement, between whom, however, great divergencies exist, were K. J. Nitzsch († 1868), J. Müller († 1878), K. Ullmann († 1865), J. A. Dorner († 1884). A. Ritschl († 1889), too, deserves a place here, though in his hands the theory assumed a new shape, and also received a better foundation. His disciples are now very numerous. His great work was *Justification and Reconciliation* (Engl. Trans. 1872). Bg. by O. RITSCHL, 2 vol. 1892–96 ; A. E. GARVIE, *The Ritschlian Theology*, 1899.

Other noteworthy and voluminous writers were : H. A. W. Meyer († 1873) with his critico-exegetical commentary on the New Testament (16 vol. 1829 ff.), frequently re-edited by other scholars ; K. von Tischendorf, the Bible critic († 1874) ; J. B. Lightfoot (*Epistles of St. Paul : The Apostolic Fathers* ; † 1889).

From out of a great number of periodicals the following may be selected : *Theologische Studien und Kritiken* (since 1828) ; *Zeitschrift für historische Theologie* (1832–75) ; *Zeitschrift für Kirchengeschichte* (1877) ; *Theologische Jahrbücher* (1842–56) ; *Zeitschrift für wissenschaftliche Theologie* (1857) ; *Jahrbücher für deutsche Theologie* (1856–78) ; *Jahrbücher für protestantische Theologie* (1875–92) ; *Zeitschrift für Theologie und Kirche* (1891) ; *Theologischer Jahresbericht* (1881 ff.) ; the *Journal of Theol. Studies* (London, 1899 ff.), the *Church Quarterly Review* (London, 1875 ff.), the *American Journal of Theol.* (Chicago, 1897 ff.), the *Princeton Theol. Review* (Philadelphia, 1890 ff.), and the independent *Hibbert Journal* (London, 1902 ff.). A *Real-Encyklopädie für protestantische Theologie und Kirche* has been edited by J. J. Herzog (21 vol. 1854–68), 3rd ed. 1896 ff. (cp. SCHAFF-HERZOG, *Religious Encyclopædia*, 1882). W. Smith and G. Wace also issued a *Dictionary of Christian Biography, Literature, Sects, and Doctrines* (4 vol. 1877–88), and J. H. Blunt a *Dictionary of Sects, Heresies, &c.*, 1874.

§ 219

Belief and Unbelief [1]

Whilst during this period faith was again displaying its power of adaptation, unbelief was also gaining ground, and whereas in the previous period its inroads had been confined to the higher classes, it now carried its attack into the ranks

---

[1] W. STUDEMUND, *Der moderne Unglaube in den unteren Ständen*, 1901 ; *Hist.-pol. Bl.* 1901, vol. 127, fasc. 8–9.

of the proletariate. In France the Revolution was responsible for atheism being declared the religion of the State, and though this condition of things did not last, its effects were to be experienced long after. Ever since, unbelief has reigned supreme throughout large sections of the French population. In Germany, too, since the middle of the nineteenth century, it has been steadily increasing, industrial development and the war now beginning between labour and capital greatly contributing to its progress. The labour leaders were all of them enemies of Christianity. Their views, spread abroad by word of mouth and by the press, soon reached the masses, who received it all the more willingly because they had been told not only that the Christian Faith had been disproved by science, but that it was a hindrance to the establishment of that new order of society which Social Democracy stands pledged to introduce. The extent to which such a view has pervaded society may be gauged by electoral results, even making all due allowances for the fact that many who belong to the party do not share its antipathy to all religion. The number of Social Democrats elected to the imperial Parliament and to the various diets and local councils has steadily grown from year to year. It is now the most numerous non-Catholic party in Germany, and it is no secret that it has now obtained the support of a large part of the Catholic population.

Society is everywhere, in greater or lesser degree, split into two camps, and though that of the believers remains by far the larger, the other has greatly gained in strength. The opposition between the two has already led to conflict, possibly worse awaits us in the future. What the ultimate upshot will be cannot be foretold, but of one thing we may be sure, the new social order will be the less likely to bring happiness the less room it gives to Him without whom there is no salvation (*Acts* iv. 12).

§ 220

Conclusion

Christians in the course of the centuries have separated into many societies. Some of these societies, after existing for a time, have perished ; others have survived to the present day. The greatest rent occurred in the eleventh and in the sixteenth century. In the former case West and East were split asunder ; in the latter a large portion of the West severed its connection with the Church of Rome, the schism extending even to the new world which had just been discovered, and of which Catholics and Protestants took divided possession.

These schisms cannot but be a subject for grief. The heart of the true Christian yearns not for schism, but for union, mindful of the injunction of Scripture, ' Careful to keep the unity of the spirit, the bond of peace. One body, one spirit, as you are called in one hope of your calling, one Lord, one faith, one baptism, one God and Father of all, who is above all, and through all, and in us all ' (*Eph.* iv. 3–6). For the West the greater misfortune was the schism of the sixteenth century, yet, however regrettable, it was not without wholesome results. It has often been questioned whether, had it not occurred, a reform of the Church would have been possible. To return a simple negative to the question would indeed be to despair of the Church's vitality and of Providence. On the other hand, there can be no doubt that the reforms were far too long delayed, and that they were introduced only when the Church had been shaken to her foundations, and when a large fraction of the world had already abandoned her in disgust. History also shows us that the wholesale apostasy not only preceded, but actually caused the reforms within the Church ; hence there can be no doubt that the Church's improvement is closely bound up with the Protestant Reformation.

Protestantism had also still more far-reaching results. The Catholic Church, being now faced in the West by another, determined to gain in strength what she had lost in numbers. To the new-found solidarity of the whole Catholic Church must be ascribed the fact that since the Reformation there has been no schism, whilst the papal elections have been performed in the greatest good order. Even the mingling with Pro-testant sects, which has replaced the previous exclusiveness, has not proved an unmitigated evil, in spite of some bad results. In those countries in which this is the case, Catholic life, at least at the present day, throbs more vigorously than where the old circumstances still prevail. The fact is too patent to require proof, nor is its explanation far to seek; the existence of an opposition is naturally, to every denomination, an incentive to good behaviour, and to the display of additional zeal.

Seen in this light, recent developments tend to assume an appearance somewhat less unsatisfactory. Yet, when all is said, schism must still be deemed an evil; this feeling is widespread, not only among the Catholics but even among the Protestants. Division amongst Christians is, however, a reality, and such it is likely to remain for long. Under these circumstances, we must perforce console ourselves with the considerations already adduced, never, however, losing confidence in the Church's Founder, who, though He seems to lead His children by dark ways, continues unceasingly to extend over the Church His protecting hand, true to His parting promise to His disciples: ' I am with you all days, even to the consummation of the world ' (*Matt.* xxviii. 20).

CHRONOLOGICAL TABLES

I. THE POPES[1]

1.	St. Peter	† 67	33.	Silvester I	314–35
2.	St. Linus	67–79 (?)	34.	St. Mark	336
3.	St. Anencletus	79–90 (?)	35.	St. Julius I	337–52
4.	St. Clement I	90–99 (?)	36.	Liberius	352–66
5.	St. Evaristus	99–107 (?)		Felix II	355–65
6.	St. Alexander	107–16 (?)	37.	St. Damasus I	366–84
7.	St. Xystus (Sixtus) I	116–25 (?)		Ursinus	366–67
			38.	St. Siricius	384–99
8.	St. Telesphorus	125–36 (?)	39.	St. Anastasius I	399–401
9.	St. Hyginus	136–40 (?)	40.	St. Innocent I	401–17
10.	St. Pius I	140–54, 5(?)	41.	St. Zosimus	417–18
11.	St. Anicetus	154, 5–66	42.	St. Boniface I	418–22
12.	St. Soter	166–174		Eulalius	418–19
13.	St. Eleutherus	174–89	43.	St. Celestine I	422–32
14.	St. Victor	189–98	44.	St. Sixtus III	432–40
15.	St. Zephyrinus	198–217	45.	St. Leo I	440–61
16.	St. Callixtus	217–22	46.	St. Hilary	461–68
	Hippolytus	217–35	47.	St. Simplicius	468–83
17.	St. Urban I	222–30	48.	St. Felix II (III)	483–92
18.	St. Pontian	230–35	49.	St. Gelasius I	492–96
19.	St. Anterus	235–36	50.	St. Anastasius II	496–98
20.	St. Fabian	236–50	51.	St. Symmachus	498–514
21.	St. Cornelius	251–53		Lawrence	498–505
	Novatian	251–58 (?)	52.	St. Hormisdas	514–23
22.	St. Lucius I	253–54	53.	St. John I	523–26
23.	St. Stephen I	254–57	54.	St. Felix III (IV)	526–30
24.	St. Xystus (Sixtus) II	257–58	55.	St. Boniface II	530–32
				Dioscorus	530
25.	St. Dionysius	259–68	56.	John II (Mercurius)	533–35
26.	St. Felix I	269–74			
27.	St. Eutychian	275–83	57.	St. Agapetus I	535–36
28.	St. Caius	283–96	58.	St. Silverius	536–37
29.	St. Marcellin	296–304	59.	Vigilius	537–55
30.	St. Marcellus I	308–9	60.	Pelagius I	556–61
31.	St. Eusebius	309 or 310	61.	John III	561–74
32.	St. Miltiades (Melchiades)	311–14	62.	Benedict I	575–79
			63.	Pelagius II	579–90

[1] Cp. *KL.* 2nd ed. vol. IX, 1424–42, where the exact length of each pontificate is clearly indicated. Z. V. Lobkowitz, *Statistik der Päpste auf Grund des Papstverzeichnisses der Gerarchia Cattolica*, 1905.

64.	St. Gregory I	590–604		110.	Stephen V	885–91
65.	Sabinian	604–6		111.	Formosus	891–96
66.	Boniface III	607		112.	Boniface VI	896
67.	St. Boniface IV	608–15		113.	Stephen VI	896–97
68.	St. Deusdedit	615–18		114.	Romanus	897
69.	Boniface V	619–25		115.	Theodore II	897
70.	Honorius I	625–38		116.	John IX	898–900
71.	Severinus	640		117.	Benedict IV	900–903
72.	John IV	640–42		118.	Leo V	903
73.	Theodore I	642–49		119.	Christopher	903–4
74.	St. Martin I	649–53		120.	Sergius III	904–11
75.	St. Eugene I	654–57		121.	Anastasius III	911–13
76.	St. Vitalian	657–72		122.	Lando	913–14
77.	Adeodatus	672–76		123.	John X	914–28
78.	Donus	676–78		124.	Leo VI	928
79.	St. Agatho	678–81		125.	Stephen VII	929–31
80.	St. Leo II	682–83		126.	John XI	931–35
81.	St. Benedict II	684–85		127.	Leo VII	936–39
82.	John V	685–86		128.	Stephen VIII	939–42
83.	Conon	686–87		129.	Marinus II	942–46
	Theodore	687		130.	Agapetus II	946–55
	Paschal	687–92 (?)		131.	John XII	955–64
84.	St. Sergius	687–701		132.	Leo VIII	963–65
85.	John VI	701–5		133.	Benedict V	964
86.	John VII	705–7		134.	John XIII	965–72
87.	Sisinnius	708		135.	Benedict VI	973–74
88.	Constantine I	708–15			Boniface VII	
89.	St. Gregory II	715–31			(Franco)	974
90.	St. Gregory III	731–41		136.	Benedict VII	974–83
91.	St. Zachary	741–52		137.	John XIV	983–84
	Stephen	752		138.	Boniface VII	984–85
92.	Stephen II	752–57		139.	John XV	985–96
93.	St. Paul I	757–67		140.	Gregory V	996–99
	Constantine II	767–68			John XVI	997–98
	Philip	768		141.	Silvester II	999–1003
94.	Stephen III	768–72		142.	John XVII	1003
95.	Adrian I	772–95		143.	John XVIII	1003–9
96.	St. Leo III	795–816		144.	Sergius IV	1009–12
97.	Stephen IV	816–17		145.	Benedict VIII	1012–24
98.	St. Paschal I	817–24			Gregory	1012
99.	Eugene II	824–27		146.	John XIX	1024–32
100.	Valentine	827		147.	Benedict IX	1032–44
101.	Gregory IV	827–44		148.	Silvester III	1045
	John	844		149.	Gregory VI	1045–46
102.	Sergius II	844–47		150.	Clement II	1046–47
103.	St. Leo IV	847–55		151.	Damasus II	1048
104.	Benedict III	855–58		152.	St. Leo IX	1049–54
	Anastasius	855		153.	Victor II	1055–57
105.	St. Nicholas I	858–67		154.	Stephen IX	1057–58
106.	Adrian II	867–72		155.	Benedict X	1058–59
107.	John VIII	872–82		156.	Nicholas II	1058–61
108.	Marinus I	882–84		157.	Alexander II	1061–73
109.	Adrian III	884–85			Honorius II	1061–69

158.	St. Gregory VII	1073–85	198.	Benedict XII	1334–42
	Clement III	1084–1100	199.	Clement VI	1342–52
159.	Victor III	1087	200.	Innocent VI	1352–62
160.	Urban II	1088–99	201.	Urban V	1362–70
161.	Paschal II	1099–1118	202.	Gregory XI	1370–78
	Theodoric	1100–2	203.	Urban VI	1378–89
	Albert	1102		Clement VII	1378–94
	Silvester IV	1105–11	204.	Boniface IX	1389–1404
162.	Gelasius II	1118–19		Benedict XIII	1394–1424
	Gregory VIII	1118–21	205.	Innocent VII	1404–6
163.	Calixtus II	1119–24	206.	Gregory XII	1406–15
164.	Honorius II	1124–30	207.	Alexander V	1409–10
	Coloetino II	1124	208.	John XXIII	1410–15
165.	Innocent II	1130–43	209.	Martin V	1417–31
	Anacletus II	1130–38		Clement VIII	1424–29
	Victor IV	1138		Benedict XIV	1424 . . . ?
166.	Celestine II	1143–44	210.	Eugene IV	1431–47
167.	Lucius II	1144–45		Felix V	1439–49
168.	Eugene III	1145–53	211.	Nicholas V	1447–55
169.	Anastasius IV	1153–54	212.	Calixtus III	1455–58
170.	Adrian IV	1154–59	213.	Pius II	1458–64
171.	Alexander III	1159–81	214.	Paul II	1464–71
	Victor IV	1159–64	215.	Sixtus IV	1471–84
	Paschal III	1164–68	216.	Innocent VIII	1484–92
	Calixtus III	1168–79	217.	Alexander VI	1492–1503
	Innocent III	1179–80	218.	Pius III	1503
172.	Lucius III	1181–85	219.	Julius II	1503–13
173.	Urban III	1185–87	220.	Leo X	1513–21
174.	Gregory VIII	1187	221.	Adrian VI	1522–23
175.	Clement III	1187–91	222.	Clement VII	1523–34
176.	Celestine III	1191–98	223.	Paul III	1534–49
177.	Innocent III	1198–1216	224.	Julius III	1550–55
178.	Honorius III	1216–27	225.	Marcellus II	1555
179.	Gregory IX	1227–41	226.	Paul IV	1555–59
180.	Celestine IV	1241	227.	Pius IV	1559–65
181.	Innocent IV	1243–54	228.	St. Pius V	1566–72
182.	Alexander IV	1254–61	229.	Gregory XIII	1572–85
183.	Urban IV	1261–64	230.	Sixtus V	1585–90
184.	Clement IV	1265–68	231.	Urban VII	1590
185.	St. Gregory X	1271–76	232.	Gregory XIV	1590–91
186.	Innocent V	1276	233.	Innocent IX	1591
187.	Adrian V	1276	234.	Clement VIII	1592–1605
188.	John XXI	1276–77	235.	Leo XI	1605
189.	Nicholas III	1277–80	236.	Paul V	1605–21
190.	Martin IV	1281–85	237.	Gregory XV	1621–23
191.	Honorius IV	1285–87	238.	Urban VIII	1623–44
192.	Nicholas IV	1288–92	239.	Innocent X	1644–55
193.	St. Celestine V	1294	240.	Alexander VII	1655–67
194.	Boniface VIII	1294–1303	241.	Clement IX	1667–69
195.	Benedict XI	1303–4	242.	Clement X	1670–76
196.	Clement V	1305–14	243.	Innocent XI	1676–89
197.	John XXII	1316–34	244.	Alexander VIII	1689–91
	Nicholas V	1328–30	245.	Innocent XII	1691–1700

246. Clement XI	1700–21	254. Pius VII	1800–23
247. Innocent XIII	1721–24	255. Leo XII	1823–29
248. Benedict XIII	1724–30	256. Pius VIII	1829–30
249. Clement XII	1730–40	257. Gregory XVI	1831–46
250. Benedict XIV	1740–58	258. Pius IX	1846–78
251. Clement XIII	1758–69	259. Leo XIII	1878–1903
252. Clement XIV	1769–74	260. Pius X	1903
253. Pius VI	1775–99		

II. ROMAN AND BYZANTINE EMPERORS

Augustus	30 B.C.–A.D 14
Tiberius	14–37
Caius Caligula	37–41
Claudius I	41–54
Nero	54–68
Galba, Otho, Vitellius	68–69
Vespasian	69–79
Titus	79–81
Domitian	81–96
Nerva	96–98
Trajan	98–117
Adrian	117–38
Antoninus Pius	138–61
Marcus Aurelius	161–80
Commodus	180–92
Pertinax	193
Septimius Severus	193–211
Caracalla	211–17
Macrinus	217–18
Elagabalus (Heliogabalus)	218–22
Alexander Severus	222–35
Maximinus Thrax	235–38
Pupienus and Gordianus	238
Gordianus the Younger	238–44
Philippus Arabs	244–49
Decius	249–51
Gallus and Volusian	251–53
Valerian	253–60
Gallienus	260–68
Claudius II	268–70
Aurelian	270–75
Tacitus	275–76
Probus	276–82
Carus	282–84
Diocletian	284–305
Maximian	286–305
Constantius Chlorus	305–306
Galerius	305–11
Constantine I the Great	306–37

Maximin	308–13
Licinius	308–23
Constantius	337–61
Constantine II	337–40
Constans I	337–50
Julian the Apostate	361–63
Jovian	363–64
Valentinian I	364–75
Valens	364–78
Gratian	375–83
Valentinian II	375–92
Theodosius I	379–95
Honorius	395–423
John the Tyrant	423–25
Valentinian III	425–55
Avitus	455–56
Majorian	457–61
Severus	461–65
Ricimer	465–67
Anthemius	467–72
Olybrius	472
Glycerius	473
Julius Nepos	474
Romulus Augustulus	475
Arcadius	395–408
Theodosius II	408–50
Marcian	450–57
Leo I	457–74
Leo II and Zeno	474–91
Basiliscus	476–77
Anastasius I	491–518
Justin I	518–27
Justinian I	527–65
Justin II	565–78
Tiberius II	578–82
Mauritius	582–602
Phocas	602–10
Heraclius	610–41
Constantine III and Heracleonas	641

Constans II	641–68	Romanus IV (Diogenes)	1067–71
Constantine IV (Pogo-		Michael VII (Para-	
natus)	668–85	pinakes)	1071–78
Justinian II	685–95	Nicephorus III (Botan-	
Leontius	695–98	iates)	1078–81
Tiberius III	698–705	Alexius I (Comnenus)	1081–1118
Justinian II *bis.*	705–11	John II (Com.)	1118–43
Philippicus Bardanes	711–13	Manuel I (Com.)	1143–80
Anastasius II	713–16	Alexius II (Com.)	1180–83
Theodosius III	716–17	Andronicus I (Com.)	1183–85
Leo III the Isaurian	717–41	Isaac Angelus	1185–95
Constantine V (Cop-		Alexius III	1195–1203
ronymus)	741–75	Alexius IV	1203–4
Leo IV	775–80	Alexius V (Murzuflus)	1204
Constantine VI	780–97		
Irene	797–802	LATIN DYNASTY	
Nicephorus I	802–11		
Michael I	811–13	Baldwin I	1204–6
Leo V the Armenian	813–20	Henry	1206–16
Michael II the		Pierre de Courtenay	1216–17
Stammerer	820–29	Jolante	1217–19
Theophilus	829–42	Robert de Courtenay	1219–28
Theodora	842–56	Baldwin II	1228–61
Michael III the		Jean de Brienne	1230–37
Drunkard	842–67		
Basil I the Macedonian	867–86	TREBIZOND AND NICENE	
Leo VI the Wise	886–912	EMPIRES	
Constantine VII	912–59		
Alexander	912–13	Theodore I (Lascaris)	1204–22
Romanus I	919–44	John III (Vatatzes)	1222–54
Romanus II	959–63	Theodore II (Lasc.)	1254–58
Nicephorus II (Phocas)	963–69	John IV (Lasc.)	1258–61
John Zimisces	969–76		
Basil II	976–1025		
Constantine VIII	976–1028	CONSTANTINOPLE	
Zoe	1028–50		
Romanus III	1028–34	Michael VIII (Palæo-	
Michael IV	1034–41	logus)	1259–82
Michael V	1041–42	Andronicus II	1282–1328
Constantine IX		Andronicus III	1328–41
(Monomachus)	1042–54	John V (Pal.)	1341–91
Theodora	1054–56	John VI (Cantac.)	1341–55
Michael VI	1056–57	Matthias	1354–56
Isaac Comnenus	1057–59	Manuel II (Pal.)	1391–1425
Constantine X (Dukas)	1059–67	John VII (Pal.)	1425–48
		Constantine XII	1448–53

III. WESTERN (*i.e.* GERMAN) EMPERORS AND KINGS [1]

Charles I the Great		Lothar I	840–55
(Charlemagne)	800–14	Lewis II	850–75
Lewis I the Pious	814–40	Charles II the Bald	875–77

[1] German Kings who were not likewise Emperors have an asterisk before their names.

Charles III	881–87	*Frederick of Austria	1314–30
Guido of Spoleto	891–93	Charles IV of Bohemia	1346–78
Lambert of Sp.	892–98	*Wenzel of Bohemia	1378–1400
Arnulfus	896–99	*Rupert of the Pala-	
*Lewis III the Child	900–11	tinate	1400–10
Lewis III of Provence	901–2	Sigismund of Hungary	1410–37
*Conrad I	911–18	*Albert II	1438–39
Berengar of Friuli	915–24	Frederick III	1440–93
*Henry I	919–36	Maximilian I	1493–1519
Otto I the Great	936–73	Charles V	1519–56
Otto II	973–83	Ferdinand I	1556–64
Otto III	983–1002	Maximilian II	1564–76
Henry II	1002–24	Rudolf II	1576–1612
Conrad II	1024–39	Matthias	1612–19
Henry III	1039–56	Ferdinand II	1619–37
*Henry IV	1056–1106	Ferdinand III	1637–57
Henry V	1106–25	Leopold I	1657–1705
Lothar II the Saxon	1125–37	Joseph I	1705–11
*Conrad III	1138–52	Charles VI	1711–40
Frederick I	1152 90	Charles VII	1742–45
Henry VI	1190–97	Francis I (Consort of	
*Philip of Swabia	1198–1208	M. Theresia)	1745–65
Otto IV of Brunswick	1198–1215	Joseph II	1765–90
Frederick II	1215–50	Leopold II	1790–92
*Henry Raspe	1246–47	Francis II	1792–1806
*William of Holland	1247–56		
*Conrad IV	1250–54	EMPERORS OF AUSTRIA	
Interregnum (Richard			
of Cornwall and		Francis I	1806–35
Alfonso of Castile)	1256–73	Ferdinand I	1835–48
*Rudolf of Habsburg	1273–91	Francis Joseph I	1848
*Adolfus of Nassau	1292–98		
*Albert I of Austria	1298–1308	EMPERORS OF GERMANY	
Henry VII of Luxem-		William I	1870–88
burg	1308–13	Frederick I (March 9)	1888
*Lewis of Bavaria	1314–47	William II (June 15)	1888

IV. FRENCH KINGS

Carolings		*Capetians*	
Charles II the Bald	840–77	Lewis V (Fainéant)	986–87
Lewis II the Stammerer	877–79	Hugh Capet	987–96
Lewis III	879–82	Robert	996–1031
Carlman	879–84	Henry I	1031–60
Charles III (emperor)	885–87	Philip I	1060–1108
Otto (Eudes)	887–98	Lewis VI the Fat	1108–37
Charles III the Simple	898–923	Lewis VII the Young	1137–80
Robert I	922–23	Philip II (Augustus)	1180–1223
Rudolf	923–36	Lewis VIII the Lion	1223–26
Lewis IV (Overseas)	936–54	Lewis IX the Saint	1226–70
Lothar	954–86	Philip III (le Hardi)	1270–85

Capetians—continued

Philip IV the Fine	1285–1314
Lewis X the Quarreller	1314–16
John I	1316
Philip V the Tall	1316–22
Charles IV the Fair	1323–28

House of Valois

Philip VI	1328–50
John II the Good	1350–64
Charles V the Wise	1364–80
Charles VI	1380–1422
Charles VII	1422–61
Lewis XI	1461–83
Charles VIII	1483–98
Lewis XII	1498–1515
Francis I	1515–47
Henry II	1547–59
Francis II	1559–60
Charles IX	1560–74
Henry III	1574–89

House of Bourbon, &c.

Henry IV	1589–1610
Lewis XIII the Just	1610–43
Lewis XIV the Great	1643–1715
Lewis XV the Beloved	1715–74
Lewis XVI	1774–92
First Republic	1792–1804
The Convention	1792–95
The Directory	1795–99
The Consulate	1799–1804
Napoleon I (emperor)	1804–14
Lewis XVIII	1814–24
Charles X	1824–30
Louis Philippe (of Orleans)	1830–48
Second Republic	1848–52
Napoleon III (emperor)	1852–70
Third Republic	1870

V. KINGS OF ENGLAND

Anglo-Saxons

Egbert	c. 800–837
Ethelwolf	837–56
Ethelbald	856–60
Ethelbert	858–66
Ethelred I	866–71
Alfred the Great	871–900
Edward I	900–24
Athelstan	924–40
Edmund I	940–46
Edred	946–55
Edwy	955–59
Edgar	959–75

Danes and Anglo-Saxons

Edward II the Martyr	975–78
Ethelred II the Un-ready	978–1016
Sweya (Suanon)	1014–15
Canute the Great	1015–36
Edmund II Ironside	1016–17
Harald I	1036–40
Canute II	1040–42
Edward III the Con-fessor	1042–66
Harald II	1066

Normans

William I the Conqueror	1066–87
William II (Rufus)	1087–1100
Henry I Beauclerk	1100–35
Stephen of Blois	1135–54

Plantagenets

Henry II	1154–89
Richard I Lionheart	1189–99
John Lackland	1199–1216
Henry III	1216–72
Edward I	1272–1307
Edward II	1307–27
Edward III	1327–77
Richard II	1377–99

House of Lancaster

Henry IV	1399–1413
Henry V	1413–22
Henry VI	1422–61

House of York

Edward IV	1461–83
Edward V	1483
Richard III	1483–85

House of Tudor

Henry VII	1485–1509
Henry VIII	1509–47
Edward VI	1547–53
Mary I	1553–58
Elizabeth	1558–1603

House of Stuart

James I	1603–25
Charles I	1625–49
Commonwealth	1649–60
Charles II	1660–85
James II	1685–88

William III and Mary II	1689–1702
Anne	1702–14

House of Hanover

George I	1714–27
George II	1727–60
George III	1760–1820
George IV	1820–30
William IV	1830–37
Victoria	1837–1901
Edward VII	1901–1910
George V	1910

VI. KINGS OF SPAIN

Ferdinand the Catholic (of Aragon)	1479–1516
Isabella the Catholic (of Castile)	1474–1504
Joanna and Philip I (of Castile)	1504–7
Charles I	1516–56
Philip II	1556–98
Philip III	1598–1621
Philip IV	1621–65
Charles II	1665–1700
Philip V (of Bourbon)	1700–46
Ferdinand VI	1746–59
Charles III	1759–88
Charles IV	1788–1808
Joseph Bonaparte	1808–13
Ferdinand VII	1814–33
Isabella II	1833–68
Don Carlos V	1833–45
Dictatorship of Serranos	1869–71
Amadeus of Savoy	1871–73
Republic	1873–75
Don Carlos	1869–76
Alfonso XII	1875–85
Alfonso XIII	1885

INDEX

THE END

PRINTED BY
SPOTTISWOODE AND CO. LTD., COLCHESTER
LONDON AND ETON